# FASHION SUPPLY CHAIN MANAGEMENT

# FASHION SUPPLY CHAIN MANAGEMENT

MICHAEL P. LONDRIGAN

LIM College

JACQUELINE M. JENKINS

**FAIRCHILD BOOKS**

NEW YORK · LONDON · OXFORD · NEW DELHI · SYDNEY

FAIRCHILD BOOKS
Bloomsbury Publishing Inc
1385 Broadway, New York, NY 10018, USA
50 Bedford Square, London, WC1B 3DP, UK

BLOOMSBURY, FAIRCHILD BOOKS and the Fairchild Books logo are
trademarks of Bloomsbury Publishing Plc

This edition published 2018
Reprinted 2019 (twice), 2020

Library of Congress Cataloging-in-Publication Data
Names: Londrigan, Michael P., author. | Jenkins, Jacqueline M., author.
Title: Fashion supply chain management / Michael P. Londrigan, LIM College, Jacqueline
Jenkins.
Description: 1 Edition, | New York City : Fairchild Books, An imprint of Bloomsbury Publishing
Inc, [2018] | Includes index.
Identifiers: LCCN 2017050407 | ISBN 9781501317781 (pbk.) | ISBN 9781501317804 (pdf)
Subjects: LCSH: Clothing trade. | Business logistics.
Classification: LCC HD9940.A2 L66 2018 | DDC 746.9/20687—dc23 LC record available at
https://lccn.loc.gov/2017050407

ISBN: PB: 978-1-5013-1778-1
ePDF: 978-1-5013-1780-4
ePUB: 978-1-5013-1781-1

Typeset by Lachina
Printed and bound in the United States of America

To find out more about our authors and books visit
www.fairchildbooks.com and sign up for our newsletter.

# contents

# extended contents

**6 Sourcing and Production**  99

**7 Quality Assurance**  119

**8 Logistics**  137

# preface

While supply chain management occurs in just about every industry that produces a product, the fashion supply chain is unique because of the factors that drive this sector. Fashion is a global business that is influenced by the whimsical nature of consumers, economic conditions, social norms, political developments, natural disasters, and new retail business models. *Fashion Supply Chain Management* is a practitioner's guide that takes a comprehensive look at the functions, industry partners, trends, and key decisions throughout the global fashion supply chain.

## A REAL-WORLD PERSPECTIVE

In today's world of fashion, where companies are being built around the concepts of fast fashion, ecommerce, and mass customization, brands are looking for supply chain solutions that focus on getting the right product to the right customer at the right time at the right price. The industry needs supply chain professionals who understand the fundamentals of supply chain management and sector-specific issues, such as the production calendar, corporate social responsibility, customer demand, and quick turnaround for ecommerce delivery options. The goal of this book is to give its readers a foundational knowledge of supply chain management; it also includes fashion company case studies, industry interviews, and author insights that provide a real-world perspective on the challenges and opportunities being presented in the global fashion supply chain.

The book captures the evolution of the fashion supply chain from the point of view of the industry professional. Both authors have fashion industry experience and are currently academicians in the business of fashion. Upon completion of *Fashion Supply Chain Management*, readers will be able to assess what makes fashion so unique from a supply chain perspective, understand the roles of internal and external partnerships throughout the supply chain, and gain exposure to the technical and managerial skills needed to be successful as a fashion supply chain management professional. Because the authors have chosen to look at supply chain management in its totality, the book includes insight into areas such as finance. *Fashion Supply Chain Management* also recognizes the importance of the retailer and the customer and concludes by focusing on these aspects of the fashion supply chain.

## THE FOCUS OF THE CHAPTERS

Because *Fashion Supply Chain Management* was written with the goal of educating those who aspire to succeed in the supply chain of the fashion business, the book's content is representative of what industry leaders are grappling with today. Each chapter addresses a specific area of fashion and the supply chain. *Fashion Supply Chain Management* starts off in **Chapter 1** with an overview of the fashion industry. **Chapter 2** provides insight into the global nature of the fashion supply chain, detailing the leading and emerging areas of manufacturing, trade agreements, and sourcing strategies that minimize risks. **Chapter 3** deals with corporate social responsibility, a game-changer for apparel manufacturing. Because the organizational structures and communications throughout a fashion business are key to building a nimble, resilient supply chain, **Chapter 4** gives an insider's look at the players within a fashion business and how they work collaboratively. **Chapter 5** focuses on the use of raw materials in the production process. **Chapter 6** offers insight into fashion manufacturing by emphasizing sourcing and production. **Chapter 7** details the importance of quality assurance in maintaining a competitive advantage. Logistics, the subject for **Chapter 8**, is a key component of the supply chain with regards to information management and movement of goods. **Chapter 9**, on the flow of information, helps readers understand how the collection and analysis of data support decision-making throughout the supply chain network. As fashion companies grow, the financing of their supply chain becomes a critical element in the operations of their business. **Chapter 10** outlines financing instruments that cater to the needs of businesses that conduct international trade transactions. Readers will gain insight into the evolution of retailers and their impact on the supply chain through the content of **Chapter 11**. Since fashion is all about understanding the consumer, **Chapter 12** concludes the book by focusing on fashion customers and their expectations.

## FEATURES

To enable students and instructors to maneuver easily through the contents of the book, the authors have added the follow learning resources within each chapter.

- Learning Objectives tell readers the subject areas and management insight that they will gain from the chapter.
- Key Terms are bolded and defined within the chapter text to highlight new and/or important vocabulary.
- *Tables and Illustrations* highlight key points or show an actual example of a fashion concept. *Fashion Supply Chain Management* includes several tables and pictures that guide students visually throughout the book. The tables can also serve as a study guide.
- Because the authors believe in the value of real-world insight and application, each chapter includes an Industry Interview. These professionals were selected because of the contributions that they have made to the industry.
- *Case Studies* provide students with an opportunity to apply the takeaways from the chapter while also learning about a company's supply chain or retail strategy. In addition to being a learning tool, the case studies provide current insight that students can discuss in a job interview to demonstrate their knowledge of the fashion industry.

- At the conclusion of each chapter, students have an opportunity to test their knowledge by completing the *Chapter Review Questions* and *Chapter Exercises*. These exercises are a way for students to collaborate with their classmates on the learnings from the chapter.
- Because the authors have experienced firsthand the challenges and opportunities presented in the book, they share their personal insights through *Notes from the Field*. These notes are informative stories that reflect on what they have experienced and learned while working in the fashion industry.

## INSTRUCTOR'S RESOURCES

- The Instructor's Guide provides suggestions for planning the course and using the text in the classroom, as well as supplemental assignments and lecture notes.
- A Test Bank includes sample test questions for each chapter.
- PowerPoint© presentations include images from the book and provide a framework for lecture and discussion.

Instructor's Resources may be accessed through www.FairchildBooks.com.

## ACKNOWLEDGMENTS

Just as supply chain management is a network of internal and external partners working together to meet the demands of the consumer, the development of *Fashion Supply Chain Management* included key industry partners, colleagues, and personal supporters who contributed to the completion of the book. The authors would like to acknowledge LIM College for its commitment to the business of fashion. We would like to send a special thank-you to the team at Bloomsbury Publishing for their guidance: Amanda Breccia, Corey Kahn, Joseph Miranda, and Edie Weinberg. We would also like to thank the industry professionals who allowed us to include their interviews in the book: Mary A. Alonso, Mary G. Cally, Craig Dana, Michael Gilson, Amy Hall,

Edward Hertzman, Rick Horwitch, Regine Lahens, Mark A. Messura, Chad Schofield, and Deborah L. Weinswig.

Jacqueline M. Jenkins would like to extend her gratitude to those who lent their time and insight toward the creation of the book: Robert Burton, Judith Erwin, Michael Gilson, Kyla Marshell, Kimberly Minor, Sudhir Sachdev, Heather Schooler, Irv Varkonyi, Jeffrey A. Wurst, and Nioka Wyatt. Jacqueline would like to also thank her friends in New York and her family in Philadelphia for their support: Joan Jenkins (mom, behind-the-scene editor), Jocelyn, Shoshauna, Jan, and Gary.

Michael P. Londrigan would also like to thank those in the LIM College community for their continued support of his academic pursuits. In addition, he would like to extend a very special thanks to his loving wife, Dr. Marie Truglio-Londrigan, for her constant support and editing, as well as to Paul, Jacklyn, Leah, Chris, and Greyson, who mean the world to him. A special thanks to Dr. Guy Adamo, who got him back in the game, and to Dr. Alfred Sloan for his continued support and guidance.

**The Publisher wishes to gratefully acknowledge and thank the editorial team involved in the publication of this book:**

**Acquisitions Editor: Wendy Fuller**
**Development Editor: Corey Kahn**
**Assistant Editor: Kiley Kudrna**
**Art Development Editor: Edie Weinberg**
**In-House Designer: Lachina**
**Production Manager: Claire Cooper**
**Project Manager: Chris Black**

# The Supply Chain and the Fashion Industry

## LEARNING OBJECTIVES

Upon completion of this chapter you will be able to:

- Establish a working definition for supply chain management from a scholarly and business practitioner's perspective.

- Survey the history of supply chain management in relation to the dynamic nature of the fashion industry.

- Discuss how the changes in the fashion industry are impacting the fashion supply chain.

- Predict how the supply chain will advance to meet the demands of the modern consumer.

# DEFINITION OF SUPPLY CHAIN MANAGEMENT

Bain & Co., in its 2015 Management Tools publication, defines supply chain management as "the complex collaboration of suppliers, manufacturers, distributors, dealers, customers, and so on to ensure a seamless production and delivery of finished goods." The circular image depicted in Figure 1.1 shows the multiple points of impact along the route that goods travel while moving through the supply chain, such as the sourcing for raw materials (upstream and downstream), the capital required to produce and distribute goods (cash-flow), and the operational functions (distribution, logistics, and inventory management). Throughout the supply chain, vendors add value to products, information is leveraged to improve speed, customer profiles are made, and markets are analyzed. These various elements are supply chain contributors.

Because fashion is driven by the whimsical, ever-changing desires of consumers, success in the fashion industry is driven by a retailer's ability to deliver product to the market in a timely and cost-efficient manner. Since a retailer must have inventory to generate sales, supply chain management can easily be described as the lifeline of the fashion industry. Regardless of how well a product is marketed, a retailer is unable to sell what it doesn't have available. This book examines the role that supply chain management plays in turning design concepts into garments that are delivered to retailers to meet a consumer's desired timeline, price point, and quality expectations.

In this chapter you will learn how the changes in fashion industry business models, consumer preferences, and major selling channels are impacting how retailers are constructing and leveraging their supply chain processes. As the business of fashion changes, the operational infrastructure that supports the business must also change. The chapter will also provide background information about the inception, evolution, and current and future state of supply chain management. In order to keep up with the demands of fashion consumers, the fashion supply chain must change.

# ORIGINS OF THE SUPPLY CHAIN MANAGEMENT CONCEPT

The term *procurer logistics* appears as an early reference to supply chain management in the book *The Art of War*, written in 1838 by Baron Antoine-Henri Jomini (March 6, 1779–March 24, 1869), the Swiss officer who served as a general in the French army and later in the Russian service. The term showed up again in 1905 in a US article in *The Independent* newspaper about the wartime situation. It is no surprise that supply chain management, the efficient production and distribution of goods, is associated with wartime activities. Several of the apparel industry's manufacturing efficiencies developed from a military need; necessity is truly the mother of invention. In fact, men's ready-to-wear garments and standard sizes were established to meet the uniform requirements of men enlisted in the Civil War. Uniforms were initially custom-made. However, as the war progressed, manufacturers began to build factories that could quickly and efficiently meet the growing demands of the military.

The mass production of uniforms also necessitated the development of standard sizes. As sizing data were being collected, it was revealed that certain sets of

**Figure 1.1**
**Diagram of supply chain management** The diagram shows the interrelated nature of the operations that result in the production and distribution of goods.

measurements tended to recur with predictable regularity. After the war, the military measurements became the source for the first commercial sizing scales for men. Because fashion is more about prestige than practicality, ready-to-wear clothing for women could have easily grown from the standard sizing used by the military; however, it took until the beginning of the twentieth century for women's **ready-to-wear**, mass-produced clothing to gain enough acceptance from the fashion world to be a reputable source of clothing.

In the 1980s, the term *supply chain* was used in an article in the *financial times* by Keith Oliver of Booz Allan Hamilton, the management consulting firm that focuses on process efficiencies for various industries. Peter F. Drucker, whom *Business Week* hailed as "the man that invented management," is credited with establishing the organization principles of supply chain management. Drucker, an Australian-born American consultant, studied the dynamics of individuals and organizations to determine their ability to collaborate and pursue common goals.

# EVOLUTION OF THE SUPPLY CHAIN RELATIVE TO CONSUMER DEMAND

## Industrial Revolution: 1800s and Early 1900s

With the exception of the internet era, the Industrial Revolution is considered one of the periods that significantly advanced retail and production. Table 1.1 recognizes a few of the lead inventions, such as the sewing machine, that made the Industrial Revolution a key era of advancement for business and production. Another was the motor car; in 1907, Henry Ford announced that the goal for the Ford Motor Company was to create "a motor car for the great multitude."[1] Much like clothes, cars were expensive because they were being produced on a custom versus mass-market basis. To resolve this issue, Mr. Ford created a process that focused on four principles: interchangeable parts, continuous flow, division of labor, and less wasted effort.[2] By applying these basic principles of production, Mr. Ford was able to achieve his goal, as the Ford assembly line reduced the

time to manufacture a car from 12 hours to 30 minutes. The first cars cost $850, roughly $17,000 in today's market.[3] Interestingly, one of the ways that Ford was able to reduce the cost of production was by offering no factory options—not even a choice of color. As we continue to look at the evolution of the supply chain, we will see how innovations in technology will allow for mass customization down to an individual consumer.

On the fashion front, the 1850 invention of Isaac Singer's sewing machine enabled seamstresses to move to an automated garment construction process that increased speed, added durability to the garments, and enabled more decorative ornamentation. The sewing machine also created the opportunity, in a cost-effective manner, to introduce categories of clothing to meet lifestyle changes such as sports, leisure, and sleepwear. As already mentioned, ready-to-wear was invented to meet the needs of the military. But while the sizing and garment construction process created new efficiencies, women shoppers still preferred custom apparel versus apparel produced for the masses. However, for rural markets, Aaron Montgomery Ward's 1872 mail-order catalog was retail's first movement into a more standard order and fulfillment process for consumer consumption.

| Table 1.1 Industrial Revolution Advancements That Impacted Retail | |
|---|---|
| **Supply Chain Evolution** | **Retail Advancement** |
| 1807 Francois Isaac de Rivaz invented a car fueled by an internal combustion engine. | 1844 R. H. Macy opened his first store—a sewing supply store—in Boston. |
| 1850 Isaac Singer invented an affordable sewing machine for home and commercial use. | 1857 The first commercial elevator was installed in E. V. Haughwout & Co. department store, located at Broadway and Broome Streets, New York. |
| 1913 The Ford assembly line forever changed mass production. | 1872 Aaron Montgomery Ward produced the first mail-order catalog. |

The inventions of the industrial revolution provided the key mechanical and process innovations that directly impacted the retail environment. For example, one of supply chain's lead inventions is the invention of the sewing machine by Isaac Singer in 1850.

# Before and after World War II: 1940s and 1950s

There is a belief among historians that if you want to know what is going on in society take a look at what people are wearing. This thought holds true when we look at the fashions before and after World War II. At the beginning of World War II, the fashion houses of Europe such as Coco Chanel and Jeanne Lanvin were the true trend setters of fashion. American designers hadn't yet hit the international fashion scene. Because of fabric rationing in Europe, prewar fashions were tailored and used less lavish materials to fit the economic constraints of the war-torn world. Once the war was over, fashion began to bloom with color, styling, and draping that ushered in collections such as the 1947 Christian Dior Corelle, which means the "New Look" (Figure 1.2).

**Figure 1.2**
**Christian Dior's first collection: Corelle ("New Look")** The collection was accented by the use of fur and generous amounts of material to reflect a post–World War II mindset.

**Table 1.2** Inventions and Retail Advancements before and after World War II

| Supply Chain Evolution | Retail Advancement |
|---|---|
| 1952 US patent no. 2612994 was issued for an apparatus that classified and recognized images according to photo-line responses, also called barcoding.[4] | 1940s Western films created the first iconic retail clothing item, jeans. |
| 1956 Standard steel shipping containers were invented.[5] | 1947 Christian Dior's first collection hit the runway: Corelle ("New Look"). |

Table 1.2 shows the technological advancements that supported fashion interests before and after World War II. While the fashion world was moving from drab to fab, the supply chain began benefiting from advancements such as the 1952 patent issued to Norman Woodland and Bernard Silver for a barcoding system that allowed for inventory to be tracked in stores. Woodland and Silver were graduate students at the Drexel Institute of Technology[6] who were attempting to solve the issue of inventory tracking in the highly items-oriented grocery business. After they modified the type of ink used to print the code and applied a coding methodology inspired by Morse code, a patent was granted for the "Classifying Apparatus and Method."

As with many innovations, the accompanying technology has to catch up with the invention and application of the concept. The barcode was no different. For barcode technology to become the key means of tracking items, there needed to be a way to read the code quickly and a standardization process to facilitate transactions across multiple platforms. This technology would arise as grocers saw a need to monitor inventory more efficiently.

In 1955, the idea of a global supply chain became a cost reality with the introduction of **standard shipping containers,** steel shipping containers with standardized dimensions. Malcolm McLean, an American and the industrious owner of the largest trucking fleet in the South, obtained the first patent for the shipping container. Over his thirty years of owning his trucking business, he observed the inefficiencies that were created by loading and unloading odd-sized wooden crates. Like a true entrepreneur, he began to work on standardizing

**Figure 1.3**

**Standardized shipping containers carrying cargo** The picture shows multiple containers being shipped.

the trucking container business. He then saw that the next big opportunity was to take his extensive truck hauling experience coupled with his goal of standardization and move this logic to ocean cargo carrying. After purchasing the Pan Atlantic Tanker Company, he perfected the process of loading and unloading trucks and ships. McLean's final container design was super strong, uniform in design, theft-resistant, stackable, and easy to load, unload, truck, rail, ship, and store. If you were to go to any major port today, you would see the large standard boxes that McLean conceived.

As with many inventions, the adoption of the innovation takes place overtime and centered typically around a particular need. Thus, it was the efforts in the US Navy in the 1970s that enabled the shipping container to be accepted by every shipping line and every county in the world. Much like the introduction of the Model T assembly line reduced costs, the standard steel shipping container drove shipping costs from $5.86 for loose cargo to $0.16 per ton.[7] This made the idea of shipping cargo around the world a financial reality. For the manufacturing-intensive needs of the fashion industry, global shipping drastically changed apparel production. Figure 1.3 shows the mass of cargo able to be transported with the use of the standardized shipping container.

## The Age of Social and Economic Change: 1960s to 1980s

While the period from the 1960s to the 1980s will be known for its prolific political and social change, such as the culminating years of the civil rights movement and the era of the Cold War, there were also technological

**Table 1.3** Innovations of the Age of Economic and Social Change

| Supply Chain Evolution | Retail Advancement |
|---|---|
| 1960s electronic data interchange (EDI) and material resource planning (MRP) were invented. | 1962 Sam Walton founded Walmart. |
| Mid-1980s FedEx provided near real-time information about package deliveries. | Fast fashion commenced with the founding of H&M, a Swedish multinational company. Since then: Gap 1971  Inditex (Zara parent company) 1975  Fast Retailing Group (UNIQLO parent company) 1983 |

advancements that supported the creation of new business models that evolved around the efficiencies of the supply chain (Table 1.3). **Fast fashion,** a retailing business model based on the rapid production of new designs, was primarily founded through this period's launch of Gap, Inditex, and Fast Retailing Group. It should be noted that H&M (Hennes & Mauritz), the Swedish behemoth retailer that exists in sixty-one countries with a store base of 3,700 locations, was founded in 1947.

A key driver of efficiency is the ability to successfully transport information throughout the entire supply chain. There would be no efficiency if a shipper couldn't communicate with a vendor about an estimated time of arrival or if a production team were unable to share measurement requirements to a production house. That is why the 1960s invention of **electronic data interchange (EDI),** the electronic transfer of information applying a standardized format, was so critical. Like so many supply chain innovations, EDI was developed to solve a military challenge.

Thanks to EDI, operations managers were able to create business documents to track and store information that was able to be shared between different computers. The 1961 invention of a material resource planning (MRP) system by Josef Orlicky enabled one to track demand and required components for end products. MRP helps organizations maintain inventory levels and also plan manufacturing, purchasing, and delivering activities.

Since the late 1880s, there has been an interest in creating an automated means to track and monitor stock. The punch card introduced in 1899 by Herman Hollerith was essentially the precursor to the computer because of its ability to read data by using a chip. Hollerith went on to found the world's first computer company, IBM. Through numerous iterations of the early punch card technology, in 1967 IBM created the first computerized inventory management and forecasting system. This system reduced the costs of carrying inventory because it enabled retailers to minimize inventory obsolescence, reduce carrying costs, lessen the need to expedite inventory shipping, and improve ordering and handling processes.

In 1972, the first modern scanning system was installed by RCA at a Kroger's grocery store. With this scanning system, one could quickly and efficiently read barcoding with minimal manual effort. To further support the adoption of barcoding technology, other data capture inventions were implemented, such as the railway tracking system invented by David Collins from Sylvania, a North American light manufacturer.

Much like standardization of sizes was needed to support the advancement of ready-to-wear garments, there was a need for standardization of barcodes. In 1971, an IBM consultant, George Lauer, created the twelve-digit barcode that is used in stores today (Figure 1.4).

**Figure 1.4**
**Example of a barcode**

**How to Read the Uniform Product Code**

- The first six digits start with a 0 followed by the five-digit code of the manufacturer.
- The last six digits identify the item the bar code is affixed to.

Lauer went on to create the precursor to point-of-sale (POS) technology. He was also one of the leading forces behind the establishment of the **uniform product code (UPC),** a standard means to recognize the product manufacturer, product category, and selling country. As UPC was initially invented for the grocery trade, it was originally known as the universal grocery productions identification code (UGPIC). In June of 1974, the first UPC scanner was installed at a supermarket in Troy, Ohio.[8] To much amazement, the first product to have a barcode included was a pack of Wrigley's gum.

Some additional key supply chain evolutions include JC Penney's 1975 installation of the first real-time **warehouse management system,** a software application that supports the daily operations of a warehouse. Then the logistics side of the supply chain got a boost with 3M Transportation's creation of centralized transportation planning, which allowed companies to take advantage of network synergies. Considering that the retail world is dominated by ecommerce companies that primarily exist because of flexible shipping capabilities, the mid-1980s FedEx execution of near real-time information about package deliveries was truly an innovative solution. It is hard to imagine what retailing would be like today if one couldn't track deliveries.

## The Dot-Com Boom: 1990 to Early 2000s

During this period, as shown in Table 1.4, companies like Hewlett-Packard and Georgia Pacific introduced supply chain advancements such as Hewlett Packard's distribution requirements planning (DRP) system, which addressed the challenges of inventory planning by linking distribution activities (outflows) with manufacturing activities (inflows). Through centralized logistics planning, Georgia Pacific was able to create $20 million in annual savings by implementing a centralized logistics planning initiative. While all of these advancements played a role in the evolution of the supply chain, the landscape for local manufacturing was forever changed by the growth in imports from China between 1995 and 2006. Because of open trade policies and access to a cheaper production base, imports from China grew from $45 billion to $280 billion during this period.

**Table 1.4** The Dot-Com Boom Welcomes Internet Shopping Capabilities and Online Consumer Content

| Supply Chain Evolution | Retail Advancement |
|---|---|
| Early 1990s Hewlett-Packard linked distribution activities with manufacturing activities (DRP). | 1990 First World Wide Web server and browser were created. |
| 1994 Georgia Pacific implemented a centralized logistics initiative across the organization; creates $20M annual savings. | 1995 Microsoft released Internet Explorer 1.0. |
| 1995–2006 US imports from China grew from $45 billion to $280 billion. | 1995 Amazon and eBay were founded. |

These businesses were called "Dot Coms" because they were primarily internet-based businesses.

More details on the globalization of the supply chain will be provided in Chapter 2.

## Highlights of the Internet Evolution

As retailers learned how to use technology to support the sale of goods, the consumer started moving from bricks to clicks. It is hard to imagine what the shopping experience today would be like if we couldn't search the internet, if retailers didn't have websites, and if individuals weren't able to purchase items with online payment. However, the game-changing reality of ecommerce was brought on by a series of technological and consumer adoption advancements that spanned over several decades with contributions from the military, research institutions, the private sector, and innovative entrepreneurs that were looking for a means to create the multiple commerce platforms that coexist today.

As with many of the supply chain advancements, internet advances were primarily driven by military needs. During the Cold War, to answer the need to allow communication between computers in different geographic locations, the US Department of Defense funded the Advanced Research Project Agency (ARPANET), which created the precursor to the **World Wide Web (WWW)**, an information space where documents can be accessed by the internet. In the 1980s, the first company domain name, Symbolics.com, was registered to a computer manufacturer located in Massachusetts. Table 1.5 summarizes the key points of advancement for internet technology and adoption. In the 1990s, the web became used commercially because of its search engine capability.

## Father of the Internet

*"In those days, there was different information on different computers, but you had to log on to different computers to get at it. Also, sometimes you had to learn a different program on each computer. Often it was just easier to go and ask people when they were having coffee."*

SIR TIM BERNERS-LEE

**Table 1.5** Inventions and Technology Adoptions for Internet Capabilities[10]

| | |
|---|---|
| 1950s | First electronic computers were invented. |
| 1960s | US Department of Defense funded the Advanced Research Projects Agency (ARPANET) to allow communication between computers in different geographic areas during the Cold War. This was the precursor to the World Wide Web. |
| 1970s | Internet Assigned Numbers Authority (IANA) was established to oversee the assignment of internet protocol addresses, domain names, and internet protocol parameters. |
| 1980s | Domain name protocols continued to advance. The first dot-com domain name, Symbolics.com, was registered by a Massachusetts-based computer manufacturer. |
| 1990s | The internet became open for commercial use. Search engine capability enabled users to surf the web. |

While the internet supports commercial use today, the concept was initially utilized to support the interests of the military.

**Table 1.6** Today's Reality of an Omnichannel Shopping Environment

| Supply Chain Evolution | Retail Advancement |
|---|---|
| Customer-focused, differentiated supply chain plans were created. | 2000 Net-a-Porter was founded. |
| There was cross-functional integration within the supply chain. | 2007 Apple released the iPhone. |
| Training in knowledge-based learning (talent management) began. | c. 2000 Omnichannel and the demand chain concepts were introduced. |

Because of consumers' steady adoption to online shopping, today's retailers are leveraging multiple buying channels to support the diverse means that consumers engage and purchase product.

Sir Tim Berners-Lee, a British computer scientist, was the lead inventor of the World Wide Web. Although computers existed, there wasn't a way for individuals to share information. Berners-Lee's work allowed individuals to collaborate by sharing information through a web of hypertext documents: hence the name, the World Wide Web. He wrote the first World Wide Web server, "httpd," and the first client, "WorldWideWeb" a what-you-see-is-what-you-get hypertext browser/editor that ran in the NeXTStep environment. This work was started in October 1990; the program "WorldWide-Web" first was made available in December, and on the internet at large in the summer of 1991.[9]

## Today's Reality: 2000 to the Present

Whatever a consumer can dream—from one-hour delivery, to clothes that change color based on your mood—the continuation of supply chain evolution and retail advancements makes those dreams a reality. In the very early days of the supply chain, the focus was on availability and reliability. As seen in Table 1.6, availability and reliability are still the most desired outcomes from an effective supply chain; however, technology and new retail business models have created a selling environment that enables consumers to be a part of the production process. For example, Shoes of Prey is a custom shoe company that leverages **computer-aided design (CAD)**, the use of computer systems to aid in the creation and modifications of designs. These changes are all due to the adoption of web-based selling and mobile technology that has created the opportunity for consumers to shop on an integrated platform model called "omnichannel."

As manufacturers and retailers continue to leverage manufacturing capabilities such as 3D printing and big data, demand-driven supply chain networks are becoming a reality. Demand-driven supply chain networks focus on consumer preferences in a proactive manner to deliver the right product to the right consumer at the right time. By focusing on actual demand versus forecast, retailers are able to maintain lower inventory levels, reduce waste due to obsolescent products, and increase the ability to meet customer demand. While a demand-driven network optimizes resources, this means of production and order fulfillment is a significant change from traditional supply chain planning.

## FASHION INDUSTRY DISRUPTORS AND THE IMPACT ON THE FASHION SUPPLY CHAIN

The $1.2 trillion global fashion industry is being disrupted by market forces such as online shopping, fast fashion, and changes in consumer buying preferences driven by a shift in market demographics. Today's supply chain professionals are grappling with how to improve the speed of production and distribution while operating in a retailing environment where the multitude of brands has resulted in a shift of buying power from retailers to consumers. As consumers gain more buying power, retailers must look for new means to engage their market and strengthen a business's operating procedures to reduce costs while also elevating the value and/or experience of the product offering. All of these changes have a direct impact on the fashion supply chain. The unwillingness of customers to pay for shipping is causing retailers to redesign delivery routes to reduce costs while dramatically improving the speed of delivery. The millennial consumer also wants goods produced in a socially responsible manner, causing retailers to seek alternative, environmental, and labor-friendly production processes.

For many of these reasons, it is no surprise that the behemoth online retailer, Amazon, has made the business-savvy decision to leverage its supply chain infrastructure and brand recognition to compete in the fashion industry (Figure 1.5). As a result of Amazon's dominance in the ecommerce market, retailers are making strategic acquisitions and business model modifications to compete against the presence of Amazon in the market. For example, Walmart's 2016 $3 billion acquisition of Jet.com, an ecommerce shopping solution startup, is a demonstration of how retailers are concerned with Amazon's ability to steal market share from existing brands because of Amazon's core competency of sourcing, distributing, and performing customer service within the online shopping business model.

In 1994, Jeff Bezos, the founder and CEO of Amazon.com, took advantage of two key factors for retailing success: a product category with seemingly unlimited inventory and a hassle-free means to access consumers, the internet. Over the years, Amazon has expanded its product offering, set industry standards for online product delivery, and for many retailers has become the aspirational online retailing model to emulate. Amazon is an example of how supply chain management has evolved to be a leading differentiator for a retailer.

## THE CONSUMER'S ABILITY TO SHOP ANYTIME AND ANYWHERE

Over the past decade, the fashion industry has experienced dramatic changes in where consumers shop, how they engage with the product, and what their perceptions are about price and value. Figure 1.6 shows how a handheld personal digital assistant (PDA) functions as a virtual cart to allow consumers to browse ecommerce sites and place purchases into their virtual baskets. **PDAs** are devices that combine the functionality of a computer, a telephone, the internet, and networking. Additionally, significant retail consolidation and consumers' preference to purchase online instead of at brick-and-mortar locations are forcing retailers to re-create their business models to meet the

**Figure 1.5**
**A 1998 photo of Amazon founder and CEO Jeff Bezos as he demonstrates his concept of an online shopping cart for books** Books were selected as the first Amazon product offering because of the limitless titles that could be accessed through the Amazon website. However, it was Amazon's mastery of its supply chain that enabled the business to dominate the retailing sector.

**Figure 1.6**
**The mobile shopping cart** The mobile shopping cart is disrupting traditional retailing models and their supply chain networks.

demands of the modern consumer. For example, several retailers have reconfigured their store space and salesperson responsibilities to support a **click and collect** purchasing option, by which consumers purchase online and retrieves the item from their local store. Essentially, this feature is turning retail locations into mini-**fulfillment centers**, locations where incoming orders are processed for delivery. Stores like the Gap and Zara have dedicated space on the selling floor for online purchase pickup.

## Brick and Mortar versus Online Sales

As major retailers such as Macy's planned to close one hundred stores by August 2017, it is no surprise that online is the **sales channel** with the most growth potential. A sales channel is a means to reach consumers. While brick and mortar represents the largest sales channel, online sales is the channel that is outpacing store sales. According to Forrester Research Inc., a global research and advisory firm, online sales are expected to reach $523 billion by 2020, up 56 percent from $335 billion in 2015.[11]

The shakeup due to the growth of the online channel and the convergence of online and in-store, multichannel, and omnichannel retailing is dramatically changing fashion business models, the supply chain focus, and consumer engagement strategies. As a result, there will be great opportunities in the future for advancements in production and distribution networks in fashion.

## Omnichannel versus Multichannel Retailing

Retail technology advances are beginning to connect all aspects of the overall shopping experience.[12] Thus, retailers no longer have the luxury of pursuing marketing and merchandising strategies that assume that the shopping experience is a simple one; it is actually an integrated process driven by customers' desire to shop either on their mobile device or in the store. Table 1.7 shows the differences between omnichannel and multichannel retailing. **Omnichannel retailing** pursues the consumer wherever the consumer chooses to engage, whereas in **multichannel retailing** the consumer must opt into a specific channel. The messaging for multichannel retailing lacks the customer-centric messaging of an omnichannel strategy. In

| **Table 1.7** Omnichannel versus Multichannel Sales ||
|---|---|
| **Omnichannel** | **Multichannel** |
| Retailer proactively reaches a consumer wherever and however the consumer chooses to shop. | Retailer reactively engages the consumer once the consumer opts into a specific channel of engagement. |
| Messaging, branding, and ordering are coordinated along with multiple mobile devices and in-store displays. | No common mobile device strategy is used to reach the consumer. |
| Data-driven customer profiles are developed to target marketing. | The consumer obtains untargeted product information from mass distribution points of internet searches, in-store promotions, and print ads. |
| Projected sales per transaction are greater. | Projected sales per transaction are lower. |

Source: http://www.omni-channel.biz/

omnichannel retailing, there are multiple, individualized marketing touch points based on what consumers prefer from their web searches. As a result, consumers purchase more with omnichannel compared to multi-channel sales.

## FAST FASHION

Social media, with its endless ability to promote new fashions coupled with consumers' ongoing quest for almost instant gratification, is fueling **fast fashion**, a retailing culture focused on the production of new fashion concepts, at a reduced price point, in a short period of time. The following is a summary of fast fashion statistics.

**Fast Fashion Facts**[13]

- From 2000 to 2014, global production of garments doubled. Consumers' garment purchasing increased by 60 percent.
- Across essentially every category of clothing, consumers are keeping clothing half as long as they did fifteen years ago.
- Between 2000 and 2011, European brands on average increased the number of clothing collections produced from two a year to about five a year.

To keep up with the pace and volume of fast fashion, retailers have had to slash production times by identifying alternative material sourcing solutions, establish vendor relationships that are able to produce items right off the runway within a narrower production window, and use manufacturing capabilities that enable costs to maintain relatively low. For example, Zara offers twenty-four new clothing collections each year, and H&M offers twelve to sixteen collections[14] that are refreshed nearly weekly. For these reasons, **near-shoring**, the movement of production closer to the consumer, is being used by retailers to reduce production lead times. In the late 1990s, production was moved offshore to take advantage of cheaper labor rates. However, the push for fast fashion is causing labor costs to be only a portion of the production consideration. The ability to meet consumer demand, the need to produce on-trend fashions, and the increased need to beat other brands to market are dramatically impacting the fashion supply chain.

Fast fashion is also challenging the supply chain to address concerns about fast fashion's adverse impact on the environment, such as the waste of water and energy used in garment manufacturing and the rise of **landfills**,

waste disposal locations that are rapidly filling because of the amount of clothing being discarded each year. For example, Americans, some of the world's largest consumers of apparel items, throw away approximately 70 pounds of textile items per year. This amount of garbage is equivalent in weight to two hundred men's T-shirts, and most of this waste ends up in landfills.[15] Chapter 3 on social responsibility provides more details on this topic.

## CONCLUSION

With the Department of Labor projecting a 22 percent growth in supply chain management jobs between 2012 and 2022, it's evident that there are numerous changes occurring within the field of supply chain management. Supply chain management has evolved from a back-office function to a critical component of any organization that produces and/or distributes goods and services. With the complexity of competing in a global marketplace coupled with the challenges associated with ecommerce business models, the inner workings of the supply chain have become the lifeline for fast fashion companies looking to succeed in today's retail environment.

The increasing complexity of the supply chain is causing companies to grapple with issues such as global logistics, in-store distribution management, multivendor relationships, and risk management. Thus, retailers are seeing how an efficient and reliable supply chain can be a tremendous value to a fashion business. As mentioned previously, a retailer can only sell inventory that is available.

While it is often thought that technology is the key to success for supply chain management, effective communication and relationship building are actually the critical components to the success of the supply chain network. Relationships are built on trust that the mill or factory will meet the specifications of the production team. For their part, the mill and factory are committed to meeting the requests to ensure a vendor relationship that will enable long-term growth and profitability for both parties. Within this book, you will see how collaborative relationships throughout the supply chain enable retailers to meet the ever-changing demands of today's consumer.

## INDUSTRY INTERVIEW: DEBORAH L. WEINSWIG, THE HEAD OF GLOBAL RETAIL RESEARCH & INTELLIGENCE AT FUNG BUSINESS INTELLIGENCE CENTRE (FBIC)

During the Retail's Big Show 2016, hosted by the National Retail Federation, I had the pleasure of seeing Deborah L. Weinswig, the Head of Global Retail Research & Intelligence at Fung Business Intelligence Centre (FBIC), present a perspective of the future of the global supply chain. FBIC is the research division of Li & Fung that collects and analyzes market data on sourcing, supply chains, distribution, and retail. Prior to joining the Li & Fung team, Ms. Weinswig worked for investment firms where she held several senior leadership roles that focused on analysis of the consumer products market.

Ms. Weinswig is very involved in thought leadership in her industry and was one of the founding members of the Oracle Retail Strategy Council; she is also an active member of the International Council of Shopping Centers (ICSC) Research Task Force. In 2012, she received ICSC's Researcher Award for Outstanding Service and was also ranked as one of the 36 Best Analysts on Wall Street by *Business Insider*. Since 2002, Ms. Weinswig has been identified as the top-ranking earnings estimator by the Retailing/Broadlines Industry and was ranked second or third place as a stock picker by StarMine.

**Interviewer:** *As you look at the evolution of the fashion business, what are the major changes occurring in the global fashion supply chain?*

**D.W.:** There is a definite increase in the amount of investment that companies are making in their supply chain. This is a day and age where the supply chain is becoming increasingly a differentiation point. As the time from the catwalk to the selling floor has become more compressed, the supply chain has become more of a selling point for fashion. Your supply chain is your differentiator. From talking with various retailers, I can see how their conversation has changed from how they are viewing their supply chain as more than just a mere operation; they are viewing it as a strategic advantage. Investments in supply chain management are changing the game like never before because of the way in which consumers expect to receive goods—click and get. Because of ecommerce, today's consumers have an expectation of speed.

The other significant change is the need for retailers to develop reverse logistic solutions that are incredibly complicated. While consumers may purchase online, many will go to the store to return items. This is causing a challenge for retailers because stores are being forced to take in products that fall outside of their normal inventory. Once products that are only sold online or not sold at a particular location get returned to a store, the retailers must make the decision of whether to hold the item at full price or take an immediate markdown to ensure movement of the item. This is something that every retailer is struggling with as the store and online worlds converge. To solve the problem of a customer buying in one store and returning items in another store, one retailer has a van that shuttles between the retailer's two largest stores to transport product between the two locations because the product mix between the stores is so different. Retailers must figure out what is going to work.

Another evolving trend is the number of pure play ecommerce retailers that are moving into a physical space. The supply chain is impacted because now the ecommerce model is being challenged to stock inventory in multiple locations while still meeting the customer's expectations with regards to product availability, speed to market, and price.

Customer service is another key aspect that ecommerce businesses are trying to get a handle on. Retailers must decide how they want to address the customer service aspects of their business. Amazon has defined the standard for great customer service by its ease of ordering and return procedures, multiple delivery options and its limitless, diverse categories of inventory. Retailers must figure out the customer service challenges because failure to do so will result in disappointments in the customer's overall experience. An outcome that no retailer wants to face.

**Interviewer:** *How has digital retailing disrupted supply chain management?*

**D.W.:** Everyone wants things much faster on a more personalized basis. Because of these reasons retailers are placing smaller manufacturing orders

with factories. The competitive nature of the fashion industry is causing retailers to get purchases to consumers when they want it and on their own terms. Retailers are doing more orders that are customized, localized, and personalized. That is how today's consumer wants things.

Consumers want experiential retailing. What does this mean? Retailers must raise their service level expectations. Ecommerce retailers are finding a need to have a brick-and-mortar location so that consumers have the opportunity to experience the product before they make a purchase. While ecommerce is still about convenience, customers still want to touch and feel the product. This desire to create an experience has an impact on the logistics side of the business with regards to how inventory is stocked and the types of product assortments placed in stores.

An example of an online retailer that has been successful with its push to meet customer expectations is the shoe retailer Zappos. A part of its success might be attributed to the fact that Zappos is a single category business. However, Zappos is all about customer service. Zappos strives to make the consumer have an unbelievable experience. Zappos understands the value of servicing the customer in her own space, on her own terms. It [Zappos] just wants to take care of her. Because the online options for consumers are increasing exponentially, it is much more difficult for retailers. Additionally, the amount that consumers are spending on apparel is decreasing. This goes back to the first question of why retailers are investing in their supply chain; they need a competitive advantage. Retailers are in a race to have the best options for their customers.

Because it is so much easier to buy product anytime and anywhere, the idea of speed to develop and deliver product is becoming that much more important. The free shipping model is a challenge for retailers. Retailers understand that by having the right product at the right time, they are able to sell more items at full price. Once again, speed is key.

This is causing more retailers to move their production onshore. While the majority of the production and fabric is in China, retailers are giving consideration to having their production located closer to their markets. The idea of more product being made in America is becoming a reality.

However, an area where onshoring is not an option today is luxury goods. The access to high-end materials and quality craftsmanship limits the ability for luxury products to be produced outside of the traditional luxury locations. That is why lower price point goods that are more basic in their design and construction are being considered for onshore production.

**Interviewer:** *During your Retail's Big Show 2016 presentation, entitled* The Future of Digital Retail, *you spoke about sixteen digital tech trends such as smart malls, virtual reality, and drone deliveries. Which trend will be the most challenging for retailers to address from a supply chain standpoint?*

**D. W.:** 3D printing is going to be one area of advancement that will have a significant impact on the supply chain. Instead of having stores filled with inventory, retailers will be printing products in stores, on demand. Since customers want more customization, 3D printing enables customization whereas the traditional supply chain lacked this ability due to factory constraints and costs. 3D printing has the potential to increase sales because 3D printing allows consumers to get things that are made just for them within a reasonable amount of time at a reasonable price point.

Big data is another area of advancement that will impact the supply chain. Big data provides a means for retailers to better understand their customer, production requirements, and market changes. By understanding data patterns, retailers can begin to tailor their offerings to consumers in advance of production decisions. A challenge with big data is understanding the source of the data and evaluating whether the data will produce reliable results. However, the bigger issue is having analytical talent to be able to evaluate and utilize the data.

**Interviewer:** *Where do you see opportunities for innovations in supply chain management?*

**D. W.:** There are still opportunities to reduce the time for production. Companies like Under Armor, the Maryland-based athletic company, are applying innovation and local manufacturing tactics to the supply chain to reduce product lead times. To pursue local manufacturing, companies need opportunities for tax breaks and incentives so that they are able to invest in the talent and equipment needed to produce locally. To truly reduce lead times, companies must have the manufacturing capabilities for onsite production of soft and hard line items such as some of the customization initiatives that are occurring in the footwear industry.

With regards to voids in the supply chain, there is always an opportunity for increased digitization of information throughout the supply chain. The digitization of information will facilitate the movement of information throughout the supply chain, which ultimately will enable brands to make better production, delivery, and selling decisions.

## Questions Pertaining to Interview

1. Based on the examples raised by Deborah Weinswig, how has the supply chain become a point of differentiation for a brand? What does a brand need to do to make these points of differentiation sustainable?
2. The interviewer discusses the disruptions in the fashion business, such as the new business models that center on ecommerce. What are the pros and cons to these disruptions from a supply chain perspective?
3. Beyond the examples given by Deborah Weinswig, how will 3D printing change the supply chain and retail channels?

## Company Background

Li & Fung Group was founded in 1906 as an export trading business located in the port city of Guang-zhou, China. The company's founder started the business by translating trade documents from Chinese to English. Today, the business is being run by the third generation of the Fung family, Victor and William. The company operates a global supply chain network of over 25,000 individuals in 300 offices and distribution centers around the world, with a vendor base of 15,000 factories, mills, and logistics partners.[16] Li & Fung is a leader in sourcing and logistics. The company's offerings encompass the full spectrum of supply chain management services, such as design, sourcing, and logistics. The company has also taken on a retail element of the business. Because of the number of factories that Li & Fung controls through its extensive third-party agree-ments, Li & Fung is a leading player in the apparel and footwear manufacturing business.

Historically, the company has primarily grown by means of acquisitions. In 2013, the company spent $432 million on five acquisitions after the business had acquired ten other companies the prior year.[17] While Li & Fung has significant control over its factory base throughout Asia, the company doesn't maintain ownership of the majority of the factories that it uses as sources of production. It is the combined volume of the Li & Fung business that makes this entity the leading player in fashion manufacturing.

In 2013, over 81 percent of the Li & Fung $20 billion annual revenue came from the United States and Europe.[18] Essentially, the company is a powerful intermediary between Western apparel retailers. The company's client list reads like the occupant list for a major mall, with brands like Walmart, Sears, Target, Coach, Hudson's Bay, Tommy Hilfiger, DKNY Jeans, Kate Spade, American Eagle, Aeropostale, and Sean John on the list, just to name a few.[19] In 2014, the company spun off its Global Brands Division, Li &

Fung's branded division that owns, licenses and offers brand management services to well-known brands such as Juicy Couture, Lucky Brand Jeans, Quiksilver, Calvin Klein, Under Armor, Frye, Cole Haan, and Spyder.

## Market Opportunity[20]

With a network of 15,000 vendors in 60 countries, Li & Fung is the world's largest sourcing agent. As such, the company has access to all forms of pre- and postproduction data information. In addition, the organization also has access to buying trends, local and global sourcing considerations, and future mar-ket innovations. In 2012, Li & Fung acquired Catalyst, initially a provider of electronic artificial surveillance that began to provide radio frequency identification (RFID) solutions with the potential of impacting the entire Li & Fung customer base. The RFID solutions provide insight into the customer's experience in the store, inventory management support, and theft prevention.

While collecting store data using RFID, the lead-ership team at Li & Fung identified an ability to harness the company's data to provide solutions to current and future challenges that exist with apparel manufacturing. The solution was called the **digital supply chain**, a means to capture sourcing and logistics data remotely while storing this information in a cloud for access by multiple parties. The digital supply chain enables retailers to collect metadata that can be acted upon to assess issues like where the bottlenecks are in the supply chain and where there is duplication of tasks. The solution also pro-vides insight into what data are missing with regards to management decision-making.

As the concept of compliance continues to grow in significance for apparel manufacturing, the digital supply chain provides a means to track production without increasing labor costs and to improve the overall ability to meet the standards for compliance testing. This concept has proven successful in automotive and aerospace industries, where similar concerns arise with regards to production parts malfunctioning, inventory tracking, and evaluation of consumer demand.

Robert Burton, executive vice president of Li & Fung Sourcing, was grappling with the question of how to increase visibility throughout the entire Li & Fung factory base without dramatically increasing costs and implementing cumbersome processes to capture factory information within a fairly short period of time. The solution was the digital supply chain, which was established to address the following issues and opportunities within the business.

### Production Costs

There are several factors that increase the cost of production, such as labor, raw materials, equipment, and transportation. In addition, there are costs due to poor production processes that create waste in the fabric, rejections for poor quality, theft, and production delays, to name just of few of these added costs. The digital supply chain provides a means to obtain real-time information that can be acted upon before more goods are produced that might be flawed because of previous unseen issues. With this information, factories are able to better balance their line to improve the progress of garments. Because the margins in mass-produced apparel are relatively small, an ability to manage controllable costs through the production process can result in a tremendous impact on the bottom line. The digital supply chain creates greater cost visibility through its ability to track and monitor costs from start to finish of the production cycle.

### Consumer Expectations

Consumers are forcing retailers to dramatically bring down production lead times. This means that gone are the days when retailers had six months to produce and deliver a line. Once again, the factors that retailers are able to control, such as the speed of making decisions, the ability to minimize errors, and smarter insight into consumer demand, enable retailers to achieve the goal of getting the right product to the right consumer at the right time. Visibility into the production process from a cost and timing perspective will enable sourcing and other operational areas of the business to make more informed production decisions.

### Need for Middle Management Oversight

The labor-intensive nature of apparel manufacturing forces management to emphasize containing costs on such items as salaries for middle management. However, middle management expertise is often needed to monitor the various aspects of the production process. The digital supply chain creates a means for information to be gathered remotely from multiple locations without the need for onsite management at each location. It also ensures consistency and makes tampering with data impossible. While the retailer might find the information helpful for future orders, the sharing of information could put the factory in a vulnerable state with regards to its performance. For this reason, it is important for there to be a mindset of collaboration versus a transactional perspective that is primarily focused on short-term outcomes to emphasize the value of long-term relationships with factory partners.

### Vendor Transparency

Another challenging issue that retailers face is minimizing subcontracted work to unauthorized vendors, which is a concern from a compliance and quality standards perspective. By having an ongoing means to track production, a retailer can easily tell whether a garment has been produced at an unauthorized factory. Since today's consumers are holding retailers accountable for socially responsible production practices, it is in the best interest of retailers to have a clear understanding of all vendors throughout the supply chain that participate in the production of their goods.

### Aggregate Data Collection and Analysis

While individual factories might collect data, until the data are examined at an aggregate level, meaning from all mills and factories, it is relatively impossible to identify trends such as flaws in material that result in garment defects, production delays due to the need to wait for fabric, and misreading of specification packages because of the transmission of wrong information. Since large retailers often use multiple mills and factories, the ability to look at all combined production data provides insight into the overall production performance. Robert Burton, Li & Fung's digital supply chain leader, made the following comment: "Retailers are finally able to connect the dots. The aggregation of data also provides a means to easily train and correct errors by sharing common mistakes and best practices throughout the entire supply chain network."

**Case Study Questions**

1. While the digital supply chain presents tremendous benefits for the retailer, what benefits do you see for factories that would provide data for the digital supply chain? What is the downside for factories? Is there a way to create a balance so that both retailers and factories are in a win-win situation?
2. How might the concept of the digital supply chain affect retailers' decision to bring production back onshore?
3. While the digital supply chain addresses many operational hurdles, what challenges does it fail to resolve?

## CHAPTER REVIEW QUESTIONS

1. Based on the points covered in this chapter, why is supply chain management considered the backbone of the fashion industry? How does the supply chain impact designers, retailers, and consumers?
2. What is the correlation between the fickle nature of the fashion consumer and the ability to plan from a supply chain management perspective? To meet the demands of apparel shoppers, how must a brand think about its supply chain lead times, production costs, and inventory planning?
3. As the global fashion supply chain has evolved, how has it become more efficient? What are the opportunities for future efficiencies? How will these efficiencies impact future retail business models?

## CLASS EXERCISE

To understand the impact of a global fashion supply chain, develop a perspective of being either a factory owner or a retailer. If you were a factory owner, what would be the pros and cons of a global fashion supply chain? If you were a retailer, what would be the pros and cons of a global fashion supply chain? What benefits and challenges exist for both factory owners and retailers with regards to the concept of a global fashion supply chain?

## KEY TERMS

ready-to-wear
standard shipping containers
fast fashion
electronic data interchange (EDI)
uniform product code (UPC)
warehouse management system

World Wide Web (WWW)
computer-aided design (CAD)
PDAs
click and collect
fulfillment centers
sales channel

omnichannel retailing
multichannel retailing
near-shoring
landfills
digital supply chain

## REFERENCES

1. History of Ford Motor Company, company website.
2. Ibid.
3. http://historical.whatitcosts.com/facts-modelT.htm.
4. www.SUPPLYCHAINOPZ.COM, 2013.
5. World Shipping Council Partners in Trade, History of Containerization, 2016. Available online: http://www.worldshipping.org/about-the-industry/history-of-containerization.
6. Heroes of Capitalism, October 22, 2012, http://drexel.edu/now/archive/2012/October/Barcode-60th-Anniversary/.
7. http://www.priceandspeed.com.au/about-us/history-shipping-containers/.
8. History of Barcodes, https://www.barcodesinc.com/articles/history.htm.
9. http://inventors.about.com/od/bstartinventors/p/TimBernersLee.htm.
10. http://www.livescience.com/20718-computer-history.html.
11. Linder, M. (2016), "Online Sales Expected to Reach $523 Billion in the Next Five Years, Up 56% from $335 Billion in 2015," *Internet Retailer*, January 29.
12. Haims, A. (2014), "Omni-Channel Finally Becomes Mainstream in 2015," Marketing Land, December 22. Available online: http://marketingland.com/omni-channel-finally-becomes-mainstream-2015-111366.
13. Remy, N., E. Speelman, E. Eveline, and S. Swartz (2016), *Style That's Sustainable: A New Fast Fashion Formula*, McKinsey & Company.
14. Ibid.
15. Confino, J. (2016), "We Buy a Staggering Amount of Clothing and Most of It Ends Up in Landfills," *HuffPost*, September 14.
16. Li & Fung Annual Report 2015.
17. Yin, D. (2013), "Li & Fung Falls Out of Favor," *Forbes Asia*, September.
18. Ibid.
19. Ross, R. J. S., D. Patterson, B. Dana, B. Yadegari, and C. Wegemer (2014), "A Critical Corporate Profile of Li & Fung." Mosakowski Institute for Public Enterprise, Paper 31. Available online: http://commons.clarku.edu/mosakowskiinstitute/31.
20. R. Burton, NRF 2016 Presentation, January 2016.

# The Global Factors That Impact the Fashion Supply Chain

## CHAPTER 2

## LEARNING OBJECTIVES

Upon completion of this chapter you will be able to:

- Assess how the dynamics of operating in a global environment impact the fashion supply chain.

- Trace the evolution of manufacturing locations around the world and understand its impact.

- Evaluate the role and outcome of government policy on apparel manufacturing.

- Formulate global sourcing strategies that minimize risks while meeting the fashion industry's business model objectives of speed to market and cost containment.

# THE GLOBAL FASHION SUPPLY CHAIN

The **American Apparel and Footwear Association (AAFA)**, a trade organization that focuses on public policy and legislative concerns that relate to the apparel and footwear industry, reported that in 2015, 98.4 percent of shoes and 97.3 percent of clothes sold in the United States were imported.[1]

Apparel and footwear production is truly a global supply chain that incorporates vendors, factories, and professionals around the world, but primarily in North America, South America, Europe, and Asia (Figure 2.1). As production shifts, there are expected opportunities for an increased presence of Africa in the global fashion supply chain. Asia continues to be the dominant manufacturing continent, with China producing the majority of the world's apparel exports. As labor costs rise in China, apparel and footwear companies are seeking lower-cost countries for production because the typical fashion consumer is unwilling to bear a rise in costs. BMI Research, a macroeconomic research firm, reported that the labor prices in China are four times greater than in Bangladesh, Laos, Cambodia, and Myanmar.[2] To maintain **margins**, a percentage of sales that is derived by subtracting the costs of manufacturing a good from the sales price, companies must seek cheaper and more efficient sourcing options. For these reasons, there have been several new entrants into the apparel production market, such as Bangladesh, Vietnam, and India.

This chapter will discuss the history of various countries' involvement in the supply chain, the characteristics that enabled these countries to succeed in apparel manufacturing, and the emerging trends that are resulting in an increase in onshore versus offshore production. It will also provide insight into the emerging countries that are increasingly involved in apparel production. Additionally, it will explore the key relationships throughout the

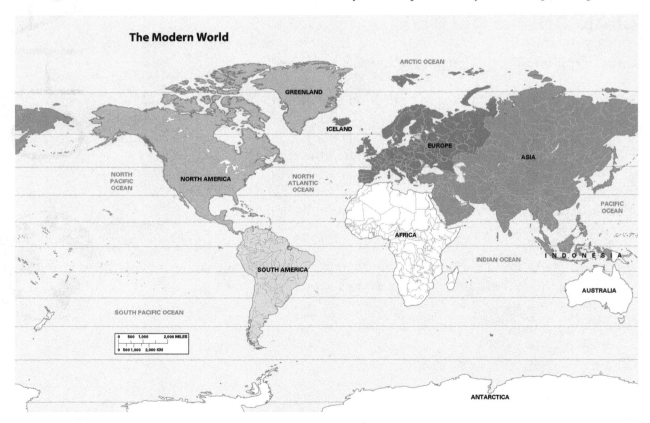

**Figure 2.1**
**The global fashion supply chain** This chain is the network of fabric mills, factories, logistics partners, and distribution centers located on four of the seven continents: North America, South America, Europe, and Asia.

global supply chain and explain how effective management of these relationships can mitigate risks, improve quality, and reduce costs.

## THE HISTORY OF QUOTAS

Given the labor-intensive nature of apparel manufacturing, labor costs have always been a key factor in deciding where to locate manufacturing. Another key factor is governmental support and/or restrictions on production. For example, the United States has sometimes used **quotas**, which restrict the quantity of textiles and apparel being imported into the country for certain categories, such as men, women, and children.

As seen in Figure 2.2, under the Reciprocal Trade Agreement Act (RTAA), passed during the presidency of President Franklin Delano Roosevelt, US presidents were given the authority to negotiate **bilateral trade agreements**, contractual relationships that governed the exchange of goods and investment between two countries, without seeking congressional approval. Bilateral trade agreements also included the setting of tariffs and quota restrictions that impacted trade. RTAA was enacted to stimulate a free-flowing global trade environment. Instead of practicing a trade philosophy of **isolationism**, an economic policy that makes a country self-reliant rather than a participant in a global trading market, the United States was taking a more liberal stance and becoming involved in the global trade environment. RTAA also gave presidents a key role in the shaping of US trade policies, a role that is still being implemented by the current presidential administration.

After RTAA, the next major trade policy to impact apparel manufacturing was the 1962 Trade Expansion Act passed by President John F. Kennedy. As a result of the industrialization driven by post–World War II expansion, textile production had grown. However, the United States and the United Kingdom were importing significantly more textiles than they were exporting. Kennedy's Trade Expansion Act was passed with the goal of increasing jobs and economic opportunities for the United States and its allies.[3] It was felt that RTAA did not usually succeed in balancing imports and exports because the race for cheaper labor continued to drive manufacturing outside the United States and the United Kingdom.

As the trade imbalance in textiles and apparel continued to grow, the United States and EU countries decided to limit the amount of goods able to be imported from developing countries; the result was the **Multi Fibre Arrangement (MFA) of 1974**. This period of restrictions and quotas lasted from 1974 to 2005. During the early phases, there was a quota on raw materials like cotton, man-made fibers, and silks. Quotas were put in place to limit the impact of emerging countries entering into the apparel manufacturing market, which had been dominated by the United States and the European

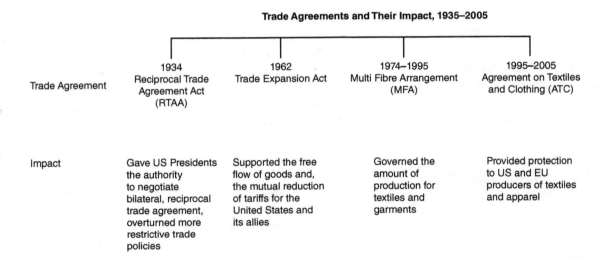

**Trade Agreements and Their Impact, 1935–2005**

| Trade Agreement | 1934 Reciprocal Trade Agreement Act (RTAA) | 1962 Trade Expansion Act | 1974–1995 Multi Fibre Arrangement (MFA) | 1995–2005 Agreement on Textiles and Clothing (ATC) |
|---|---|---|---|---|
| Impact | Gave US Presidents the authority to negotiate bilateral, reciprocal trade agreement, overturned more restrictive trade policies | Supported the free flow of goods and, the mutual reduction of tariffs for the United States and its allies | Governed the amount of production for textiles and garments | Provided protection to US and EU producers of textiles and apparel |

**Figure 2.2**

**Chronology of US trade policy, 1930s–2005** This chart shows some major milestones in the progression of liberal trade policy.

Union. However, the elimination of quotas had a detrimental impact on the US apparel manufacturing market because of the reduced labor costs of emerging economies that were doing apparel manufacturing.

In 1995, the **World Trade Organization (WTO)** established the **Agreement on Textiles and Clothing (ATC)**, which mandated a ten-year phaseout of quota protection. This legislation gave companies the freedom to select manufacturing locations without restrictions on the volume of production. It was part of the 1995 Uruguay Round Agreement, which involved negotiations among 123 countries. A period of ten years was selected to allow for the apparel manufacturing market to prepare for the impact of a globally diverse sourcing geographic footprint dominated by locations with the cheapest cost of production.

Because labor costs continue to be the driver in why companies choose to manufacture in a particular country, the elimination of quotas facilitated the unhindered movement of production to countries with cheaper labor costs, such as China. During the quota phaseout period, the United States lost over 900,000 apparel manufacturing–related jobs.[4] As US labor wages rose, what had once been the US cottage industry of apparel manufacturing moved to overseas production in countries with cheaper labor costs.

When quotas were eliminated, the apparel-manufacturing market became favorable for emerging economies such as India, Pakistan, and Bangladesh because of their relatively cheaper labor costs. The final phase of the quota was lifted on December 31, 2004. The impact of the quota elimination wasn't actually felt until the final phases because established manufacturing countries like the United States, Canada, and the European Union were not obliged to use the quota eliminations until the final phases; hence the dramatic shift of production from established to emerging countries at this time.[5]

# HISTORICAL LOOK AT SUPPLY CHAIN MANAGEMENT BY COUNTRY

## United States

As seen in Figure 2.3, the 1950s, right after the end of World War II, was considered a period of economic boom for the United States. At this time many former

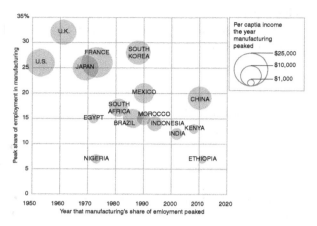

**Figure 2.3**

**Evolution of the global apparel manufacturing market, 1950s–2020** The chart shows that initially the United States was the dominant manufacturer of textiles and apparel. However, through the shifts in the aforementioned trade policy, US dominance lessened over time. Today China produces over 80 percent of the apparel and textiles consumed by the United States.

uniform and parachute factories transitioned into manufacturers of civilian clothes. Because of the wartime investment in machinery and worker training, these factories were efficient for their time, and the increased employment supported the creation of the US middle class. This fact is significant because the wages of the middle class during this time of economic boom enabled the average US worker to purchase many of the ready-to-wear fashions that the factories were producing. Clothing was no longer made at home but was made in US factories and sold from stores.

By 1960, American households were spending, on average, 10 percent of their income on apparel and footwear. In today's dollars, this amount of spending roughly translated into $4,000 of annual purchases. Individuals purchased less than 25 garments a year, of which 95 percent were manufactured in the United States.[6] Large-scale retailers like the Gap and JC Penney began to chase better profit margins and stopped being **vertically integrated**; that is, they stopped relying on their internal production departments and instead relied on external vendors to manufacture goods. During this period, companies began to outsource their production to **offshore manufacturers**, factories that existed in countries or locations outside the company's home country. Companies like Liz Claiborne and The Limited retained the design and marketing functions of the brands, the highest profit areas, and outsourced the less profitable and in some instances the most risky aspects of the business, their apparel manufacturing. Essentially, these companies became "manufacturers without factories."[7] This shift in strategy was a key turning point for the fashion industry because by removing the manufacturing element of the business, these companies repositioned their balance sheets to no longer require the investment in hard assets associated with owning and running factories. The financial implications of this change in production strategy are further explained in Chapter 10.

Additionally, these companies have transitioned to relying on a cheaper labor base. In essence, they've reduced their cash requirements while also freeing up capital for long-term asset investments, a move that ultimately drives profitability without significantly changing the product or market focus.

In the book *Overdressed: The Shockingly High Cost of Fast Fashion*, the author states that by 2003 the Gap was placing production orders with 1,200 factories across four different countries.[8] A garment was pieced and assembled throughout the entire supply chain instead of being started and finished by the same workers in one factory. This new production strategy ultimately drove down costs, but it also made the United States a much less competitive market because US factories weren't organized this way and US workers weren't trained to function in such a manner.

The year 1978 was the peak year for US manufacturing jobs.[9] Because of increased competition from abroad and the trade agreements discussed earlier in this chapter, from 1978 onward the United States was in a downward spiral for apparel manufacturing jobs. Since 1990, the apparel, leather, and allied products markets have fallen by a dramatic 84 percent and 912,000 jobs have been lost, primarily in California, New York, Texas, and North Carolina. These four states employed 50 percent of the apparel labor for the United States. In 2013 California was the largest employer, at 35 percent.[10]

## Apparel Imports to the United States[11]

Figure 2.4 shows that in 2013–2014 Vietnam, Bangladesh, and Indonesia together imported $18.1 billion in apparel into the United States, an amount that is only

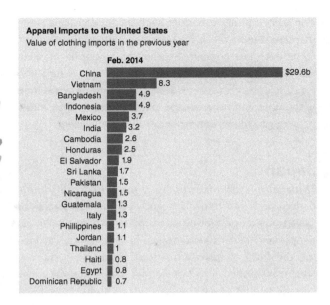

**Apparel Imports to the United States**
Value of clothing imports in the previous year

**Feb. 2014**

|  |  |
| --- | --- |
| China | $29.6b |
| Vietnam | 8.3 |
| Bangladesh | 4.9 |
| Indonesia | 4.9 |
| Mexico | 3.7 |
| India | 3.2 |
| Cambodia | 2.6 |
| Honduras | 2.5 |
| El Salvador | 1.9 |
| Sri Lanka | 1.7 |
| Pakistan | 1.5 |
| Nicaragua | 1.5 |
| Guatemala | 1.3 |
| Italy | 1.3 |
| Phillippines | 1.1 |
| Jordan | 1.1 |
| Thailand | 1 |
| Haiti | 0.8 |
| Egypt | 0.8 |
| Dominican Republic | 0.7 |

**Figure 2.4**
**Apparel imports to the United States by country, 2013–2014** The figure shows that China led significantly as a producer of apparel imports into the United States, with Vietnam the next largest importer.

61 percent of the top importer, China. Even after the Rana Plaza factory fire that killed over 1,100 garment workers, Bangladesh garment manufacturing continues to grow for two primary reasons: because of the relatively cheap labor costs and because Bangladeshi garments have duty-free access to Eastern European markets.[12] Having abundant access to raw materials is another way for countries to rise in value within the supply chain. For example, Pakistan has been able to advance because of its access to cotton.

## United Kingdom

By the 1960s, the United Kingdom began to take the lead in manufacturing (see Figure 2.3), primarily for the same reasons that the United States saw a boom after World War II. This was an age of political and social change that was supported by the undercurrent of economic growth and opportunities. However, the United Kingdom's thrust in production was eclipsed by the challenges of labor costs, a rise in imports from countries with a cheaper labor source, and ultimately, a drain in talent. On the labor front, the 1999 introduction of pro-labor legislation such as the national minimum wage (NMW) resulted in higher labor rates.

For labor-intensive sectors such as apparel, this wage increase caused the UK apparel-manufacturing market to be even less competitive than its emerging markets that were trading market access for fair wages. By 1999, the UK apparel market was at a steep point of decline, without glimpses of hope in the workwear, quick response fashions, and technical textiles markets.[13]

## Japan

With an eye on maintaining a sense of world dominance, since the mid-nineteenth century the Japanese government has continued to make investments in its people and its infrastructure. These investments, taking the form of heavily financed government entities, later transitioned into large-scale private ventures that had the benefit of developing under a highly subsidized startup period. However, Japan's dominance was toppled by the devastation of World War II, when 40 percent of the country's factories and industrial infrastructure was destroyed.[14] Though at first it seemed that the manufacturing sector would be greatly set back, Japan seized the moment to do as it has done in the past: it bet on its future. Through public and private sector ventures led by the Japanese government, Japan retooled and rebuilt its economy and became an economic leader. Capital investment and political change drove the reinvention of the Japanese manufacturing business.

Because Japan was essentially starting from scratch to rebuild after World War II, it had an advantage over other competing countries that were trying to make do with outdated equipment, skill sets, and infrastructure. Instead of building on what was and relying on cheap labor to achieve competitive pricing, Japan built with an eye to the future by investing in technology to meet future production demands. Unlike labor, which over time necessitated increased wages, better work conditions, and safer work environments, technology enabled Japan to be competitive without the pressures of growing with a low-skilled, high-volume workforce.

To foster growth, the Japanese government also introduced large, modern industrial groupings called **keiretsu** that shared resources and talent and focused on a common area of industry.[15] The keiretsu dynamic enabled Japan to leverage capital, talent, and innovative ideas across a platform of like-minded entities.

Education became Japan's secret weapon. Japan's heavy investment in education after World War II resulted in the country's high literacy rate, which in turn enabled the country to become a manufacturing powerhouse. Japanese workers were known for their ability to increase efficiencies, and a talented workforce was able to tackle complex manufacturing tasks. Often Japanese workers were cross-trained to be able to complete multiple jobs on the production line. However, Japan didn't have an advantage in low-cost production of mass-market goods like the apparel sourced for fast fashion retailers.[16] Because of the simplicity of mass-market, low-cost garments, the talents of the Japanese worker were not needed in this area, and Japan failed to adequately transition the skill sets of the Japanese worker to the lower margin business.

While Japan seemed to be on track to be the leading overseas manufacturer, things began to slow down in the 1970s. As Japan was highly dependent on petroleum, the 1973 oil crisis was a significant blow to its economy. Eventually, a significant portion of Japanese apparel manufacturing moved away. To replace this loss in manufacturing revenue, Japan placed its focus on the electronics and automotive sectors, areas in which it could compete because of its ability to create innovative businesses and the level of talent of the Japanese worker. In short, the skills and production technique developed for apparel transitioned successfully to more competitive markets such as electronics for the Japanese labor market, an area where the Japanese still maintain dominance.

## South Korea

By the 1980s Asia was the top continent for producing and selling garments. Asia was an attractive manufacturing market because of its access to key resources to support manufacturing, such as competitive wages, a significant raw material base, and an untapped market for the goods that were being produced. Seoul, Korea, became one of the first Asian manufacturers of apparel. With strong investment by the government and public-private partnerships, the factories in Seoul were built with the latest technologies to enhance the overall competitiveness of this region. By 1980, 24 percent of South Korea's manufacturing was in textiles, clothing, and leather goods. Footwear was also a lead area of production.[17] As wages increased, however, South Korea lost its competitive edge and manufacturing declined.

## China

In addition to being a source of cheap labor, China was a vast, untapped market for US apparel. While access to a cheap labor source is key for apparel manufacturing, companies also received an additional benefit by relocating sourcing production near new markets for consumption. For example, Nike, which started in 1964 by importing and distributing sneakers from Japan, moved its production to China in the late 1970s. This move created an entry into the growing Asian market.[18] At that time, the population in China was slightly under two billion, while the US population was roughly 24 percent that of China.[19] In addition, the US market had been tapped by retailers from the United States and abroad for quite some time. China became a production and selling market of choice.

In 1978, after the Chinese government loosened control on the country's equipment and allowed the formation of public-private partnerships, the country tried to restart its economy by encouraging business ownership, easing pricing controls, and investing in educating its growing workforce.[20] Research by the **International Monetary Fund (IMF)**, an international financing organization, reported a 42 percent productivity growth for China from 1979 to 1994. In addition to investing in workforce development, China pursued advanced robotics and other technological innovations that contributed to a jump in productivity. China's investment paid off. In 2000, it produced a mere 8 percent of US apparel imports. The US apparel and footwear market is primarily being supplied by China. In 2015, imports from China accounted for $48.9 billion, up 3.6 percent following a small increase of 1.6 percent in 2014.[21]

## India

Behind China, but growing quickly in production capability and capacity, is India with 11,000 factories and 1.258 million people.[22] With a goal of emulating the production boom of China a mere two decades ago, India is investing capital in labor, infrastructure, and equipment to boost its manufacturing performance. India is not only producing goods for export, but is also producing goods for its own consumption. Increased population coupled with the rise of double-income households is causing India to be one of the fastest-growing markets. India's prime minister, Narendra Modi, described India in 2016 as having the "three Ds": democracy, demography, and demand.[23] India, an economy that had primarily been built on the service sector, has been making inroads into the apparel manufacturing sector since the elimination of quotas in 2005.

As stated earlier in the chapter, raw material sourcing and manufacturing have moved to different areas of the world due to rising labor costs. Other factors that are also causing companies to relocate manufacturing are the uncertainty of the political climate, a growth in infrastructure investment, and new market access in emerging economies. Of note for apparel companies is the fact that 55 percent of mid-market apparel will be sold in emerging markets by 2025.[24] For example, not only has India become attractive for production, but its appetite for consumer goods such as apparel and footwear also makes it an attractive consumer market. The change in demographics to a younger population, the rise in disposable income, and investments in retail-related real estate have created tremendous growth in the Indian market.

## Africa

As labor costs continue to rise in China, companies are looking for other destinations to strengthen their growing supply chain network. South Africa is identified as one of the fastest-growing emerging markets. In 2013, the **United States Agency for International Development (USAID)**, a US government agency responsible for delivering humanitarian aid, partnered with the American Apparel Footwear Association (AAFA) to identify potential opportunities for building the manufacturing sector in South Africa.

In 2012, the United States and South Africa established a **Trade and Investment Framework Agreement (TIFA)** to analyze the future outlook on trade and investment. Furthermore, the United States has a Trade Investment and Development Cooperative agreement with the South African Customs Union (SACU). Both agreements prevent double taxation on merchandise that is exported from the United States to South Africa.

**Partner Africa** is a leading nonprofit social enterprise driven by a mission to improve the livelihoods of workers and producers and to enhance access to global markets. Partner Africa offers ethical trade services to global brands and suppliers. The organization also offers capacity building, training to certify manufacturers, and trade development to enhance the marketability of regions such as South Africa and the European Union.

Other areas of Africa, including East Africa, Ethiopia, and Kenya, are drawing interest from global retailers for the purpose of apparel production. Global retailers like H&M, Primark, and Tesco are using these countries primarily for bulk production of core, basic items such as T-shirts. This selection of production item is reflective of the stage and comfortable level that companies have with production coming out these areas. A core, basic item doesn't require design and other advanced manufacturing capabilities, so the production of the item matches the production capabilities of the area.

Companies are interested in the African market partly to increase their market presence and produce their products. It is an opportunity for companies to test the market on a small scale and to create a brand presence in Africa. Brands are willing to emphasize Africa because of the previous and current challenges, such as adequately developed manufacturing infrastructure, access to stable electric resources, and a skilled workforce. throughout the country. In addition, a study by the United Nations projected that sub-Saharan Africa will experience the highest growth of individuals able to work over the next twenty years. By 2035, the working population of this region will be equivalent to the current labor pool in China: more than 900 million laborers.[25] The **African Growth and Opportunity Act (AGOA)** is also a major attraction for companies who are producing in certain regions in Africa because products can be shipped to the United States duty-free. For this reason, 92 percent of Kenya's production went to the United States in 2013.[26]

In addition being a vast labor source, Ethiopia in particular has the potential to be a major supplier of raw materials. Of the 3.2 million hectares of land that is conducive for the cultivation of cotton, less than 7 percent is being utilized.[27] Later in this chapter, the book will further explain why a key benefit of a manufacturing area is its ability to provide raw materials for the production process.

While Africa presents opportunities for manufacturing and some market presence, it still faces several challenges relating to communication infrastructure and poor roads before it can support a robust supply chain network. The overall economy tends to be slow-paced and is hampered by complex business practices and political concerns. Africa also lacks some of the basic supplies and components necessary to create a vertical supply chain system. However, because of their projected labor outlook, both Ethiopia and Kenya are investing in these areas while also actively obtaining foreign investments from other countries that have a vested interest in the manufacturing advancement of this region.

## Notes from the Field

It goes without saying that the fashion industry is key to the global economy, and it might be the most global of all businesses, especially in the United States, where approximately 97 percent of all apparel and accessories are imported. As evidenced in this chapter, the fashion industry supply chain has totally embraced the global economy. During my career with the various companies I worked for, our goal was always to satisfy the customer, which in most cases was a retailer. My global travels took me from Honduras to Bangladesh and many stops in between. At one point I had 400,000 frequent flyer miles! Many of my contemporaries in the industry had the same number or more; as the global economy grew and new areas for production opened up, we all followed like lemmings. People thought this was glamorous, but the point was to conduct business, and the apparel, textile, and accessory factories, except for a few, were generally located in an industrial setting far from any tourist attractions. It was important work—enjoyable at times, difficult at other times—but a job that the global economy offered and that I always relished.

# FACTORS THAT DETERMINE LOCATIONS FOR APPAREL MANUFACTURING

## Labor

Throughout this chapter, there will be an ongoing emphasis on the significance of labor in the apparel-manufacturing process. Apparel manufacturing is one of the most labor-intensive, low-skilled manufacturing processes. On average, 40 percent of garment production is labor. Given the potential for human rights violations such as unfair wages, denial of workers' rights, and lack of safety on the job, the fashion industry has continued to improve its labor compliance. Chapter 3 further discusses the impact of labor abuses on the apparel-manufacturing process and how retailers have addressed these concerns by practicing compliance and strengthening vendor relationships throughout the global fashion supply chain.

By far, the majority of apparel workers are women working in lower-level production roles such as cutting and sewing. Because of lack of jobs, access to education, and cultural norms, low-level apparel manufacturing is often the only option available for women who need to earn a living. The majority of apparel-manufacturing jobs require low skill levels; however, these are essentially the lowest-paid and most easily exploited positions. On average, only 3 to 4 percent of apparel jobs are those of machine assistant, planner, or operational support[28] and are not related to production. Since there is often a shortage of talent to fill these roles, these positions are often held by expatriates or are covered offsite at the company's headquarters.

While garment production is typically a low-skilled job, some schooling is expected, and this is often factored into the decision to pursue manufacturing in a particular country or region. One of the reasons that Western companies built manufacturing plants in Mexico and Turkey in the 1970s was that a quarter of the children in these countries went to secondary schools.[29] And one of the reasons that companies are looking more hopefully at Africa for manufacturing is that the rate of child education is on the rise. Increased manufacturing depends on government investment in education and infrastructure.

Because labor is such a critical factor in the manufacturing process, companies are continually trying to identify cheap labor sources for production. Prior to the phaseout of the Multi Fibre Arrangement (MFA) quota systems, which governed the amount of production for textiles and garments between 1974 and 2004, factories were set up and maintained because they had the capacity to produce garments within the constraints of the quota. This meant that the primary reason a factory was selected for production was that it had the capacity to produce, not that it had the talent and/or manufacturing processes that guaranteed a quality, efficient assembly line. For this reason, countries could establish a manufacturing base with minimal investment in training and with the expectation of paying low wages.

After the quota constraints ended in 2005, companies began to select factories on the basis of performance. As factories moved to a focus on performance versus costs, they had to invest in talent, increased their management costs, and pay fair wages. To remain competitive, mature manufacturing countries also started to face requests for greater compliance, increased vendor transparency, and lean sourcing capabilities. Because these requests require more oversight and talent compared to basic assembly-line work, mature manufacturing companies started to invest in management training and certification programs, which are often funded through public-private partnerships between government and private corporations.

While manufacturing often starts with low wages, as the workforce matures there is often a push from labor for improved wages, improved working conditions, and management opportunities. To achieve these objectives, workers often organize themselves to create unions or go on strike. The main role of a union is to advocate for workers' rights, wages, benefits, and other opportunities. Union fees can vary based on the country, region, and size of the union. One of the disadvantages of unions is the potential of workers to go on strike. In the global supply chain process, sourcing agents and other key departments should assess the company, country, and region to identify if they are heavily populated with unions. In the case of Cambodia, one factory can have an infinite number of unions. For example, Factory A can have five unions while Factory B can have thirty unions. This situation can pose a risk for fashion retailers if a union goes on a strike. Although the human rights of workers are important, an excessive number of strikes will create a delay in merchandise shipments.

## Infrastructure

The political climate and infrastructure are also factors that impact the global fashion supply chain. Governments play an instrumental role in supporting or limiting the global supply chain. Because manufacturing typically is the economic generator that creates jobs and access to foreign investment, countries choose to pursue manufacturing relationships that support their development.

There is a reason that manufacturing plants are strategically located within areas that have access to roads, rail, and sea. As areas become more accessible, factories typically move farther inland where the costs of land might be cheaper; however, moving inland can also increase costs due to the greater distance and potential challenge of locating workers.

## Access to Natural Resources

While apparel manufacturing is heavily labor-intensive, textile manufacturing is capital-intensive, with higher barriers to entry. Unlike apparel manufacturers, there isn't an abundance of textile mills. The capital-intensive nature of the textile business, coupled with the advanced skill set that is required to run a mill, makes countries with a textile base attractive areas for production. Textile mills require equipment, technology, and advanced talent to operate the machinery, factors that give textile production a more elevated function in the supply chain network. There is also a significant reduction in production and transportation costs if the fabric mills and factories are located within close proximity of each other. A company with textile and manufacturing resources within the same area potentially reduces risks associated with time delays due to raw material deliveries while also facilitating transportation and coordination throughout the production cycle.

### *Cotton: The Key Raw Material*

To further emphasize the point that countries with access to raw materials such as cotton are more than likely to

**Table 2.1** Top Cotton Importers and Exporters, 2015[30] (dollars in billions with the exception of Germany)

| Imports | Exports |
|---|---|
| China $10.3 | China $15.8 |
| Bangladesh $4.5 | India $7.5 |
| Vietnam $3.8 | United States $5.9 |
| Turkey $2.3 | Pakistan $3.1 |
| HongKong, China $2.1 | HongKong, China $2.3 |
| Indonesia $1.6 | Vietnam $1.8 |
| South Korea $1.3 | Turkey $1.7 |
| Italy $1.3 | Italy $1.5 |
| Pakistan $1.3 | Brazil $1.4 |
| United States $1.1 | Germany $998.9 million |

This table shows the lead importers and exporters of cotton, the key raw material for apparel production.

show advancement on the apparel production value chain, Table 2.1 shows top ten importers and exporters of cotton. While China is the highest producer of cotton, it is also the greatest importer of cotton. Because China is the lead producer and most advanced manufacturing company of today, its cotton consumption far exceeds that of other countries. The United States, which has significantly reduced its apparel-manufacturing capacity, is the third largest exporter of cotton, with an annual export amount of $5.9 billion. This trend of countries with increased manufacturing capability having access to raw materials is further demonstrated when you look at Bangladesh's import amount of $4.5 billion.

## MOVEMENT ON THE SUPPLY CHAIN VALUE CHAIN

The apparel industry is often how countries enter into and gain a stake in the manufacturing sector. Figure 2.5 depicts the stages of evolution for countries during their evolution in apparel manufacturing. Since the majority of the tasks associated with basic garment production are primarily low-skill and laborious processes, countries with large pools of unskilled labor tend to partake in apparel manufacturing. Competitive labor rates and an ability to take advantage of trade agreements often position countries to pursue garment making.

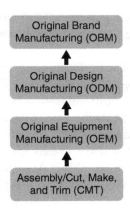

**Figure 2.5**
**Movement on the supply chain value chain** This diagram shows how countries evolve up the value chain in apparel manufacturing.
Source: The Apparel Global Value Chain Economic Upgrading and Workforce Development[31]

Countries typically enter the business doing **Cut, Make, and Trim (CMT)**, the process of hiring contractors to perform the apparel-manufacturing functions of cutting, making, and trimming. While this is the area of production with the fewest barriers to entry, such as capital or talent constraints, it's also the area with the least amount of return. Modern manufacturers often use laser cutters to cut multiple layers of material with increased accuracy and efficiency. The "Make" in CMT is the actual sewing of the garments. In low-skill production lines, workers often stitch one piece of the garment and pass the garment to the next point on the production line. The repetitive nature of the piece-by-piece assembly improves efficiency throughout the production line because workers gain expertise in a single aspect of production versus having to be trained to master multiple production tasks. The final aspect of CMT is that garments are trimmed with embellishments and finishing touches before they are packed for shipment. Because of its repetitive nature, CMT essentially requires the least amount of skills.[32] Hence, CMT is often the point of entry for many countries just entering the manufacturing arena.

CMT often occurs in **export-processing zones (EPZ)**, designated economic zones that support export production, or areas that offer tariff reduction to support the export of goods to the buyer's country, such as the export agreement between Pakistan and the United Kingdom.[33] The training offered within this segment

of the value chain is often hands-on rather than formal training from a vocational or institutional curriculum.[34]

As one moves up the value chain, the level of talent required advances slightly because the **Original Equipment Manufacturing (OEM)** stage of the apparel manufacturing value chain typically focuses all production activities to create a finished good, such as the sourcing of raw materials and production of the item. Because the sourcing, production, and distribution at the OEM level is more involved than CMT manufacturing, there is also an introduction of management talent to support production supervision, logistics, and procurement during this stage.

**Original Design Manufacturing (ODM)** encompasses the CMT and OEM while also assuming the responsibilities of garment design. The design aspect of production is one of the more profitable tasks. It requires that the ODM factory have access to talent with technical design skills and some knowledge of market trends and forecasting.

The highest value-added segment of the apparel manufacturing chain is **Original Brand Manufacturing (OBM)**, that is, factories that produce and sell their own lines of garments. These factories take on the functions of design, assembly, finishing, distribution, planning, and general management. Hence, the OBMs are often seen in countries where the government has established public-private partnerships that support workforce training and provided some infrastructure requirements such as roads and a stable utility source.

## IMPACT OF TRADE POLICY ON APPAREL MANUFACTURING

Because the government's role is key in the import and export of goods, this section highlights key trade agreements that support the advancement of the global fashion supply chain.

The **North American Free Trade Agreement (NAFTA)** was established to eliminate barriers to trade and to support the cross-border movement of goods among the three powerful North American countries of the United States, Canada, and Mexico. In 1992, NAFTA was signed by President George H. W. Bush, Mexican president Carlos Salinas de Gortari, and Canadian prime minister Brian Mulroney.[35] In addition to the restriction of goods available among these countries, there was an imbalance of trade due to the inequitable tariffs that existed. For example, the tariff for Mexico's imports into the United States was 250 percent higher than Mexico's tariff on US imports into Mexico.[36] In addition to improving the trade relations among these countries, NAFTA also had the following impact on the global apparel manufacturing market:

| | |
|---|---|
| **Rise of Exports**[37] | After NAFTA was signed, Mexico and the United States experienced tremendous export growth as goods were traded between the two countries.<br><br>In 1993, Mexico exported $39.9 billion in goods to the United States. This amount grew to $210.8 billion by 2004 (437 percent growth), a 46 percent GDP increase for the period stated.<br><br>From 1993 to 2004, the United States's exports to Mexico increased by 242 percent, a 50 percent GDP increase for the period stated. |
| **Foreign Investment** | To support the advancement of production in Mexico, the United States invested heavily in Mexico's apparel-manufacturing sector to create efficiencies that ultimately improved the trade relations between the two countries. Since many US firms leveraged the manufacturing firms in Mexico for assembly, the United States is the largest foreign direct investor (FDI) in Mexico. |
| **Job Growth**[38] | As exports grew for each of these countries, there was an overall improvement in the quality of life due to the rise of employment. |

The **Free Trade Area of the Americas (FTAA)** is currently being negotiated. The passing of the FTAA trade agreement would essentially extend the NAFTA to every country in North America, Central America, South America, and the Caribbean, with the exception of Cuba.

The **Central American Free Trade Agreement (CAFTA)** was passed by Congress in July 2005. Similar to FTAA, CAFTA is an expansion of NAFTA to include five Central American nations (Guatemala, El Salvador, Honduras, Costa Rica, and Nicaragua) and the Dominican Republic.

The **Trans-Pacific Partnership (TPP)** is a trade agreement between the Pacific Rim countries and the United States, Canada, Mexico, Chile, and Peru to strengthen trade among these countries by eliminating tariffs on textiles and garments. The twelve initial countries included in TPP were the United States, Japan, Malaysia, Vietnam, Singapore, Brunei, Australia, New Zealand, Canada, Mexico, Chile, and Peru. This bloc of countries represents 12 percent of the world's trade.[39] In January 2017, the United States exited the TPP agreement.

# SUPPLY CHAIN SOLUTIONS OF TODAY

## Onshoring versus Offshoring

A principle of **corporate social responsibility (CSR)** is that transportation costs should be reduced because trains, trucks, and ships emit significant amounts of carbon waste that pollute the earth. In addition, as ecommerce brands continue to promote same-day delivery and fast fashion makes ever-growing demands, retailers can no longer survive a manufacturing process that requires six months of production. These factors are causing retailers to seek solutions that promote production sources closer to the consumer. Hence, retailers are looking to reduce production time by **staging goods**, or separating production of a garment into various stages of production, and supporting local manufacturing. While it will take several years to reduce production in China, companies are pursuing the **China Plus One Strategy**,[40] the selection of another area of production in Asia in addition to maintaining production in China. This strategy moves production to a cheaper labor source, diversifies the supply chain network, introduces the company to a new potential market, and prepares for reduced production in China in anticipation of the rise in wages. Some production has moved further inland to other Chinese provinces; in addition, Vietnam, with its introduction to the World Trade Organization in 2007, is a country that has benefited from the China Plus One Strategy. Companies are moving production and investment to hedge against potential market declines in China.[41]

Movements such as Buy New York, launched in the New York Garment District, and emerging production areas such as Brooklyn, New York, are marketing campaigns that are making consumers aware of the benefits and opportunities of supporting manufacturers. While these movements are generating some local support, countries like the United States lack the knowledge of workers skilled in aerobatics to support large-scale local manufacturing because of the manufacturing void that occurred when apparel manufacturing moved offshore.

## Evolution of Global Supply Chain Risks

As production became more complex, the supply chain risk factors became more of a challenge. Figure 2.6 is a timeline that tracks the evolution of supply chain risks and retailers' strategies for mitigation.

During the Industrial Revolution, the supply chain network was highly localized, with the raw material source, production facilities, and market in close proximity. As shown in Figure 2.6, because there was no need to transport goods or materials, the supply chain risks were minimized, with the exception of local issues such as stagecoach robberies. The introduction of the assembly line meant that companies began to use standardized models and were vertically integrated: the parent company often owned the factories, raw material mills, and distribution networks. Although there were risks due to concentration, there was less risk than in today's global

environment because the parent company maintained primary control of all operations.

The 1950s to 1960s was an era of internationalization, driven by access to enhanced shipping capabilities and an interest in pursuing cheaper labor sources. Because of advances in shipping capabilities, companies began establishing offshoring relationships that were still vertically integrated but existed beyond the borders of the parent company. This offshoring parent company relationship created increased risks because companies were being operated outside their familiar markets and therefore were vulnerable to uncertainties caused by geographic changes.

After companies moved away from vertically integrated models, retailers entered into outsourcing relationships that were built on the premise of cheaper labor costs and, in some cases, access to new markets. Such was the case for the emergence of China in the 1980s. When the majority of the supply chain was outsourced across multiple continents, supply chain risks became a reality of advancing a business.

In today's world of political, social, and weather-related disasters, it's realistic to think that a company's supply chain network is highly vulnerable to acts that might block access to raw materials and production facilities. But while retailers are continuing to face concern over supply chain disruptions, consumers do not accept production stoppage or an inability to access materials as reasons for being unable to purchase an item. This is another reason that retailers are looking to establish

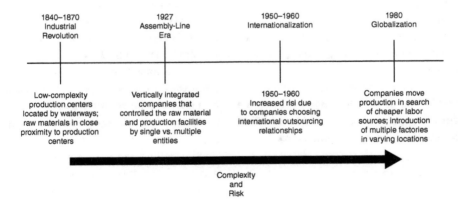

**Figure 2.6**
**The evolution of global fashion supply chain risks** This figure depicts how risks increase as the supply chain grows in complexity.
Source: Bosman, R. (2006), "The New Supply Chain Challenge: Risk Management in a Global Economy," FM Global.

collaborative relationships with key suppliers and factories: these working relationships enable them to troubleshoot supply chain issues and resolve disruption issues more quickly; retailers might also avoid a problem by using proactive monitoring and communication with their supply chain network.

Because of the ripple effect of a supply chain malfunction, companies are starting to look at the supply chain from a holistic perspective that looks beyond the sourcing, production, and distribution aspects of the business. Retailers are also evaluating and planning for supply chain challenges and how they might impact the marketing aspects of the business: the promotional calendar, floor layouts and customer promotions, and ultimately financial losses caused by loss sales (sales that are missed because the product is unavailable), markdowns due to late arrivals, and additional costs that might be associated with transporting goods by air to minimize delays.

In addition to having established relationships, retailers should also have in place a **disaster recovery plan** that provides a roadmap on how to address everything from a facility being unable to open to how to identify alternative sourcing partners if a particular region is experiencing a disaster. While insurance is provided to guard against such disasters, there is the unquantifiable loss that occurs once a retailer loses the confidence of its consumers. Therefore, the desire for reduced production and raw material costs must be balanced with the risk and ability of retailers to manage in the face of such occurrences.

When utilizing few vendors to maximize economies of scale, companies must also look at the risks of concentrating production sources. To reduce this risk, companies split production sources and even go to the extreme of diversifying the areas of production to allow for localized issues such as weather or politically related issues. Although this solution addresses the risks, companies must also consider the impact on the profit margin caused by the additional costs or time required to achieve production in a decentralized production footprint.

# SOURCING STRATEGIES TO MANAGE GLOBAL RISKS

While moving production to areas of cheaper labor sources and pursuing new market opportunities by moving production closer to local markets are valuable

business objectives, each of these efforts means a change in the supply chain structure or, in many instances, the introduction of new suppliers in new locations. As a company's supply chain becomes more complex, the risk potential for labor, production, and natural occurrence disruptions rises dramatically. Therefore, companies are constantly balancing the risk-rewards scenario for supply chain expansion and modifications. For example, the 2015 West Coast port closure had a tremendously adverse impact on retailers that depended on West Coast ports to receive shipments of goods from Asia. Kurt Salmon, the management consulting firm that specializes in supply chain management, reported that the West Coast closure could cost retailers approximately $7 billion in 2015, with the chance of spillover costs in subsequent years.[42] To avoid further delays in products reaching the ports and then not being able to be processed for distribution, retailers were turning to air freight. Except for fast fashion retailers such as Zara or H&M, the cost of airing freight was an unexpected hit in profitability because traditional retailers typically priced their goods without the expectation of air costs.

Since the fashion business is driven by consumer whimsy, both unpredictable and impulse-driven, retailers are always looking to provide the right product, at the right time, for the right consumer. However, a breakdown or even just a delay due to problems with the supply chain can result in lost revenues, and worse, a loss in consumer confidence. Because of the immense impact of a supply chain breakdown, a study by a professor from Georgia Institute of Technology and a professor from the University of Western Ontario projected that it can take approximately two years or more for companies to rebound from a supply chain failure.[43] In a retail environment where there is minimal brand loyalty, supply chain resiliency is a key area of emphasis to protect against customer loss due to unforeseen inventory delays.

In a study of eight hundred companies, the same professors also tracked that the year prior to the production failure the company also faced a drop in sales growth (7 percent), increased production costs (11 percent), and a rise in inventory (14 percent).[44] This finding further demonstrated that the resiliency of a company's supply chain is not only a business objective but also a key differentiator that provides long-term benefits to a business.

## Notes from the Field

This chapter discusses the growth of the global economy, but one must remember that this phenomenon has had a relatively short life span, with tremendous growth occurring only since the 1980s. Global trade in the fashion industry began slowly after the Korean War and continued to pick up steam as more countries started to produce apparel and accessories and as trade agreements were established around the world. As the global economy expanded, so did sourcing and production opportunities. One such opportunity presented itself while working with one of our agents, who told us of wonderful factories in Cairo, Egypt. It just happened that I had a large order for some men's knit shirts that needed to be at a very low price and I was struggling with where to produce them. So off to Cairo I went to evaluate four factories. My agent at that time set up the appointments, I met the driver, and we spent the next two days visiting four factories. I liked what I saw, they made samples,

and we struck a deal with two of the factories. I went back home and requested more samples; half came in beautiful from one factory and the other half were terrible, with footprints on them and bad sewing, just terrible. I inquired with the agent and learned that at this particular time in Egypt many of the factories were still government owned and they were told what and when to make products and did not really care about outside orders. Of course, no one told me this on the trip, and the government-owned factory was very gracious and presented well. Needless to say, I was not happy. I flew back to Cairo to see if I could salvage the order, but to no avail, and we canceled it and started from the beginning. The one factory that did perform well did not have the capacity to complete the order in time. These are the challenges and risks associated with expanding apparel manufacturing to new suppliers.

# CONCLUSION

The global fashion supply chain is a network of vendors that support the sourcing, production, logistics, and distribution aspects of raw and finished goods. Because of the constant need to increase production while minimizing costs, production locations have been selected based on labor costs. A factor that also supports the movement of apparel manufacturing is the intervention of governments in the form of trade agreements and public-private partnerships. Countries recognize the economic benefits that a vibrant apparel manufacturing sector can create.

Given the demands of today's consumers, brands are seeking supply chain solutions that enable them to get the right product, to the right consumer, at the right time. To achieve this goal, the supply must be flexible and able to support reduced lead times. Hence, brands are beginning to explore the possibilities of onshoring production. Consumers are also seeking socially responsible

manufacturing practices that guarantee a fair wage, support safe working conditions, and offer environmentally favorable production processes. While the emphasis on socially responsible products adds a possible layer of costs because of the required compliance and monitoring, the benefits of meeting consumer demands and creating a good brand perception are causing brands to focus on socially responsible manufacturing.

As the global fashion supply chain continues to stretch around the world, brands are incurring additional risks caused by the basic reason that production is occurring around the world rather than in a single location. Brands must identify opportunities to mitigate these risks by reducing redundancies throughout the supplier network, pursuing strategies to deal with geographic constraints, and establishing working relationships throughout the supply chain to facilitate an efficient, effective decision-making process.

# INDUSTRY INTERVIEW: CRAIG DANA, SENIOR SUPPLY CHAIN PROFESSIONAL LIVING IN HONG KONG

For this chapter, I had the pleasure of interviewing my former boss, Craig Dana. Craig is an experienced supply chain professional who has spent the past decade in Hong Kong overseeing supply chain operations for major retailers like Tory Burch and Ann Taylor. Craig started his career as a market research analyst for Coopers & Lybrand, where he quickly ascended the ranks to become a principal consultant for the firm's retail practice. Craig earned his MBA from the New York University–Stern School of Business.

**Interviewer:** *Since you have been in Hong Kong, what have you found most interesting about your work in supply chain management?*

**C. D.:** The change in the China production patterns has been most interesting. There has been a huge influx of production to China. However, on a percentage basis, there has been a huge outflux of production from China. The country's production profile has changed because the cost of doing business there changed.

The pressure on the supply chain to drive down costs is another area that I have found fascinating. If you walk down 34th or 125th Street in New York, everything is on sale all the time. This is because there are too many stores. The US and European retailers are struggling with the demands of being a public business. The demands of being a public company are causing these businesses to keep opening stores. However, the increase in stores creates a glut of inventory. This puts pressure on the supply chain to drive down costs because retailers know that they won't get full-price sell through for these items. Therefore, the supply chain gets taxed to produce at the lower costs. Then retailers must go to lower-cost factories or work with suppliers in a more collaborative manner to drive down costs.

For big-volume countries, retailers are just pushing for the lowest costs. Retailers are squeezing suppliers for the lowest costs. However, a retailer can take a different view and have a more integrated supply chain. This would mean that the retailers are willing to take costs out of the equation, and the retailers are now working on a more long-term basis with a factory to drive down costs.

To reduce costs, the retailer would work with the factory to eliminate duplicative efforts. For example, every factory has compliance, and a brand will typically have a third party do compliance to ensure that there isn't an issue with the production. While it is necessary for the retailer to ensure compliance, this duplicative inspection adds costs and time to the production. If a retailer is working on a transactional basis, meaning they are shopping for the cheapest production costs, there is no incentive for the factory to work with the retailer in a collaborative manner. There is more of an incentive to cut costs because the factory is trying to guarantee the cheapest price for production. The factory has more of an incentive to cut corners. However, if there is a strategic relationship, meaning that the retailer is working on a balance scorecard, there is more of an emphasis on collaboration, quality compliance, and product development. Since the balanced scorecard focuses on performing against specific measures versus costs, the factory will perform to these factors.

When there is a collaborative relationship, brands will do things like support factories doing more testing, having their own fabric labs, and pursuing other quality control procedures. The key to a collaborative supply chain relationship is that you must take the factors of time and money out of the equation. However, this often unrealistic because the supply chain is driven primarily by costs and speed.

**Interviewer:** *Over the past ten years, what has been the biggest change in the global supply chain?*

**C. D.:** The impact of quotas and the emergence of new production countries. In the early years, suppliers were moving to countries for quota purposes. As long as factories had quota, they could get orders. That is why production areas like Mauritius and Madagascar went away once quotas went away from these production areas. They weren't necessarily prepared for production. They just had quotas.

Quotas dictated a company's supply chain strategy. Brands had to produce with suppliers that had a legal ability to export product. Quotas created an artificial barrier in the market. For example, because of quotas, from 2005 to 2006 a retailer like an Ann Taylor manufactured in over twenty countries. For that reason, business flooded into China. As China got more growth, China became expensive, so that is when you saw a push by brands for production in Vietnam, Bangladesh, and India. However, these countries matured rapidly due to supply and demand. This drove up the cost of production for these countries. Supply and demand are the key drivers of the supply chain.

Countries like China with quotas and a relatively large, cheap labor force created a great source for production. To start a factory in China, there were relatively low barriers to entry. To start a factory didn't require a lot of capital, so you would see barns with sewing machines. Countries that had factories that were required to move because of quotas were more competitive, such as Korea and Taiwan. These suppliers that moved offshore succeeded because they were able to move quickly to open factories outside of their home country. These businesses now had a model for production that could be duplicated.

Another thing that has happened is that brands are focusing on social compliance and human rights. This is a danger with new countries that might not have labor laws that support minimum wages. That is why Korea and Japan are a challenge for production.

Because they don't have the media focus and human rights compliance considerations, they are able to open factories that potentially lack socially responsible business practices. Western countries are focused on human rights compliance such as tracking age verification.

**Interviewer:** *What do you think of the pace of today's supply chain? How is this pace impacting retailers and consumer expectations?*

**C. D.:** The supply chain has had to become that much faster. Ten years ago, every US company was working on a rigid four-season calendar. Brands worked a year in advance. They had a process that started with visiting fashion shows and creating designs off the interpretations from the shows. In retrospect, this was a very slow, methodical supply chain that allowed brands to focus on details such as having a coordinated line. With the continuing influence of fast fashion and the customer mindset that they are no longer looking for what everyone else wanted, this interest in coordination and a slower supply chain has begun to go away.

In the 1990s, there was a point in time when the basic product was cool, such as the Gap's Khaki line. Everyone wanted Abercrombie. There was a time when women were focused on quality and investment pieces. Professional women had six pieces that they wore interchangeably every day.

Today, people want to be trendy. You don't have a uniform. Plus, the supply chain capabilities of a Zara or H&M allow brands to meet the trendiness that consumers want. It doesn't matter if the item only lasts for a season because the consumer isn't wearing the style that long. High-quality, timeless style at a relatively high cost is losing out because consumers are voting with their wallets. Thus, a brand must have a much faster supply chain.

A brand must be willing to determine what is most important—speed, quality, or costs. Because US brands try to deliver it all, they struggle because it is hard to segment a supply chain tasks. If you are a brand whose business model is built on a coordinated collection, then fast fashion doesn't work with that.

How do you meet the customer's demand if you have been ordering a different pants fit and the trend moves to wide leg boots pants? How do you make changes to your marketing, because much of that is set a year in advance? For these reasons, it is difficult for design teams to work on multiple seasons.

The key to fast fashion is having access to raw materials. Therefore, you must commit to your fabric early. This is the most costly part of the process. In fast fashion, you copy a design, and you produce based on the fabric that you have. Speed to market trumps all. All of these steps take time. If the fabric isn't quite right, it is ok because speed to market is key. The fast fashion companies continue to drive supply chain decisions.

If all your processes are hardwired to wardrobe collections, then moving to fast fashion will be a challenge. It is very difficult to have parallel processes. To address this problem, retailers tend to have a core and fast fashion track. Brands need to be able to take calculated risks because it's fashion. Some things will work, and some things won't work.

**Interviewer:** *What are your thoughts on the impact of ecommerce?*

**C. D.:** Ecommerce is driven on consistency and fit. You will sell more if the customer knows that your sizing is true from a fit perspective. If the consistency and fit aren't there, the customer won't buy, or you will have high returns. The fit is important. Many shoppers are accustomed to just returning. Everyone has free shipping, so it's no big deal for customers to return items. Ten years ago, you made money on shipping. Now you lose a lot because everyone returns.

**Interviewer:** *Within the industry, there is a buzz around the concept of a collaborative supply*

*chain. How easy or challenging is it to create collaboration throughout a global supply chain?*

**C. D.:** In theory, it isn't hard. What is critical beyond collaboration is trust. That takes time. If a supplier doesn't believe that you will do what you say you will do, it doesn't work. In order to hold factory space, the factory must know that you are going to use it or pay a charge for it. Opportunistic factory relationships are hard in fast fashion. To be opportunistic in fast fashion, you must have the fabric at the factory. Once you send fabric to another factory, you will have to pay taxes on it. The trust is the biggest barrier.

## Questions Pertaining to Interview

1. Why are retailers constantly being confronted with the cost of their production? How does cost impact the sales of product? What does this mean from a supply chain perspective?
2. Were quotas a benefit or a disadvantage for brands? Were quotas a benefit or a disadvantage for factories? How could quotas be a winning proposition for both parties?
3. In addition to the planning challenges mentioned in the interview, what other challenges does fast fashion present to traditional retailers that operate with a four-season calendar? How might these retailers overcome these challenges within their supply chain?
4. Why are fast fashion retailers willing to take a gamble on a design, unlike more traditional retailers that plan production with a four-season calendar?
5. Why is trust a challenging concept in the world of chasing production costs? How should supply chain professionals think about trust in their supplier relationships?

Hennes & Mauritz (H&M) is the behemoth Swedish retailer that is known for its success with fast fashion around the world. The company targets women and men between the ages of eighteen and forty-five. H&M also dresses children and produces its own brand of cosmetic products. With a store footprint of 4,000 retail locations in 62 markets and ecommerce sites in 13 countries, H&M is one of the fastest-growing retailers.[45] The top three countries by store locations are Germany (449), USA (415), and China (353). H&M employs 148,000 individuals around the world. The company's plan is to grow its store base by 10 to 15 percent a year and to maintain comparable sales per store volumes. Essentially, H&M is looking to increase its market penetration without cannibalizing its current store volumes. The company is also expecting growth in its ecommerce business.

While H&M's business model is built around today's trend of fast fashion, the first H&M store opened in 1947 as Hennes, the Swedish word for "hers." Later the company acquired the hunting and men's clothing store Mauritz Widforss; hence the name H&M. The company is a family-owned business that is in its third generation of family management, and Germany is still the company's largest market. H&M opened its first store outside of Sweden in 1964 in Oslo, Norway. To fund the business's expansion plans, the company went public in 1974. HM Group is the parent company, which operates H&M, COS, Monki, Weekday, Cheap Monday, and Other Stories brands. The company also offers home furnishings through H&M Home.

H&M is known for its fashionable, often trendy styles that look like they came right off the runway. In fact, the company has been known to partner with big fashion designers such as Karl Lagerfeld, Stella McCartney, Roberto Cavalli, Matthew Williamson, and Versace.[46] These iconic design collaborations further position H&M as the go-to retailer for fashionable looks at a fraction of the cost. On the company's website is posted the company's philosophy: "Fashion and quality at the best price in a sustainable way." As today's consumers are increasingly focused on stylish value retailing options, H&M continues to grow in popularity around the world.

While the company owns no factories, the business still maintains significant control over its production because of the volume of product that the company places with its vendor network each year. This control enables the business to follow manufacturing practices that produce quality products. According to the company website, H&M's Global Quality Department supports 500,000 product tests for issues such as shrinkage, twisting, colorfastness, and pilling, as well as chemical and product safety tests for issues like flammability. Given the company's presence in the children's market, the company tests rigorously for product safety and requires that all vendors in its supply chain network comply with its safety and sustainability standards. H&M has also been one of the outspoken retailers looking to increase standardization in the children's wear market.

In addition to ensuring safety and compliance, the business focuses on managing costs. Given its low price points, H&M makes its profits from the volume of goods that it is able to produce in a cost-effective manner. It uses in-house designers, works directly with its vendors instead of using agents, projects the right fashions for the appropriate markets, and has an efficient logistics network.

### Case Study Questions

1. Given the global success of the H&M brand, identify the areas in the case study that explain why H&M has dominated the fast fashion industry. Is this success sustainable? If you think it is, why? If you don't think so, why?

2. H&M competes against other retailers through its volume of stores, prices, and design capabilities; what does this mean about the H&M supply chain? What must the H&M supply chain do to maintain the company's competitive advantage?

3. At the end of the case study, there is a summary of how the company cuts costs, such as by using in-house designers. What additional risks does the company assume by pursuing these cost savings? How could these risks be mitigated? How could the return on these potential savings be greater than the risks?

## CHAPTER REVIEW QUESTIONS

1. Considering the countries identified in the evolution of the global fashion supply chain, explain what factors aided in the rise and demise of each of these countries with regards to their role in apparel manufacturing.

2. To further understand how trade agreements play a major role in the production of apparel, research the benefits and downsides for each of the trade agreements listed in the chapter. How do these agreements impact labor costs, access to raw materials, and market access?

3. How would the trend of onshoring impact supply chain lead times and production capacity? Identify a retail brand that would benefit from the implementation of an onshoring supply chain strategy. To implement this strategy, what factors must this brand consider?

## CLASS EXERCISE

Develop recommendations for the following scenarios.

**Scenario 1:** If you were a senior leader of a large retail brand that sources product around the world, what risk mitigation strategies would you implement? How would you build relationships with your supplier network? What factors would you consider to ensure that you get the right product, to the right consumer, at the right time?

**Scenario 2:** A major retailer is looking to diversify its supplier base because the company currently depends on a small vendor base located in a country that has a volatile political environment and is experiencing rising labor costs. What recommendations do you have for identifying a new supplier base? To avoid the risk of a production error, how would you plan to transition to the new supplier base? What risks do you anticipate with this change?

## KEY TERMS

American Apparel and Footwear Association (AAFA)
margins
bilateral trade agreements
quotas
isolationism
Multi Fibre Arrangement (MFA)
World Trade Organization (WTO)
Agreement on Textiles and Clothing (ATC)
vertically integrated
offshore manufacturer
keiretsu
International Monetary Fund (IMF)

United States Agency for International Development (USAID)
Trade and Investment Framework Agreement (TIFA)
Partner Africa
African Growth and Opportunity Act (AGOA)
Cut, Make, and Trim (CMT)
export-processing zones (EPZ)
Original Equipment Manufacturing (OEM)
Original Design Manufacturing (ODM)
Original Brand Manufacturing (OBM)

North American Free Trade Agreement (NAFTA)
Free Trade Area of the Americas (FTAA)
Central American Free Trade Agreement (CAFTA)
Trans-Pacific Partnership (TPP)
corporate social responsibility (CSR)
staging goods
China Plus One Strategy
disaster recovery plan

# REFERENCES

1. American Apparel and Footwear website, https://www.aafaglobal.org/AAFA/ApparelStats_and_ShoeStats_at-a-glance.aspx.
2. Magnier, M. (2016), "How China Is Changing Its Manufacturing Strategy," *Wall Street Journal*, June 7.
3. Kennedy, J. F. (1962), "Remarks upon Signing the Trade Expansion Act," October 11. Available online: G. Peters and J. T. Woolley, *The American Presidency Project*, http://www.presidency.ucsb.edu/ws/?pid=8946.
4. "U.S. Textile and Apparel Industries and Rural America," US Department of Agriculture. Available online: https://www.ers.usda.gov/topics/crops/cotton-wool/background/us-textile-and-apparel-industries-and-rural-america.aspx.
5. Ibid.
6. Vatz, S. (2013), "Why America Stopped Making Its Own Clothes," KQED, May 24. Available online: http://ww2.kqed.org/lowdown/2013/05/24/madeinamerica/.
7. Anz Insights Commercial Banking Asia—Textile and Garment Industry, July 2012. Available online: http://anyflip.com/musm/nkdj.
8. Ibid.
9. Morss, E. (2011), "The Loss of American Manufacturing Jobs: What Are the Facts?" Available online: http://www.morssglobalfinance.com/the-loss-of-american-manufacturing-jobs-what-are-the-facts/.
10. "Made in America: Apparel, Leather, and Applied Products," US Department of Commerce. Available online: http://www.esa.doc.gov/sites/default/files/ApparelandLeatherIndustryProfile.pdf.
11. Chalabi, M. (2014), "Where the U.S. Gets Its Clothing, One Year after the Bangladesh Factory Collapse," *FiveThirtyEight*, April 23.
12. "Bursting at the Seams: Bangladesh's Clothing Industry" (2013, October 26), *The Economist*, 409. Available online: https://www.economist.com/news/business/21588393-workers-continue-die-unsafe-factories-industry-keeps-booming-bursting-seams.
13. Jones, R. M., and S. G. Hayes (2004), "The UK Clothing Industry: Extinction or Evolution?," *Journal of Fashion Marketing and Management: An International Journal*, 8 (3): 262–78. Available online: https://doi.org/10.1108/13612020410547798.
14. Dolan, R. E., and R. L. Worden (eds) (1994), *Japan: A Country Study*. Washington: GPO for the Library of Congress. Available online: http://countrystudies.us/japan/98.htm.
15. Ibid.
16. Special Report (2014), "(Still) Made in Japan—Manufacturing in Japan," *Economist*, April 10.
17. *South Korea: A Country Study*. Andrea Matles Savada and William Shaw, editors. Washington: GPO for the Library of Congress, 1990. Available online: http://countrystudies.us/south-korea/50.htm.
18. Wilsey, M., and S. Lichtig (n.d.), "The Nike Controversy." Available online: https://web.stanford.edu/class/e297c/trade_environment/wheeling/hnike.html.
19. http://populationpyramid.net/china/1975/.
20. Hu, Z., and M. S. Khan (1997), "Why Is China Growing So Fast?" International Monetary Fund, IMF Economic Issues No. 8. Available online: https://www.imf.org/external/pubs/ft/issues8/issue8.pdf.
21. Freund, K. (2015), *Textiles and Apparels Changes in 2015 from 2014*, United States International Trade Commission. Available online: https://www.usitc.gov/research_and_analysis/trade_shifts_2015/textiles.htm.
22. McKinsey & Company (2013), "The Global Sourcing Map—Balancing Cost, Capacity, and Compliance."
23. "India: India Push to Become Manufacturing Hub Hinges on Easing Investment (2016), *Asia News Monitor*, February 18. Available online: https://www.voanews.com/a/india-push-to-become-manufacturing-hub-hinges-on-easing-investment/3192756.html.
24. Keller, C. (2014), "Succeeding in Tomorrow's Global Fashion Market," McKinsey & Company, September.
25. Berg, A., S. Hedrich, and B. Russo (2015), "East Africa: The Next Hub for Apparel Sourcing," McKinsey & Company, August.
26. Ibid.
27. Ibid.
28. "The Apparel Global Value Chain: Economic Upgrading and Workforce Development," in Duke (2011) (PDF), *CGGC Apparel Global Value Chain*.
29. Ababa, A. (2014), "Manufacturing in Africa: An Awakening Giant," *Economist*, February.
30. Workman, D. (2017), "Cotton Imports by Country." Available online: http://www.worldstopexports.com/cotton-imports-by-country/. Workman, D. (2017), "Cotton Exports by Country." Available online: http://www.worldstopexports.com/cotton-exports-by-country/.
31. Duke (2011) (PDF), *CGGC Apparel Global Value Chain*, http://citeseerx.ist.psu.edu/viewdoc/download?doi=10.1.1.233.1379&rep=rep1&type=pdf.
32. "Cut Make Trim: What Does It Mean?" Available online: https://cutmaketrim.wordpress.com/2012/04/15/cut-make-trim-what-does-it-mean/.
33. Duke (2011) (PDF), *CGGC Apparel Global Value Chain*.
34. Ibid.

35. Amadeo, K. (2017), "History of NAFTA and Its Purpose,"The Balance, July 7. Available online: https://www.thebalance.com/history-of-nafta-3306272.

36. Ibid.

37. Sommer, H. (2008), "The Economic Benefits of NAFTA to the United States and Mexico," National Center for Policy Analysis, June 16. Available online: http://www.ncpa.org/pub/ba619.

38. Daniel, H. (2011), "Benefits of NAFTA for Canada," July 21. Available online: http://benefitof.net/benefits-of-nafta-for-canada/#ixzz47M89Ju1G.

39. "TPP: What Is It and Why Does It Matter?" (2016), BBC News, July 27.

40. Anz Insights Commercial Banking Asia—Textile and Garment Industry, July 2012. Available online: http://anyflip.com/musm/nkdj/basic.

41. Dezan Shira & Associates (2015), "The China Plus One Model and the Competitive Advantages of Manufacturing in Vietnam," Emerging Strategy, October. Available online: http://www.emerging-strategy.com/article/china-plus-one-and-the-competitive-advantages-of-manufacturing-in-vietnam/.

42. Reagan, C. (2015), "West Coast Ports: Retail's $7 Billion Problem," CNBC Website, February.

43. Bosman, R. (2006), "The New Supply Chain Challenge: Risk Management in a Global Economy," FM Global. Available online: http://www.fmglobal.com/~/media/assets/pdf/p0667_Chainsupply.pdf.

44. Ibid.

45. Hoovers, "H & M Hennes & Mauritz AB Company Profile." Available online: http://www.hoovers.com/company-information/cs/company-profile.HM_Hennes__Mauritz_AB.1bdef5deeef07f57.html.

46. Bjornback, E. (2013), "Family Business," March 22. Available online: https://www.scribd.com/doc/133039076/H-M-Family-Business.

# Corporate Social Responsibility and Sustainability

## CHAPTER 3

## LEARNING OBJECTIVES

Upon completion of this chapter you will be able to:

- Describe corporate social responsibility (CSR) and sustainability.

- Summarize the current philanthropic philosophy of CSR and the sustainable business practices in the fashion industry.

- List the key players in the fashion industry—brands, educators, designers, retailers, consumers—and explain how they portray CSR and sustainable business practices.

- Analyze the value that third-party certification adds to CSR and sustainable business practices.

- Explore alternative points of view concerning CSR and sustainable business practices.

- Explore the impact of CSR policies and practices on the supply chain.

- Propose potential solutions to address concerns surrounding CSR policies and practices.

# CORPORATE SOCIAL RESPONSIBILITY (CSR)

The European Commission (2017) defined **corporate social responsibility (CSR)** in the following way: "Corporate social responsibility (CSR) refers to companies taking responsibility for their impact on society" (para 1). CSR and sustainability have been inextricably linked in the fashion industry, yet there is no one definition that describes the two concepts and explains how they relate to the supply chain. Instead each participant or sector of the industry applies the two concepts as it sees fit.

Interest in CSR began in earnest in the 1950s when several highly acclaimed business authors discussed the merits and value of responsible practices. Some trace the origin to an earlier time (1930s), but a formal discussion probably began in the 1950s with the publication of Howard R. Bowen's landmark book *Social Responsibilities of the Businessman*, Selekman's *Moral Philosophy of Management*, and Heald's *Management's Responsibility to Society: The Growth of an Idea*. Yet for individuals involved in the fashion industry—including apparel, textiles, and accessories—a strong understanding of the importance of CSR came fairly late and can be traced to the Kathie Lee Gifford fiasco in 1996 (see Figure 3.1). In an article from the *New York Times* titled "A Sweetheart Becomes Suspect; Looking behind Those Kathie Lee Labels," Stephanie Strom (1996) put into perspective the event that most point to as the defining moment in the CSR movement as it relates to the fashion industry. In this article Strom brought Kathie Lee to task for having a clothing line that was being manufactured by thirteen- and fourteen-year-olds in Honduras and for using other questionable business practices.

This single event brought to light how all individuals are responsible for the totality of their actions, whether known or unknown. These issues, however, have always existed. Some have been more serious than the Kathie Lee Labels episode, but it took a celebrity to bring to light a flaw in the supply chain, one that unfortunately continues to be exploited today in various shapes and forms. This entire article provides an in-depth understanding of just how serious an event this was and how it became the catalyst for the CSR movement in the fashion industry.

**Figure 3.1**
**Kathie Lee Gifford exiting a press conference, 1996**
The photo shows angry protesters outside a press conference in 1996 where Kathie Lee Gifford was trying to defend her company's sourcing practices. The Kathie Lee Gifford episode galvanized various stakeholders to call for action surrounding sweatshops around the globe.

CSR is about improving the quality of life for those in the apparel, textile, and accessories industry who do not have a voice—about improving the lives of workers, their families, and the community in which they reside and society at large. The other important concept, **sustainability**, means meeting the needs of the present without compromising the future. In order to achieve the goals of CSR, sustainability must be factored into the business equation.

# SUSTAINABLE POLICIES AND PRACTICES IN THE FASHION INDUSTRY

The event just noted prompted concern and was considered the catalyst that further facilitated interest in CSR practices in the fashion industry. The industry, however, had already attempted to address the importance of CSR through **vendor compliance**. The exact method by which vendor compliance was managed varied from fashion company to fashion company. For example, a menswear wholesaler in the past may have had several shelves filled with large three-ring binders of vendor compliance manuals that were developed by the various companies the wholesaler did business with. All these manuals were essential because each retailer, brand, and designer had its own set of standards that needed to be met. Individuals who worked for the menswear wholesaler (generally in the production or sourcing department) were required to read the entire manual and sign a confirmation verifying that the manual was read and the policies understood, thereby securing compliance. The signed document was then communicated back to the originator of the manual and formed a contract stating that the vendors would abide by the principles and practices set forth. The vendor compliance manuals essentially documented the policies, procedures, and protocols for sourcing, inspecting, and shipping products.

However, the process of vendor compliance did not address some of the key CSR issues that are being addressed today, such as freedom of association, fair wages, sanitary work conditions, adequate breaks, and paid overtime. These are specific issues that focus on social justice and care of people and the environment, rather than on the process of the work that needs to be carried out. Furthermore, big three-ring binders—of course—are now a thing of the past, are cumbersome, and leave room for error.

# VIEWPOINTS OF KEY INDUSTRY PARTICIPANTS

The fashion industry is composed of key participants that include brands, designers, retailers, third-party certification organizations, educational participants, and finally consumers. Each of these key participants may have alternative viewpoints that ultimately influence the decisions they make about CSR. For example, some in the fashion industry focus on corporate philanthropy, doing good works and providing a potential benefit to the consumer.

There are many companies in the fashion industry that perform good works and have solid, sustainable, CSR practices—far too many to present in this text. TOMS® and Warby Parker are often considered models not only for their CSR practices but also for their philanthropic work. In addition, these companies have a transparent supply chain and treat their employees fairly and by giving back, which is one of their strengths and how they connect with the consumer. An example of

giving back is TOMS "with every purchase, TOMS will help a person in need." The consumer feels good about helping someone else with a purchase. Being mindful of their employees creates a win-win situation. Glavas and Kelley (2014) noted that employees for these companies are committed to their organizations, feel that their organizations support them, and are generally satisfied.

## Brands

*TOMS®.* **TOMS®** focuses on both the environment and corporate philanthropy (see Figure 3.2). For example, TOMS® shoes are made with vegan materials and are made using sustainable practices. Furthermore, TOMS® gives back to the community in a variety of ways, demonstrating its corporate responsibility and accountability not only to the environment but also to the people it employs and to communities in need. For a full accounting of how TOMS® demonstrates responsibility and philanthropy, one can visit its extensive website: http://www.toms.com/. The section titled "How We Give" provides evidence of this brand's commitment.

*Warby Parker.* Another brand that models CSR along with corporate philanthropy is **Warby Parker** (see Figure 3.3). Warby Parker's goal is to offer designer eyewear at an affordable price. The goal was conceived from a personal experience:

**Figure 3.2**
**Some of the many shoe designs TOMS® offers** TOMS® sells footwear, eyewear, and apparel and focuses on CSR and sustainable business practices; it leads by example.

Every idea starts with a problem. Ours was simple: glasses are too expensive. We were students when one of us lost his glasses on a backpacking trip. The cost of replacing them was so high that he spent the first semester of grad school without them, squinting and complaining. (We don't recommend this.) The rest of us had similar experiences, and we were amazed at how hard it was to find a pair of great frames that didn't leave our wallets bare. Where were the options? (Warby Parker n.d.: para 1)

Additional information about Warby Parker may be viewed at its website: https://www.warbyparker.com/. The brand is also committed to people globally who do not have access to glasses and so have poor vision. Without the ability to see, these individuals have trouble achieving educational goals, gaining employment, or carrying out the activities of daily living. This problem spurred Warby Parker to partner with nonprofits for the expressed goal of ensuring that glasses are distributed to those in need.

*PVH Corp (formerly Phillips-Van Heusen Corporation.* A publicly traded company, **PVH Corp** (see Figure 3.4) is also well known in the industry for its social and environmental emphasis as well as its philanthropic efforts, although not many consumers would put it in the same class as TOMS® or Warby Parker because its practices are more behind the scenes. Many of these efforts are documented on its website: http://www.pvh.com/. More specifically, PVH is one of the largest global apparel companies in the world and considers itself a global leader in the apparel industry. This leadership is observed throughout the website, particularly in the statement on corporate responsibility:

> Corporate Responsibility is central to how we conduct business and applies across all stages of our operations and supply chain. As an industry leader, we recognize the great responsibility and opportunity to make positive impacts—from source to store—by empowering the people we work with, preserving the environment and supporting our communities. (PVH 2015: para 4)

A bold example of this responsibility and commitment to its people is an initiative through which brand owners, retailers, international unions, and factory workers are collaborating to prevent fires and structural failures. Additional information is given on the company website.

## Designers

One only has to do a search to see the notable and not so notable designers in today's fashion industry. Design is a major component of the fashion industry, with the

**Figure 3.3**
**Photo from Warby Parker headquarters** Warby Parker believes everyone should be able to afford good eyewear. It has taken a strong stance in corporate philanthropy by providing glasses to those who cannot afford them.

**Figure 3.4**
**One of PVH's many storefronts** PVH has a long history in the fashion industry and continues to work to achieve goals of CSR and sustainability.

most famous and easily identifiable designers working in the offices of major brands, retailers, and manufacturers. These individuals have the ability to practice CSR and sustainability through the designs they are inspired to create. They work not only for large companies but also from their homes or smaller storefronts selling their fashions. To address each of these individuals, therefore, would not be possible or the point of this chapter. Rather, we will focus on one designer who values CSR and sustainability: **Stella McCartney** (see Figure 3.5).

*Stella McCartney.* McCartney's website may be accessed at http://www.stellamccartney.com/. The website shows that there are essentially three concepts at the core of McCartney's work ethic: being responsible, being honest, and making decisions and practicing with an eye toward the future. This means engaging in practices that will sustain not only the business but also the environment and the people residing in that environment. There are also secondary ethical concepts embedded in McCartney's website: respect, trust, and the need for the fashion industry to practice reflection every day of its work. Decisions that are right and just, not only for brands, designers, and retailers but also for the environment and people, ultimately will build trust between all of the key participants in the fashion industry. Sometimes difficult questions must be asked so that difficult decisions can be made that take into account CSR and corporate philanthropy.

"Many if not most people want to make the ethical choice—they just need help getting there" (Brown 2014: para 10). Providing information to consumers about the supply chain from fiber to finished garment will also facilitate trust, and one of the outcomes is a consumer who feels free to ask questions. "If consumers then begin to ask questions and demand accountability—if humanitarian, health, and environmental concerns start to drive the fashion industry—ethically sourced fashion will become the norm" (Brown 2014: para 11). McCartney is following Brown in that she is helping consumers make the ethical choice through her designs.

## Well Dressed?

A publication titled *Well Dressed?* (University of Cambridge Institute for Manufacturing 2006) discusses the present and future sustainability of clothing, designs,

**Figure 3.5**
**Stella McCartney in one of her retail shops** Stella McCartney developed her business by focusing on caring and social responsibility. She prides herself on living the life that she espouses through her designs and is a role model for future fashion designers.

and textiles in the United Kingdom (UK) and around the globe; it also looks at broadening the role of the designer to some degree. The authors discuss durable clothing and the idea that to be more sustainable and lessen the impact on the environment one should produce and purchase clothing that has a lasting value.

> Fashion by its very definition, isn't designed to last long. Consumers often wear garments too little, wash them too often, and at too high a temperature. All bad news for the environment. Can designers help to change the situation? Can clothes be designed that help us develop an emotional attachment to them, that have stories and origins that make us want to cherish them and to look after them well? (University of Cambridge Institute for Manufacturing 2006: 31)

This is certainly a worthy approach, but how does one convince the consumer? The larger question is, how does one convince retailers to buy and market clothes that last long, that one can develop an attachment to? This very concept goes against what most retailers seek—profits—and to derive profits one must sell products. If we

## Notes from the Field

Corporate social responsibility takes many different forms in the fashion industry. This box focuses on sustainability and the perceived differences between male and female purchase decisions. As you read the chapter, think about your own personal decisions to buy fashion products: do they sync with what the author is thinking? My career has traditionally focused on menswear, and therefore most if not all of my experiences documented in the text are based on this product category. It has been my perception that the male consumer practices more sustainable purchasing than the female consumer when it comes to apparel. This is not a very popular idea among my colleagues in the fashion industry and one that is not empirically supported; it is based on my own personal shopping habits and observations of males in the consuming public. A man buys a dress shirt, and if that dress shirt is properly cared for, it can last years and does not go out of style. Conversely, a woman purchases a blouse and wears it for a season or two and then moves to the next style. Similar examples can be seen in trousers, suits, and sport shirts. Traditionally males have purchased pieces for their wardrobe as investment pieces with the idea that they will last long and not need to be replaced that regularly, whereas the female consumer purchases more for fashion and replaces her purchases on a more frequent basis (again my own theory). However, in recent years, with the advent of fast fashion, the younger male consumer has been swept up in this concept and has started to buy on a more frequent basis, particularly sportswear. This trend could perhaps be driven by the fashion industry itself.

as a consuming world bought less, what impact would this have on the overall economy? Certainly, the authors of *Well Dressed* raise an interesting point that leads the reader to more questions. Questions are good; they enable the dialogue that is important in CSR and sustainable practices.

Let's explore the idea presented in the article *Well Dressed*. What would happen if designers made a conscious decision to design garments that lasted longer and the consumer developed this attachment to fewer products? The consumer would buy two shirts per year (hypothetically) rather than the traditional ten. Retailers would now have to stock less, and their profits or sales volume would need to be adjusted if they were to remain profitable at the diminished sales volume. This would lead to less production required around the globe and therefore less need for factories, which in turn would put people out of work. The change would affect those very people in developing countries who desperately rely on consumers to consume apparel and accessories so that they can keep their jobs and feed, house, and clothe their families; these are the people who could be potentially affected by the good intentions of the global fashion industry. Thus sustainability

and sound CSR can have interesting, unanticipated consequences if not carefully practiced.

## Retailers

Just as brands and designers play a role in CSR and in sustainable practices, so do retailers. One might question this idea and see the retailer solely as a place to *sell one's wares*, but others would consider retailers as major players who have the ability and responsibility to model responsible practices. Two examples that will be incorporated in this chapter include California Cloth Foundry and Nike. As noted in this chapter, there are many examples of brands and designers who adhere to sound business practices, and so too are there many retailers. They would fill a separate book, but this text focuses on providing viable examples.

*California Cloth Foundry.* On the retail side of the fashion industry, a recent entry into the sustainable market is **California Cloth Foundry** (see Figure 3.6). It has taken a unique approach that borrows from the farm-to-table theme by touting itself as "grown to sewn in the U.S.A.," a completely sustainable American supply chain. California Cloth Foundry is about trust and about developing and creating "the most sustainable cloth, and clothes, possible . . . This means that from farm to fashion each aspect of production has been labeled, barcoded, registered, inspected, and thoughtfully designed to meet the highest ecological and ethical standards" (California Cloth Foundry n.d.: para 1). The California Cloth Foundry has developed a clear structure and process to ensure positive CSR and sustainable practice outcomes. It is not only environmentally responsible but also cares for its employees, who work daily to ensure their practices are in place and carried out with fair wages and safe working conditions.

*Nike.* One other example from an international retail perspective is **Nike** (see Figure 3.7). A major force in the fashion industry not only in retailing but also in manufacturing, Nike has set goals for increased transparency in its supply chains with a target date of 2020. During 2015 the company shipped over one billion items while reducing carbon emissions and increasing water efficiency in its manufacturing processes. This was accomplished by eliminating factories that could not meet their performance targets. Nike has put in place a rating system that is self-monitored and that has produced strong results. In addition, the company has improved the use of environmentally preferred materials. Indeed, the Beaverton, Oregon–based active apparel and footwear giant has come a long way from its scandal-packed days of alleged sweatshop manufacturing, but it knows its business model is still far from perfect (Nike 2014–15).

**Figure 3.6**
**Apparel products offered by California Cloth Foundry** California Cloth Foundry provides the consumer with an authentic, socially responsible experience. It is an example of how to create a fashion business that represents a strong point of view.

**Figure 3.7**
**Nike's iconic logo** Nike continues to make strides in its supply chain management by reducing its environmental footprint.

Nike has set itself three new goals that it's hoping to hit for fiscal 2020: (1) minimize its environmental footprint, (2) transform its manufacturing, and (3) unleash human potential (McGregor 2016). McGregor (2016) interviewed two Nike executives about their views on CSR and Nike's three new aims. During the interview Mr. Parker, president and chief executive officer of Nike, stated, "At Nike, we believe it is not enough to adapt to what the future may bring—we're creating the future we want to see through sustainable innovation." Parker further stated, "Today our teams are advancing ambitious new business models and partnerships that can scale unprecedented change across our business and the industry" (para 4). In the same article, Hannah Jones, chief sustainability officer and vice president of the company, stated, "We've set a moonshot challenge to double our business with half the impact. It's a bold ambition that's going to take much more than incremental efficiency—it's going to take innovation on a scale we've never seen before" (para 5).

## Third-Party Certification Organizations

One of the outcomes of the Kathie Lee episode was that President Bill Clinton called a meeting involving multinational companies, colleges and universities, and NGOs to discuss sweatshop and environmental issues.

An outcome of these meetings was the emergence of associations, organizations, and coalitions, nationally and internationally, that are steadfast in their attempts to develop policies and practices that address corporate social irresponsibility (Kang, Germann, and Grewal 2016).

Many of these policies and practices focus on being transparent in all aspects of business. Transparency means that anyone who is interested in a business practice has access to the information and can literally "see" what is being done. In other words, a company is upfront with its customers about how it operates its supply chain. That being said, authors Granados, Gupta, and Kauffman (2010) note that the concept of transparency is complex and can be rather elusive. For example, from a transparency standpoint, what information does the sender wish to send and what information does the sender wish to hold back? How will the information be communicated and through what channels? How will the sender or the organization ensure that the message is accessible? Who will ensure that the message being sent is being developed in a way that is easily understood and accessible to the targeted audience (Granados, Gupta, and Kauffman 2010)? These are some important questions that need to be considered with regard to transparency. What follows is a brief introduction to some organizations that have a clear mission to enhance transparency in an attempt to facilitate CSR practices.

*Fair Labor Association.* The **Fair Labor Association**'s main mission is to improve the lives of workers by addressing "abusive labor practices." It fulfills its mission by offering resources to companies as well as educational programming. It also uses advocacy as a strategy (Fair Labor Association 2012). For example, it advocated on behalf of children in Uzbekistan who were being sent out of school to pick cotton. Additional information may be gathered from http://www.fairlabor.org/.

*Social Accountability International (SAI).* **Social Accountability International**'s main mission is to ensure human rights in the work environment. To accomplish this mission, it develops structures and processes that need to be in place in the work environment to protect workers. One of its main functions is to offer educational programming to ensure compliance with

regard to worker rights (Social Accountability International 2012). A recent addition to the programs offered by SAI is its "TenSquared" initiative. TenSquared is a program that helps teams of workers and managers find innovative solutions to health and safety challenges in the workplace. The program encourages participating teams to move past existing power dynamics and helps them translate their shared interests into bold action in a mere one hundred days. Social Accountability International (2017) relates the following success story: "A Brazilian company changed its assembly line processes to help prevent worker injuries. The effort not only improved employees' safety at work, but it saved the company USD120,000 per year." Additional information may be gathered from http://www.sa-intl.org/.

*Worldwide Responsible Accredited Production.* The main mission of **Worldwide Responsible Accredited Production** is to ensure that workers are safe and treated in an ethical way. The major efforts are carried out via certification educational programs offered at individual facilities (Worldwide Responsible Accredited Production 2017). Additional information may be gathered from http://www.wrapcompliance.org/.

*Sustainable Apparel Coalition.* The **Sustainable Apparel Coalition** focuses specifically on footwear and textiles and works to prevent environmental harm and to create positive outcomes for people and their communities (Sustainable Apparel Coalition n.d.: para 1). This coalition also works with the **Higg Index**, a measurement tool developed to measure sustainability performance. By being able to measure sustainability, the coalition can identify areas of deficiency and thereby develop strategies for improvement (Sustainable Apparel Coalition n.d.: para 1). In this way, the industry can address inefficiencies, eliminate damaging practices, and achieve the environmental and social transparency that consumers are starting to demand. Additional information may be gathered from http://apparelcoalition.org/.

*OIA Sustainability Working Group.* The Outdoor Industry Association's Sustainability Working Group **(OIA Sustainability Working Group)** assists companies in achieving environmental and socially best practices. The group is a collaboration of over three hundred outdoor stakeholders, all working together to achieve a business ethic aimed at responsible practice (Outdoor Industry Association n.d.). Additional information may be gathered from https://outdoorindustry.org/advocacy/working-groups/sustainability-working-group/.

## Third-Party Certification Organizations in Practice

The organizations just discussed have moved the conversation from how to get the product to market to how to treat those who make the product. Shareholders, CEOs, and other stakeholders such as the consumer have become involved in this conversation. In addition, the idea of becoming more transparent has entered into the conversation. The main idea is to provide information to the consumer and the investing community that illustrates just what the industry or company is doing about these very important topics, which in the past had been discussed behind closed doors. Some would argue that companies jumped on the bandwagon as a way to increase sales through marketing: *look at us and look at what we are doing to make the world better.* The truth is that companies should be practicing sustainability and sound CSR practices when no one is looking. When it comes to CSR and sustainable practices, it should not be about the money but about doing the right thing,

although there is evidence to suggest that a positive link exists between CSR and financial profits (Mikolajek-Gocejna 2016; Orlitzky, Schmidt, and Rynes 2003).

As with any industry when a new policy, process, or procedure is implemented, cost is a consideration in developing sound CSR and sustainable business practices. The company must consider what the value is that is added to the organization and how important it is. Some of the organizations listed above charge a fee for their services, depending on the level of commitment to a specific program; specific information regarding fee for service can be found on their websites. Companies around the globe have created entire departments to deal with CSR issues—some with one person, others with dozens—and all of these people add to the payroll and therefore the cost of doing business. Other cost considerations involve the actual product itself. Was a decision made to use only organic cotton? Will the product be produced domestically? Are the inputs used (textile dyes, for example) environmentally friendly? All of these factors may lead to increased cost to the company and therefore to the consumer. There are no easy answers, and each company will approach these issues in a different manner.

One can take the example of California Cloth Foundry discussed earlier. The executives who founded the company took a serious look at the environment and

### Notes from the Field

California Cloth Foundry has hit upon a recipe to help educate consumers and drive business while supporting many of the important tenets of CSR and sustainability discussed in this chapter. Like California Cloth Foundry, I too wanted to make a difference. In 1992 I was working for a men's cut and sew knit and woven shirt wholesaler, and we had the opportunity to acquire a designer name to help market our products. I worked with our team and decided that it should be an environmentally friendly line of men's knit tops. We believed back then in the importance of creating a product that was different and would satisfy a customer need. We used a fabric from Burlington Knits (not to be confused with Burlington Coat Factory) that used low-impact dyes and less water in

its production. We produced the shirts in our factories in Mississippi, we used 100 percent cotton buttons and natural twill tape in the neck, our hang tags were printed on recycled paper, and the shirts were actually shipped in paper bags using no plastic clips, pins, etc. This of course was before the internet, so we had to sell to traditional retailers. We had moderate success at the specialty store level but no success at the larger department or chain stores. They loved the product and the concept but feared what it would say about the rest of the knit shirts they were selling in their store! They did not know how to successfully market the product. If we launched today with our own website, who knows what the results would be?

the supply chain and made the conscious decision to be different, and that decision cost money. Could they have decided to create beautiful clothing from other fiber sources? Could they have decided to save on labor costs by sourcing their production in a lower-cost country? Of course they could have, but that was not what they decided to do because it was not what they stood for, and most notably it was not in accordance with their mission. California Cloth Foundry has a specific ethos that all members believe in and support, and hopefully the consumer will also see the value in their decisions. One advantage that the Foundry has today that did not exist a decade ago is that it can connect directly with the consumer via the internet. This provides the company with the opportunity to tell its story to consumers who are like-minded and believe in what the company is doing.

CSR, sustainability, and transparency can potentially have a broad impact on the overall supply chain, not just the factory. Also key is the call for standards that will ensure that these practices are carried out. No universal standard exists, but the hope is that all factories will adopt one of these standards or adhere to CSR policies established by the retailer or brand. It is also clear that these associations, organizations, coalitions, and general working groups have demonstrated the need to work collectively and collaboratively in partnerships with one another to achieve sustainable goals.

The organizations previously discussed, as well as countless major retailers and brands around the globe, have their own standards that are embedded in their individual CSR policies. From a supplier point of view, however, following CSR standards can be complex, confusing, and daunting. It is challenging to remain compliant because any one factory may be supplying product to brands or retailers with different standards. There has been a movement to have a universal set of standards for all to adhere to, but this industry goal has not been reached.

## Educators

Educators and those involved in educational endeavors are also key players in the CSR and sustainability movement. The question is, does education drive practice or does practice drive education? Or is there an alternative possibility? Is it possible for there to be synergistic movement between both practice and education, each influencing the other and creating movement forward with regard to CSR and sustainability practices? To address education, this section will cover first educators for responsible business practices and later consider the educators' point of view.

*Educators for Socially Responsible Business Practices.* It is incumbent on the educators of the world to make sure that they are preparing students for

### Notes from the Field

Universal standards for CSR have proven to be an elusive goal because many competing organizations work with thousands of companies, each with differing standards. Several of these competing organizations are listed in this chapter, and although they all are interested in CSR, they do exist in some measure to support their own internal and external stakeholders. I once visited a factory that was in the process of preparing for an audit and witnessed something that I thought was very interesting. The factory was actually changing the color of the floor lighting that showed workers the way to the exits in case of an emergency. First I thought, good for them for even having the system in place, but I was puzzled by the

activity, so I asked the factory manager just what they were doing. He explained that one auditing body demanded that the emergency path lights be red and another organization that was coming to conduct a factory audit the next day had guidelines that required that the floor lighting be amber (yellow), so they actually had to switch the color of the lights to pass the audit. Such is the life of a factory manager trying to comply with the many different standards and to remain compliant in order to be in a position to do business with multiple companies. It is not an easy feat and one that obviously detracts from the daily running of a factory, and of course it costs money.

successful careers in the fashion industry and to instill in them what sound CRS practices are and how the topic of sustainability fits into the conversation. To this end, an organization titled "Educators for Socially Responsible Apparel Business (ESRAB)" was formed under the guidance of several like-minded educators, principally Marsha Dickson of the University of Delaware. ESRAB was founded as a collaborative learning community whose members collectively share their knowledge and experiences to build awareness and foster campus and community engagement.

The nine founding members initially worked to develop the organization using the International Textile and Apparel Association's (ITAA) annual conference as a platform to meet and disseminate information surrounding critical issues affecting the fashion industry. ITAA provided opportunities to publish and present the findings of the group and to invite educators from all campuses that have fashion-related curricula to participate and share ideas on how to educate the next generation of students so that there will be an increased awareness of CSR practices. ESRAB has grown to over eighty member schools since 1999.

Educators for Socially Responsible Apparel Business is now known as **Educators for Socially Responsible Apparel Practices** (ESRAP), a subtle change but one that better reflects the changing industry. With the name change an additional formal goal was established, which was to work on a global scale to affect changes in curriculum to better reflect the current state of CSR in the fashion industry and to empower students to become change agents with newly acquired knowledge from the programs that they are enrolled in. Currently, the identified goals of ESRAP are to "change curriculum on a global scale to better reflect the current state of Corporate Social Responsibility (CSR) and sustainability in the fashion industry, and to empower students to become change agents" (ESRAP 2015: para 1).

ESRAP will have an impact. Each individual faculty member who teaches a fashion class at a college, university, or technical school around the world can play a part by instilling his or her own philosophy on these topics. In addition, each faculty member, by participating in partnerships, research, and organizations such as ESRAP, along with presenting publications at conferences, has the potential to initiate major changes related to CSR and sustainability in the fashion industry. Members of ESRAP have worked with the Sustainable Apparel Coalition HIGG Index to develop a set of learning goals that will be shared with the education community worldwide. This work started in 2015 at the International Textile and Apparel Association's annual meeting.

*Educators' Point of View.* In the opening of the chapter it is noted that CSR and sustainability have been linked to the fashion industry. Each company, designer, brand, and retailer has its own ideas on what sustainability in the fashion industry means and how it relates to the supply chain. ***Sustainable Fashion*** is a groundbreaking book by Janet Hethorn and Connie Ulasewicz, faculty members at schools that have fashion programs. The authors of this text set out to help the reader understand what is currently going on in the fashion industry as it relates to sustainability.

> "Echo chic," "environmentally conscious," "ethical consumerism," and "clothing with a conscience." Terms such as these abound. But what do they mean for people that design and develop clothing? What do they mean for the people who buy and wear clothing? Most want to wear clothing made in "'responsible" ways and that do not harm the planet, but how do we factor this in along with other considerations as we shop for and put together what we wear each day? (adapted from Hethorn and Ulasewicz 2008: xiii)

There are other important questions to consider: What do these terms mean in the development of the clothing we wear from a supply chain standpoint? Do fashion companies make conscious decisions when it comes to answering these questions, or do they just make apparel that they think will sell?

It is generally assumed that sustainability has to do with the environment: for instance, what resources are used as inputs into the clothing that we buy and wear and how the clothing is developed. Companies talk about organic cotton and wool, zero waste design, and creating clothing that will last. But there has also been talk and action regarding fast fashion. In other words, there is a trend toward the development of disposable clothing, which goes against the concept of sustainability. So, while educators and some in the industry are talking about CSR, the question remains: Are we talking the talk but not walking the walk? If we are to be a sustainable world, does what is sometimes categorized as disposable clothing (fast fashion) have a negative effect on the environment, and ultimately the fashion industry? The fashion industry is based on creating newness, and if we slow or halt that newness, what happens to the economics of the fashion industry and the people who work in it?

Hethorn and Ulasewicz (2008) identified three areas in which to explore the concept of sustainability: people, processes, and environment, as presented in Table 3.1. Readers can further explore the ideas of these two authors and others in their text. These authors discuss in detail the three concepts listed in Table 3.1 and deal with the real question for the industry and those working on various supply chains: What is meant by sustainability? Sustainability, or the ability to sustain, is used in conjunction with other terms in order to craft some common definitions. For example, according to the World Commission on Environment and Development (1987), **sustainable development** "meets the needs of the present without compromising the ability of future generations to meet their own needs" (section 3, para 27). Clearly, this definition, on the face of it, goes against almost everything that the fashion industry stands for.

| **Table 3.1** Exploration of Concepts Related to Sustainability | |
|---|---|
| People | People consume clothing. They have basic needs that fashion can address. Sustainability works both ways here; as people can sustain the environment by addressing their clothing choices, fashion can also sustain people in various ways. |
| Processes | Processes, both production and economic, have an impact on the direction that sustainability takes. The way we approach making fashion goods guides the resulting ecological footprint. |
| Environment | Environmental concerns and opportunities are closely tied to fashion. Since garments are made of materials (e.g., fibers, fabrics, notions) there are direct physical environmental impacts connected to the use, reuse, resilience, and sustainable actions that surround fashion. |

Source: Hethorn and Ulasewicz 2008: xiv.

The fashion industry constantly consumes resources, and only a minority of companies invest in and develop strong sustainable business practices coupled with viable CSR policies.

## Notes from the Field

In order to impact the future, students must have the tools to be the change agents that educators hope they will be. You often hear the phrase that we are educating future leaders, and this is true no matter what educational institution or level is involved. It is incumbent upon the faculty to share their knowledge and expertise with students so that students can make informed decisions surrounding CSR and sustainability. The classroom provides the perfect place for this interaction to take place, and today that can be in a face-to-face scenario or in a distance learning setting. In most of the classes that I teach, whether at the undergraduate or graduate level, I ask the following question on an exam: If you had the opportunity to take a position with your dream company and between the interviews and the offer you found out that the company employed poor CSR practices (child labor, no paid overtime, to name a few), would you accept the position when offered? Of course there is no right or wrong answer. Generally I give the most points to students who say they will accept the position in order to be a change agent and have a positive impact on the company's CSR policies. As we all know, this would not happen overnight, but I always respect and applaud those students who are passionate enough to believe that they can make a difference.

# Consumers

The conversation would not be complete without bringing the consumer into the picture. How does the consumer interact with CSR and sustainability in the fashion industry? The simple answer is by buying the products that the retailers offer. But do consumers really care if the garments and accessories they purchase are made using sustainable methods and following CSR policies? How many consumers thoroughly research companies and their policies before making their purchase decision? Are consumers willing to pay more for the added value that sound CSR and sustainable practices bring? Ann-Taylor Adams (2014) states, "Fifty-five percent of global online consumers across 60 countries say they are willing to pay more for products and services provided by companies that are committed to positive social and environmental impact" (para. 1). However, she also brings into question consumer attitudes about CSR:

> Finding consumers around the world who say they care about the environment or extreme poverty is relatively easy. But does care about issues convert to action when it comes to buying decisions? Some fifty-two percent of global respondents in Nielsen's survey say their purchase decisions are partly dependent on the packaging—they check the labeling first before buying to ensure the brand is committed to positive social and environmental impact. Millennials (age 21–34) appear more responsive to sustainability actions. Among global respondents in Nielsen's survey who are responsive to sustainability actions, half are Millennials; they represent 51 percent of those who will pay extra for sustainable products and 51 percent of those who check the packaging for sustainable labeling. (para 5)

Not to be outdone by the millennials (see Figure 3.8), Generation Z (born roughly in 1995–2009) also has strong views on sustainability and CSR practices. "New research into Generation Z in the US reveals that it's time for businesses to 'confess' more openly that their sustainability and social programs are designed to make them more money" (Salt Communications 2015). It was further noted that 57 percent of Gen Zs that were surveyed felt that it was okay for a business to make a profit

**Figure 3.8**
**A group of Millennials** Millennials make up the largest consuming group in the United States today, surpassing baby boomers for that title. Millennials have been reported as having a strong propensity to be responsive to sustainable policies and practices. Will the industry feel and respond to their values?

while making the world a better place. This is a bit of a departure from what the millennials think and shows a changing thought process that the retailers of tomorrow will have to address in their marketing plans. Members of Generation Z feel strongly about rewarding organizations that are making the world a better place. Approximately 61 percent say they are willing to go out of their way to buy products and services from businesses that are sustainable and socially responsible, while 59 percent of the same respondents rank working for a company that helps make the world a better place as important a consideration as salary (Salt Communications 2105).

The message seems to be clear: the consuming public does in fact care and does pay attention and most importantly shows the results at the register—good news indeed. However, there is some question about this good news. Habel, Schons, Alavi, and Wieseke (2016) noted that although the positive benefits of CSR give the consumer a "warm glow" (p. 84), their qualitative focus groups revealed some interesting information about consumer perceptions. For example, although consumers did in fact identify the benefits of CSR, there was a concern about the cost of CSR engagement and price fairness. "Under certain circumstances the positive effect of CSR engagement on perceived price fairness through benefit perceptions might prevail, while under other circumstances the negative effect through price markup perceptions might prevail" (p. 88). These "certain circumstances" hinge on whether or not the consumer thinks the company's decision about CSR is related to extrinsic factors such as self-interested financial motives or to altruistic motives that focus on taking CSR actions for the greater good (see Du, Bhattacharya, and Sen 2007).

The interaction of the consumer with the supply chain is discussed in more detail in Chapter 12.

## An Alternative Viewpoint

For all the good that has been done in the area of CSR and sustainability, there are those in the fashion industry who think that more needs to be done and in fact challenge the notion that any good has been accomplished at all. In an article that appeared on the *Ecotextile News* website, Brett Mathews reported on Sharan Burrow, the general secretary of the International Trade Union Confederation. Sharan Burrow spoke about the CSR programs of major brands and how retailers have had "little if any positive impact on guaranteeing workers' rights" and have "deferred addressing underlying structural issues" (Mathews 2016: para 1). Furthermore, Mathews claimed that "there are now serious global governance gaps concerning global supply chains" (para 1). The author of this text believes, however, that much progress has been made and through sound CSR practices and sustainability movements many more lives have been improved than not.

## CONCLUSION

This chapter offers a broad view of CSR and sustainability practice in our contemporary fashion industry. The initial overall definition of CSR presented in the opening paragraph is just that—overall and general. The principles of CSR are enacted in many forms, including philanthropy and human and environmental justice (Walker-Said and Kelly 2015). Actions associated with CSR and sustainability are necessary for business and to support ethical practice. CSR and sustainable business practice also require the implementation of formal compliance standards. Fashion companies, retailers, educators, and consumers are all key players as the industry makes strides toward being social responsible and actively engaging in sustainable practices.

There are opposing viewpoints, but they can stimulate conversation from which we learn so we can then apply this learning to CSR policies. Readers of this text can take time to reflect on their own ideas, values, and beliefs about CSR and sustainable business practices and determine where they stand. What is the overall impact of positive CSR and sustainable practices? How can you be a part of that conversation? What solutions can you provide? What role will you play in the future? More importantly, what role can you play now as a student? You can start now by challenging your professors to include more detailed content about CSR and sustainable practices in your coursework. In Chapter 4 we will look at the interrelationship of various departments within a fashion company and how they communicate with each other to develop the CSR/sustainable story.

# INDUSTRY INTERVIEW: MARY G. CALLY, INDUSTRY EXECUTIVE

I had the opportunity to discuss CSR and sustainability with Mary G. Cally, a fashion industry executive. Our interview with Mary looks at several different themes that tie directly into this chapter. Mary is an entrepreneurial, highly creative global apparel and home fashions executive with a talent and passion for developing strategic sourcing programs and products through cultivation of deep and extensive global alliances and partnerships. Ms. Cally is recognized in the industry for significantly impacting the growth of multimillion-dollar global businesses through an innovative, dedicated, visionary leadership style and business approach. She spearheaded the strategy, creation, and growth of multiple fashion lines and home products. Mary has an innate ability to improve margins and production processes, has strong analytical and problem-solving skills, and has a keen aptitude for balancing design esthetics with compliance standards.

**Interviewer**: *How would you define corporate social responsibility (CSR)?*

**M. C.:** In the broadest sense, by definition a company's CSR policy functions as a self-regulatory mechanism whereby a business monitors and ensures its active compliance with the spirit of the law, ethical standards and national or international *norms*. Some firms' implementation of CSR goes beyond compliance and engages in actions that will further some social good, beyond the interests of the firm and that which is required by law, such as philanthropic activities.

**Interviewer**: *How are your CSR principles and policies reflected in your supply chain?*

**M. C.:** In our supply chain we follow the principles of self-regulation in that we actively monitor all of our suppliers domestically, as well as internationally. This includes fabric and trim suppliers, factories, warehouses, as well as all traffic functions. So in effect we are monitoring the entire supply chain. We have a list of principles which is embodied in our Code of Conduct, which all suppliers must read and agree to. We conduct on-site visits on a yearly basis. If we find any grievances, we send a formal report advising of the CAP that needs to be completed and based on the offense we allow a certain amount of time for

stated issues to be corrected, and if the violations persist or are flagrant we will cease doing business with that company. On a corporate level we follow these principles within our own office structure.

**Interviewer**: *What roadblocks and opportunities does CSR present within your supply chain?*

**M. C.:** There can be several roadblocks based on the country as well as level of supplier. It is the responsibility of our company to ensure all suppliers understand our goals and expectations in working with them. On the positive side, having strong CSR policies in place can enhance our position with our customers and ultimately the consumers who purchase our products, so the opportunity to tell a positive story that resonates with the consumer can be a powerful message.

Some suppliers may have a lack of knowledge or understanding of the benefits of following a CSR policy. The upside for our suppliers is the opportunity to learn and strengthen their image in the marketplace, which make them a more valuable resource for both a manufacturer and for the worker they wish to attract. For the manufacturer as well, it is important that retailers know that we abide by these principles and they can be verified by an audit by the retailer's qualified auditing firm.

**Interviewer:** *Where does the CSR department fit in the overall corporate structure? Does it stand alone?*

**M. C.:** Our CSR area, Social Compliance and Customs Trade Partnership Against Terrorism (C-TPAT), is housed within the Production Operations area. C-TPAT is a voluntary supply chain security program for manufacturers as well as retailers, freight forwarders, brokers, and warehouses.

**Interviewer:** *Is it embedded in sourcing? Whom does the department report to?*

**M. C.:** Reports to the SVP of Production and Operations.

**Interviewer:** *How do your consumers view your CSR policies? Do they care? Is it reflected at the register?*

**M. C.:** Consumers are becoming much more aware of social compliances as more information is available through all forms of media. I do not think at this time, the consumer is willing to pay more for an item knowing that it has been ethically sourced and manufactured. The expectation is that a company will follow a responsible CSR program which includes a living wage for workers, fair treatment, and a safe environment. There is, of course, a cost absorbed by the manufacturer to be able to implement policies, such as the addition of trained personnel, cost of auditing, etc. In today's society it is becoming second nature for consumers to assume that you are following sound CSR policies, but as we all know that is not always true.

**Interviewer:** *Your concluding thoughts on the future of CSR.*

**M. C.:** In general, CSR is growing in the industry as more companies become aware of the need for the consumer to be assured that ethical policies are followed. Throughout the supply chain there has been a great deal of pressure placed on retailers by outside human rights and watchdog groups, to make certain the brands they carry follow a policy which embodies the general principles and standards of such a program.

## Questions Pertaining to Interview

1. Consider Mary G. Cally's definition of CSR. What verbs does she use in her definition that articulate the "action" necessary for CSR?
2. Mary G. Cally speaks about policies for CSR. How do you suppose policies ensure CSR and sustainability?
3. How will communication and education assist an organization to ensure policy implementation and compliance?
4. Within the context of this interview, what are the core factors for the successful implementation of CSR and sustainability practices in a company?

# CASE STUDY: Nike

Much has been discussed about companies and how they interact with all their stakeholders, especially what consumer expectations are for their products and companies. Nike is featured here as a representative company in the retail sector that also manufactures its own products. "At Nike, we believe we have a responsibility to conduct our business in an ethical way. We expect the same from our business partners, and focus on working with long-term, strategic suppliers that demonstrate a commitment to engaging their workers, safe working conditions and environmental responsibility" (Nike 2016: para 1). Nike takes its CSR very seriously. Given the size and scope of its global operations, Nike has undertaken steps to redesign its supply chain (see its website, *www.nikeresponsibility.com*, for more specific information). Nike has created a strong code of conduct that it expects all its trading partners to adhere to; if they don't or simply can't, Nike will stop using them. In most cases when Nike inspects a facility that it wishes to use, it will give the company the opportunity to correct deficiencies if they are deemed not too serious in order to comply with Nike's code of conduct. In some instances, this cannot be accomplished, and Nike will make the difficult decision not to work with that specific factory. In other instances Nike might find new violations of its code on subsequent visits that will need to be mitigated in order for the factory to continue producing products for the brand. The issue of CSR and sustainability is ongoing 24/7, as all it takes is one incident to tarnish the reputation of a major brand.

Nike has introduced technology to support its manufacturing process and has taken steps to improve the lives of the workers making its products. Nike is a global powerhouse and one of the most recognized brands in the world, yet it still faces CSR and sustainability challenges in the work that it does. One challenge in an increasingly competitive marketplace is subcontracting that has not been approved. For example, suppose Nike develops a partnership with a factory and it performs all of its CSR protocols and deems the factory a good partner and in good standings according to Nike's code of conduct. Nike thoroughly vets the company and agrees that it is one that it can trust, so Nike places business with the company. Three months later one of the certifying organizations listed in the chapter is performing an inspection for another client in the same area where Nike has recently placed new business, and it finds Nike apparel being made in a factory that has not been approved by Nike. This is a factory that another client is contemplating using, and it is the first inspection by this regulating body. Unbeknownst to Nike, evidence of child labor and poor working conditions with forced overtime at regular pay are documented by this organization. As a courtesy, this organization, which has previously performed inspections for Nike, raises the alarm by contacting Nike directly.

## Case Study Questions

1. Using the information in this chapter and on Nike's website, answer the following question: How did this sourcing problem happen?
2. How can Nike, who manufactures in so many countries, have eyes everywhere?
3. The negative repercussions of such an incident for the brand are enormous; what plans can Nike take to prevent this from happening again?

## CHAPTER REVIEW QUESTIONS

1. Conduct a web search and find brands, designers, and retailers who specifically speak about CSR and sustainability practices. What are the similarities and differences between these brands, designers, and retailers? As you consider your findings, do you see any glaring omissions that need to be addressed?

2. What is the initial step that a fashion industry company should take if it wishes to make a commitment toward CSR and sustainability?

3. Which company that was featured in the chapter is a benchmark organization for CSR/sustainability? What is your rationale?

4. What are your personal ideas, values, and beliefs about CSR and sustainable business practices?

5. Given the knowledge you have obtained about CSR and sustainability, what is the greatest gift you can bring to your work environment now or in the future?

## CLASS EXERCISES

1. Identify three publicly traded companies and compare and contrast their CSR policies. Determine if these policies add to the overall marketability of the company and its products from a consumer standpoint.

2. The *Ecotextile* article cited in the text provides an alternative viewpoint. Do a search to find other such articles and determine if there is any validity to their point of view. How does this match up with other research?

## KEY TERMS

corporate social responsibility
   (CSR)
sustainability
vendor compliance
TOMS
Warby Parker
PVH Corp
Stella McCartney
California Cloth Foundry

Nike
Fair Labor Association
Social Accountability
   International
Worldwide Responsible
   Accredited Production
Sustainable Apparel
   Coalition
Higg Index

OIA Sustainability Working
   Group
Educators for Socially
   Responsible Apparel Practices
*Sustainable Fashion*
sustainable development

# REFERENCES

1. Brown, E. (2014), *Ethical Chic: How Women Can Change the Fashion Industry*. Available online: http://www.forbes.com/sites/yec/2014/01/14/ethical-chic-how-women-can-change-the-fashion-industry/#664cf4471ea3.

2. California Cloth Foundry (n.d.), *Farm to Fashion*. Available online: http://www.triplepundit.com/2016/05/farm-fashion-california-cloth-foundry/.

3. Du, S., C. B. Bhattacharya, and S. Sen (2007), "Reaping Relational Rewards from Corporate Social Responsibility: The Role of Competitive Positioning," *International Journal of Research in Marketing*, 24 (3): 224–41.

4. ESRAP (2015), *About Us*. Available online: http://www.esrapglobal.org/about-us.html.

5. European Commission (2017), *Corporate Social Responsibility (CSR)*. Available online: https://ec.europa.eu/growth/industry/corporate-social-responsibility_en.

6. Fair Labor Association (2012), *Improving Workers' Lives Worldwide*. Available online: http://www.fairlabor.org/.

7. Glavas, A., and K. Kelley (2014), "The Effects of Perceived Corporate Social Responsibility on Employee Attitudes," *Business Ethics Quarterly*, 24 (2): 165–202.

8. Granados, N., A. Gupta, and R. J. Kauffman (2010), "Information Transparency in Business-to-Consumer Markets: Concepts, Framework, and Research Agenda," *Information Systems Research*, 21 (2): 207–26.

9. Habel, J., L. M. Schons, S. Alavi, and J. Wieseke (2016), "Warm Glow or Extra Charge? The Ambivalent Effect of Corporate Social Responsibility Activities on Customers' Perceived Price Fairness," *Journal of Marketing*, 80, 84–105.

10. Hethorn, J., and C. Ulasewicz (2008), *Sustainable Fashion: Why Now? A Conversation about Issues, Practices, and Possibilities*, New York: Fairchild Books.

11. Kang, C., F. Germann, and R. Grewal (2016), "Washing Away Our Sins? Corporate Social Responsibility, Corporate Social Irresponsibility, and Firm Performance," *Journal of Marketing*, 80, 59–79.

12. Mathews, B. (2016), "Unions Note the 'Failure of CSR,'" *Ecotextile News*, June 1. Available online: http://www.ecotextile.com/2016060122149/social-compliance-csr-news/walmart-gap-h-m-slammed-in-new-reports.html.

13. McGregor, L. (2016), "Nike Raises Its Sustainability Game, Sets New Supply Chain Goals for 2020," *Sourcing Journal*, May 12. Available online: https://sourcingjournalonline.com/nike-raises-its-sustainability-game-sets-new-goals-for-2020/.

14. Mikolajek-Gocejna, M. (2016), "The Relationship between Corporate Social Responsibility and Corporate Financial Performance: Evidence from Empirical Studies," *Comparative Economic Research*, 19 (4). Available online: https://doi.org/10.1515/cer-2016-0030.

15. Nike (2014–15), "NIKE, Inc. FY14/15 Sustainable Business Report," Sustainable Brands. Available online: http://www.sustainablebrands.com/digital_learning/csr_report/next_economy/nike_inc_fy1415_sustainable_business_report.

16. Nike (2016), *Nike Supply Chain Disclosure*. Available online: https://help-en-us.nike.com/app/answer/article/supply-chain/a_id/20878/country/us.

17. Orlitzky, M., F. L. Schmidt, and S. S. Rynes (2003), "Corporate Social Responsibility and Financial Performance: A Meta-Analysis," *Organizational Studies*, 24 (3): 403–41.

18. Outdoor Industry Association (n.d.), *Sustainability Working Group*. Available online: https://outdoorindustry.org/advocacy/working-groups/sustainability-working-group/.

19. PVH (2015), *Corporate Responsibility*. Available online: http://www.pvh.com/responsibility.

20. Salt Communications (2015), *Gen Z*. Available online: https://mullenlowesalt.com/blog/2015/06/generationz-us/.

21. Social Accountability International (2012), *About SAI*. Available online: http://sa-intl.org/index.cfm?fuseaction=Page.ViewPage&pageId=472.

22. Strom, S. (1996), "A Sweatheart Becomes Suspect; Looking behind Those Kathy Lee Labels," *The New York Times*. Available online: http://www.nytimes.com/1996/06/27/business/a-sweetheart-becomes-suspect-looking-behind-those-kathie-lee-labels.html?pagewanted=all.

23. Sustainable Apparel Coalition (n.d.), *Apparel Coalition*. Available online: http://apparelcoalition.org/.

24. Sustainable Apparel Coalition (n.d.), *The Coalition*. Available online: http://apparelcoalition.org/the-coalition/.

25. Taylor Adams, A. (2014), "Global Consumers Are Willing to Put Their Money Where Their Heart Is When It Comes to Goods and Services from Companies Committed to Social Responsibility," *Nielsen*. Available online: http://www.nielsen.com/us/en/press-room/2014/global-consumers-are-willing-to-put-their-money-where-their-heart-is.html.

26. TOMS (2016), *Corporate Responsibility*. Available online: http://www.toms.com/corporate-responsibility.

27. University of Cambridge Institute for Manufacturing (2006), *Well Dressed? The Present and Future Sustainability of Clothing and Textiles in the United Kingdom*. Available online: http://www.ifm.eng.cam.ac.uk/uploads/Resources/Other_Reports/UK_textiles.pdf.

28. Walker-Said, C., and J. D. Kelly (2015), *Corporate Social Responsibility? Human Rights in the New Global Economy*, Chicago: University of Chicago Press.

29. Warby Parker (n.d.), *History*. Available online: https://www.warbyparker.com/history.

30. World Commission on Environment and Development (1987), *Report of the World Commission on Environment and Development: Our Common Future*. Available online: http://www.un-documents.net/wced-ocf.htm.

31. Worldwide Responsible Accredited Production (2015), *WRAP for the Public*. Available online: http://www.wrapcompliance.org/en/wrap-for-the-public.

# Key Players and Departments

## LEARNING OBJECTIVES

Upon completion of this chapter you will be able to:

- Describe the interrelationship of departments within a fashion company.

- Identify the various departments that support the fashion supply chain.

- Determine best practices for setting up departmental relationships.

- Understand the importance of communication within a fashion company.

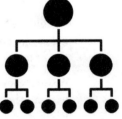

# ORGANIZATION AND DEPARTMENT STRUCTURE

The fashion industry has traditionally been driven by manufacturing. In the United States this scenario existed for the most part until the late 1960s and early 1970s, when consumers developed their strong voice and demanded products that manufacturers were not making. This shift caused the fashion industry to move from a manufacturing economy in which retailers sold what the fashion companies made to a market-driven economy in which consumers told the fashion companies (manufacturers) what they wanted to buy.

In the fashion industry today, various departments are interrelated. This chapter focuses on the structure of the fashion organizations and the interrelationship between the key players and departments within the supply chain. We can define a fashion company as any company that is engaged in a commercial enterprise that is related to the apparel, accessory, and textile industry. This would encompass retailers, wholesalers, manufacturers, and designers of apparel and accessory products. There are four distinct levels in the fashion business:

Primary level: This level is composed of the growers and producers of the raw materials of fashion: the fiber, fabric, leather, and fur producers who function in the raw materials market.

Secondary level: This level is composed of manufacturers and contractors that produce the semifinished or finished goods from materials produced on the primary level.

Retail level: This level is a direct distribution channel to the consumer and is composed of many different facets [see Chapter 11].

Auxiliary level: This is the only level that functions with all the other levels simultaneously. This level is composed of all the support services that work to keep the consumer aware of fashion trends; it includes advertising, visual, and fashion consultants and researchers. (Stone 2015)

The fashion industry functions because of the structure and processes of the supply chain, the chain of operations in which each link has a direct effect on the preceding and following links (see Figure 4.1). The

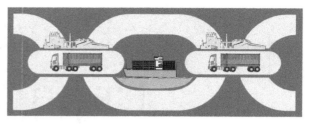

**Figure 4.1**

**Picture of the supply chain** The supply chain is depicted by an actual chain identifying various steps in the process. An understanding of the details and corresponding complexities of this chain ensures seamless movement from the initiation of product development to the satisfied consumer.

departments that work together within a fashion company are linked in the same manner, with each department having a direct effect on the other departments and with communication flowing between departments. These departments are determined by the type and size of the company (see Figure 4.2). Sole proprietors who are responsible for every facet of the business operate side-by-side with large multinational fashion corporations employing thousands of people with decision-making spread out over many departments. While acknowledging that there are smaller companies in the fashion industry, this chapter focuses on larger companies with multiple departments.

No two fashion companies are exactly alike. Each company may use a similar model as the one portrayed in Figure 4.2; however, the department structure that is developed, as well as the processes used for communication and for the working of the company, will be individualized to meet individual company needs. There is a process or a flow within each department as well as a process or flow that takes place between departments. Without a comprehensive structure and without detailed processes in place, chaos will reign.

## Organizational Chart of a Fashion Company

The model illustrated in Figure 4.2 gives the reader a visual representation of the structure of a fashion company and the varying departments within that company. However, the formal representation of company structure is known as the **organizational chart**, which

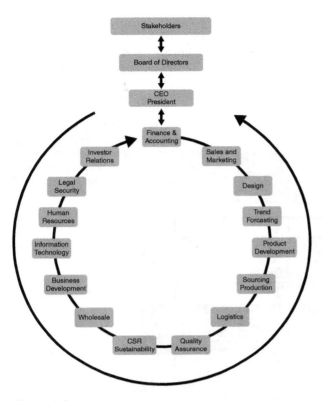

**Figure 4.2**
**Departments within a fashion company** This model portrays the typical structure of a publicly traded global fashion company and the various departments that make up the company. It also hints at how the processes that take place, including communication, are bidirectional.

illustrates key players in an organization (Ebert 2006). Ebert (2006) noted the complexities of an organization and discussed the formal and informal authority of its key players: "The structure of a company, however, is by no means limited to the organizational chart and the formal assignment of authority. Frequently, the **informal organization**—everyday social interactions among employees that transcend formal jobs and job interrelationships—effectively alter a company's formal structure" (Ebert 2006: 192).

Ideally the departments visualized in an organizational chart are depicted with solid lines and dotted lines expressing the formal lines of authority and of communication. See Figure 4.3A and 4.3B. These two organizational charts are obviously very different. In the large publicly traded company, for each departmental box on the chart there are multiple subgroups that report to the individual managers, and in some cases hundreds and even thousands of employees could be working for that organization (particularly if the company owns its own factories). In a small-scale fashion company there can be a total of four people running the business, and in some cases as few as three. The small fashion companies typically tend to be startup companies that have a limited product or a niche within the industry. As often happens in the fashion industry, several people who work for a particular company or several different companies see an opportunity to start a business. These individuals then develop their product and ultimately take customers and/or product away from an existing company. They do this by relying on relationships that have been built up over time.

## Types of Organizational Structures and Charts

A literature review of organization structures and charts can help individuals understand that there are many ways to create a chart or organizational structure. Individuals would consider the size of the company and the type of industry in which the organization functions. An organizational structure can also be seen as a communication tool. The chart should use clear lines that symbolize communication flow as well as lines of authority. This is important because lack of communication, inefficient communication, and miscommunication all may result in production issues.

Leo Sun (2016) in the *Business Dictionary* looked at several of the most common forms of organizational charts, including functional, product, and regional charts. **Functional organizational charts** have at the top the executive, with middle managers below all reporting to the top executive. The **product organizational chart** represents a structure in which there may be a number of top executives, each responsible for his or her own product. An example in the fashion industry is Polo Ralph Lauren, which has multiple divisions—retail, wholesale, men's, women's, children's—each with a group president reporting to the CEO. The **regional organizational chart** would depict a larger national or global organization that is represented by regional executives. These executives are responsible for the execution of work within their targeted location, possibly

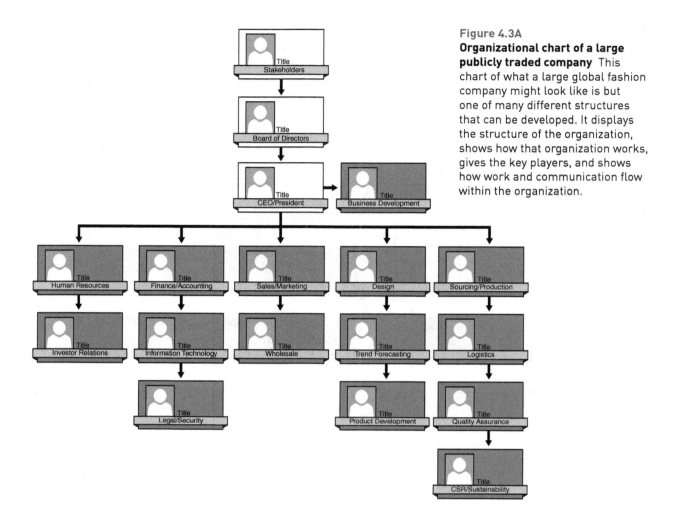

Title
Stakeholders

Title
Board of Directors

Title
CEO/President

Title
Business Development

Title
Human Resources

Title
Finance/Accounting

Title
Sales/Marketing

Title
Design

Title
Sourcing/Production

Title
Investor Relations

Title
Information Technology

Title
Wholesale

Title
Trend Forecasting

Title
Logistics

Title
Legal/Security

Title
Product Development

Title
Quality Assurance

Title
CSR/Sustainability

**Figure 4.3A**
**Organizational chart of a large publicly traded company** This chart of what a large global fashion company might look like is but one of many different structures that can be developed. It displays the structure of the organization, shows how that organization works, gives the key players, and shows how work and communication flow within the organization.

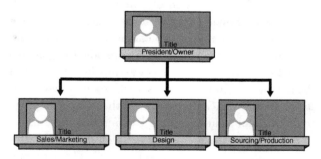

Title
President/Owner

Title
Sales/Marketing

Title
Design

Title
Sourcing/Production

**Figure 4.3B**
**Organizational chart of a small fashion company** This shows what a small company might look like in the fashion industry. Often in small companies there may be no need for a formal chart.

reporting to a regional vice president, who in turn would report to the CEO. In this instance a significant amount of power is granted to local executives because they would be considered the resident experts in their particular region (Sun 2016).

## Key Players Represented in an Organizational Chart

In the large multinational fashion company (publicly traded), the focus is on creating shareholder value through increased profits. At the top of the chart are the **shareholders** demanding a certain level of performance from the CEO/president and the board of directors (see Figure 4.2). The shareholders are those individuals and corporate investors who have taken a stock position in the company; they own stock that has been purchased

**Figure 4.4**

**A board of directors** In today's complex world of fashion, it is important for boards to be composed of people with varying attributes, as depicted by the bubbles. Each board member brings something different to the table.

through a brokerage house. The amount of stock can vary from one share (based on market price) to millions of shares. The **board of directors** is a body of elected or appointed members who jointly oversee the activities of a company or organization (see Figure 4.4).

The **CEO/president** works with the board of directors to set the goals for the company and, in conjunction with the finance department, creates the budget. The CEO/president is often chosen by the board of directors at large publicly traded companies, but with smaller companies that position can be filled from within or through an outside recruiting organization. Most fashion companies work with a top-down budget process, with the CEO/president working with the board of directors to set an overall sales goal that includes projected profits, which become the basis for the budget. Once the revenue projections are set, a plan is put in place based on intended markups to achieve that goal. Each individual department is then allocated a fixed amount of money to spend to achieve those goals, and that is communicated from the top down.

For example, suppose Company X is a large publicly traded fashion company with sales in excess of $7.4 billion. This sales revenue is made up by the retail and wholesale divisions. To understand the impact of a top-down budgeting approach, we can look specifically at one division: the men's knit shirts wholesale division. Let us say the target for the men's knit shirt wholesale division is $41 billion and the target markup is 50 percent. Based on this scenario, the person(s) in charge of that division (most likely a group president or vice president) will be responsible for developing a plan to achieve

$1 billion in sales by selling into the many wholesale accounts that Company X has around the globe. At a 50 percent markup, the cost of goods will need to come in at $500 million, allowing for a gross markup of the same amount given the target of 50 percent markup. This process would then be repeated throughout the entire organization, with each division being allocated a sales or budget goal to meet at a specified markup to achieve the overall desired results.

In this instance we are talking about product that will ultimately be sold to the consumer, as there are many other top-down budget decisions that go into running a company, such as payroll, benefits, rent, and equipment. This description may tend to oversimplify the process, but it has worked well for many fashion companies. All of these decisions have a direct effect on the supply chain because the amount of money that is budgeted will determine where and how the company produces products to satisfy customer needs.

# INTERRELATIONSHIPS AND COMMUNICATION

How companies are structured and organized is important. An equally important aspect is how the organization functions and operates: the processes. These processes involve the interrelationships that exist within one organization or between multiple organizations in the supply chain.

## Departments within a Fashion Company

The various departments portrayed in Figure 4.2 depict a large publicly traded fashion company. What are the functions of each department, and how do they interact with the overall supply chain? The previous example discussed top-down budgeting and how the shareholders, board of directors, and the CEO/president work together, but the real work surrounding the supply chain happens in the individual departments.

### Finance and Accounting

The **finance and accounting department** works in conjunction with the CEO/president to develop the top-down budget. The responsibility of the finance and accounting department is then to communicate with each individual department the amount of money it will be allocated to achieve the overall company goals and projections. Budget meetings would be set up, reports created and monitored during the year, and revised as needed. The accounting function pays the bills while sharing monthly updates with finance to ensure that departments remain on track. The Institute of Chartered Accountants in England and Wales (ICAEW) (2011) identified five key functions carried out by the finance department:

1. **Accounting:** to record the financial consequences of organizational activities
2. **Compliance:** to meet the requirements of government and other regulatory bodies
3. **Management and control:** to produce and use financial and related information to inform, monitor and instigate operational actions to meet organizational objectives
4. **Strategy and risk:** to inform and influence from a financial perspective the development and implementation of strategy, and to manage risk
5. **Funding:** to inform and engage with investors and funders, both current and potential, to obtain and maintain the necessary financial resources for the organization. (3)

The finance department plays an important role especially in mid- to large-size fashion businesses because it determines whether there is success and failure, with funding being one of the most critical functions. Without

proper funding the company and hence the supply chain would cease to exist. Funding a fashion company means developing relationships with banks and other lenders to ensure a solid cashflow on which to run the business. Although not unique in this aspect, the fashion company must have enough cash on hand or, as will be discussed in Chapter 10, work with factors to secure funding in order to produce the orders necessary for the business. Given the nature of lead times to produce the goods and the terms with which the retailers operate, this can be a lengthy process.

For example, suppose fashion company X receives an order for 10,000 shirts, which it sells to retailer Y at $10.00 each at a 50 percent markup. The order is worth $100,000 to company X, and it needs to spend $50,000 to finance the order. The retailer needs delivery by June 1, and company X receives the order on March 15. Company X now has to produce and finance that order approximately 75 days prior to shipment, and the retailer's terms are net 60 days from receipt of goods. This means that company X will have to put out the $50,000 a full 135 days prior to being paid. If one magnifies that by hundreds of orders for a mid- to large-size fashion company, one can see how important the finance function can be and how it is related to the rest of the organization.

## Sales and Marketing

Without a **sales and marketing department** a company would find itself with no orders to produce. Martin

---

### Notes from the Field

The cost of doing business as viewed in this chapter can take many different forms, all of which have an effect on the bottom line. When selling, there is information that can provide an advantage in the negotiating process, and those who ask the right questions can save their company money and therefore provide a better value to the consumer. While working in the industry, one of the questions often asked by knowledgeable buyers when making a sales call was "do you carry your own paper or are you factored?" If factored, the buyers will know that you have to pay

an additional fee to secure funding (see Chapter 10), and this will provide them with additional leverage to negotiate the price of the goods, as they do not see the need to help you finance an order that they are buying from you. On the other hand, if you respond that you do carry your own paper, you are signaling that your company is financially sound (not that those that are factored are not, but carrying your own paper adds a measure of security), has funding in place to conduct ongoing business, and does not need the services of a factor.

(2015) stated, "Marketing is the most important part of any business activity. It is what creates customers and generates income, guides the future course of a business and defines whether it will be a success or a failure" (para 1). Martin (2015) continues by stating:

> The Marketing Department is the key to good marketing and sales. It promotes and establishes a business in its niche, based on the products or services the business is offering. It identifies the areas in which the product fits and where the business should focus its marketing strategy and, therefore, spend its budget for the maximum coverage and results. The marketing department helps a business to do the following:
>
> > Build relationship with the audience: Creates awareness of the business and its products as well as provide inputs that create interest for the audience. It brings in new customers and creates new business opportunities for the enterprise.
> >
> > Involve the customer: It engages existing customers, tries to understand them and hear what they have to say. It monitors the competition, creates new ideas, identifies outlets, plans the strategy to involve customers and retain them.
> >
> > Generate income: Finally, the aim of the marketing department is to generate revenue. All its activities are aimed at broadening the customer base and finding opportunities that would create more revenue for the enterprise. (para 3)

Traditionally, management would produce a product and the sales department was expected to sell it, regardless of what it was. Today that has changed, and all fashion companies use a marketing strategy that includes market analytics, research, social media content, product development, advertising, and promotion, all focused on a consumer-centric outlook. Marketing and sales communicate the wants and needs of the consumer and translate those wants and needs into orders, thus having a direct effect on the supply chain.

## Design

The **design department** relies on information that is developed by the sales and marketing teams. It develops its own ideas and concepts through functional areas such as trend forecasting and product development. Trend forecasters predict the colors, fabrics, textures, materials, prints, graphics, beauty/grooming, accessories, footwear, street style, and other styles that will be presented on the runway and in the stores for the upcoming seasons (see Figure 4.5).

**Product developers** work to ensure the profitability and quality of the fashion items they are responsible for producing. They oversee the decisions for the day-to-day operations while interacting with the design team to ensure that the integrity of the design vision is maintained. They may also be responsible for the technical requirements and deciding what materials will be used. The product developing function varies from company to company.

Unlike product developers, fashion designers are responsible for creating original clothing, accessories, and footwear. They may sketch designs or use computer-aided design (CAD) methods to record their creations. In addition, they select fabrics and patterns and give instructions on how to send the products they designed to the various departments responsible for

**Figure 4.5**
**Design development** These two industry professionals are working to solve a design issue prior to creating a finished sample. The design process goes through many different phases and can include draping on a form, as illustrated in the photo. Others designers may opt to develop their patterns and concepts using computer-aided design tools.

executing their visions. Although not generally stated in designers' job descriptions, research has become a major part of what they do. In order to understand what the consumer wants and needs, the designer must always be on the lookout for new ideas and inspiration. To accomplish this, the designers (in a mid to large fashion company) would have working with them a team that might include trend forecasters and product developers. These groups, with the support of marketing and sales, would help the designer understand what is happening from a political, social, and economic standpoint, which in turn will help the designer create what the consumer wants and needs at any particular time in the season.

**Trend forecasting** companies exist in the fashion industry to serve the design community by helping them supplement their creative ideas (see Figure 4.6). Companies such as the Doneger Group, WGSN, Edelkoort Inc., and Fashion Snoops are just a few of the companies that serve the fashion industry. Sherman (2014) carried out an interview with Newbold, the managing director of WGSN trends, who stated, "We're a real, trusted resource for validation, ... Things are moving so fast. We give you the tools to know that what you're making is going to be commercially viable" (para 4). Sherman (2014) continued by interviewing Kevin Silk, the WGSN chief commercial officer, who stated, "Color libraries, CADs, those are just gravy." He added, "What we do is distill this massive amount of information through our experts down to usable, actionable insights" (para 8).

Product developing teams also create product and will sometimes be a standalone department or report to a design group. The product developers might hold

**Figure 4.6**

**Example of a trend board** A key tool that is used by trend forecasting companies is the trend board, sometimes referred to as the mood board because it sets the theme for upcoming seasons. Even today, with all the technology that is used in the fashion industry, this is one aspect that trend forecasters still cling to. It might be created in 3D via a CAD program, but it is still a vital tool for helping clients decide on what to buy.

design degrees or come with years of merchandising experience in the fashion industry. Although not technically designers (although some might argue this point), they rely on working with existing products in the fashion world and reinterpreting them to meet a specific target market. Design teams and product developers have a direct impact on the fashion supply chain because it is their ideas that are put into action to create tech pacs and develop sourcing strategies. (A tech pac [or pack] is an informative sheet that designers create to communicate with a manufacturer all the necessary components needed to construct a product.) One small change after

## Notes from the Field

A key to success in the design of fashion products is finding inspiration, and design inspiration can come from anywhere at any time. As illustrated in this chapter, the design process can be simple or complicated; with a designer you never know when the opportunity for inspiration will come. I was walking the streets in NYC one day with a friend who happens to be a designer for a major brand, and we were discussing

the upcoming season and the color trends that we were seeing (I from a marketing and sales perspective and she from a design standpoint). My friend was having difficulty coming up with a green color to represent her ideas, and suddenly she looked down and found a green wrapper to a chewing gum, picked it up, and declared, "I found my new green!" Design inspiration can come from anywhere at any time!

the order has been taken and sent to the factory for production can have significant effects on the efficiency of that supply chain, which can affect the cost of the finished goods and shipping costs, as well as taking a toll on human capital.

For example, a retail buyer places an order based on a set of designs. These designs are communicated to the factory via a tech pac with all product specifications included. One month later the buyer decides to change the buttons and makes it known that there will be no extension on the delivery date. This is a real-life scenario that sometimes happens. How is the supply chain affected? There may be several ways to deal with this issue. First, the fashion company may say no, which could negatively affect the relationship between the buyer and the fashion company. The fashion company may say yes, which could increase the cost of goods to the buyer but have a far greater effect on the supply chain by disrupting the flow of the order. For example, in this case the originally purchased buttons would need to be returned, or they could be used in another order. There would in all probability be an extended wait period for delivery of the new buttons. But the buyer has already stated that there will be no extension on the delivery date. Therefore, there may need to be negotiation in terms of work overtime to make the ship date, which will take a toll on human capital. Thus one seemingly small change can totally disrupt the entire supply chain.

## Sourcing and Production

The **sourcing and production department** is composed of several subsets: logistics, quality assurance, CSR/sustainability, and legal/security—all key departments that interact with the supply chain at such high levels that each one of these warrants its own chapter. Communication between all departments is paramount. Once an order is taken by a company and the sourcing and production department has decided to place it in a specific factory, logistics must get involved to ensure that the goods can be shipped in a timely manner to meet the customer needs (see Figure 4.7).

Will we have to fly the goods, or will they be shipped via sea on a large container ship? The answer to these questions depends on the size of the order and the ability of the factory to meet the production schedule. Communicating the requirements from sourcing

**Figure 4.7**
**Logistics** Logistics is a key element in the fashion supply chain, as the cost of shipping finished goods can vary greatly depending on the mode selected. Logistics can cover the shipping of fashion goods by sea, air, or truck. The choice is often determined by the clients' need for speed to market and the cost associated with each method.

and production becomes critical because the difference in cost between sea and air is very substantial, with air being more expensive and limited in space. Sea is much more common and cost effective. If the order was taken by the marketing and sales team with air freight in mind and costed using sea, there would be a large discrepancy in the final cost of the goods, creating an issue.

Quality assurance plays a major role in providing confidence in the finished product. The question that needs to be addressed is, who will carry out the inspection of goods in the factory, prior to release of the shipment from the producer, and upon receipt at the warehouse? The answer to each question will have a cost consideration and can also affect the timing of delivery. Middle to large fashion companies can produce product in hundreds of factories around the globe, and having individuals from the home company present in each factory is not feasible, so inspection companies or agents are often used. A key point to remember is that every time someone touches the product, it costs money.

## Corporate Social Responsibility (CSR)
CSR/sustainability departments now play a major role in the fashion supply chain. In their original iteration,

many of the large companies housed the CSR departments in their legal office because they were just looking at the concept from a legal standpoint. Today there is still a legal and public relations relationship, with many if not all of the CSR roles being assumed by varying members of the sourcing and production functions. In the past there was the potential for a conflict of interest to exist between sourcing and CSR because the sourcing department had the responsibility to place orders in factories that could deliver the product at the price they needed within a specific time frame. It was not always the case that these factories were fully vetted from a CSR perspective, and in some cases they were considered in violation of human rights. Thankfully, times have changed, and public opinion and consumer demands have impacted the entire CSR discussion in a positive way. There are still bad actors in the industry that place business in factories that are not fully CSR-compliant, but their numbers are declining. Having CSR as part of sourcing has changed the reporting dynamic and allowed the departments to function more cohesively.

Some companies feel that legal departments can be instrumental in furthering the role of CSR in the fashion industry. In a presentation titled "How Your Legal Team Can Be Instrumental in Advancing Corporate Social Responsibility," Fernando Garcia (2016) stated:

> Practically speaking, just meeting legal statutory requirements is the role of compliance; CSR means going above and beyond that, to recognize the obligations a company has to its shareholders and broader stakeholders (employees, society, environment, etc.). To understand why CSR is so important to today's in-house legal departments, we can contrast the role of various departments, such as sales versus the in-house legal department. Whereas sales targets range from month to month or quarter to quarter, the legal department is the gatekeeper ensuring that the quest for short-term gain does not create risk or compromise long-term sustainability. The role of legal is best described by the definition of sustainable development, which is meeting the needs of today, without compromising the needs of tomorrow. (para 3)

As evidenced by this point of view and the larger discussion in Chapter 3, CSR continues to be addressed in several different departments, with the key focus on having a CSR department housed within the sourcing department.

## Wholesale

The **wholesale department** in a fashion company would have responsibility to sell to other retailers and even its own outlet stores if applicable. It affects the supply chain through the sourcing and production department by placing orders for merchandise that has already been approved in the fashion line or by potentially working with buyers to develop new product. If the latter, the wholesale department would also be communicating with the product development team and in some cases the design department. The precise setup of the wholesale department will vary, but one of its key functions will focus on sales.

## Business Development

The **business development department** has a significant impact on a supply chain and in some instances is influential in directing a company to redefine itself and restart itself from ground up. For example, an existing fashion company that focuses on one aspect of the fashion industry might create a brand extension by adding a men's to a women's line of product or going into the accessories business if the main focus is apparel. With the addition of a new business that is unfamiliar to an existing structure, there is a need to redefine or create a new supply chain. Communication of potential plans either prior to or during discussions of new business developments is critical for a successful transition.

## Information Technology

Information technology (IT), which is often overlooked in the supply chain or sometimes taken for granted, has the ability to transform how companies do business. In a recent article by Tara Donaldson (2016) in the *Sourcing Journal* titled "For Supply Chains, It's Digitize or Die," Donaldson spoke with leading executives from Li & Fung, a global fashion sourcing powerhouse, about the changes in technology that are currently impacting supply chains around the world. The executives from Li & Fung took the view that in order to remain competitive one must incorporate a digital strategy in the supply chain or perish.

The driving force, as with much of the fashion industry, is the consumer. Consumers refuse to waste time and energy on things that are neither innovative nor efficient. In the same article Donaldson (2016) interviewed Sinclair, the COO of Li & Fung's sourcing business, who believed that the way forward is a balanced process. The question asked by Donaldson of Sinclair was, *are we as efficient, are we as streamlined and lean as we could be*? Sinclair responded:

> The answer to that question is no, [we're] not ... The solution is collaboration between manufacturers of textiles, bags, shoes, in conjunction with the brand owners and retailers. Align productivity through the supply chain. It's not looking at one as a standalone, you have to look at the supply chain holistically. Duplication, triplication, cut that out. And a digital supply chain will address that. (para 10)

Manufacturing is very labor-intensive, both at the factory level and administratively in the office. Tracking and tracing products takes up the majority of one's time. IT departments have the ability to reduce the amount of time and energy spent on functions better suited to new technologies. Sinclair (Donaldson 2016) noted, "If you were to digitize the manufacturing process so that RFID [radio frequency identification] picks up the movement of all of the things just described, that sends it to pre-formed reports in the cloud, it's being tracked and traced automatically" (para 23). In addition, IT functions as one of the main communicators within any organization through intranets, extranets, emails, phones, and so on. Without a strong commitment to an IT department, the supply chain would come to a screeching halt. See Figure 4.8.

## Human Resources (HR)

One of the last departments that is referenced here is the **human resource department (HR)**, and like the other departments, HR plays a critical role in fashioning the supply chain by making sure that the right people are in the right positions at the right time and for the right cost. For a large multinational fashion company, that can be a daunting challenge because at any moment in time there may be thousands of employees in dozens of countries. Not only is having the right people in place important, but providing a framework for communication can also be challenging, particularly if there are several languages

**Figure 4.8**
**Diagram of an information technology department**
The ability of information technology to communicate with the various stakeholders involved in the supply chain is critical to profitability. Depicted here are various elements that make up an IT department and the recent addition of the "cloud" to the mix. Today's fashion industry supply chain is technology dependent, and with advances in technology occurring practically on a daily basis, IT departments must stay on top of new and exciting technologies that will help companies stay competitive.

spoken across multiple countries, not to mention time zones. In "Ten Steps to a Global Human Resources Strategy," Quelch and Bloom (1999) state:

> The scarcity of qualified managers has become a major constraint on the speed with which multinational companies can expand their international sales. The growth of the knowledge-based society, along with the pressures of opening up emerging markets, has led cutting-edge global companies to recognize now more than ever that human resources and intellectual capital are as significant as financial assets in building sustainable competitive advantage. (para 1)

Companies are only as good as the people they employ; therefore, spending time and resources to develop and sustain an effective workforce will only serve to strengthen all companies across the supply chain.

## Investor Relations

The last department listed in Figure 4.2 is the **investor relations department.** This department would only pertain to those fashion companies that are publicly traded and have a responsibility to provide information and services to shareholders. The National Investor Relations Institute (NIRI) (2003) defines investor relations (IR) as "a strategic management responsibility that integrates finance, communication, marketing and securities law compliance to enable the most effective two-way communication between a company, the financial community, and other constituencies, which ultimately contributes to a company's securities achieving fair valuation" (para 2).

The IR department also works in conjunction with the **public relations (PR) department** to help shape public opinion of the company. It does this by providing positive news stories on the company's CSR practices as well as general news that consumers are interested in. In addition, if and when there is a negative story surrounding the company, the PR department will respond to the situation to maintain the company's profile. It is here that the IR and the PR departments have the potential to interact with the supply chain. All too often there has been negative news surrounding a fashion company and its sourcing practices, and it has been the role of the PR department and to a lesser extent the IR department to address these issues. However, the role of PR in sharing news can be misleading and at times questioned as to

motive and accuracy. As often stated in this book, practicing sound CSR polices is doing the right thing when no one is looking, and if this adage is followed, then shouting what you are doing through your PR department could be called into question; conversely, if the PR department's function is to dispute or obfuscate negative information that arises surrounding the supply chain, then something is wrong with the overall process.

## Communication among Departments

The organizational charts previously offered clarify the structure of the organization and also offer an introduction to the processes of an organization, such as communication. In any organization there needs to be a natural flow of information and material from one department to another (bidirectionally). Although each department may be considered a standalone department, it is reliant on the next with one critical goal in mind: ensuring that the departments function as they should via communication. In other words, there needs to be open, transparent communication throughout the varying levels of the organization depicted in the organizational chart (Hassell 2016).

Successful fashion companies perfect the art of communication by making communication a part of the culture of the organization. They break down the silos that are common to any company, whether they be top-down or lateral. Hassell (2016) identified several key concepts to facilitate this culture of communication: building open and transparent communication via trust, respect, and honesty, all of which will be facilitated by collaborative efforts (para 8). This is not as easy as it sounds. Consider, for example, the complexity of the supply chain and the complexity of the departments within an organization. The routes of communication are extremely complex and leave room for errors due to miscommunication or even lack of communication.

Often lack of communication or miscommunication can alter the efficient working of a fashion company and by extension disrupt the supply chain flow. Office politics is sometimes unavoidable and can be mitigated by clear, transparent leadership from the top down (Kosicek, Soni, Sandbothe, and Slack 2012). For example, just as there is a formal line of communication as depicted in the organizational chart, there may also be an informal line of communication perpetrated by groups of people who may be interacting with one another in an informal way not depicted on a formal organizational chart. These groups can exist within the formal structure or in a social setting where individuals meet for coffee or at lunch or for drinks after work. A common term used to describe these informal groups and the resulting informal communication is the "grapevine":

> The grapevine is an informal communication network that can run through an entire organization. Grapevines are found in all organizations except the very smallest, but they do not always follow the same patterns as formal channels of authority and communication, nor do they necessarily coincide with them. Because the grapevine typically passes information orally, such information often becomes distorted in the process. (Ebert 2006: 193)

Unfortunately, informal communication may be working from erroneous information and thus lead to decision-making that may lead to negative outcomes. Leadership and a culture of communication are two ways to prevent this type of miscommunication. Establishing internal communications where employees feel that they are partners in the working of the organization and key participants in quality initiatives may prevent negative "offroading" (Ash 1992).

The grapevine is typically word of mouth; however, with the advent of electronic communications the old grapevine has adopted a new venue for informal communication and miscommunication. Today's electronic communication, email, twitter, Facebook, and so on are changing the way companies and individual employees interact. Like society in general, the faceless communication and ability to hide behind written words can and does lead to communication issues within organizations. Morgenstern (2016) addressed issues with messaging and productivity issues: "Why is e-mail so bad? It's like an overstuffed toy box full of miscellaneous stuff—missives from your boss, requests from clients, FYIs, news feeds, social-media alerts, junk. We spend more time sifting through it all than getting anything done" (15).

While informal groups and communication may lead to issues in the organization, it may be possible to enlist these informal workings in a synergistic way. At times organizations even encourage informal groups to exist because experienced managers recognize that they cannot be avoided and can also be used to reinforce the more formal side of the organization. As Ebert (2006) notes, "Some firms support a process called **intrapreneuring**: creating and maintaining the innovation flexibility of a small-business environment within the confines of a large, bureaucratic structure" (193).

## CONCLUSION

In order to have a viable company, one must determine what the structure of that organization will be. A formal organizational chart must be drawn up and lines of communication established. Although formal lines of communication will exist, a company must also work with informal lines because they will be a part of any organization. There are many departments that make up a large multinational fashion company, and each has a prominent position in ensuring that the company remains profitable. Top-down budgeting is one way to maintain control over the budgeting process in a large organization. As with any industry, there are small companies (sometimes startups) that are composed of only a few people, each taking on multiple roles to ensure success. Whether you are a large company or a small one, communication between departments is necessary to be successful, and it all starts and ends with having the right people in the right place at the right cost.

# INDUSTRY INTERVIEW: AMY HALL, EILEEN FISHER

In this chapter we discussed how various departments within a fashion company interrelate and how they act to support the fashion industry supply chain. Key to the success of the various departments that we have discussed are the very people who staff those departments. Poor leadership can have a devastating impact on the organization, and it is the successful companies that find the right mix of people to carry out the required tasks. I had the opportunity to discuss this topic with Ms. Amy Hall from EILEEN FISHER, a leading women's wear company headquartered in Irvington, New York, that has a simple but weighty mission statement: "Our mission embraces simplicity, sustainability, and great design."

Ms. Hall is the director of social consciousness and has been with Eileen Fisher for over twenty-two years. Amy explains that she has had the good fortune to lead the social consciousness commitment (human rights, environmental sustainability, and support of women, girls, and the community) at this incredible company. In addition, Amy serves on the company's Leadership Forum and coleads the People and Culture area along with her visionary colleagues. Through her work she influences teams and individuals to integrate values, of which social consciousness is one, into their everyday practices. This is patient and persistent work, where small steps can lead to big leaps. It is also highly collaborative, both internally and externally, engaging company leaders, suppliers, peers at like-minded brands, advocacy organizations, policymakers, customers, and the media.

**Interviewer:** *In your role your focus is social consciousness; how does Eileen Fisher approach this as it relates to the various departments within the organization?*

**A. H.:** My role has and continues to be one of a facilitator where I integrate social values surrounding the environment and human rights into our everyday business practices. I believe that I inspire our teams and individuals by leading the company in our Social Consciousness challenges. This has been accomplished in more of an evolutionary fashion over a long period of time. It has been about breaking down barriers within and across departments so that there is no tension, no we/they syndrome, sort of a business philosophy where we view ourselves as one entity. In addition, we have engaged the services of outside consultants to help build a CSR system around product, creating more collaborative thinking. It is more of a nudge factor, more give and take.

**Interviewer:** *In your keynote talk at the International Textile and Apparel Association Conference in October 2015, you spoke about mapping and how it created an Ah ha moment for you and the company; can you tell me about that experience?*

**A. H.:** The idea was to come together to discuss how we as a company could reduce our carbon footprint. We enlisted the help of a consultant to undertake a process called "system mapping." We brought together twenty-two individuals from across the "system of the product." We quickly realized that the process itself would be never-ending and would not provide one single answer but rather a path for the future. It forced us to look at our business in a new and different way, and we realized that if we were serious about this effort, we had to make tough decisions about how we thought about the company as well as our consumers. We needed to look at the entire design process from fiber choice to fabric, manufacturing, logistics, and fulfillment. We realized how a simple change in a product design could have drastic effects on the supply chain and how those changes had the potential to impact the very workers that we are concerned about. We had to look at the corporate culture and make decisions surrounding reorders: was it the right thing to do? If we said yes, what impact did that decision have throughout the supply chain? By forcing our supply chain to accept a reorder, did it prevent the supplier(s) from carrying out its work in an ethical and/or sustainable manner? In many instances we found the answer to be yes, so we are now exploring how to restructure our internal processes so that we support, rather than prevent, our suppliers to do the right thing.

**Interviewer:** *What challenges do you face in coordinating all the departments to have the same voice when it comes to social consciousness?*

**A. H.:** The major challenge is to make sure that all of our associates have the same brand vision. We are a growing company with 1,200 employees operating in twenty states plus Canada and the UK, with three corporate offices. We are what I would consider decentralized, so yes, it is a challenge. We have strong internal communication systems in place to ensure that all of our associates feel engaged and are part of the culture that Eileen projects. We encourage and welcome personal perspectives to be shared; we want people to feel engaged in the culture. We try to provide a consistent message across the corporation. We use an intranet system to provide video messaging, we set up Q&A sessions, and we provide a team page and have valuable resources within our technology platform. We host monthly talks similar to Ted Talks. It helps that we have a consistent message in our Vision 2020 and how it relates to our company "Manifesto," strategic objectives, and triple-bottom-line strategy. Our vision is for an industry where human resources and sustainability are not the effect of a particular initiative, but the cause of a business well run, where social and environmental injustices are

not unfortunate outcomes, but reasons to do things differently.

**Interviewer:** *Within the organization is there one department that feels more ownership of your social platform?*

**A. H.:** I would like to say that no, there is no one department that feels more ownership, but I would be remiss if I didn't say that I believe that the social consciousness team is a key voice. We are building toward an overall collaborative effort, including all the teams from our artisan partners to our design, sourcing, and store groups, basically everyone that is involved with the product.

**Interviewer:** *What opportunities are there to strengthen the relationship between departments?*

**A. H.:** Consistent messaging around our Vision 2020 strategy as it relates to our broader company objectives. Individuals need to make the commitment; they need to determine that this is the right company for them, that there is fit. It is not just about showing up to work every day; you have to believe in what we are doing and that we can make a difference. On an executive level we meet on a regular basis (one hour per week) to share and discuss key topics. In addition we hold full-day retreats once per month to have more in-depth discussions on strategy. We like to use those opportunities to close the loop on issues and look for ways to continuously improve.

**Interviewer:** *If you think about the consumer, are there one or two departments that have the strongest connection to the consumer? Or are all equally important?*

**A. H.:** I would have to say that the retail and ecommerce departments would be the closest to the consumer, more so the retail associates, as our ecommerce platform accounts for about 5 percent of our total business. Our sales team and marketing team would also be key contributors, but by far the retail team, who interact with our consumers on a day-to-day basis, are our first contact. For that reason it is even more important for them to embrace the ethos of the company. To that end we do have a strong training program and are very selective on whom we employ at that level.

**Interviewer:** *Closing comments? What is the vision for the company as it relates to interdepartmental coordination?*

**A. H.:** Through consistent messaging, our efforts around mapping and dedication to Vision 2020, the coordination between departments will evolve naturally and we will achieve our business core values.

**Questions Pertaining to Interview**

1. What are some positive outcomes in an environment where social values are present and respected?
2. What is Eileen Fisher doing well? What could it be doing better?
3. Reflect upon the interview. Did you experience an Ah ha moment with regard to your own social values? If yes, what was the Ah ha moment, and what changes do you see you need to make within your own life and/or educational endeavor? How will this alter your views on your own future professional endeavors?

## CASE STUDY: MPJL

In this case study we have created a fictitious company that operates on the large side of the fashion industry but still struggles with the same issues presented in the chapter. Normally discussions surrounding people are reserved for texts on human resources or psychology, but to fully understand and appreciate the fashion industry supply chain, a discussion of people must occur. MPJL is a major fashion company operating on a global scale and is responsible for developing fashion products for major retailers and wholesalers. The company is organized to include design, product development, sourcing/manufacturing, and logistics. These functions are housed in one location in the corporate headquarters located in New York City.

MPJL prides itself on managing its supply chain in a socially responsible business environment. One of the cornerstones of the business philosophy is delivering quality products with the highest standards while addressing every aspect of the supply chain. The key to its success is meeting customer needs by providing fashion products at competitive prices,

at the right time, in the right quantity, with excellent quality that the consumers demand.

In order to better serve its customers, MPJL uses its extensive network of resources to position itself as the leader in the fashion sourcing and manufacturing business. MPJL has developed cutting-edge technology, distribution channels, and supplier networks to solve the production needs of an ever-changing global fashion industry. MPJL also utilizes the services of agents and certifying bodies to ensure that its strict Codes of Conduct are continuously met.

Key to its success is the thousands of people it employs around the world. From design in the New York offices to production in all parts of the world, it is the people and the ability to communicate effectively that has provided MPJL with financial stability in the past and hopefully for the foreseeable future.

MPJL operates with over 12,000 suppliers in over thirty countries, in addition to its own offices around the world. Communication is one of the keys to success. Given the size and complexity of a global fashion company, it would be easy to have a communication mishap. Operating in thirty countries, the language and cultural differences alone could cause major breakdowns in communication. The chapter has provided some insights into how one could mitigate communication breakdowns, but by no means is this an exhaustive listing. Use the chapter as well as your own research and critical thinking skills to answer the following questions.

**Case Study Questions**

1. Create a communication plan that will keep everyone informed and will provide strong customer value.

2. In addition to communicating internally, what methods would you recommend to communicate with external stakeholders, and how often?

3. Are there specific technology packages that you can recommend through your research that can be employed to foster effective communication with the design department in NYC and the many factories MPJL works with around the globe?

## CHAPTER REVIEW QUESTIONS

1. What do you see as the major stumbling blocks in communicating within a fashion organization?
2. What role should technology play in communicating within a single office? Globally?
3. How does technology facilitate communication?
4. In what way(s) is technology a barrier to communication?

5. In your opinion, what department is the most important in a large-sized fashion company? Why?
6. Is top-down budgeting the best method for setting a budget for a mid- to large-size fashion company? Explain.

## CLASS EXERCISES

1. Scan the web and identify fashion companies of interest. Once a fashion company of interest is found, search its website for its organizational chart. Discuss the similarities and differences between the fashion companies found. What do you suppose the reasons are for these similarities and differences?

2. Reflect upon one of your past work experiences. Does one employment experience rank as "the best" work experience? If yes, tell a story about what made it a "best" experience. What was it about the company that made it a best experience? Were there social values in place that made it "the best"? Describe what those were.

## KEYTERMS

organizational chart
informal organization
functional organizational chart
product organizational chart
regional organizational chart
shareholders
board of directors
CEO/president

finance and accounting
   department
sales and marketing department
design department
product developers
trend forecasting
sourcing and production
   department

wholesale department
business development
   department
human resource department
investor relations department
public relations (PR) department
intrapreneuring

## REFERENCES

1. Ash, R. W. (1992), "The ABCs of Developing TQM," *Security Management*. Available online: https://www.questia.com/magazine/1G1-13574332/the-abcs-of-developing-tqm.
2. Donaldson, T. (2016), "Li & Fung: For Supply Chains, It's Digitize or Die," *Sourcing Journal*. Available online: https://sourcingjournalonline.com/li-fung-supply-chains-digitize-die-td/.
3. Ebert, R. J. (2006), *Business Essentials* (6th ed.), Upper Saddle River, NJ: Prentice Hall.
4. Garcia, F. (2016), "The View from Canada: The In-House Role in Corporate Social Responsibility." Available online: http://legalexecutiveinstitute.com/role-corporate-social-responsibility/.
5. Hassell, D. (2016), "Open Communication: Vital to Business Success," American Management Association. Available online: http://www.amanet.org/training/articles/Open-Communication-Vital-to-Business-Success.aspx.
6. ICAEW (2011), *The Finance Function: A Framework for Analysis*. Available online: https://charteredaccountantsworldwide.com/wp-content/uploads/2016/09/Developing-effective-finance-functions-for-the-unique-contexts-within-which-they-operate.pdf.
7. Kosicek, P. M., R. Soni, R. Sandbothe, and F. Slack (2012), "Leadership Styles, Industry Fit, and Quality Focus," *Competition Forum*, 10 (2): 49–54.
8. Martin (2015), *Marketing Department: Organization, Tools & Responsibilities*. Available online: https://www.cleverism.com/marketing-department-organization-tools-responsibilities/.
9. Morgenstern, J. (2016), "E-mail's Not the Issue," *MIT Technology Review*, 19 (2): 14–15.
10. National Investor Relations Institute (2003), "Definition of Investor Relations." Available online: https://www.niri.org/functionalmenu/about.aspx.
11. Quelch, H. J. A., and H. Bloom (1999), "Ten Steps to a Global Human Resources Strategy," Strategy+Business. Available online: http://www.strategy-business.com/article/9967?gko=db7b9.
12. Sherman, L. (2014), "Trend Forecasting: What Is It Good For?" Fashionista. Available online: http://fashionista.com/2014/08/trend-forecasting.
13. Stone, E. (2015), *The Dynamics of Fashion*, New York: Bloomsbury.
14. Sun, L. (2016), "Which Organizational Structure Is Right for Your Business?" *Business Dictionary*. Available online: http://www.businessdictionary.com/article/557/which-organizational-structure-is-right-for-your-business/.

# Raw Materials

## LEARNING OBJECTIVES

Upon completion of this chapter you will be able to:

- Establish the Industrial Revolution as a context for understanding the roots of the fashion industry in the United States.

- Describe the differences between natural and synthetic fibers.

- Conceptualize how fabrics are made.

- Explain how tariffs can affect raw material choices.

- Outline the design process.

- Consider the importance of the World Trade Organization (WTO) as it relates to raw materials.

- Explore how textile and yarn technology interact with the fashion industry.

# THE INDUSTRIAL REVOLUTION

From the 1790s through the 1830s, the United States transitioned from an agrarian economy to an industrial economy. The 1790s proved to be the pivotal time, as this was when Samuel Slater opened the first industrial mill in Pawtucket, Rhode Island. Slater immigrated to the United States from Great Britain under the ruse of being a farmer. What was the reason for this deception? It was prohibited by the British government to leave the country if you had been working in the textile sector because the British did not want to lose the financial edge they had created within their own Industrial Revolution. Slater had worked in a spinning mill and memorized the workings of the equipment. He used that knowledge to set up shop here in the United States and is credited by many as being the father of the American Industrial Revolution because he developed machinery based on the technology from the British model (Figure 5.1). These innovations in the United States greatly increased the speed and efficiency with which cotton thread could be spun into yarn (Londrigan 2009).

To delve into the Industrial Revolution in depth is beyond the scope of this text. A brief introduction is warranted, however, because it is one of the triggers that spurred growth and expansion and resulted in a greater ability to produce apparel in larger quantities (Londrigan 2009). For example, during this time natural fibers such as cotton and wool were the fibers of choice in the United States, although it was only a matter of time before synthetic fibers were introduced, also known as man-made or manufactured fibers. In a very basic sense, the cultivation of natural fibers and the production of man-made fibers could also be considered the start of the fashion industry textile supply chain and by extension the overall fashion industry supply chain. This chapter focuses on the apparel and textile side of the fashion industry supply chain and also on raw materials: natural and synthetic fibers.

# INTRODUCTION TO RAW MATERIALS

Synthetic fibers or natural fibers, faux fur or real fur, polyvinyl chloride (PVC) or leather—which raw material is the right one? In the fashion industry supply chain

**Figure 5.1**
**Worker during the Industrial Revolution** A worker tends to a yarn-winding machine in a turn-of-the-century weaving mill in the United States.

the choices of **raw materials** are endless, with today's consumer driving much of the decisions in terms of which raw materials to use. Raw materials are the basis of the apparel and home goods fashion industry supply chain, so one has to ask, what raw materials should one choose to be successful? To answer that question, one has to ask what type of business one is going to be in and what customers one is going to serve. The key to being successful in the fashion business is to properly identify one's target market. Is there a problem or opportunity in the market that needs to be addressed? Who will be my customer? Many new businesses will tell you that they want to sell to everyone, but that is not possible. A clear definition of your target market will allow you to focus your marketing efforts on those who will most likely buy your product, allowing you to create the most efficient use of your resources. This decision will also help to inform what raw materials you decide to use. We cannot lose sight of the fact that the cost of raw materials is a dominant factor in determining which to use based on the target market. The price of a real fur intended for the luxury market will be vastly different than the cost of a faux fur positioned at the middle consumer market. The same can be said for fiber choice: synthetic or natural? Who is the end user?

In today's market the consumer is a very powerful end user who drives many of the fiber choices. This was not always the case. Historically (1900s–1960s), it was the manufacturers who made the decisions on which raw materials to use based on the type of equipment at their disposal. The country had not yet entered the stage known as a marketing-based economy. Rather, it was a manufacturing-based economy, with the manufacturers producing what was in their best interest, not necessarily the consumers' (Austin 1989). Similar to the overall fashion industry supply chain, there is also a textile supply chain. The origin or the starting point of the textile supply chain is the fiber, which is then spun into yarn, which is then made into fabric (fibre2fashion n.d.). For the purpose of this chapter, fiber will be classified into synthetic and natural.

## Synthetic Fibers

Generally speaking, **synthetic fibers** are thought to be durable and easy to work with. They are made in a filament form—a long continuous strand—so that they run better on the equipment. Ease of production is a primary reason why spinners and mills preferred synthetic fibers. The innovation of synthetic fibers in the 1950s ushered in the easy care revolution, with DuPont's Dacron (tradename in the United States) and Terylene (tradename in the United Kingdom) leading the way (see Figure 5.2). Synthetic fibers gained a strong foothold in the fashion industry, creating new and exciting products for the consumer, while the chemical companies spent large sums of money to promote and market the fibers to the fashion industry (Alfred 2009).

Synthetic fibers are not only created from chemicals but can also have origins in natural materials such as wood pulp. Regardless of their origin, they all undergo a chemical process to transform them into a yarn. Most synthetic fibers are created by forcing a chemical compound, a chain of synthesized molecules, through what is called a spinneret. The chemical compound forms a continuous filament, which is the basis for a synthetic yarn (IEEE GlobalSpec 2016). The spinneret is similar to a shower head, with many small holes through which the chemical compound passes; when the chemicals hit the air after passing through the spinneret, they harden to form the yarn. With the advances in technology these

**Figure 5.2**
**Man in a Dacron suit** This photo depicts a man in a polyester leisure suit. Polyester was one of the synthetic fibers to be accepted by the menswear market and created new opportunities for what was considered fashion-forward garments and colors for the male consumer.

filament yarns have steadily been reduced in thickness. In today's consumer market the term that is most associated with a fine synthetic yarn, fabric, or garment is *microfiber*. The industry term for the circumference of the yarn is *denier*.

Weight per unit length (linear density) is the measure of a continuous filament or yarn, used traditionally in textile industry. It expresses weight in grams of nine kilometers (9000 meters) length of the material. Therefore lower the denier number, finer the material; and higher the denier number, coarser the material. In most countries other than the US, it has been replaced by the Tex system where one denier equals 1/9th of a tex or 10/9th of decitex. (*Business Dictionary* 2016: para 1)

There are many synthetic fibers, yarns, and fabrics. Some examples of these fibers are listed here with an accompanying description.

- **acetate and triacetate fibers:** This type of fiber is known as a regenerated man-made material. Acetate is developed from cellulose. The cellulose is the result of a chemical process using wood pulp as its base. These fibers are commonly seen in linings and even women's lingerie.
- **acrylic and modacrylic fibers:** These fibers have an uneven surface, and they are formed by additional polymerization of at least 85 percent by weight of acrylonitrile or vinyl chanide. These are used primarily in the manufacturing of sweaters and scarves.
- **aramid and polyimide fibers:** These fibers are created via a wet or dry processing technique and spun from the polymer. Protective gear is the end product produced from these fibers.
- **elastomeric fibers:** These fibers are created by cross-linking natural and synthetic rubbers. The resulting fibers are spandex fibers and anidex fibers. These fibers can stretch and recover fully and rapidly.
- **spandex or elastoester:** This is a manufactured material that is both lightweight and can be stretched over 500 percent without breaking. A substitute for spandex is Elastoester. Both of these are used primarily in sports-related apparel and considered elastomeric fibers (see Figure 5.3).
- **nylon:** Nylon is made of polyamide. The material is resistant to wrinkling, does not absorb water, and dries quickly. Nylon has many uses in the fashion industry in both apparel and accessories, not to mention home furnishings.
- **polyester:** This is an important synthetic fiber. The manufacturing process uses melt-spinning so the size and shape can be adjusted for specific applications. Polyester has multiple uses in the fashion industry, from dresses to shirts and blouses.

**Figure 5.3**
**Spandex** Spandex running tights and athletic tops provide form-fitting apparel perfect for working out in. Elastomeric yarns have greatly increased the potential to create athletic apparel and have helped create demand for what has become known as athleisure wear, which has exploded over the past several years to become a separate category in the fashion industry.

Its application, however, extends far beyond the fashion industry, and it has many industrial uses.

- **polypropylene:** This is a vinyl polymer, similar to polyethylene. The structure has a methyl group attached to every other carbon in the backbone chain. It is excellent for base layers while hiking and camping in cold weather.
- **polyvinyl chloride (PVC):** This leather look-alike is used to simulate leather products in the fashion industry.
- **rayon/lyocell:** This includes textile fibers and filaments composed of regenerated cellulose, excluding acetate. It is produced from naturally occurring polymers. The fiber is sold as artificial silk, and it has a serrated round shape with a smooth surface. It is a hybrid because it starts out as a natural product but then undergoes a harsh chemical process to create a usable yarn for the fashion industry.

## Natural Fibers

**Natural fibers** are hairlike raw materials that are obtained directly from plants, animals, vegetables, and minerals. Natural fibers are different from synthetic fibers. They are short fibers that are twisted together, with the exception of silk, which is the only natural fiber to come in a filament form. As a result, there is a tendency for natural fibers to break during production, causing downtime and lost profits. There are many natural fibers, yarns, and fabrics. Some examples of these fibers are listed here with an accompanying description.

- **cotton:** Cotton is a fiber that is obtained from the cotton plant. It is the preferred fiber because it is durable. Cotton absorbs moisture, is smooth to the touch, and drapes well. One potential negative quality of cotton fabric is that it takes time to dry. It creases easily, requiring regular ironing unless treated with wrinkle-free or wrinkle-resistant chemicals. Even with a fiber such as cotton, you still have additional choices, such as, should it be organic? What about Pima cotton, or Egyptian long-staple cotton? Choosing cotton as a raw material still requires further decisions, with the key being who the target market is. See Figure 5.4.

- **linen:** Linen fabric is one of the oldest fabrics known to modern man. The properties of linen are similar to cotton fabric. It is moisture-absorbent and durable. In addition, it creases easily and also requires ironing. End uses in the United States are summer apparel and home textiles. Linen is a staple in many wardrobes around the globe, especially in arid climates.

- **jute:** Jute has been used in the textile industry for ages. It is obtained from the jute plant. Jute has high tensile strength and can be used in packing materials, and in recent years it has become common in home furnishings such as rugs.

- **silk:** Silk is the only natural fiber that comes in a filament form. The discovery of silk in China dates back centuries. Silk is produced by caterpillars often called silk worms. Silk fiber has a unique sheen. It is very smooth to the touch while exhibiting strong tensile strength.

- **spider silk:** Scientists have also discovered a way of producing silk from spiders. Since this is relatively new, the production costs are quite high, so there is limited production and use in the fashion industry (see Figure 5.5).

- **wool:** Wool is a fiber that has traditionally been used in the textile industry, and it is obtained primarily from sheep. Wool fabric is soft. In addition, it provides warmth and is easily dyed, making it a consumer choice for winter apparel.

- **yak:** The yak, found in the Himalayas in India and Tibet, supplies hair that offers warmth for colder weather.

- **camel hair:** Camel fiber has been traditionally used for the production of winter apparel, most often seen in the development of coats.

- **llama:** Llamas are typically found in South America, although there has been a spread of llama

**Figure 5.4**
**Cotton** Cotton has always been an important aspect of the fashion industry supply chain, especially in the United States. Here cotton plants are growing in an open field under a cloudy sky. This photo could represent any cotton-producing farm in the world, as the basic practices of raising cotton are fairly consistent around the globe.

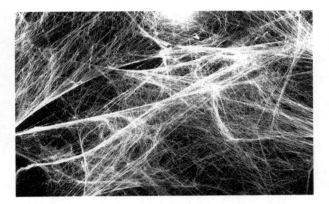

**Figure 5.5**
**Spider silk** Spider silk created from spider webs has only recently been introduced to the world of fashion. It is a difficult medium to work with and therefore is costly, time-consuming, and limited in its applications.

production in the artisan communities throughout North America. Llamas produce a soft fiber used in the production of apparel, and courser hairs/fibers are used in the production of rugs and wall hangings.

- **alpaca:** There has been an interest in the Alpaca, resulting in the development of small farms throughout the United States. Similar to sheep wool, Alpaca fiber is prized for winter wear and has been described as lighter in weight and softer and warmer than sheep's wool. The use of the Alpaca has gained increasing popularity in recent years, possibly because raising Alpacas seems to have a smaller negative impact on the environment as compared to other wool-bearing animals.

- **ramie:** Ramie fiber is obtained from the Ramie plant. It has been used in the textile industry for centuries. The fabric produced is strong, silky, and shiny and does not crease easily. In spite of this, it is not used extensively because it is costly to produce. It is useful in the production of sewing thread, filter clothes, fishing nets, and packaging material. As a fiber ramie is often mixed with cotton to create a ramie cotton blend, thereby mitigating to a degree the cost of production of ramie while adding strength to the cotton.

- **angora:** Angora fiber is obtained in two ways, from the Angora rabbit and the Angora goat. The hair of the Angora rabbit is long and soft. Angora wool is frequently produced from the Angora goat, and this wool is often blended with rabbit.

- **cashmere:** Cashmere fiber is obtained from the hair of the Cashmere goat, found in Kashmir and Himachal Pradesh in India, Pakistan, Nepal, Iran, Mongolia, and China. At the present time, China is the largest producer of Cashmere fiber. It is soft, lightweight, fine, and warm, and the best fibers are harvested from the underbelly of the Cashmere goat. The quality of Cashmere is based on the length of the hair and where on the animal it is harvested from. It is considered a luxury fabric.

- **mohair:** The hair from the Angora goat is called Mohair fiber. It is described as possessing warmth and being lightweight, crease resistant, durable, and soft. Because of these qualities it is used in the production of winter apparel, but also in the production of blankets, rugs, and scarves.

- **soybean:** Recently, experts have developed the concept of obtaining fiber from soybean. It is lustrous and strong and dyes easily. Moreover, it is soft to the touch and lightweight. It is ideal for use in summer wear, underwear, sleepwear, sportswear, children's wear, and home textiles. As with any new fiber, the cost of production is high because the demand is low.

- **bamboo:** Bamboo fiber is a recent innovation in the textile industry. Obtained from the bamboo plant, it possesses several qualities such as smoothness and durability. In some circles it is labeled environment-friendly, although in order to change into a usable fiber it must undergo a very caustic chemical reaction similar to rayon unless it is retted like flax, which is transformed into a yarn through a mechanical process. This fiber can be put in the hybrid category because it starts out as a natural fiber but undergoes a transformation using chemicals similar to synthetic fibers. Bamboo fabric is emerging as a fabric of choice in the textile industry. It is largely used in the production of ready-made apparel and home textiles.

Apart from these natural fibers, experts are trying to develop fabrics from plants such as wheat, rice, and beetroot. One innovative company has developed what can be considered a natural fiber out of spoiled milk, marketed as Qmilch. For additional information, see *www.qmilkfiber.eu*. There are also other synthetic and natural fibers that can be considered when making choices for raw materials. For example, additional synthetic fibers such as polyolefin, polyethylene, vinyon, or vinal may be considered, as well as other natural fibers such as corn, coir, and sisal.

## Findings and Trims

Although not a focus of this text, findings and trims are nonetheless an important aspect of the fashion industry supply chain. Whether you are talking about buttons, zippers, ribbons, beads, thread, sequins, or other materials that fall into this category, they all have a direct effect on the cost and production of the finished goods. Identifying trims is an important function of the overall design process (see Chapter 4). It is often a good practice to work with one's manufacturing partners to identify findings and trims that work well with the other materials that have been chosen in one's designs. There are far too many choices for one person or one department to be an expert in all the various findings and trims that are available. For a button for a men's dress shirt, for example, one could pay $.15 for a plastic button or $3.75 for a mother of pearl button, and with up to seventeen buttons on a men's dress shirt, the cost can easily affect the retail value.

One additional aspect when deciding what findings and trims to use in the final product centers around quality and quality assurance. Knowing the properties of the findings and trims selected is crucial in ensuring that they are fully compatible with all the components of the finished product, and this is where the expertise of the manufacturers who are responsible for making the finished product can be a valuable resource. Sewing thread is considered a finding, and it is not common for a designer or merchandiser to specify a particular thread (unless there is a strong reason to do so, such as to produce contrasting colors), and most manufacturers know what thread to use with what fabrics that will ensure adherence to the performance standards that were established for the finished product.

## Accessories

**Accessories** are fashion items that contribute to the overall look of the wearer (Figure 5.6). For the accessories market the availability of leather and fur dictated the fashions for quite some time, until the introduction of faux fur in the early 1900s and PVC in the 1920s. These innovations provided the fashion industry with new materials to experiment with and for the consumer to choose from. Many times the consumer uses these choices to demonstrate social and political positioning. For example, today's faux products have made great strides and many designers use them, as it has become difficult to tell the difference between real and fake in certain products. In years gone by furs were seen as status symbols; however, this status symbol seems to have gone by the wayside, possibly due to the concerted efforts of animal rights groups and public awareness campaigns. Hines (2015) noted:

> As technology improved, manufacturers were able to create fur effects in silk—resembling leopard, gazelle, and mole—and eventually,

**Figure 5.6**

**A collection of accessories** Fashion accessories come in all shapes and sizes. Shoes, bags, jewelry, hats, scarves, and ties are just some that are popular with men and women, and they pose interesting challenges to the fashion industry supply chain because they have a variety of inputs and may be produced in many different ways and in many different places.

synthetic pile fabrics like Orlon and Dynel, created in 1948 and 1950, respectively. By 1957, fake furriers were trying their hands at replicating mink, beaver, chinchilla, seal, raccoon, ermine, pony, and giraffe, some with more success than others. At best, one could hope to convince the eye, if not the touch. (para 5)

Leather, considered today a byproduct of the meatpacking industry (Stone 2013), was a staple of the fashion industry long before anyone knew what fashion was. Leather is still considered by many to be the product of choice for handbags, small leather goods, and footwear, and so it continues to be a choice for many fashion companies. Synthetics such as Ultrasuede and PVC are considered inexpensive substitutes for leather and at times have taken market share away from leather products because they have provided a cost-effective alternative (Stone 2013).

## TEXTILE SUPPLY CHAIN FLOW

Up to this point there has been an overall discussion about raw materials and synthetic and natural fibers, all of which have been considered as individual components, but in actuality there is also a process that needs

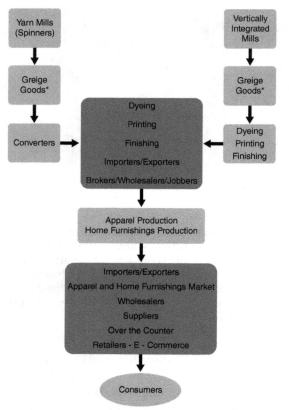

*Greige goods are unfinished textiles that are knit or woven in their raw state with no color or finishing added.

**Figure 5.7**
**Textile supply chain flow**

to be considered. Figure 5.7 is a visual representation of this process. As already noted, when it comes time to determine what raw materials to use to satisfy the end consumer, the wide variety of choices could have a tendency to complicate the decision-making process. The key to success is properly identifying the target market. The model that is depicted in Figure 5.7 provides a visual representation of the flow of textiles from fiber to consumer. This model is reproduced all over the globe in many different countries with the same end result, a garment that is available for sale to the consumer. It is typical of the overall process, although of course there are variations depending on the individual companies involved in the process of developing fiber, yarns, and fabrics. Companies that would be considered fully vertical would complete every step of the process, whereas others would be involved in one or more of the steps.

## Fabric Construction

The process of **fabric construction** goes from fiber to yarn to fabric. Generally speaking, there are three ways to make a fabric: knit a fabric, weave a fabric, and form a fabric, also called a nonwoven fabric. Knitting is the interloping of yarns, and weaving is the interlacing of yarns. Nonwoven fabrics are created through several different processes that include, but are not limited to, entanglement, adhesive application, and felting.

Within the textile industry there are two sectors that are involved in the construction of fabric. The primary sector is composed of mills and converters. These organizations are the ones that actually produce and/or finish fabrics. The secondary sector includes those companies and individuals that are involved in the resale of yarns and fabrics. This sector includes jobbers, brokers, wholesalers, retail stores, and manufacturers. The roles of these organizations have changed over the years, as there are fewer and fewer jobbers, brokers, and wholesalers operating in the global apparel and textile industry today. In the past thirty-five years there has been a decline in this entire sector, primarily because of imports and because the retail industry has assumed the role of product developer by creating its own private-label programs. In the past there were dozens of these secondary companies vying for business. Jobbers had **greige goods** on hand (in stock) (unfinished textiles that are knit or woven in their raw state with no color or finishing added) in many different fabrics, either knits or wovens, and could "convert" them into a finished fabric, generally by adding color, patterns, or texture, on a very short lead time (Figure 5.8). Jobbers usually specialized in one type of fabric, either knit or woven, and served a specific group of customers in the fashion industry. Brokers were intermediaries in the marketplace; they rarely took ownership of a fabric but consummated transactions between buyers and sellers of fabrics, earning a commission on the sale.

## The Design Process

The fashion **design process** comes in many shapes and sizes and is primarily predicated on the size of the company, the number of employees, and who the customers are. A typical fashion design process is presented in Figure 5.9. The first step in any design process, whether

**Figure 5.8**
**Finished textile fabrics** Before textiles are finished (dyed into colors), they all start out as greige goods, which are unfinished textile fabrics in a natural state before any solid color has been applied.

formal or informal, is the research phase. Designers must consider what is happening within their local market as well as around the globe, as many companies today have a global presence. Research can be paid for or developed by visiting stores and traveling around the world; although the internet can be a ready source of information, there is nothing like seeing firsthand the various trends that are taking place. Once the research is complete and the necessary information is gathered, it is time for conceptualization or "product ideation": just what products will be considered for today's consumers? The next phase is the actual design of the garments or accessories, which can be achieved through sketching or the use of technology (computer-aided design). The process does not end there because with many companies several review processes take place to support or encourage further work on the "line" or "lines" that have been developed by the design team. The greater the input from senior management, as well as the sales and marketing teams, the better chances the company has for success. Upon final approval of the design, the line is passed to sourcing and manufacturing to have the technical packages (tech pacs) completed and disseminated, which can be done physically or through computer-aided manufacturing (CAM) processes. With this step complete, the process moves rapidly to sampling, approvals, production, and delivery.

Amarasiriwardena (2013) stated, "Developing great clothing faces challenges with cost of iterative development, high customer expectations and scaling barriers. Nevertheless, there's a lot that can be learned from the rapid development and customer insights" (para 3). Furthermore, he stated, "In an ideal world, products are always designed with the end user in mind. However, for many clothing brands that rely on retailers to distribute their apparel, it adds a layer between the designer and the end user—where the apparel brand's customer is in fact the buyer at a retailer—not the consumer" (para 4). For this reason it is essential to identify the target market unless you are the retailer or selling directly to the consumer via the internet. Therefore, designers must design with a dual purpose in mind: satisfy the retailer first and then the consumer.

In Figure 5.9, the first step in the process is to perform trend research, which Amarasiriwardena also suggests doing. When looking at a very broad topic such as *raw materials*, it is important to remember that each company, designer, and product developer operates within a specific aspect of the fashion industry. For example, within the menswear category there may be a focus on knits, which may be further broken down into men's cotton knit shirts as opposed to sweaters or some other form of knit top. Raw materials in the fashion textile/supply chain must be understood as a very broad and complex set of subsets that all need to be taken into account. Some fiber companies provide trend information to assist with research. One such company is **Cotton Incorporated**, which provides trend information primarily on cotton. For additional information visit their website at *www.cottoninc.com*. Trend researchers can also attend fabric (textile) trade shows such as Premiere Vision, a world-renowned textile trade show held in Paris every year, along with a smaller show in New York City produced by the same organization that produces Premiere Vision. Additional trade shows include TexWorld, held in several cities around the world throughout the year, as well as the many local textile shows that also provide valuable trend information. Trend information may also be available via paid services such as the Doneger Group, WGSN, and Edelkoort Inc. The opportunity to perform trend research is only limited by two things: time and money.

One of the first steps that designers might undertake is the creation of a trend or mood board that sets

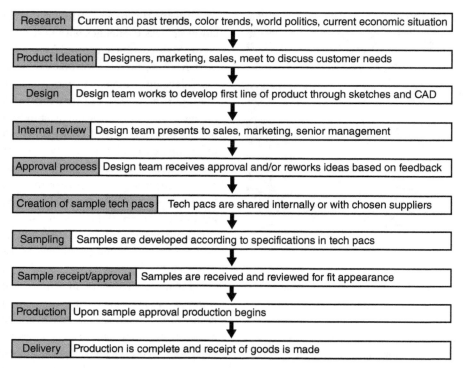

| Research | Current and past trends, color trends, world politics, current economic situation |
| Product Ideation | Designers, marketing, sales, meet to discuss customer needs |
| Design | Design team works to develop first line of product through sketches and CAD |
| Internal review | Design team presents to sales, marketing, senior management |
| Approval process | Design team receives approval and/or reworks ideas based on feedback |
| Creation of sample tech pacs | Tech pacs are shared internally or with chosen suppliers |
| Sampling | Samples are developed according to specifications in tech pacs |
| Sample receipt/approval | Samples are received and reviewed for fit appearance |
| Production | Upon sample approval production begins |
| Delivery | Production is complete and receipt of goods is made |

**Figure 5.9**
**The typical design process** The process depicted in this figure provides the reader with a general idea of the design process. This process will vary from company to company and is provided to illustrate one such example.

the tone for the line of products that they will be working on for a specific season or time period (Figure 5.10).

**Figure 5.10**
**Mood board** As trends develop, designers and merchandisers create mood boards to communicate their ideas for upcoming seasons, providing a visual representation of where fashion is heading.

Once the trend or trends have been properly identified, the next step would be to further evaluate the viability of these decisions for one's specific market(s) and then decide on which raw materials to pursue. In many instances, especially if one is importing finished goods into the United States, one would rely on a third party for help with securing the raw materials. If the process is controlled internally, one would have someone on staff responsible for procuring the materials to make samples and test the concept. If one uses an importer who uses a third party (agent), the importer would be responsible for supplying the various options that one has decided on based on the trends. In the case of imports, the decision of which raw materials to use may not be based solely on trends but may be influenced by the cost and tariffs (duty) related to the product. So not only must one review trends, but one must also once again look at the end consumer and/or retailer to determine if the choice one has made fits the price proposition that one expects.

# EXAMPLE OF A COST DIFFERENTIAL: COTTON VERSUS POLYESTER

Because of many factors, including tariffs, the choice of raw materials will have a direct effect on the cost of the finished product, as evidenced in Table 5.1, which looks at the cost differential between a men's 100 percent cotton woven long-sleeve sport shirt and one made from 100 percent polyester. The initial cost of the polyester fabric is less than that of the cotton fabric, creating a different final cost, even though the duty rate on the synthetic (polyester fabric) is higher than that on the cotton fabric. Based on this comparison, one must decide what fabric (raw material) should be used for the target market and what product best fits that market and at what price point. The costs of fabric, labor, trims, freight, drayage, and miscellaneous are estimated in Table 5.1.

# COUNTRY OF ORIGIN AND THE CONSUMER

The choice of raw materials in the fashion industry supply chain is further complicated by **country of origin** rules. When consumers purchase a piece of apparel, an accessory, or even a bolt of cloth from a local fabric store, they do not really know where the entire product is from. Do brands, retailers (via private-label programs), and design houses provide enough information to the consumer when it comes to country of origin? For the sake of transparency in the supply chain, should they be compelled to? The US government requires that the country of origin be permanently affixed and visible at the point of purchase. However, it does not require the maker of the product to list the country of origin of all of the components that were used in the production of the apparel, textile, or accessory product.

The **Institute of International Trade** noted that in the Rules of Agreement **World Trade Organization (WTO)** members need to ensure that country of origin is defined as the place where the product is produced and that the "rules of origins are transparent, that they do not have restructuring, distorting or disruptive effects on international trade, that they are administered in a consistent, uniform, impartial and reasonable manner, and that they are based on a positive standard" (Institute of International Trade 2009: para 6).

There are two primary methods that countries use to adhere to these guidelines set forth by the WTO: the substantial transformation method and the value-added percentage test. The method most commonly used in the fashion industry is the substantial transformation method. This method essentially confers country of

| Table 5.1 Cost Differential: Cotton and Polyester | | | |
|---|---|---|---|
| **100% cotton men's long-sleeve woven sport shirt** | | **100% polyester men's long-sleeve woven sport shirt** | |
| **Category 338 6105.10.00** | | **Category 438 6205.20.20** | |
| Fabric $2.50 per yard at 1.25 yards per garment | $3.12 | Fabric $.80 per yard at 1.25 yards per garment | $1.00 |
| Trims, including buttons, tags, labels | $1.25 | Trims, including buttons, tags, labels | $1.25 |
| Labor per piece | $3.50 | Labor per piece | $3.50 |
| Total first cost | $7.87 | Total first cost | $5.75 |
| Tariff (duty) at a rate of 17.6% | $1.55 | Tariff (duty) at a rate of 32% | $1.84 |
| SubTotal | $9.42 | SubTotal | $7.59 |
| Freight | .25 | Freight | .25 |
| Drayage (moving the product out of the port) | .25 | Drayage (moving the product out of the port) | .25 |
| Miscellaneous | .25 | Miscellaneous | .25 |
| Total | $10.17 | Total | $8.34 |
| Wholesale at 30% margin | $14.52 | Wholesale at 30% margin | $11.91 |
| Retail at 65% margin | $41.48 | Retail at 65% margin | $34.02 |

Developed by: Michael P. Londrigan.

origin based on where the greater value is added to the product. In many instances this occurs at the factory level where the product is assembled because the labor costs generally outweigh the inputs (fabric and trim) that constitute the finished product. Additionally, the value-added percentage test defines the degree of transformation required to confer origin on the good in terms of a minimum percentage of value that must come from the originating country or of the maximum amount of value that can come from the use of imported parts and materials. The consumer remains in the dark as to the origin of the sewing thread, fiber, yarn, fabric (raw materials), finishing, and packaging. All that the consumer sees listed is the country where the item underwent a substantial transformation.

Over half of the upland cotton exported by the United States (on average) finds its way into China, where much of it is converted into fabric that finds its way into garments that are then imported back into the United States. For example, a potential trail of a men's 100 percent cotton knit shirt may appear as follows. The cotton is picked, ginned, and baled here in the United States and then exported to China, where it is spun into yarn, knit into greige fabric, dyed, finished, and shipped to Bangladesh, where it is cut, sewn, and packaged into a finished garment before being shipped back to the United States. What does the consumer see as far as country of origin? The label reads "Made in Bangladesh" because the greater value (the labor) was added to the garment in Bangladesh.

The industry as a whole focuses a great deal of energy on corporate social responsibility (CSR) and ethical issues, as it should, but much of it is aimed at the factory level. Greater transparency is warranted in terms of the entire fashion supply chain if we are to provide consumers with all the information they require to make an informed purchase decision. The example of the men's knit shirt is fairly straightforward, and if all parties to the process have adhered to sound CSR policies, the country of origin would be considered a nonissue given the global nature of the fashion industry today. The dynamics of the issue change when pieces of the supply chain employ poor CSR practices. Let's say the factory in Bangladesh passed the various litmus tests for good CSR practices but the mill that knit the fabric used child labor or discharged its dye effluents into the local river. Then what? How are consumers to know all of the components without full disclosure on the label, so that if they wanted to they could learn more about the companies producing the product? One main reason that this does not occur is cost. It would cost money to track the various origins and to verify their accuracy, and most consumers would not want to pay the extra money required to be fully knowledgeable about what they buy and wear.

Dr. Linda Greer of the Natural Resources Defense Council also reminds us to look at the health and environmental impact our decisions have as they relate to our raw material yarn and textile choices. Dr. Greer states that "four areas in the textile industry have the biggest potential environmental impact: the types of fabrics you choose, the mills that dye and finish these fabrics, the way the goods are transported and the consumer care directions provided to the consumer" (Greer 2015: para 5). The bottom line is that research needs to be done so that the entire textile/supply chain, from fiber to consumer, can be made transparent so that choices are based on informed decisions regarding the health of the planet. There is no sense choosing the "right" fiber if it is going to be woven or knit and then dyed and finished at mills that are polluting the waterways and emitting harmful chemicals into the atmosphere. It is all well and good to buy organic cotton, but if it is not processed under strict guidelines (such as the Global Organic Textile Standard, GOTS), then the resource of good fiber is wasted and there is deception of the consumer.

Additional areas of concern that Dr. Greer raises are transportation and care of the finished garments. Container ships and rail transport have the smallest carbon footprint, with air being the worst second only to trucking. Unfortunately, in the United States, as in most places around the world, trucks move freight, and until an alternative method, such as trucks powered by a more sustainable power source, is employed, we are stuck with that aspect of the business. Additionally, washing and caring for garments not only damage the garments but also add to the environmental impact through electricity and water usage, as well as through detergents, which can prove harmful. One way to lower the impact is to handwash and line-dry apparel. Although it sounds old school, this method does have a lesser impact on the overall environment, as many of the chemicals used in detergents can have a toxic effect. The concerns that Dr. Greer has raised are real and have been echoed by others in the industry, and it will take a concerted effort by all stakeholders to usher in change.

## Textile Certification

A recent development in the textile industry has been certification programs for textiles. These key programs include the Global Organic Textile Standard (GOTS) and the Oeko-Tex® Standard 100. In addition, there are various certification programs that were developed to certify organic cotton. Certification programs vary by country. In the European Union, the Council Directive on Organic Farming defines production and certification

requirements of organic crops. In the United States and in Asia, the National Organic Program (NOP) and the Japanese Agricultural Standard (JAS), respectively, do the same. Each of these certifying organizations has standards that have a direct effect on the textile supply chain, and as such they add time and money to the process. This is not to say that using these programs places the textile supply chain at a disadvantage. Certification programs and standards ensure the value of the process and therefore provide added value to the end consumer. The following two sections provide more detail on two main standards.

Global Organic Textile Standard The **Global Organic Textile Standard (GOTS)** is the worldwide leading textile processing standard for organic fibers. The aim of this organization is to

> define world-wide recognised requirements that ensure organic status of textiles, from harvesting of the raw materials, through environmentally and socially responsible manufacturing up to labelling, in order to provide a credible assurance to the end consumer. Textile processors and manufacturers are enabled to export their organic fabrics and garments with one certification accepted in all major markets. (GOTS 2014: para 4)

This standard covers the "processing, manufacturing, packaging, labelling, trading and distribution of all textiles made from at least 70% certified organic natural fibres. The final products may include, but are not limited to fibre products, yarns, fabrics, clothes and home textiles" (GOTS 2014: para 6).

OEKO-TEX® Standard 100 The **OEKO-TEX® Standard 100** is a "certification system for textile raw, intermediate and end products at all stages of processing" (OEKO-TEX® Standard 100 n.d.: para 1). The standard tests for controlled substances and chemicals known to be harmful. Part of the decision-making process regarding these standards concerns how the product will be used by the consumer. For example, products that come in contact with skin may have stricter requirements than products that do not. For a product to be certified, it must be in compliance with certain criteria, which also apply to nontextile accessories such as buttons, zippers, and rivets.

# Textile Innovation

There is a saying in the fashion industry that fashion is evolutionary, not revolutionary, and for the most part this is an accurate statement. But the changes in the industry of textiles and yarns are, in fact, revolutionary. In an article posted in the *Cornell Chronicle* authored by Boscia (2016) titled "Cornell, Partners Seek to Revolutionize Textile Industry," there is a discussion about a public-private partnership that aims to fast-track innovation in "smart" fabrics for use in apparel, transportation, electronics, and consumer products, as well as protective gear for soldiers and first responders. Part of the conversation centered on the Advanced Foundational Fabrics of America (AFFOA) institute, which "promises to accelerate breakthroughs in fiber science and manufacturing that will lead to fabrics that see, hear, sense, communicate, store and convert energy, regulate temperature, monitor health and change color" (para 2). In this article, Juan Hinestroza, associate professor in the Department of Fiber Science & Apparel Design at Cornell, goes on to say that "with the creation of AFFOA, we are taking a major step forward in revolutionizing the textile industry and speeding scientific breakthroughs that will transform many aspects of our society, as textiles are all around us—in toothbrushes, pillows, car seats, airplanes, protective gear, fashion and more" (Boscia 2016: para 5).

It is an amazing time to be involved with fibers and textiles, and with the creation of these new products the textile/supply chain will have to adapt. Some of what is discussed in the Cornell piece just noted is happening today: fabrics that change color, textiles that detect heat, smart fabrics in the athletic market (see Figure 5.11). Ghent University (Universiteit Gent 2016), for example, has identified six areas that comprise the current wearable technology components:

- Sensors to detect body or environmental parameters
- A data processing unit to collect and process the obtained data
- An actuator that can give a signal to the wearer
- An energy supply that enables working of the entire system
- Interconnections that connect the different components

**Figure 5.11**
**Technology and fabrics** An example of a shirt using the latest technology to create the ultimate consumer experience. Sensors are knitted into the fabric to detect and monitor bodily functions such as heart rate. With such innovations a new category termed "wearable technology" has emerged.

- A communication device that establishes a wireless communication link with a nearby base station (para 1)

Today's athletic market is using several of these components to enhance the consumer experience with apparel products.

Innovation in textiles is the next new frontier for the apparel and accessories industry. Globe Manufacturing Company was invited to present at the first-ever Smart Fabrics Summit in Washington, D.C., in April 2016. Globe and its project partner, Propel, presented its Wearable Advanced Sensor Platform (WASP), the system for real-time monitoring of physiology and location designed for firefighters and first responders. The US secretary of commerce Penny Pritzker stated:

> Recent advances in technology have brought together the apparel, technology, and textile industries to develop new capabilities in fabrics with the potential to change how athletes, patients, soldiers, first responders, and everyday consumers interact with their clothes and textile products . . . Known as smart fabrics, these new high-tech products have the capability to interact with their user or environment, including by

tracking and communicating data about their wearer or environment to other devices through embedded sensors and conductive yarns. (Innovation in Textiles 2016: para 3)

Not only is the industry looking at ways to connect consumers to their garments for athletic and health applications, but it is also looking at how to further improve the functionality of fabrics through washing and other applications. A group of researchers from RMIT in Australia have developed a new, cheap, and efficient way to grow special nanostructures, which can degrade organic matter when exposed to light that is directly shined onto textiles. The work paves the way toward nano-enhanced textiles that can spontaneously clean themselves of stains and grime simply by being put under a light bulb or worn out in the sun. If this technology can be used in the mainstream, a great amount of water and electricity will be saved, not to mention the cost of cleaning products. These and other innovations are truly revolutionary and will need to be considered when reviewing individual supply chains (existing and new textile and fashion chains) in the fashion industry.

## CONCLUSION

The choices for consumers and therefore designers and manufacturers, although finite, appear endless when viewed through the lens of fashion. Consumers lead the way based on prices and trends, and they vote with their wallets and purses by accepting or rejecting the fashions that are offered in today's marketplace. How products are produced and the country of origin play a role with particular regard to how corporate and social responsibility may affect choice. In addition, the tariff system can affect the cost of goods sold. The textile supply chain is being transformed through technology and textile and yarn innovations. You can reflect upon the information that you now know and ponder what may be trending in the future and the direction consumers may set their sights on. Furthermore, think about the evolution of fabrics over the years. Now, think about what the future revolutionary changes may be for the consumer and for the environment. Most importantly, what ideas do you have to spark a revolution? Finally, what are the ways and means that you can remain current in today's dynamic changing fashion industry?

## INDUSTRY INTERVIEW: MARK MESSURA, COTTON INCORPORATED

As the main focus in this chapter is the raw materials used in the production of products in the fashion industry, I invited Mark A. Messura, senior vice president of global supply chain marketing for Cotton Incorporated, to discuss how cotton interacts with the fashion industry supply chain. As discussed in the chapter, procuring raw materials (after product ideation and design) is one of the first steps in the fashion industry supply chain process. One could say that the raw materials are the lifeblood of the process, and cotton is one of the most important raw materials.

Mark Messura is responsible for his company's global marketing programs with retailers, brands, and manufacturers. He is a frequent speaker on topics such as fiber economics, supply chain strategy, and sustainability in textiles and agriculture. Mr. Messura currently serves as chairman of the International Forum for Cotton Promotion. He is also a member of the Industry Advisory Board to the Textile Development and Marketing Department at the Fashion Institute of Technology and is chairman of the Industry Advisory Board, Fashion and Textile Management Program at North Carolina State University. He is also an adjunct associate professor in the College of Textiles at North Carolina State University. He serves on the Advisory Board to the Apparel, Merchandising, Design and Textiles Department at Washington State University.

Cotton Incorporated is funded by US growers of upland cotton and importers of cotton and cotton textile products, and it is the research and marketing company representing upland cotton. The program is designed and operated to improve the demand for and profitability of cotton.

**Interviewer:** *The supply chain has many components, with fibers being one of the starting points. What role does cotton play in the fashion supply chain? Is it the fiber that is thought of first?*

**M. M.:** We know that generally, style, fit, and price are the three most important factors for consumers when they are shopping for clothes. Because cotton is a key ingredient in clothing, the versatility of cotton, both in terms of fashion and function, makes the consideration of cotton use an important first step in the supply chain. Trend and design inspiration flow very easily from the technical attributes of cotton—its soft hand, its adaptability to technologies such as laser and ozone finishing, and its sustainability advantages as a natural fiber. As for whether cotton is the first choice would depend on the end use. For athletic wear it would be polyester and nylon for performance, but when you talk about casual and athleisure apparel for men, women, and children, cotton is still a top choice.

**Interviewer:** *What is the current state of US cotton production?*

**M. M.:** The United States is the third largest cotton-producing country in the world, accounting for approximately 13 percent of global production. This trend should hold steady for the foreseeable future, with yearly fluctuations based on weather and global demand. We do see some farmers moving from cotton to food-based crops in the current year because of relative commodity prices, but this is normal and will not have a significant impact in the long run.

**Interviewer:** *From a cost perspective, how does the price of cotton affect the cost of the finished garment?*

**M. M.:** Typically, fiber cost is about 60 to 75 percent of the total cost of producing a pound of yarn. Depending on the final product that is made, the cotton component cost can be very small. For example, given current fiber prices and retail prices, cotton fiber cost accounts for about 4 percent of the final product selling price of a pair of denim jeans.

**Interviewer:** *What role does Cotton Incorporated play in the global supply chain?*

**M. M.:** Cotton is produced in 77 countries worldwide and manufactured into products in more than 160 countries. Most of the cotton fiber that is produced ends up in apparel (approximately 80 percent), with about 15 percent in home textiles and the balance used in many other products and applications. Cotton Incorporated works to promote cotton use globally in a wide variety of products. Although based in the United States, the company is global in scope, reflecting the reality that more than 95 percent of the textiles sold in the US consumer market are imported and the result of truly global supply chains. Cotton Incorporated works with companies throughout the supply chain—manufacturers, equipment suppliers, chemical suppliers, sourcing companies, brands, and retailers—to inspire and support their use of cotton in products. Interestingly enough, we are seeing some movement back to the US with foreign investment in spinning mills in South Carolina by Chinese investors.

**Interviewer:** *Who are the leading cotton producers? Do you anticipate shifts moving forward?*

**M. M.:** Over the last decade the most important change among the leading cotton-producing countries has been the emergence of India. India is expected in 2015/2016 to be the largest cotton-producing country, narrowly edging out China. The tremendous increase in Indian production over the last decade is largely the result of genetically engineered seed varieties that have dramatically improved yields, reduced pesticide applications, and improved farmer health and safety.

**Interviewer:** *Corporate social responsibility (CSR) plays an increasing role in the supply chain. Most people focus on the factory. How can we increase transparency from the fiber perspective, especially in light of countries like Uzbekistan and the use of child labor to pick the cotton?*

**M. M.:** As supply chains around the world wrestle with the challenge of improving responsible production, it really begins with transparency in the supply chain. For companies and consumers that means knowing how your products are produced and what goes into them. When it comes to cotton, the fibers are not identifiable once they have their packaging and labeling removed. That means that fibers that claimed to be organically produced cannot be verified simply by looking at the fiber alone. Transparency in production and use of cotton fiber is greatest when supply chains use US cotton. Whether genetically modified, conventional varieties, or organically produced, the US Department of Agriculture has the best systems in the world for identifying and labeling cotton in the supply chain. Every bale of US cotton is labeled with a unique number identifying its origin all the way back in the supply chain to the location of the cotton gin, which is where the fiber and seed are separated after arriving from the farm.

**Interviewer:** *What does the future hold for cotton as a fiber in the global economy?*

**M. M.:** Cotton is the number one consumer-preferred fiber. It's also the fiber consumers consider the safest for the environment. As we move forward, we can expect to see cotton in a wide variety of technical and fashion apparel and home textile products as well as in products such as disposable wipes, hygiene, medical, and industrial uses. Technology will continue to drive the industry forward, with new innovations in moisture management systems that rely on cotton to new and exciting finishing techniques that enhance cotton's performance characteristics. Where there is a need for fiber, there is a growing opportunity for cotton, provided that we can continue to deliver a value to the consumer!

## Questions Pertaining to Interview

1. Mr. Messura speaks about style, fit, and price as being key factors that make cotton a fabric of choice. Consider the greater fashion industry. What other fibers may fit the consumer in terms of style, fit, and price?
2. Cotton is a product that is used globally. What other fiber is used as extensively around the globe?
3. The term *transparency* is an interesting one when it comes to corporate social responsibility (CSR). What is the responsibility of the textile supply chain regarding transparency and CSR? What is the consumer's responsibility?

# CASE STUDY: Cotton Incorporated

Raw materials form the basis of the fashion industry supply chain, from fiber to yarn to fabric. This chapter provided a look into that world by discussing raw materials and how they interact with the fashion industry supply chain. Key to the success of companies in the fashion industry is having a good sense of all the inputs and how they affect pricing, delivery, and quality. Raw materials are a key part of that understanding. The difference between an open-end-spun cotton versus a ring-spun cotton can change the hand quality of a 100 percent cotton fabric considerably. This chapter gives a basis for understanding the industry from that perspective.

Cotton is one of the prime fibers used in the industry, and here we look at one of the premier marketing organizations, Cotton Incorporated, that has changed the way the industry and ultimately the consumer look at cotton in apparel and home textile products. In 1960, cotton apparel and home furnishings accounted for approximately 78 percent of all textile products sold at retail in the United States. By 1975, the market share of cotton had plummeted to an all-time low of 34 percent due to the successful incursion of synthetic fibers in the marketplace, threatening the extinction of cotton as a viable commercial commodity. Key to this change were two main fibers listed in the chapter, polyester and nylon.

Historically, cotton farmers ended their involvement with a cotton crop at their point of sale, which would have been the fiber itself. The farmers were confident in the market's ability to take up the cotton crop. But the new competition from petroleum-based fiber producers presented a major disadvantage for cotton, as polyester was aggressively marketed and merchandised at every point throughout the supply chain: from mills and manufacturers to retailers and consumers.

Reacting to the serious erosion in cotton's consumer market share, producers in the high plains of Texas called for a collective national marketing and research effort. With support from regional producer organizations, the cotton growers were successful in petitioning Congress to pass the Cotton Research and Promotion Act of 1966. The act established a funding mechanism, based on producer assessments, for the purpose of conducting a wide-scale effort to recapture cotton's market share.

This funding mechanism led ultimately to the creation of Cotton Incorporated in 1970. From its inaugural year, the company faced a steadily declining market share, with little product available at retail except for denim jeans, T-shirts, and bath towels. In addition, consumers had become increasingly enamored of the ease-of-care synthetic products, and textile mills had moved away from the production of cotton.

From the beginning, Cotton Incorporated adopted a "push/pull" marketing strategy. The objective was to "push" cotton textile innovations into the market through product and process development, while building consumer demand, or a "pull," through advertising and promotion.

By 1983, Cotton Incorporated had succeeded in curtailing share decline, and a long steady period of increasing consumer popularity and share growth resulted. Today, cotton can be found on store shelves everywhere in most product categories, and cotton share is more than 60 percent of the US marketplace. For additional information on the cotton industry, log on to the Cotton Incorporated website: http://www.cottoninc.com/corporate/About-Cotton-Incorporated/Cotton-Incorporated-company-history/timeline.1960-1969.cfm.

**Case Study Questions**

1. Analyze cotton's current position in the fashion industry. What does the future hold for cotton as a "fiber of choice"? Are there growth opportunities for cotton on the global market?
2. With the advances in technology as they relate to synthetic products, coupled with current consumer trends in the apparel and home textiles industry, what is the future of cotton?
3. What does Cotton Incorporated have to do to position cotton as the fiber of choice in the twenty-first century?

## CHAPTER REVIEW QUESTIONS

1. What are the key differences between natural fibers and synthetic? What are the decisions that influence the choice for your supply chain?
2. Fabrics can be created in three ways. What are they, and why and how would your choice impact the supply chain?
3. Why is certification important, and is it something that every part of the supply chain needs to do?
4. Do you agree with how the WTO confers country of origin status? Is there a different method that you would recommend?
5. Textile innovation has revolutionized the way people view textiles. How do you think these innovations will impact the supply chain, positively or negatively?

## CLASS EXERCISE

Pull ten garments from your closet. Identify the country of origin and the fiber content. By US law these two pieces of information must be permanently affixed to your garments; if they are not there, then choose another garment, as you might have removed the labels.

a. How many countries did you identify?
b. Are you familiar with these countries?
c. Can you tell by examining the garments if all the materials and findings were actually from the country stated in the label?
d. Did the fiber content play any part in your purchase decision?
e. What impact did the fiber content and country of origin have on the supply chain?
f. As the consumer, did you consider if the garment was made in a socially responsible way?

## KEY TERMS

Industrial Revolution
raw materials
synthetic fibers
acetate
triacetate
acrylic
modacrylic
aramid
polyimide
elastomeric
spandex
elastoester
nylon
polyester
polypropylene

polyvinyl chloride
rayon
lyocell
natural fibers
cotton
linen
jute
silk
spider silk
wool
yak
camel hair
llama
alpaca
ramie

angora
cashmere
mohair
soybean
bamboo
accessories
fabric construction
greige goods
design process
Cotton Incorporated
country of origin
Institute of International Trade
World Trade Organization (WTO)
Global Organic Textile Standards
Oeko-Tex® Standard 100

# REFERENCES

1. Alfred, R. (2009), "May 8, 1951: DuPont Debuts Dacron," *Time Magazine, Today in Science History*. Available online: http://www.wired.com/2009/05/dayintech_0508/.

2. Amarasiriwardena, G. (2013), "What's the 'Design Process' of a Fashion Designer?" *Quora*. Available online: https://www.quora.com/Whats-the-design-process-of-a-fashion-designer.

3. Austin B. (1989), "Managing Marketing in a Commodities Manufacturing Firm: Dominion Textiles." Available online: http://www.thebhc.org/sites/default/files/beh/BEHprint/v018/p0168-p0177.pdf.

4. Boscia, T. (n.d.), "Cornell, Partners Seek to Revolutionize Textile Industry," *Cornell Chronicle*. Available online: http://news.cornell.edu/stories/2016/04/cornell-partners-seek-revolutionize-textile-industry.

5. *Business Dictionary* (2016), "Denier." Available online: http://www.businessdictionary.com/definition/denier.html.

6. fiber2fashion (n.d.), "Plant and Animal Fibers." Available online: http://www.fibre2fashion.com/industry-article/2943/plant-and-animal-fibres?page=1.

7. Global Organic Textile Standard (GOTS) (2014), [Website]. Available online: http://www.global-standard.org/the-standard/general-description.html.

8. Greer, L. (2015), "Remove Toxic Chemicals and Fabrics from Fashion's Supply Chain," *Op-ed: The Business of Fashion*. Available online: https://www.businessoffashion.com/community/voices/discussions/can-fashion-industry-become-sustainable/remove-toxic-chemicals-fabrics-fashions-supply-chain.

9. Hines, A. (2015), "The History of Faux Fur," *Smithsonian Magazine*. Available online: http://www.smithsonianmag.com/history/history-faux-fur-180953984/?no-ist.

10. IEEE Globalspec/Engineering 360 (n.d.), "Synthetic Fibers and Fabrics Information." Available online: http://www.globalspec.com/learnmore/materials_chemicals_adhesives/composites_textiles_reinforcements/synthetic_fibers_fabrics_polymer_textiles.

11. Innovation in Textiles (2016), "Globe to Present Wearable Advanced Sensor Platform at Smart Fabrics Summit." Available online: http://www.innovationintextiles.com/globe-to-present-wearable-advanced-sensor-platform-at-smart-fabrics-summit/.

12. The Institute of International Trade (2009), *International Trade—Rules of Origin*. Available online: http://www.iitrade.ac.in/kmarticle.php?topic=Rules%20Of%20Origin.

13. Londrigan, M. (2009), *Menswear: Business to Style*, New York: Fairchild Books.

14. OEKO-TEX® Standard 100 (n.d.), "Principles of the Review and Revision Process." Available online: http://www.global-standard.org/the-standard/general-description.html.
**Principles of the Review and Revision Process - Stakeholder Input**
The GOTS Founding Organizations are backed up by stakeholder based decision bodies/technical committees which has ensured that when integrating their respective existing organic textile standards into the GOTS, views of relevant stakeholders were considered from the beginning. The GOTS approved certification bodies are also actively involved in the GOTS revision process through the 'Certifiers Council'.

In order to further broaden the basis of the GOTS, the Founding Organizations are soliciting participation by international stakeholder organisations in the ongoing process of review and revision of the GOTS. For this purpose, starting with the revision to develop standard version 3.0 in 2010 a formal stakeholder input process was established. While the review process is a continuous one, standard revisions are anticipated every three years. Details of the latest revision process are provided for in section 'Revision Procedure'.

15. Stone, E. (2013), *The Dynamics of Fashion*, New York: Bloomsbury.

16. Universiteit Gent (2016), "Smart Textiles." Available online: http://www.ugent.be/ea/textiles/en/research/research-themes/smart-textiles.

# Sourcing and Production

## LEARNING OBJECTIVES

Upon completion of this chapter you will be able to:

- Describe the process of sourcing and production in the fashion industry.

- Understand the term *supplier base* as it relates to the supply chain.

- Summarize the global sourcing process.

- Identify the ethical and contractual issues faced by purchasing and supply chain professionals.

- Explain the strategic nature the product plays in the supply chain in sourcing of the product.

# INTRODUCTION TO SOURCING AND PRODUCTION

The apparel and textile industry (fashion industry) is somewhat unique, as the two terms that we are discussing in this chapter, *production* and *sourcing*, are often used interchangeably, as are the terms *manufacturing* and *production*. **Sourcing** is most often defined as "the process of finding suppliers of goods or services" (WebFinance 2016b: para 1). Terms such as *procuring*, *evaluating*, and *engaging* are used to further expand this definition. The term *sourcing*, as it relates to the supply chain, is a relatively new term that was first used in the 1980s to express a concept that incorporated much more than just the physical production of a product or providing a service. A few of the buzzwords of the 1980s and 1990s that further illustrated the expansive and broad nature of the concept of sourcing are *sourcing strategies*, *sourcing plans*, *strategic sourcing*, *cooperative sourcing*, and *sourcing optimization*. These terms reflected the need to include other components into what was becoming a more complicated process. **Production**, on the other hand (see Figure 6.1 for an example of modern spinning equipment), is defined as "the processes and methods used to transform tangible inputs (raw materials, semi-finished goods, subassemblies) and intangible inputs (ideas, information, knowledge) into goods or services. Resources are used in this process to create an output that is suitable for use or has exchange value" (WebFinance 2016a: para 1).

These are the current definitions of sourcing and production used in the apparel and textile industry today. These definitions give the impression that sourcing and production are rather simple aspects of the manufacturing process, when in fact they are highly complex. In fact, it is difficult to talk about production without considering aspects of sourcing, and these two processes are interrelated. Some aspects of sourcing and production have made these two aspects of the fashion industry to be seen as one synergistic action, as the traditional approach is no longer sufficient. An apparel or textile company can no longer rely on a third party to just "produce" a product for it; it needs to be fully immersed in what is now known as the supply chain. This textbook focuses on the term *sourcing* because that is the one that is most commonly used in the industry today.

In today's fashion industry, companies that have production departments with a singular focus on producing

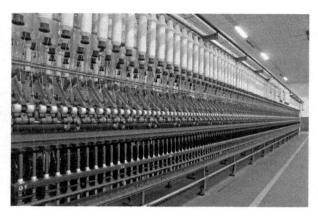

**Figure 6.1**

**A modern spinning mill** This modern spinning mill is producing yarn as one of the initial inputs to the fashion industry supply chain. The industry has advanced from the original spinning wheel that was manually operated in the home to these high-speed, technologically advanced machines capable of producing thousands of yards of yarn in a short period of time.

a product from components or raw materials have now expanded and changed titles to either sourcing departments and or sourcing/production divisions. Some of these changes have resulted in the integration of many different facets of sourcing and production, along with the hiring of an entirely new group of people with differing skill sets. Each company is unique, and the processes that are outlined here may or may not match what one would find working at any given company in a sourcing department. For example, in a large multinational corporation an individual's function may be so isolated that he or she does not know what the person down the hall or in the next cubicle is doing, whereas in a small company an individual may be involved in all aspects of the sourcing process. No two companies share the same processes in the exact same way, although there are many similarities in scope and function. Table 6.1 provides an overview of the entire sourcing and production process.

There is much information noted in Table 6.1; however, it clearly depicts that the process is a complex one that takes place on multiple levels, with decision-making embedded at every level. What Table 6.1 provides is a general framework for understanding the overall process and is by no means the only method for sourcing a fashion product. The real test for any individual working in the fashion industry will come with on-the-job training and work experience.

**Table 6.1** Sourcing and Production Process

| Title | Process |
|---|---|
| Ideation | • Identify and define the target market.<br>• Identify and define the intended product/service.<br>• Conduct research to ensure that the product and the market match.<br>• Develop the plan. |
| Design and development | • Identify materials to be used (fabric and trim).<br>• Sketch or use computer-aided design (CAD) software.<br>• Refine the sketch or CAD work.<br>• Create a pattern.<br>• Procure the necessary fabric and trim.<br>• Create the sample.<br>• Develop a tech pac (technical package fully identifying all aspects of the product to be produced, including yarn size and type and all dyeing and finishing requirements, as well as all trims and packaging and shipping methods). |
| Sourcing | • Identify potential suppliers (including in-house if that is an option). In reviewing potential suppliers, one needs to keep in mind the company policies on corporate social responsibility, as well as the legal, economic, and political conditions in the countries where potential suppliers reside and the lead time from factory to warehouse.<br>• Distribute tech pacs to all nominated suppliers.<br>• Review and analyze costs, lead times, and quality requirements submitted by suppliers.<br>• Identify a final decision as to where one will source the finished product and determine terms, letter of credit, FOB, CIF, and LDP (see text for definitions). |
| Sales and marketing | • Develop line sheets and other ancillary materials related to marketing the product.<br>• Contact buyers for appointments, attend trade shows, and collect orders. (In some cases companies will produce product for the shelf, meaning that the company projects sales based on prior history and then produces a set quantity in anticipation of orders, versus producing to orders collected from prospective customers.)<br>• Present to the buyers. |
| Production | • Finalize all details, including payment method.<br>• Execute the purchase order.<br>• Cut and sew.<br>• Do inspection, tagging, and packing.<br>• Do shipping. |
| Receiving and distribution | • Receive merchandise in warehouse or drop-ship directly to customers. (If receipt is in one's own warehouse, one might want to spotcheck to ascertain that the product meets all specifications before shipping to customers.)<br>• Distribute to customers and bill. |

Developed by Michael P. Londrigan.

# THE SUPPLIER BASE

One of the most difficult aspects of the supply chain is developing relationships with factories that can deliver the "goods" that one requires. In Chapter 5 the focus was on the raw materials that are transformed from fiber into yarn by yarn spinners and into fabrics by the textile mills. In this chapter it is the factory that becomes the focus (Figure 6.2).

There is much information written about the factories in the supply chain and the development of the **supplier base**. Establishing a reliable and trustworthy supplier base is critical to the smooth and seamless

**Figure 6.2**
**Factory sewing floor** This sewing floor in an apparel factory shows workers tending to their machines. The apparel and accessory aspects of the fashion industry supply chain are still heavily reliant on physical labor, even with the many advances in technology. This particular factory appears well lit and has the overall appearance of a well-run shop.

**Figure 6.3**
**Rana Plaza Factory collapse** This building collapse occurred because of building code violations that went unchecked, putting the factory workers at great risk. This tragedy further highlighted the need for heightened CSR policies, unfortunately at the cost of many human lives. It illustrates the importance of the supplier base and the actions that need to be taken to ensure that people working throughout the supply chain are protected.

workings of sourcing and production. As the name supplier *base* implies, it is foundational to the process of procuring the products and/or services necessary to be successful in the fashion industry.

The supplier base is those key companies (factories, mills, trim suppliers) that would be considered integral parts of the overall supply chain and that play a key role in the organization's ability to deliver the goods when the buyer needs them. It is typically in the factory that an issue may manifest itself related to corporate social responsibility (CSR). Although this is not always the case, the supply chain is complex and stretches quite far, so there are many opportunities for problems to surface that would fall under the heading of CSR. For instance, an issue could arise from the picking of cotton fiber by child labor, or a yarn spinner or textile mill might be flushing its effluents into a nearby drinking water source.

An example of a disruption of the supply chain at the supplier base was the Rana Plaza Factory collapse in Bangladesh in 2013, where 1,135 workers lost their lives and countless others were injured (Figure 6.3). The incident highlighted the need for improved oversight by the companies that were producing products in that facility, as well as by the retail labels they represented. In addition to this tragic building collapse, there have been numerous reports of fires occurring throughout the

world in apparel factories, several in Bangladesh alone. These tragedies could have been avoided. The building collapse was a direct result of the building owner skirting the law by adding three additional stories for a total of eight floors when the government had only provided a building consent (permit) to build five floors. The additional weight caused structural cracks and eventually the total failure of the structure. When the cracks were first noticed, the industrial police had requested that the factories remain closed until a structural engineer could inspect the building, but that advice was ignored. Although the building was named after the owner, there were in fact several separate factories operating in the space, and all had forced their workers to return to work. These factories were making apparel products for major retailers and brands from around the world, and with better oversight from their quality assurance teams this tragedy could have been avoided. In the aftermath *The Guardian* reported:

> A court in Bangladesh has formally charged 38 people with murder in connection with the 2013 collapse of the Rana Plaza building which killed 1,135 people in the country's worst industrial disaster. A total of 41 defendants face

charges over the collapse of the complex, which housed five garment factories supplying global brands. Plaza owner Sohel Rana is the principal accused. (*The Guardian* 2016)

Supply strategies are integral to a business's success. One strategy, James Morgan (1993) noted, is to see suppliers as "vital players in their planning process, with many organizations attributing their competiveness to their suppliers' efforts" (para 1). The resulting competitive gains can manifest themselves in a wide range of areas, from better prices and delivery times to increased opportunities to consider implementing innovative sourcing practices. Management consultant Paul Inglis noted that such improvements will not be realized without meaningful leadership from business owners and executives as "leading companies develop tailored supply strategies that are directly linked to their corporate strategies" (1998: para 10). Ultimately, these strategies construct a sound supply base from which the supply chain is operationalized.

Countless experts and business analysts have agreed that developing partnerships can provide strong benefits to all parties involved in the supply chain. No matter the size of the business, establishing partnerships can prove cost-effective and provide added benefits such as preferential treatment at the factory level when scheduling production. Having a strong partner at the factory level who is beholden to one's company for a consistent flow of business makes good sense for the consumer as well because it can provide a consistent flow of product to meet ongoing consumer demand. A partnership can also help provide cost savings that can be passed on to the retailer and ultimately to the consumer. As Morgan (1993) indicated, suppliers can be an important source of information that can help businesses improve performance and productivity. After studying a major buyer survey, he cited five general areas in which supplier involvement can help buyers compete in the marketplace:

1.  Product design, technology, or ideas for producing new products which includes ways in which materials may be used in product development.
2.  Product quality by offering suggestions that may help buyers to hold consistent tolerances in production.
3.  Product development from design to market place shortened or "speed to market."
4.  Product cost reduction as a result of the streamlining of work processes and/or substituting costly components with less expensive but still effective ones.
5.  Customer satisfaction. (para 10)

The first two boxes in Table 6.1, ideation and design and development, involve identifying the intended target market and developing the product(s) to satisfy that market. These two steps are only the beginning of the process. The remaining steps can prove challenging because they involve the development of the supplier base. As noted in Figure 6.4, a reliable means of transportation such as trucking services is a key to a successful supply chain. What resources does the supplier base need to both develop and sustain a well-established supply chain? Without this success will be difficult to achieve.

Sara Ireton is the director of customer experiences with NFI Global, formerly National Freight Inc., a family of companies founded in 1932 and dedicated to serving the supply chain industry. NFI has grown to become one of America's leaders in third-party logistics. According to Ms. Ireton (2009), there are ten key factors to consider when choosing a supplier. Detailed descriptions of these key factors are presented in Table 6.2. See

**Figure 6.4**

**A large-capacity truck**  In every country around the globe, moving freight by truck is a key to a successful fashion industry supply chain. Freight haulers can carry large quantities of fashion merchandise, most of which is in the containers that come right off the cargo ships. Without trucks it would not be possible to have a fashion industry supply chain.

| Table 6.2 Ten Key Factors in Choosing a Supplier | |
|---|---|
| **Key Factor** | **Description** |
| Total landed cost | This is the cost one would pay to have the product delivered to the port of one's choice. |
| Product quality | Product quality needs to be defined by the buyer and agreed upon by the supplier; it is key to customer satisfaction. |
| Logistics capability | Does the supplier have access to the proper means of conveyance to get the product to the market? |
| Location | Details regarding time zones and ability to communicate and visit factories can have a significant impact on the decision of where to produce. |
| Trade regulations | Regulations positively and negatively impact the ability to source from particular countries, and governmental trade agreements need to be reviewed prior to any decisions. |
| Finances | The terms of purchase and the risk of the supplier need to be considered. |
| Time to market/responsiveness of supplier | How quickly can the vendor ship and respond to changes in the marketplace? |
| Value-added services | Does the vendor provide additional services such as pretagging garments at the source of supply? |
| Communication/IT capabilities | Is the supplier a real-time, internet–savvy, information-sharing partner? Ensuring that the documentation is properly executed on a timely basis is critical to getting the goods cleared on time. |
| Human toll | Visiting and working with suppliers overseas and can affect both the individuals tasked with making those trips and their families. |

These ten key factors were described by an industry expert as important when choosing a supplier. These factors will come into play during every student's career in the fashion industry.

the NFI website for more information on the company: *http://www.nfiindustries.com/services/global-logistics/*.

Of course, there are many different scenarios that will impact which supplier(s) one chooses to strengthen or create the supplier base. For example, for the company that is well established with a strong customer base, producing and selling millions of pieces of apparel or accessories, the decision is whether to continue with the existing supplier base or to add new suppliers. A different set of decisions would also need to be made when developing the supplier base for a new business that is just starting out. In all cases, developing a supplier base is an ongoing process, with evaluation being an integral part. An example would be the company that already produces in twenty or more countries and has a very well-established supplier base. The challenge for that company is to continuously evaluate its existing supplier base to make sure that all the suppliers are meeting the criteria that have been established, such as cost, quality,

lead time, local government regulations, and CSR practices. Some suppliers might start out with no red flags, but on subsequent visits remediation might be necessary. In some situations the company might seriously consider dropping a particular supplier if it fails to maintain the original agreement for CSR, cost, or quality issues. The startups and the companies that are in between might be focused on finding a first, second, or third factory that can help them achieve success. A new startup might only require one factory that has the ability to produce small production runs. This may be a local producer whose factory may be established in the startup's own community (New York City, Los Angeles, etc.).

In addition, whether they are searching out new suppliers or benchmarking the performance of current suppliers, businesses are encouraged to consider the points explained in Table 6.3 when evaluating their options, many of which overlap ("Supplier Relations" 2015: para 10).

**Table 6.3** Points to Consider When Searching for New Suppliers or Evaluating Current Suppliers

| Key Factor | Description |
| --- | --- |
| Commitment to quality | Product satisfaction starts with excellent quality, which has to be consistent in the supply chain. |
| Cost-competitiveness | The key to any successful supply chain is competitive pricing; for a small apparel producer serving a niche market or a global organization producing millions of garments, cost will always matter. |
| Communication | Communicating with customers is critical, and one must maintain open lines of communication from supplier to end user. |
| Timely service | On-time delivery is a must in today's fashion industry; if a shipment does slip in delivery, there must be communication on a timely basis. |
| Flexibility and special services | Some suppliers go the extra mile to provide flexible hours and additional training on inventory systems. |
| Market knowledge | Being able to give the customer information about the market is added value and can help cement a successful partnership. |
| Production capabilities | Knowing one's capacity and whether one can take additional business is a key factor in maintaining timely service. |
| Financial stability | It is often difficult to ascertain if one's supplier base is financially stable; the more information one can gather to that end will help in the decision-making process. |
| Logistics/location | Transportation capabilities and the location of the factory can affect accessibility. |
| Inventory | Is the supplier a "just-in-time" supplier? Can it replenish product on a fast-turn basis? Does it stock goods? |
| Ability to provide technical assistance | Can the supplier provide additional product development skills to aid in cost savings and product ideation? |

This table lists additional data points to be used when investigating new suppliers. This process often depends on the relationships that are developed, but starting with a set of criteria is always helpful.

## Fast Fashion

Fast fashion is a theme that has already been discussed and will appear in several places in this text, as it has become a mainstay in the fashion industry. Like most new business practices, **fast fashion** started as a trend and quickly became a cornerstone of many retail apparel businesses. Fast fashion has changed how companies set up their supply chains and how they react to consumer demand. In the fashion industry, **trends** are a general direction in which something is developing or changing, and fast fashion has emerged as a leading trend in shaping supplier chains around the globe. The concept of fast fashion is to reduce the speed to market and provide the consumer with product on a more regular basis. The Boston Consulting Group (2013) noted: "Ever since the 'fast fashion' model emerged two decades ago, supply chains have become a key driver of success for apparel companies. Today, they are more strategically important than ever before, due to the added pressures brought about by several trends" (para 1).

Historically, the supply chain in the United States was usually self-controlled by the manufacturing companies themselves because they owned their own factories and produced product directly under their control. Today that situation is rare, as the overwhelming majority of US companies (brands, design groups, etc.) have divested themselves of the physical plant and equipment necessary to produce the products they sell. As a result, they are increasingly relying on the supply chain by using factories and facilities that are owned by other entities; in this environment, the supplier base is more important than ever. In other parts of the world this is not always the case; Inditex, parent company to Zara located in Spain, is an example of a company that still owns factories that produce some of its own products (Figure 6.5).

**Figure 6.5**
**Zara retail store** A leading global retailer, Zara has come to personify the retail philosophy of fast fashion, which has changed the way fashion companies look at the supply chain. Zara prides itself on changing its floor sets every few weeks and creates demand for its products by keeping inventory at levels that allow for quick-sell troughs and replenishment of new goods on a rapid cycle.

The importance of the supplier base in the supply chain has also been noted by James Clark, a professor with the London College of Fashion and industry practitioner, who provides a European view in his book *Fashion Merchandising: Principles and Practice*. While discussing the fashion supply chain, Clark (2015) states, "Fashion supply chains have been irrevocably changed by the rise of the fast fashion business model, which harnessed free-trade and technology developments to revolutionize the supply of fashion product to meet rising consumer demand" (Clark 2015: 271). He further states that "the fast fashion concept has been so well received by the consumer that it is considered ubiquitous within the fashion industry. Its precise shape and form can of course differ from business to business: Zara champions a vertical business model that focuses on in-house control, whereas the Primark model focuses on entry price points on the high street" (271).

## Emerging Trends

In addition to fast fashion, there are other trends that are presently or will ultimately affect the fashion industry from a supplier base perspective. Boston Consulting Group (BCG) (2013) conducted a study and identified several trends that should be considered in any and all decisions while developing a supply chain (in this case the factory): globalization, the digital movement, the omnichannel model, and financial factors. Globalization places increased demands on the supply chain because of the need to balance local business practices with those of countries around the globe. This adds stress to the supply chain from a shipping standpoint as well as a sales and marketing standpoint. The digital movement has necessitated transparency in pricing and the frequent replenishment of goods right to the consumer's doorstep, while constantly adding pressure on the bottom line. With technology has also come the **omnichannel** model, with consumers demanding options on how to buy and when to buy products; this puts additional stress on the supply chain. Omnichannel is a relatively new concept in the fashion industry; it is a multichannel approach to sales that seeks to provide the customer with a seamless shopping experience, whether the customer is shopping online from a desktop or mobile device, by telephone, by TV, or in a brick-and-mortar store. This model brings added stressors; for example, companies need to keep abreast of ever-changing technological trends and develop ways to get products into the consumer's hands. Does the consumer pick up in a store, order online and pick up in the store, have the product sent directly to the home, or use some other variation? With the addition of quick response (QR) codes, consumers can multitask by exploring and researching new products while determining the best price by comparison shopping.

Retailers are now figuring out how to manage these new modes of delivery. Previously retailers had two or more separate and distinct locations for service: online and brick and mortar. In a wide-ranging question-and-answer session with David Jaffe, CEO of Ascena Retail Group, that appeared in the winter 2016 edition of the *Robin Report*, Mr. Jaffe was asked, "What about omnichannel?"

> Right now we are in the process of re-platforming our e-commerce system. This will allow us to implement omni-channel programs such as DOM (distributed order management system) and BOPUS (buy online, pick up in store). The new platform will exist at all our brands and because of our shared service infrastructure, we have the size and scale to do these types

of things and learn from each other. Omni-channel is an ongoing strategic initiative, and some brands (such as Ann Taylor and Loft) are further along than others. The re-platforming will provide us with the right plumbing to continue providing a seamless shopping experience. (Lewis 2016: 19)

With today's sophisticated systems and technology, companies are figuring out how to handle multiple channels from one location, thereby maximizing profits and controlling costs. Not only are consumers shopping differently using online services, mobile apps, brick-and-mortar stores, and catalogs, but they are also demanding new means of delivery, which all has to be factored into the supply chain. In addition, one must always consider the financial aspect of the business, not only in the country where the idea for the product was conceived but also for the country within which the product is being produced. This means that thinking globally and understanding cultural nuances are imperative. Multinational corporations operating around the world need to be well versed in policy and politics, currency fluctuations, and local banking customs. BCG (2013) identified common characteristics of the best-designed supply chains: the supply chain fulfills customer orders quickly and adapts quickly to changes; is flexible in its ability to develop, initiate, and sustain processes that are efficient, from the ideation stage to finished product; and finally is effective in terms of cost of operations (para 5).

## New Models for Transparency

On a smaller scale there are other trends emerging. An example is the trend to build transparency; newer organizations are pushing this trend. One such organization is Project JUST. Natalie Grillon is the cofounder along with Al Shehail of Project JUST, whose goal is to bring transparency to the fashion supply chain. Project JUST was founded in 2014. Natalie brings a unique perspective to the company because she does not have a fashion industry background but worked for the Peace Corps as a natural resource management specialist in Mali, West Africa. She later went on to pursue her MBA in Sustainable Global Enterprise Immersion with Johnson Cornell University and spent a year in northern Uganda as an operations manager at Gulu Agricultural Development Company (GADC). While working with GADC,

she gained important financial and operational skills by helping smallholder farmers gain access to global markets for their crops. With organic certification, GADC can pay the farmers a price premium while also ensuring sustainability of the land and the consequent long-term economic benefits of these farming practices. According to Grillon (personal communication, 2015), "Just as the food industry is changing and pursuing transparency and sustainability, the time is ripe for fashion to follow suit." Grillon further states, "Disruptive innovation is needed," and provides an example: "Gulu Agricultural Development Company buys from farmers, works alongside them year-round, teaching and encouraging them to adopt organic and yield-enhancing practices, and then certifies their organically grown crops" (see Figure 6.6).

What is Natalie saying to us? She asks us all to take a look at the clothes we are wearing today. Where were they made? Under what conditions? If you're wearing natural fiber, where was it grown? Who harvested it? And were those workers treated fairly? Even asking these questions provides a platform for the emergence of the *disruptive innovations* that Natalie talks about.

Natalie recounted a time of *disruptive innovation* during which her idea for a company took hold. It was the Rana Plaza factory collapse that got her to thinking:

**Figure 6.6**

**An organic cotton farmer tending his crop in northern Africa** Organic cotton continues to grow in importance as a way to provide greater transparency in the natural product movement. Today the total world production of organic cotton can fit on one large container ship, accounting for approximately 1 percent of the world cotton production.

could the cotton she was brokering with the farmers from northern Uganda have wound up in apparel products in the factory that just collapsed? How could one trace the cotton and provide the ultimate transparency to the supply chain? The answer was tapping into the latest technology to provide information that was once not possible to consumers so that they can make an informed decision on whether to buy the product. The idea started to become a reality, and the philosophy was to connect brands with ethical suppliers to provide the consumer with beautiful garments. As of this writing, Project JUST has 170 brands on their platform using its services. The key is focusing on the Millennial generation to be change agents for the industry. Natalie believes in what she is doing and can envision a future where transparency is second nature. The Millennial generation consumes information in a totally different way than previous generations, and Project JUST is looking to provide the right information to make the right purchase decisions to change the world.

Natalie's establishment of Project JUST was her time of *disruptive innovation*. The company was conceived and developed to answer some of the questions noted here and to provide consumers with as much information as possible to make an informed decision when purchasing their apparel and accessory items. The main thrust of Project JUST is connecting designers and consumers to ethical suppliers. Natalie hopes that her company will provide greater transparency, something that we all seek in the apparel and textile industry.

## Trends and Sourcing

Ideas sometimes start out as trends and soon become embedded in the fabric of the fashion industry, particularly in sourcing and our everyday lives. There are questions about how the fashion industry will respond to these trends and make necessary adjustments to the supplier base. Tara Donaldson (2015) sat down with industry executives to get their view on trends as they relate to sourcing. These questions dealt with rising costs and how these costs affect sourcing and supply, how compliance shapes business, and how business is affected by transparency efforts, ultimately leading to how businesses will meet consumer demands and how ultimately sourcing will change the trends. Answers

to these questions are interesting and also thought-provoking. For instance, it was identified that cost will continue to rise and will be fueled by two main issues: labor and compliance. The two go hand in hand because the more compliance the industry seeks, the higher the wages will need to be to cover the health and safety costs that are directly tied to compliance issues. Furthermore, one of the individuals interviewed by Donaldson (2015) stated, "Compliance has been growing in importance . . . it's only going to become more prominent and that will impact the actions and behaviors of the sourcing community and everyone in the supply chain. There is already increased collaboration of industry players working together to address compliance challenges" (para 7). This will be true in most developing countries, where compliance and transparency recommendations will continue in the foreseeable future.

One must also consider the role of technology, which accelerates the spread of information about compliance, particularly information about workers' rights and the industry tragedies that continue to occur. The spread of this type of information only continues to increase pressure to develop policies that address these issues. In the long run, with the spread of information, we may see companies stop doing business with factories that are not compliant (Donaldson 2015). These same compliance efforts and outcomes will create an environment where the consumers will be demanding more transparency from companies so that they can make informed decisions about the products they purchase (Donaldson 2015). Consumers are demanding transparency throughout the supply chain, so companies need to reveal all of their sources of supply (from fiber to trims to packaging). Of course, the industry will never be in a position to reveal all of its supplier information for fear of giving away some or all of its competitive advantage (Donaldson 2015). In addition, those interviewed felt that the industry runs the risk of providing too much information. It may create a situation where the information becomes second nature to the consumer and therefore an afterthought. But others believe that if companies are totally transparent and provide a thorough accounting of the supply chain to the consumer, the issue of providing too much information may become a nonissue.

Another pressing topic will continue to be speed to market, or the degree to which the consumer wants the product *immediately*. The entire fast fashion movement, coupled with a generation of individuals who seek immediate gratification, creates pressure and stress on the supply chain to deliver goods as quickly as possible. Donaldson's (2015) article also addresses this issue. One way to increase speed is to source more production and inputs locally. In some cases this makes sense, but in most cases it is still cost-effective to produce finished products halfway around the world and ship them back to one's home country for consumption because the apparel industry is still very much dependent on labor as a key component to the manufacturing process.

We are seeing a trend called **near-shoring**, which has the effect of reducing lead times by sourcing locally certain aspects of the product. Near-shoring allows for sourcing to take place closer to the point of manufacture, which enables a company to cut its lead times. **Re-shoring**, or bringing production back from a foreign country to the home country, is also being discussed as a way to reduce the time to market, and this may work well for certain products and aspects of the industry, but to date re-shoring is done in a very small portion of the business and in most cases fills a niche in the market. An example would be a men's knit shirt that was once produced in South Carolina and was then sourced in China and is now being produced in South Carolina again. Re-shoring still has to overcome the cost of labor in the local community.

There is only so much time you can take out of the physical production of a product, and once you involve transportation the equation becomes more difficult. Consumers can demand faster fashion and strides can be made to accommodate them, but the bottom line is that it takes time to produce apparel in meaningful quantities. The supplier base is critical to the efficient workings of the fashion industry. It is never static but must be attentive, flexible, and able to respond to the pressures placed upon it from the consumers, policies, technology, design, and trends. The supplier base would be nothing without the product to support the sourcing companies, and as discussed, this is a marketing-driven industry, with consumers driving the demand for the products they wish to consume. In essence the product becomes the king in the fashion industry equation.

## THE PRODUCT

The product, often called the "goods" in the fashion industry, is the result of sourcing and production, which depend upon a sound supplier base (see Figure 6.7). In the fashion industry **strategic line planning** is considered necessary in developing the end product. Whether it is women's wear, menswear, children's wear, or the variety of subcategories that make up the larger classifications of apparel and accessories, the conversation always comes back to the product. What does the consumer want, or, as with many cases in fashion, what do

**Figure 6.7**

**A display of menswear and women's wear** The product is often called the "goods" in fashion industry parlance. Here is a random sample of menswear and women's wear that can be bought in many retailers.

the industry, celebrities, sports figures, and others think the consumer wants? One could argue that for an overwhelming number of consumers the question is more what they want than what they actually need. That is what fashion is all about, and in order to perform at the highest level companies are always looking at ways to perfect the assortments that they offer for sale to the consumer.

## Strategic Line Planning

Boston Consulting Group (BCG) (2013) stated:

> Through our work with numerous clients, we have found that successful supply chains that effectively meet the needs of consumers share a common denominator: strategic line planning (SLP). Leading fashion companies utilize SLP each season to build a shared vision and strategy for the brand, product line, targeted consumers, planned volumes, and relative economic performance (including factors such as price and margin). (para 9)

> Furthermore, BCG (2013) identified that part of the SLP process includes consumer research, competitive benchmarks, utilization of trend forecasting models, and historical sales analysis, all linking back to the overall corporate strategy.

Along with the concept of SLP, consideration needs to be given to the product category (men's, women's, and children's) as well as where in the world the product will be produced and who the intended target is (wholesale or retail). In addition, once the product and place of production are identified, there needs to be focus on the following (BCG 2013):

- Reducing the cost of goods sold
- Ensuring transparency
- Integrating online and retail channels
- Balancing local, regional, and global responsibilities
- Aligning trends with consumer wants

How businesses address these five points hinges on the answers to the following simple questions.

## Where?

The question of where in the world the product should be sourced is often determined by the product itself, as certain countries and regions possess an expertise in a particular category; for example, Peru produces Pima cotton and China produces silk (see Figure 6.8).

The country chosen to establish a supply chain is sometimes predetermined. This means that the remainder of the supply chain must be balanced around that country or region. If there are no restrictions according to some area of expertise, then there is more freedom of choice in terms of where sourcing will take place, and additional considerations need to be taken into account (not that these same considerations would not apply to a predetermined country). For example:

- Social and political climate: Is the country open to trade? Are there any political restrictions in place that would prevent sourcing from this country? Trade agreements were covered in Chapter 2; how do they affect this aspect of the decision?

**Figure 6.8**

**Silk in the China textile industry** Silk is a mainstay of the Chinese textile industry and a major source of the silk that is used in the global fashion industry. Here are cocoons that were produced by silk caterpillars and that will be processed into silk yarn. Silk is often considered a luxury fiber/yarn/fabric, and depending on how the fiber is produced, it goes through many different processes and therefore costs more to produce than other natural fibers. Caterpillars (not worms) need to be raised so that they can create cocoons, which are transformed into yarns and then into fabrics. It is a lengthy process.

The supply chain can be a strong ally or detrimental to one's business. The key to a successful supply chain is to ask the right questions all along the chain. In this section we discuss infrastructure and the need to be certain that when you place orders with companies they can actually do what they say they can according to generally acceptable business practices. As you will see, not asking the right questions can lead to serious consequences. I recall doing business with a company that had production facilities in the Dominican Republic, which had in the past issues with a consistent electrical supply. One order that was placed with a factory called for garment washing, which the factory did well, but it neglected to inform me that it did not have an adequate power supply to run the dryers, and this was a heavy cotton shirt. On a trip to inspect final production, I was quite surprised to pull up to the factory to see several thousand of my shirts drying on makeshift clothes lines! Lesson learned: ask the questions to ensure a good supply chain.

- Infrastructure: Does the country have adequate roads and vehicles to move the product to the nearest port? Electrical and water supplies are necessary. Some countries may need to rely on generators for backup because the power often fails.
- Proclivity to natural disasters: Certain countries are more prone to floods and earthquakes. Bangladesh has a rainy season during which moving product to the port can be challenging, so time of year might be considered as well.
- Price: As a consideration this may or may not be a determining factor, depending on the product itself and the intended target market. This consideration, although important, should not be the only determinant because the lowest price is not always the best.

So often price is the driving factor that separates a company from an order, and in negotiating prices one has to be mindful of all aspects of the negotiation and realize that price may or may not be the most important factor. I once sat in on a price negotiation where the owner of the wholesale company pushed the factory owner very hard for a specific price that I knew was below the market price, and the factory owner finally agreed to the price. I was not happy with the way the negotiations had concluded, as it was clear to me that the factory owner was agreeing just for the sake of agreeing. I had a good rapport with the factory owner, so when the meeting was over I walked him to the elevator and asked him point blank if I was ever going to see the goods that we had just agreed upon during the negotiation. He politely responded no, that he would not be making the shirts for us and that he would be walking across the street to one of our competitors, who he knew would agree to his asking price and would sell to him the production that the owner of the wholesale company had agreed to. He said he would not hold up his end of the agreement. With this information, I developed a backup plan on how to replace the production, just in case, and sure enough a month before the intended delivery we received word that all the piece goods were defective and the supplier had to cancel our order. This was the factory owner's way of saving face with the owner of the wholesale company, as there was no way to hold the factory accountable if the fabric could not be used (which I knew was a lie). There is always a fair price, and squeezing the last dime out of the negotiation is not always the best practice.

- Economic instability: This may cause difficulty when trying to control events surrounding currency. Starting out, one should have a good indication of whether the currency and the economic capital of a particular country or region is stable or not.
- Cultural differences, language, religion, and holidays: These must always be prime considerations. In many instances the countries one will be trading with do not have English as their first and primary language. Being culturally aware and sensitive and having knowledge of cultural nuances will serve one well in one's relations with factories globally. Clear, concise communication is a necessity, and it is always beneficial to check and double-check.
- Trade agreements: These are in pace around the globe and play a major role in where production is placed. Trade agreements can help determine the flow of goods as well as have a direct impact on the cost of goods because there can be preferential treatment for a specific country in regards to tariffs.
- Corporate social responsibility (CSR) policies/ethical behavior: Not only do you have to consider CSR policies, but you also have to discuss ethical behavior. In some countries offering and accepting a bribe for certain considerations is considered culturally acceptable.

There are, of course, other considerations that one needs to take into account, and each country will present challenges that cannot be accounted for in these pages. The only way to ensure the sourcing of the right product from the right country at the right price and right time is to thoroughly research the country first, then the region, and then the factory itself.

### How?

Having identified the country and having agreed upon a factory, additional considerations relate to *how* one's own organization is set up. Will the organization provide fabric, trim, and packaging? Will the organization buy a complete package? Will these steps be fulfilled by personnel who work directly for the organization, or will the organization engage an agent to facilitate the transaction? If it is decided that an agent will work best, what is the commission rate that will be paid, and what will the agent's roles and responsibilities be? If it is determined that the organization will supply the fabric and the factory will supply the labor (cut, make, and trim), then the price negotiations will be different than if a full package is purchased. Some companies like to control the purchase of the fabric and provide the markers to cut against, while other companies (a large majority) prefer the complete package method. Some companies also work directly with the mills to select fabric and assign it to the factory. Regardless of the method, the price will need to be negotiated for the services rendered, and the most used method is "free on board" (FOB). Depicted in Figure 6.9 is a cargo ship that would be used to transport fashion goods around the globe; ships are directly related to the term *free on board* or FOB and are considered the most common means of shipping freight as they are often the most cost-effective.

### Shipping Choices

The term *free on board (FOB)* or, as many in the industry say, "freight on board," is commonly used in the procurement of goods from a factory. There are two ways

**Figure 6.9**

**A cargo ship** Cargo ships are the main means of transportation for most of the apparel and accessory products that are transported around the globe. They are a key factor in the logistics aspect of the supply chain. These ships can hold thousands of containers, which are offloaded directly onto trailers at major ports for transport via truck to multiple locations.

to determine FOB: origin and destination—"FOB origin" means that the seller pays for transportation of the goods to the port as well as the loading of the goods. The buyer takes ownership once the freight is secured on whatever method one is using for transportation (air or sea). The buyer is then responsible for paying the freight and any costs associated with clearing the goods (tariffs and drayage). The risk is to the buyer once the goods are loaded on board the means of conveyance. "FOB destination" means that the seller assumes freight costs to the final destination. FOB origin is the most common method in the apparel and textile industries.

Terms that are specific to the process are important to understand for communication. For example, **drayage** is the costs that one must pay to get the freight out of the port in addition to any other transportation costs to the warehouse or directly to the stores or consumers. Other terms that are used in conjunction with FOB are **full packages**, meaning that the seller (factory) provides all services to bring the product to market, which would include cost of fabric, trims, production, and packaging. If buyers state that they are buying a full package from overseas, it is generally understood that they mean they are purchasing the product FOB origin. If the seller clears the goods for export and delivers them on board bearing the cost of freight and insurance

to the port of entry named by the buyer, the term *cost insurance freight (CIF)* is applied. In essence the buyer is still buying the full package with the seller picking up the additional costs of the freight and insurance. This method is not very common because it raises the cost of goods sold to the buyer and therefore increases the amount of duty that will be owed once the goods clear customs at the point of entry. In the instance of FOB origin, the buyer controls the cost of the freight, and this is not included in the first cost, thereby lowering the tariff. Although in the case of CIF it is in the best interest of the seller to seek the lowest possible freight rates, it is not within the control of the buyer and could result in delayed lead times or in certain instances higher costs because the first cost could increase and result in a higher duty paid.

**Land duty paid (LDP)** is another method to bring goods into the United States (or any country) and means that the seller is assuming the cost of the goods plus freight and the tariff. The buyer receives the goods at port of entry, having paid the seller for not only the cost of the goods but also the cost of the freight and tariff. In this scenario the risk is assumed by the seller until the buyer takes possession at the point of entry. Although this can be negotiated, it is not a preferred method in the apparel and textile industry.

Like other aspects of the fashion industry, the "how" will vary from company to company and is determined somewhat by the product category and the size and scope of the company. The preceding discussion provides differing frameworks from which the industry operates and by no means is a complete listing of how one would work within the supply chain, but it does provide the key concepts from which to build a supplier base.

## CONCLUSION

A strong supplier base is foundational to ensure seamless and transparent sourcing and production that lead to a product that all of the key players, and most importantly the consumers, are satisfied with. Choosing the right supplier and understanding the process of how to work with and utilize that supplier are critical to having a productive and profitable supply chain and the best end product. Given the fluid nature of the fashion industry, as seen in the ever-changing and emerging trends, one must be able to work collaboratively to ensure a favorable product that consumers demand, when they demand it. New trends in sourcing such as near-shoring and re-shoring are to be considered when developing a supply chain; they are not the panacea that everyone is talking about but can be a part of one's overall sourcing philosophy. Line planning, deciding where and how the production is placed, caps off the sourcing and production topic and puts the overall process into perspective. Readers can think about how they can develop meaningful strategies that facilitate collaborative efforts between all of the key players, from the supplier base through sourcing and production, to ensure a best product for the consumer.

## INDUSTRY INTERVIEW: EDWARD HERTZMAN, *SOURCING JOURNAL*

Edward Hertzman, CEO and founder of Hertzman Media Group, took time out of his schedule to discuss his views on sourcing and production. The Hertzman Media Group is a media company within the apparel and textile industry whose goal is to "provide the knowledge and tools necessary for industry executives to make more informed business decisions" ("About Us" 2015: para 3). The *Sourcing Journal* is an online trade publication produced by the Hertzman Media Group that focuses on sourcing and manufacturing.

In addition to his work with the Media Group, Edward remains active in the fashion business as a partner in Brand Ministry (a men's wholesale and private-label company), and he continues to consult for apparel and retail brands. Edward brings to the text years of experience in the fashion industry and has in his own words provided us with insights into the industry from a professional perspective. As a current practitioner involved in the import of men's products, Edward is well suited to build on the information contained in this chapter. He has taken his passion for sourcing and production and created tools that will help others improve their own supply chains. Edward discusses how the *Sourcing Journal* helps inform and keep industry experts current with new trends and important topics relevant to the industry.

**Interviewer:** *Where did the idea for the* Sourcing Journal *come from?*

**E. H.:** I was twenty-six years old at the time and I was working for a large multinational sourcing company called Synergies Worldwide. Cotton prices were reaching historic highs, breaking records each day with no end in sight. In addition to the cotton pricing issues, brands and retailers were trying to find alternatives to China in order to combat the rising wages and raw material prices. Sourcing executives were facing unprecedented challenges. I was traveling quite a bit to Bangladesh and Pakistan at that time, bringing clients to both countries to present opportunities. Perhaps I took for granted the information I learned on the ground by spending so much time at the factory level, or maybe because of my youth, many veteran industry executives wouldn't listen to me and I became frustrated with the lack of valuable information the industry had at its disposable.

Starting *Sourcing Journal* seemed like a no brainer. Plus, I guess I wanted to prove to those veteran executives, who considered themselves know-it-alls, that they could always learn something new!

**Interviewer:** *What was the original mission of the* Sourcing Journal*? Has it changed? What are the plans for the future?*

**E. H.:** The mission was and has been the same: to be the most comprehensive news outlet for sourcing and supply chain executives in the apparel, textile, and footwear space.

That being said, I never imagined it would take off as quickly as it did, and so my life changed along the way. I now want Hertzman Media Group to be the largest media company for the apparel and footwear industry.

I envision *Sourcing Journal* as the homepage of the apparel and textile industry. We have begun to host an annual summit of sourcing executives. We've expanded our coverage by launching Vamp and Rivet. We plan to build a network of news sites, all focused on niches within the industry, and include a job portal called Apparel Executives connecting buyers to factories, agents, and sourcing services.

**Interviewer:** *What are the top issues facing executives in making sourcing and production decisions?*

**E. H.:** The biggest issue facing this industry is a lack of information. We are an underinformed industry. We have to stop thinking we know it all and realize the world is changing faster than what our industry can keep up with. How people shop, why people shop, where people shop has all changed. The entire supply chain needs an upgrade if it is to keep up with the pace at which consumers move.

I suppose this was the reason *Sourcing Journal* was created. If you look at Wall Street, it stays glued to CNBC, reads the *Wall Street Journal*, and the *Financial Times* (FT) to make sure it does not miss a beat. This is what our industry does to stay informed? The excuse I hear as to why someone doesn't subscribe to *Sourcing Journal* is that they do not have time to

read. Another very tangible issue is margin compression. The cost of goods at the factory level continues to increase. Labor costs, energy costs, food costs, inflation at the local level, plus the increase in compliance costs, have pushed freight on board (FOB) up across the board in every producing country. Additionally, the ticket prices at the retail level keep going down.

Whether it's heavy discounting, coupons, online price comparing, or showrooming, the consumer has been trained to pay less. If consumers want to pay less, then retailers want to buy the product for less and there lies the problem. If the margins are getting compressed from both ends, how does the sourcing executive overcome that?

Another issue is diminishing capacity. In my estimation, each year more factories close than factories open. The price of land and the opportunity to expand into more profitable and prestigious industries leaves little reason for the next generation of textile families or new entrepreneurs to venture into this business. Couple this with the shrinking pool of factories and expertise along with a growing demand for apparel from the exploding middle class in China and India, and the demand for factory space will only continue to increase.

I see more and more capacity being booked in China by local Chinese brands, thus limiting capacity for all others. The Western mindset that the factories are eager for business has changed. I believe the factory owner is the new king. We need to respect that and try to create a lasting partnership. Today, how we buy is more important than how we sell. I implore everyone to rethink how they treat their supply chain. The idea of hopping factory to factory with each order is changing.

**Interviewer:** *In what countries can we expect to see more or less production coming from, and why?*

**E. H.:** From a statistical point of view China is going nowhere. While production continues to migrate from there to places like Vietnam and Bangladesh, China remains the top exporter by a long shot.

If Trans Pacific Partnership (TPP) passes we will see an even larger push for Vietnam. The country is clearly planning for it, and a lot of local and foreign investment has been made there.

There is also a lot of talk about Africa, which I think will prove to be a place of opportunity, but it will take time and investment. Companies like PVH and VF, who are vocal and public about Africa, are taking a strategic and long-term position on the region. Infrastructure needs to be upgraded. The labor force, while plentiful, needs to be trained. Africa will be a place for basic, programmed business. I do not believe Africa will be known for quick turn, fast fashion, value-added products anytime soon.

As the need for quicker turn becomes essential, near-sourcing, whether the Americas for the US or Eastern Europe for the EU, may see upticks. Still, there are price and product limitations to these regions. The percentage increases will be there, but total volume will still be quite small compared to China—even shrinking China.

**Interviewer:** *How has technology improved or changed the sourcing decision-making process?*

**E. H.:** Technology has made the sourcing process more accessible and transparent. We are able to hop on a plane and get to any country and therefore any factory in the world. We can speak to our agents, local offices, or factories in real time daily through Skype or WhatsApp. Technology is making information more accessible and faster to access. In addition companies like Lectra and Gerber Technologies are continually developing new software packages that change the way offices around the globe interface with each other.

## Questions Pertaining to Interview

1. Edward Hertzman made the comment that one of the biggest issues the industry is faced with is that it is underinformed. As you think about this statement, how do you envision yourself becoming more informed about this industry?

2. Mr. Hertzman talks about diminished capacity as it relates to factories and manufacturing. What are your thoughts about this idea of diminished capacity?

3. Consider what Mr. Hertzman means when he discusses global capacity. What are your thoughts?

## CASE STUDY: Rana Plaza Factory, Bangladesh

In this chapter we focused on sourcing and production, and that topic would not be complete without a conversation surrounding corporate social responsibility (CSR). Although we dedicated the entire Chapter 3 to CSR, it is important to revisit it here. In today's fashion industry supply chain, CSR has taken center stage; whether it is a small company focused on sustainability such as California Cloth Foundry or a mega brand like Nike, the end goal of improving CSR throughout the supply chain remains relevant. Sourcing and production touch all aspects of the fashion industry supply chain from fiber to finished goods, with much of the emphasis focusing on the factory floor. It is here that the impact on human capital can be felt the most. Instances of child labor, forced overtime, poor working conditions, lack of freedom to associate, suspect buildings, and low wages are a few of the conditions that CSR continues to address and that affect all stakeholders.

In 2013 the Rana Plaza Factory in Bangladesh collapsed, killing 1,135 people, most of them workers in the factory. The building collapse also injured thousands. This tragedy further highlighted the need for apparel companies to take action on their CSR stance. The building contained clothing factories, a bank, apartments, and several other shops. The majority of the workers in the factory accounted for most of the dead. The shops and the bank on the lower floors immediately closed after cracks were discovered in the building. Warnings to avoid using the building after cracks appeared the day before had not been acted upon. Instead garment workers were virtually forced by the factory manager to return the following day to work. The building collapsed during the morning rush hour.

Factory safety has increased, unfortunately, only after such tragedies have occurred. The certifying bodies referenced in Chapter 3 now inspect the physical plant, but more needs to be done. Although there is increased emphasis on the physical structures that house many of the factories in the fashion industry supply chain, more people need to be held accountable for the safety and well-being of those who work supplying consumers with apparel and accessories for their own personal consumption.

**Case Study Questions**

1. What, if any, responsibility should the companies that place business in these factories bear for such tragedies?
2. Where does the fault lie, with the owner of the building, the local government, and/or the retailers?
3. What lessons were learned from this and other tragedies that have occurred in Bangladesh?
4. What decisions would you make as a sourcing manager regarding placing business in factories in Bangladesh?
5. Does policy and law have a place in protecting workers? Explain.

# CHAPTER REVIEW QUESTIONS

1. What technologies do you see impacting the supply chain, either now or in the future?
2. Consider the terms *production* and *sourcing*. What do you see as the differences and similarities between the two terms? How are they interrelated?
3. The term *transparency* is used in the chapter; identify and provide examples of two different fashion companies that you feel are transparent. How is this message communicated to the consumer?
4. Can re-shoring in the fashion industry become a reality?
5. Define FOB, CIF, and LDP and give examples of how they would be used in the fashion industry.

# CLASS EXERCISE

Identify a retail organization (can be any level of distribution). As a new product developer for the retail organization, you are to set up a sourcing scenario answering the following questions:

• Identify a product category, for example, men's dress shirts, women's casual pants, or children's outerwear.

The category can be any that your retailer offers to the consumer, and just one category is required.

• Identify a country from which you will source your products.
• What type of government does this country have?

- What is the current economic condition of the country?
- Identify three factories in the country that you will source your products from. These must be real factories making the specific product that you have chosen to manufacture. Based on your research, decide on one factory where you will place your business and explain why you chose that specific factory.
- Based on your knowledge of the retailer (number of stores, floor space dedicated to your category), determine what an opening order should be for the upcoming season in units (round numbers). How many times will the inventory turn in a six-month season? How much stock will you require to hold in the warehouse? The buy will be for the entire six-month season, including initial distribution and reorders.
- What is the lead time to manufacture the products at the factory level?

- What is the transit time from factory to your warehouse?
- How will you ship from the factory? To the stores?
- How will the garments be inspected at the factory site, and by whom?
- Create an itinerary for a two-week trip, including airfare, hotel, date of departure, and return; all cost aspects for the trip must be included, such as meals. The purpose of the trip is to find new factories and to visit the three that you have selected, so the trip is to the country that you are sourcing from.
- Can you think of any other question to reflect upon during your visit that will heighten your sense of corporate social responsibility?

Some of the questions can be answered in bullet form, others in more detail.

## KEY TERMS

sourcing
production
supplier base
fast fashion
trends

omnichannel model
near-shoring
re-shoring
strategic line planning
free on board

drayage
full package
cost insurance freight (CIF)
landed duty paid (LDP)

## REFERENCES

1. "About Us" (2015), *Sourcing Journal*. Available online: https://www.sourcingjournalonline.com/about-us/.
2. Boston Consulting Group (2013), "Rethinking the Fashion Supply Chain: Fast, Flexible, and Lean," BCG Perspectives. Available online: https://www .bcgperspectives.com/content/articles/retail _supply_chain_management_fast_flexible_lean _rethinking_fashion_supply_chain/.
3. Clark, J. (2015), *Fashion Merchandising: Principles and Practice*, London: Macmillan Education Palgrave.
4. Donaldson, T. (2015), "Experts on Sourcing: What to Expect in 2015," *Sourcing Journal*. Available online: https://sourcingjournalonline.com/experts-sourcing -expect-2015-td/.
5. *The Guardian* (2016), "Rana Plaza Collapse: 38 Charged with Murder over Garment Factory Disaster." Available online: https://www.theguardian.com /world/2016/jul/18/rana-plaza-collapse-murder -charges-garment-factory.

6. Inglis, P. (1998), "Strong Supply Relationships Reduce Cost, Spark Innovation," *Purchasing*, 124 (1): 45.
7. Ireton, S. (2009), "10 Factors to Consider When Sourcing Globally," *JOC.Com*. Available online: http://www.joc.com/content/10-factors-consider -when-sourcing-globally.
8. Lewis, R. (2016), "Q & A with David Jaffe," *Robin Report*. Available online: http://www.therobinreport .com/qa-with-david-jaffe/.
9. Morgan, J. (1993), "Five Areas Where Suppliers Can Be Your Competitive Edge," *Purchasing*, 115 (8): 6.
10. "Supplier Relations" (2015), *Reference for Business*. Available online: http://www.referenceforbusiness. com/small/Sm-Z/Supplier-Relations.html.
11. WebFinance, Inc. (2016a), "Production," *Business Dictionary*. Available online: http://www.business dictionary.com/definition/production.html.
12. WebFinance, Inc. (2016b), "Sourcing," *Business Dictionary*. Available online: http://www.businessdictionary .com/definition/sourcing.html.

# Quality Assurance

## LEARNING OBJECTIVES

Upon completion of this chapter you will be able to:

- Understand the meaning of quality and how it applies to the fashion industry.

- Analyze the elements that make up quality assurance.

- Identify ways in which quality is administered in the fashion industry.

# QUALITY AND QUALITY ASSURANCE

This chapter will look at quality and quality assurance in the fashion industry as it relates to the supply chain. The industry is made up of many different players: wholesalers, jobbers, brands, designers, and retailers. Each of these organizations has its own view of what quality is, integrates processes that will ensure that quality, and uses price as one of the determining factors in defining the quality of the products that it offers. This chapter describes quality and the various models and processes that are used to ensure a quality product, with the understanding that there are many different levels of quality and various processes that are used to achieve a level of acceptable quality. To understand how ensuring quality took center stage, we can review a little history.

**Figure 7.1**

**Aftermath of bombing in Japan** Japan after World War II was in dire need of rebuilding. Depicted here is the aftermath of the bombing that occurred during the war. It is here that W. Edwards Deming first started to employ his theories of quality assurance.

## The Beginning

Quality, quality assurance (QA), total quality management (TQM), and quality management systems (QMS)—no matter what you call it, the goal is the same: to provide a quality product that the consumer wants to buy and to develop loyal customers based on that quality. W. Edwards Deming is known as the man who discovered quality (Gabor 1990). Deming first started his work in Japan helping the Japanese rebuild the country after World War II (Figure 7.1). Although Deming is not known for work in the fashion industry, the same principles and ideas that were born out of his work are still applicable to the global fashion supply chain.

Deming's work in Japan did not go unnoticed in the United States. Detroit automakers were the first to take particular notice and reached out to him seeking his help in rebuilding the US auto industry, which was losing a large market share to imports during the 1970s because of lack of quality. Deming developed a Fourteen Point philosophy that guided him and led to his success. Point number one is the point that primarily guides the quality discussion for the fashion industry; it states, "Quality is defined by the customer. Improvement in products and processes must be aimed at anticipating customers' future needs. Quality comes from improving process, not from 'inspecting out' the shoddy results of a poorly run process" (Gabor 1990: 18). The fashion industry would do well to embrace Deming's teaching, as the industry often neglects future needs and focuses on the immediate in trying to get the best possible product to the consumer.

At times people in the industry also focus too much on price to the detriment of quality. Andrew Carnegie once said:

> I have never known a concern to make a decided success that did not do good, honest work, and even in these days of the fiercest competition, when everything would seem to be a matter of price, there lies at the root of great business success the very much more important factor of quality. The effect of attention to quality upon every man in the service, from the president of the concern down to the humblest laborer, cannot be overestimated. (Forbes Quotes 2015)

As Carnegie stated, there is more to the product than just price, but it is price that helps set the value on the quality that is built into the product. One can think of a discount retail store and a high-end department store. In each of these forums, the retail prices that are charged vary widely from retailer to retailer, and it could be said that the quality does as well; however, sometimes there is a misconception regarding the price-value relationship of fashion goods. Just because it is expensive does not guarantee that it is of the highest quality.

# The Three Q's?

Quality can mean different things to different people. For some it is an intangible, as it comes down to consumer perceptions. Merriam-Webster's dictionary ("Quality" 2016) defines **quality** as "how good or bad something is; a characteristic or feature that someone or something has; something that can be noticed as a part of a person or thing; a high level of value or excellence." In the fashion industry, therefore, quality has to do with the value of every action and the end product of all actions, from the beginning of the supply chain to the product that is delivered to the consumer. Is that product what consumers expected, and consequently how satisfied are they with the product that they purchased? Does this drive them to be loyal customers?

**Quality assurance** as defined by Merriam-Webster's dictionary ("Quality Assurance" 2016) is "the activity of checking goods or services to make sure that they are good." In other words, how can those in the fashion industry assure consumers that every action taken is carried out and accomplished with quality in mind? What are the specific actions and activities that take place in the checking of goods? And what policies, procedures, and protocols have been put into place to ensure that these actions and activities are integrated into the workings of the organization and in fact the entire supply chain, consistently? According to Mahmood, Zubair, and Salam (2015), companies throughout the supply chain must be able to please the consumer base, as "any organization's main and primary focus is satisfaction of its customers" (100). Companies try to ensure that the consumer receives a quality product, and the methods used to satisfy that consumer have a direct impact on the fashion industry supply chain. The fashion industry, while developing product for sale to the consumer, should strive for a degree of excellence in order to satisfy the consumer's immediate need and to develop a loyal customer based on that level of satisfaction.

Given the importance of quality, how do those in the fashion industry ensure that the products produced are quality products? How is quality controlled for? How is quality sustained over time? **Total quality management** is one approach. According to Ash (1992), total quality management (TQM) is an alternative approach to the traditional management approaches of the past. The TQM approach requires management practices to be "restructured to improve performance and product quality and customer satisfaction" (82). This restructuring focuses on teamwork, the full participation of employees as active decision makers, as well as on leaders who are comfortable with and open to sharing power and decision-making (Glorioso 1994). Thus, there is a flattening of the organization, from a hierarchy to empowerment of the employee (Winn 1996). Furthermore, in TQM there needs to be an overall willingness to analyze the workings or the processes that are in place throughout the organization as well as the supply chain—to ensure quality by continually questioning and seeking ways to make continuous improvement and by continually being aware of the consumer's needs and desires. At first, this alternative management approach may be difficult to achieve, and it is a process that takes time to understand and integrate (Winn 1996). A more contemporary view of TQM may be gleaned from **Six Sigma** (Hashmi 2000–16), which documents TQM as "a management philosophy that seeks to integrate all organizational functions (marketing, finance, design, engineering, and production, customer service, etc.) to focus on meeting customer needs and organizational objectives. TQM views an organization as a collection of processes. It maintains that organizations must strive to continuously improve these processes by incorporating the knowledge and experiences of workers" (3).

Over time, TQM became the gold standard. However, the emphasis then changed to the quality management system (QMS):

> In the late 20th century, independent organizations began producing standards to assist in the creation and implementation of quality management systems. It is around this time that the phrase "Total Quality Management" began to fall out of favor. Because of the multitude of unique systems that can be applied, the term "Quality Management System" or "QMS" is preferred. At the start of the 21st century, QMS had begun to merge with the ideas of sustainability and transparency, as these themes became increasingly important to consumer satisfaction. The ISO 9001 audit regime deals with both quality and sustainability and their integration into organizations. (American Society for Quality n.d.: para 10)

Quality management systems and the International Organization for Standardization (ISO) are further discussed later in this chapter. What is important to note is that these more contemporary perspectives are systematic in their approaches, involve all key stakeholders, and rely on data to inform decisions about processes and quality.

# PRINCIPLES AND PROCESSES

According to the *Business Dictionary* ("Principles" 2016), principles are "fundamental norms, rules, or values that represent what is desirable and positive for a person, group, organization, or community, and help it in determining the rightfulness or wrongfulness of its actions." These norms, rules, and values are synergistic with the philosophy of TQM as documented by the previous Six Sigma definition. The International Organization for Standardization (2015: 3) noted that there are seven quality management principles: customer focus, leadership, engagement of people, process approach, improvement, evidence-based decision-making, and relationship management.

A more detailed discussion of these principles follows. First, the activities and primary actions taken by any organization should always be *customer focused* and meet the customer's expectations. To do this will require *leaders* in the organization who provide a context in which all employees are accountable and assume participatory responsibility in all matters, including decision-making. The *engagement* of employees, on all levels, will require leaders to be diligent in assessing employee needs and in developing plans to meet those needs. For example, leaders may need to educate employees so that they are able to reach a level of comfort with their participation. The education may include information on how to work in teams within the organization, as well as education concerning how to deal with conflict and negotiation as the team works toward a final decision (see Figure 7.2).

Another need may be to work together collectively in teams so that all employees are doing what they say they should do in regards to TQM. Decisions pertaining to the processes that are in place to achieve a quality end product may include, for example, discussions about product development, fiber selection, sales, and

**Figure 7.2**

**Individuals working together as a team** These employees are working on a team-building exercise. Teams help break down silos and foster better quality outcomes in the supply chain. The design team must understand not only what the sourcing and production teams are thinking but all other aspects that are affected by quality so that when they are developing their concepts they have the consumer in mind and what their expected quality outcomes are.

marketing. To carry out this type of discussion, information must be collected across the supply chain that provides *evidence* as to what works well and what needs to be improved so that it can work better (this is also where big data comes in). An organization will need to discuss what helps and what doesn't help to improve the supply chain processes that sustain quality, with an eye toward ongoing and continuous *improvement*. Assessments also need to be carried out to determine what resources may be needed. Ultimately, each organization must identify what *processes* need to be in place both within the specific organization and across all organizations in the supply chain to ensure quality.

Once these processes are identified, formal protocols can ensure that quality is achieved and sustained over time. For example, an organization that prides itself on teamwork will need to develop formal processes. What is the process for team development? Who will be on the team? How will the team function when it is decision time? Will it be by consensus or by a vote? How are members selected, and when a member leaves the group, how will new members be selected? What education will be provided to learn about building and sustaining teams? Will the members be given time to attend meetings? Will team membership only represent members from a specific organization, or will others in the supply chain be members? These are just a few of the questions that are raised about team and team building and the types of processes that need to be addressed. Finally, *relationship management* is key within an organization and across the organizations within a supply chain. How do people in any organization and across the supply chain relate to one another through communication and also through the trust that hopefully develops over time?

Implementing TQM that exemplifies these philosophies, principles, and processes is not an easy task. Over the decades ideas have evolved on how to implement systems changes that foster quality. Some models have come and gone by the wayside. This is not a sign of failure but rather a sign of success, as organizations have used evidence to ask critical questions that will enhance quality and quality processes.

## APPROACHES AND METHODOLOGIES

There are four prominent approaches to achieving quality and customer satisfaction. The first approach, Six Sigma, is an approach that is used to enhance not only a business but also the systems of the business, with the overall objective of increasing profits while at the same time sustaining customer satisfaction. Sustaining customer satisfaction is achieved by both producing a quality product and maintaining the quality of that product along with customer service. The Six Sigma approach is a systematic design to enhance the processes of an organization, and it relies on various methods.

The second approach is termed lean. "The core idea is to maximize customer value while minimizing waste. Simply, lean means creating more value for customers with fewer resources" (Lean Enterprise Institute 2000–16: para 1). Elimination of waste is a part of the lean approach. It is about improving efficiency and decreasing errors, which in turn lead to a decrease in the cost of operations and ultimately greater customer and employee satisfaction. Lean is about making improvements through small steps and is ongoing. It does this by looking at how an organization is operationalized or

how the organization accomplishes its work. Those who integrate the lean approach use information or data to drive decisions, and improvement is never-ending.

The lean approach is frequently combined with the Six Sigma approach. For example, there are eight wastes that have been documented: (1) defects in a product; (2) overproduction, which means the product lies stagnant in a warehouse or is sold below cost; (3) waiting, which wastes energy, time, and money; (4) nonvalue processing or overprocessing, which wastes time and money; (5) transportation; (6) inventory; (7) motion; and (8) underutilization of employee talent (GoLeanSixSigma 2012–2016: para 1). An organization may use TQM and apply the principles and processes of TQM in the elimination of waste.

A third approach is the application of a **quality management system (QMS)**, which is defined as a "formalized system that documents processes, procedures, and responsibilities for achieving quality policies and objectives. QMS helps coordinate and direct an organization's activities to meet customer and regulatory requirements and improve its effectiveness and efficiency" (American Society for Quality [ASQ] n.d.: para 1). There is also a fourth approach, an international standard that documents the requirements for quality management systems, known as the **ISO 9001**. The ISO 9001 is the only standard that certifies quality management systems, although this is not a requirement. There are over one million companies representing many nations who are certified to ISO 9001. This standard speaks to a number of quality management principles.

In the fashion industry some companies have formally adopted one of these processes, and some have adopted organic programs based on the goal of supplying the best possible product at the price that the consumer is willing to pay. The processes and procedures that are used in the production and manufacturing of fashion goods are often dictated by the customer. That customer could be the same company for whom the goods are being produced or a contractor whose main role is to provide finished goods. In this instance *customer* does not mean the end consumer who will ultimately purchase the product at retail but the company for which the product is being made. Much of what is dictated by the customer is contained in the vendor compliance manuals that we have discussed in other chapters.

Today some fashion companies will require you to adopt one of the formal standards in order to do business with them. It is also worth noting that in the past quality focused on the products themselves, but with current efforts toward corporate social responsibility and sustainability, the issue of quality has grown in scope to include the physical plant and equipment as well as human capital. This was not always the case; thankfully, the industry recognized the need to improve.

# ESSENTIAL STEPS IN QUALITY MANAGEMENT SYSTEMS IN THE FASHION INDUSTRY

Today, with the new thinking around QMS, the philosophy has grown and now includes seven steps: design, build, deploy, control, measure, review, and improve (ASQ n.d.: para 14). What follows is a discussion of each of these steps from a fashion industry perspective.

The *design* of a product is a creation that is carried out either by an individual (designer) or a team of product developers or merchandisers. Design generally begins by identifying products that will satisfy a consumer need. The process of designing is really the origin of the supply chain and will ultimately affect the way the supply chain is administered, based on the type of product that is designed and the ultimate market it is intended for. Furthermore, if an organization has an eye on quality, the designer will raise questions about the present workings of the supply chain and whether the supply chain is able to develop and deliver the end product that is being designed.

After the product is designed, it has to be "built" or constructed. A size specification sheet and a make detail sheet (see Table 7.1) are developed that will convey not only size information to the production facility but all the details that are required to construct the product. Much of this work today is completed using computer aided design (CAD) programs. These sheets become a roadmap for "building" the product. Table 7.1 illustrates a single stock keeping unit (sku) that is laid out in one size range (not fully graded). If the full spec sheet were present, it would show all sizes and in order to grade the garment you would add and detract measurements to complete the grading process. These two items form the basis of what is known in the fashion industry as a "tech pac." Designers, merchandisers, and product developers, as well as members of the sourcing and production teams, often refer to the "tech pac" or "tech pack" as the complete package or the roadmap for all parties to follow. Properly completed teck pacs are critical in determining costing, which informs the key decision of whether to produce the product or not. If the tech pac reveals a cost that is too high, then the decision to proceed can be halted, or the design team may be instructed to go back and review all the elements that make up the garment and/or accessory to see if they can reduce the cost by taking out elements or changing the physical makeup of the product. The tech pac further indicates the level of quality that is sought in the final product by providing vital information related to size and construction, such as number of stitches per inch. All this information is checked further down the supply line (Figure 7.3).

There is yet another aspect of building that an organization may wish to consider: the buildout of the supply chain and whether or not the supply chain and the corresponding processes can deliver the specifications identified in Table 7.1.

Today, through the use of advanced technology, companies are using product lifecycle management (PLM) systems or enterprise resource planning (ERP) systems to *deploy* and communicate all the information that is being designed and built. These systems have greatly reduced the time it takes to communicate vital information to trading partners throughout the supply chain, and hence they cut down on lead time and greatly improve the supply chain process. This involves lean thinking.

Policies, procedures, and protocols also need to be put in place to *control* the process or to ensure that the process is unfolding in a systematic way. People and resources must be used to identify areas that need to be monitored on a regular basis. For example, there is the simple need to be aware of the calendar. Given how the seasons overlap and the number of products that any given company can be working on at one time and throw into a fast fashion supply chain, one can quickly lose control if checks and balances are not in place. And how can one organization "control" what is taking place in a partnering organization that may exist across the globe? What QMS can be put into place?

**Table 7.1** Size Specification Sheet and Make Detail Sheet

| | | | | | | |
|---|---|---|---|---|---|---|
| **Company:** XYZ Menswear | | **Size Class:** Men's | **Product Type:** Tailored Dress Pants | | | |
| **Description** | **Style** | **Fabric** | **Description** | **Original Size** | **Care** | **Instructions** |
| | RN90736 | 100% Wool | Tailored Dress Pants | 34/34 | Dry Clean Only | |
| **SIZE SPECIFICATIONS** | | | | | | |
| **Size Specification with Tolerances** | **Waist** | **Seat** | **Knee** | **Inseam** | **Outseam** | **Rise** |
| | 34 +/- $^1/_2$ inch | 23 +/- $^1/_8$ inch | 10.5 +/- $^1/_8$ inch | 34 +/- $^1/_2$ inch | 44 +/- $^1/_2$ inch | 11 +/- $^1/_8$ inch |

| MAKE DETAIL SHEET | | | | | | |
|---|---|---|---|---|---|---|
| **Description** | | **Measurement** | | | | |
| Waistband | | Width = 1 $^1/_4$ inches; Length = 34 inches | | | | |
| Pockets | | | | | | |
| Backside traditional besom pocket | | Width = 5 $^1/_4$ inches; Length = $^1/_2$ inch | | | | |
| Location | | 2 $^1/_4$ inches from left and right side seams; 3 $^3/_4$ inches from top of waistband | | | | |
| Depth of pocket (inside of pant) | | 8 inches from the bottom of the waistband; 4 $^3/_4$ inches from the pocket seam | | | | |
| Backside traditional besom pocket button | | Width = $^5/_8$ inch; Quantity 2 | | | | |
| Location | | $^1/_2$ inch from top of traditional besom pocket; 2 $^3/_8$ inches from the left side of the pocket; located in both backside pockets | | | | |
| Backside tradition besom pocket | | 1 inch; Quantity 2 | | | | |
| Button hole | | how many | | | | |
| Location | | 1/2 inch from top of seam; 2 1/2 inches from the left side of the pocket; located on both pockets | | | | |
| Side Hand Pocket | | Length: 6 1/4 inches along the side crease of pants; Quantity 2 | | | | |
| Location | | 2 inches from top of the waistband | | | | |
| Depth of pocket (inside of pant) | | 12 inches from bottom of waistband; width = 6 1/2 inches | | | | |
| Front Side Belt Loops | | Width = 1/2 inch; Length = 2 inches | | | | |
| Location | | 2 inches from top of the waistband | | | | |

(continued)

**Table 7.1** Size Specification Sheet and Make Detail Sheet (*continued*)

| MAKE DETAIL SHEET | | | | | | |
|---|---|---|---|---|---|---|
| **Description** | | **Measurement** | | | | |
| Depth of pocket (inside of pant) | | 12 inches from bottom of waistband; Width = 6 1/2 inches | | | | |
| *Front Side Belt Loops* | | Width = 1/2 inch; Length = 2 inches | | | | |
| Right hand side facing pant, pant loop | | 1/2 inch form button hole flap | | | | |
| Left hand side facing pant, pant loop | | 1 inch from inside flap seam | | | | |
| *Backside Belt Loops* | | Width = 1/2 inch; Length = 2 inches | | | | |
| Right hand side facing pant, pant loop | | 1 1/4 inches from right hand seam | | | | |
| Left hand side facing pant, pant loop | | 1 1/4 inches from left hand seam | | | | |
| Right center back pant loop | | 6 1/2 inches from the right hand seam | | | | |
| Left center back pant loop | | 6 1/2 from the left hand seam | | | | |
| *Hardware* | | | | | | |
| YKK metal zipper | | Length = 8 inches | | | | |
| Location | | 1 1/4 inches from top of waistband; 12 inches from left side seam | | | | |
| *Functional Buttons and Button Holes* | | Buttons = Four Holes; Stitch = Cross stitched; Thread Color = Dyed to match | | | | |
| Inside closing button on top flap | | Width = 5/8 inch; 4 1/2 inches from end of flap; 1/2 inch from top of waistband | | | | |
| Corresponding button hole on inside flap | | Width = 3/4 inch; 1/2 inch from end of inside flap; 1 3/4 inches from top of waistband | | | | |
| Closing button on inside flap | | Width = 5/8 inch; 4 1/2 inches from end of inside flap; 1/2 inch from top of waistband | | | | |
| Corresponding button hole on outside flap | | Width = 3/4 inch; 1/2 inch from end of inside flap; 1 3/4 inches from top of waistband | | | | |
| *Labels* | | | | | | |
| XYZ logo | | Width = 1 inch; Length = 2 1/2 inches | | | | |
| Locations | | On right hand side of front of pant; 10 3/4 inches from right hand seam; 1 1/2 inches from top of waistband | | | | |

Developed by Michael P. Londrigan.

**Figure 7.3**

**Garment factory worker measuring garments**
A garment factory worker is measuring garments to ensure that they meet the specifications that were established in the development process. Quality assurance happens at various stages in the production process and involves inline inspections, random sampling, and finished garment inspections. To ensure complete compliance with the original size specifications and make details, finished garment inspections should occur at the factory prior to shipment and after the goods arrive at their destination prior to shipping to the customer.

Having systems in place is meaningless unless there are ways to *measure* performance. The points of measurement are determined by the companies involved in the process and are predetermined and agreed upon at the outset of each negotiation. Several activities to measure are the purchase of the fiber, the development of yarn, the creation of a fabric, and the production of finished garments. *Measures* in this instance may not be the physical measuring of garments but measures of how the overall process is progressing. Does the company need to intervene to remediate a certain situation, say, a late delivery or perhaps a fabric that failed a quality test? Each of these points along the supply chain requires the measurement of quality to ensure that the outcomes are as desired.

Finally, to understand how well an organization or company is working, there must be a *review* process to help determine next steps with an eye toward continuous *improvement.*

Quality practices can and should appear at any point in the supply chain and can be instituted or managed by any of the trading partners. It is about building quality throughout the entire production process and the supply chain (Burnes, Mullet, and Bryand 2016). Designers, buyers, production workers, and all employees involved in the product pipeline must work to ensure that consumers "get what they pay for." Quality becomes a winning strategy for consumers, retailers, and manufacturers when executed properly. Setting up QMS is an intensive process that is people centered and that rests on the establishment of standards. When general standards are written for specific products, they are generally called specifications. Specifications are more specific than standards and contain additional details beyond the general descriptors used in standards. To be useful to all personnel and to be viable tools in a global marketplace,

---

## Notes from the Field

Today we have tools at our disposal that did not exist while I was working in industry, and if they did, they were very expensive and only the very large companies could afford them. Today PLM and ERP systems come in all shapes and sizes and are quite affordable, but prior to the advent of PLM and ERP systems we relied on overseas curriers to send packages back and forth to our trading partners around the globe. Yes, you could "fax" a copy of a size specification sheet, but you could not send your make detail sheets, which included all your trim items (buttons, labels, hangtags, etc.), via fax. You had to physically pack and ship them. One of the companies I worked for used DHL, an international shipping service, as its preferred carrier, and every day at around 4 p.m. the receptionists would get on the public address system and announce "DHL is here," and everyone in the production department would panic trying to get the packages together. Although they knew DHL was coming, it occurred almost every day! So much for thinking lean.

standards and specifications must be easily understood, measurable, and electronically communicable. Here are several considerations for developing a working QMS for a fashion company:

- Creation of a working specification sheet (see Table 7.1)
- Creation of a make detail sheet to accompany the specification sheet (this will vary from company to company but is viewed as a comprehensive writeup describing the actual product in words) (see Table 7.1)
- Setting of tolerances (to be conveyed in the spec sheet)
- Development of a sampling plan
- Execution of the sampling plan, including physical testing
- Review of data
- Adjustments to product (if necessary) based on review of data
- Preproduction samples
- Production samples
- Finished garment audit
- Decisions based on the review of data

The specification sheet will be predetermined by the design team, product developer, and/or merchandiser and will be based on consumer expectations for this particular product. Size specifications vary from designer to designer, company to company, and retailer to retailer. The fashion industry does not have universal size specifications, and it is generally accepted that it is the designer's idea of what the consumer wants that will dictate the actual size specifications.

It is important to understand how a sampling plan (which will determine how many units would need to be inspected to verify that the shipment meets the original standards that were established) is developed. For years military standard 105 (formally known as MIL-STD-105E) was used as a guide for establishing the sampling plan and was based on a statistically significant random sampling model. Today Ansi ASQ Z1.4 has replaced military standard 105 as the method for developing a sampling plan based on physical attributes of the end product. In addition to the actual measuring of the garments, there are physical tests that must be conducted on fabric, findings, trim, and full garments. Following is a list of the various points in the supply chain at which a quality inspection of some sort should take place for apparel:

- Fiber, whether natural or synthetic, must be inspected and meet certain standards because it is the beginning of the process; if the fiber is of poor quality, the rest of the product will follow suit.
- Yarn, which is required to knit, weave, or create a nonwoven, must be of a certain quality or the fabric and finished garment will not meet the standards that have been set up.

## Notes from the Field

One topic that is not generally discussed in the same sentence as the supply chain is ethics. All along the supply chain there are opportunities to abuse the system and to make money if you do not value your own personal ethics. My ethics were tested many times over the years; once while I was in a country working with one of my customers, the owner of the company that I was employed with asked me to conduct a quality inspection of some woven shirts that we were producing for a retail customer. I arrived at the factory, and since the order was for 15,000 shirts, I had set up the entire day to complete the audit. Using military standard 105 with an accepted quality level of 1.0 and a double sample method, my chart told me that I had to randomly select and inspect 315 garments. Out of the 315, if 5 or fewer failed, you accepted the lot, or if more failed, you rejected the lot. In this case I had to reject the lot. The factory owner was not happy because the factory would have to resize the entire 15,000 shirts to conform and be accepted. He promptly offered me a cash bribe of $10,000.00 to look the other way. I of course rejected the bribe and the shipment!

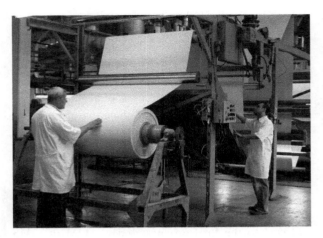

**Figure 7.4**

**Worker inspecting fabric for defects** Fabric inspection is a critical aspect of the quality assurance protocol. If a defect is detected, it is mapped so that when the fabric is cut into garment pieces the cutter knows just where the defect will appear. If there are too many defects the fabric will be rejected. This process can occur at the mill before the goods are shipped and again upon receipt at the factory before cutting occurs.

- *Fabric* inspections are made before the fabric leaves the mill as well as when it is received by the manufacturer (see Figure 7.4). At the manufacturer, fabric can be inspected on the roll and then again on the cutting table.

- Finished garments are inspected in the manufacturing line while the garments are being produced and generally at the end of production prior to packing to make sure that the final product adheres to the original specifications. In addition, final customers may or may not execute their own inspections. If the garments were purchased with a letter of credit (LC), discussed in Chapter 10, the bank will require a completed certificate verifying that the shipment was inspected to the satisfaction of the customer before releasing funds to the manufacturer.

As with all things related to the supply chain, when individuals touch the product, whether it is at the fiber stage or finished garment stage, they want to be paid for their services, and this holds true even if the people responsible for the inspections are on the company payroll, as there is a cost associated with their time that must be accounted for. Thus quality assurance involves cost considerations as well.

# ADMINISTERING QUALITY PROGRAMS IN THE FASHION INDUSTRY

## Internal Quality Assurance

Large fashion companies (brands and retailers) often have in-house departments that are responsible for the quality aspect of the products that they produce and sell to the consumer. Many of these companies have teams that report up through the sourcing and production departments, whose departmental structures will vary. Whether to have an internal team or an external team is generally determined by the size and scope of the company and the number of products that it offers for sale. It is also not uncommon for large companies to have an internal team with specific responsibilities, supported by an external partner (discussed in the next section). In addition to having quality assurance personnel on staff at a central location (headquarters), large companies may employ auditors who travel around the globe inspecting factories and production based on company protocols.

To keep tight control on both internal and external quality assurance processes and procedures, companies today also use the existing functionality that is built into enterprise resource planning (ERP) systems or product lifecycle management (PLM) systems to assist in the quality assurance process. Clear communication of requirements during the product development and production process is essential to ensuring quality in the supply chain. In addition to the systems used in the production process, there are specific products that are used in quality assurance, such as OneSource from Bureau Veritas, which is designed to provide a holistic overview of quality assurance, including testing, inspections, and factory audits. There are many way to approach quality assurance from a recordkeeping and systems standpoint, and these are but a few of the methods and systems used in the fashion industry supply chain.

## External Quality Assurance

The decision to use the services of an external quality assurance organization is often based on several factors. It could be required by the company that is buying the product, as is the case with many retailers, who will require certified physical test results before approving production. The decision could also be based on the needs of the company that is producing the product for sale, as is the case with many large companies that are producing in hundreds of factories around the globe and need to have inspections completed on finished goods.

To facilitate an external quality assurance program, one could engage the services of an agent to inspect finished goods at the factory on one's behalf based on the specifications and make detail sheets. In most cases the agent is limited to performing audits and does not get involved in physical testing. If the requirements call for physical testing, setting up quality assurance programs, or helping to train personnel, one would then have to engage the services of one of the organizations that are set up to perform those duties. There are numerous companies that can perform textile testing (from fabric to finished garments), assess manufacturing facilities, ensure compliance with various standards and regulations, and provide training. Three such companies are Intertek (www.intertek.com), SGS Group (http://www.sgs.com/), and Bureau Veritas (http://www.bureauveritas.com/). These are full-service companies and integral parts of the supply chain. The interview at the end of the chapter provides more insight into this aspect of the industry.

## CONCLUSION

The process of striving for quality plays a major role in the fashion industry. The quality of one's product represents who the fashion company is and what it stands for. There are many different levels of quality, and they are not always dependent on the function of cost. The consumer will often equate high value with having high quality, but it is often the perception of the consumer that affixes a level of quality based on price. The achievement of a quality product via TQM or QMS is frequently based on the integration of processes and measures throughout the supply chain, which does add cost to the final product. Today, TQM or QMS involves a team of employees, whether that team be internal or external to an organization. Whichever the case, resources are needed to ensure the quality of the product and ultimately to satisfy the consumer. It is clear that over time the literature on quality and how quality is addressed in organizations has evolved. Contemplate some of these changes. Given what you now know about quality and the fashion industry, what do you see as the next evolutionary change that will be introduced in the world of quality improvement?

## INDUSTRY INTERVIEW: RICK HORWITCH, BUREAU VERITAS

Bureau Veritas is one of the leading supply chain quality assurance companies in the world. I had the opportunity to speak with Rick Horwitch, who was able to provide further insight into the world of quality assurance. Rick shared with us his expertise and brought to life some of the current thinking and best practices that are currently being employed in the field of quality assurance.

Rick Horwitch is vice president of Solutions Business Development and Marketing for Bureau Veritas–Consumer Products Services. Bureau Veritas is the world's oldest and one of the largest providers of quality, health, safety, environmental, and sustainability (QHSES) services. Its customers include 48 of the top 50 retailers in North America and 41 of the top 50 consumer product brands. Rick's focus is on developing quality assurance solutions to encompass the entire supply chain and to help his company's customers manage risk, protect their brands, and reduce cost.

Rick has thirty years' experience in the consumer products industry, covering all facets of business: sales, marketing, operations, sourcing, manufacturing, and information technology.

**Interviewer:** *Can you describe your understanding of quality assurance in the fashion industry specifically as it relates to the supply chain?*

**R. H.:** I would describe the supply chain as every step of the process from design to delivery (to the consumer) of a product. Some companies are extending this definition to include analysis of customer returns (especially for quality-related issues). Within this very broad spectrum, every touch point is critical. Often we find that production and/or quality-related issues are a direct cause of poor design (especially technical design) and a lack of understanding of how different materials can, or cannot, work with each other. Color, fit, specifications are all critical components. Moving into sourcing and production, I often find that companies narrowly define "supply chain" as whoever is making the product. This approach fails to take into account numerous touch points: material, components, trims, thread, yarn, fiber, dying, finishing, chemical, etc., suppliers. I once spoke at a "supplier summit" for a major denim manufacturer. I was told the audience would be their supply chain. I thought this meant a dozen people. Wrong! There were over two hundred people, representing dozens of companies. The owner had invited his entire supply chain, which included the suppliers of his suppliers. The point the owner made was that everyone in the room contributed to the denim he was making, and thus had a stake in the quality of the product.

**Interviewer:** *Can you tell me what services BV offers, and why would a company use those services?*

**R. H.:** Bureau Veritas is the oldest (founded in 1828) and one of the largest providers of testing, inspection, and certification (TIC) services in the world. We have eight divisions covering all areas of business: Marine, Aerospace/Transportation, Energy, Construction, Infrastructure/Industrial/Facilities, Certification, Health/Safety/Environment/Sustainability, and Consumer Products. Bureau Veritas–Consumer Products Services (BVCPS) provides a wide range of quality, compliance, and consulting services. From a macro level, our services can be broken down into

four areas: Testing, Inspections, Audits, and Consulting. We cover all consumer products, including apparel and footwear, toys and juvenile products, furniture, home goods (and a wide range of hard goods), health, beauty, food, automotive, electrical, and wireless/connected devises. The following is a brief overview:

- Testing: physical, performance, regulatory, and compliance

- Inspections: preproduction, in-line/during-process, final random, DC, in-store, mold prevention (especially for footwear and leather goods)

- Audits: Social Compliance, Environmental Compliance and Management Systems (including chemical management), Factory Assessments (for capabilities, capacity, and quality management process/systems), Security Assessments (to C-TPAT requirements), Facilities Safety (structural and electrical systems)

**Interviewer:** *It has been several years since I was involved in quality assurance. Can you take me through the process that is used today for an apparel company? Where do you start, and where do you end up?*

**R. H.:** As mentioned above and below, there needs to be a collaborative process between all departments and stakeholders. Our testing, inspection, and audit data show that the majority of problems can be averted is there is better collaboration and communication. Companies that are doing the best job in quality understand this. The quality teams are part of the design and product development process (providing technical, regulatory, and compliance advice). This includes development of trims and materials (not just product designs). Sourcing engages with factory assessment audits before a new supplier is on-boarded. These audits validate whether a factory has the capabilities, capacity, and internal QC processes to make the products.

**Interviewer:** *I recall using military standard 105 with various acceptable quality levels (AQLs) when I worked in the menswear industry and had to be called upon to inspect goods in a country; is this standard still used today? What, if any, software programs are in use for apparel and accessory companies to assist in the delivery of quality assurance?*

**R. H.:** The same basic standard is being used today, although it has now been made a national standard referred to as Ansi ASQ Z1.4.

Regarding systems, several companies offer ERP (enterprise resource management) and PLM (product lifecycle management) systems specifically designed for the apparel and footwear industries. Clear communication of requirements during the product development and production processes is essential to quality assurance in the supply chain. Specifically for quality assurance, there are several platforms, including industry-leading OneSource from Bureau Veritas, that are designed to provide a holistic overview of quality assurance, including testing, inspections, and factory audits.

**Interviewer:** *Who are the key players from a quality assurance standpoint? Other than your organization, which are some of the dominant companies?*

**R. H.:** While there are numerous companies around the world who perform many of the services I have described, there are only a handful of "dominant" global service providers who provide a wide range of services. In addition to Bureau Veritas, I would include Intertek, SGS, UL, TUV-SUD, and TUV-Rhineland.

**Interviewer:** *In the supply chain, where does quality assurance start? Design, product development? Functional teams within the various departments?*

**R. H.:** Quality starts with the CEO. Every CEO I have ever met says, "we strive to provide our customers with the highest quality product, and experience,

possible. Quality is a foundational pillar of our company." When I ask if they view the services that we (and our competitors) provide as strategic or tactical, the majority answer "tactical." Quality is often assumed to exist. Validating quality is viewed as a policing function that adds cost and time. If the message from the top is about margin/profit and speed, this is often interpreted as cut corners (and costs).

**Interviewer:** *Can you describe a typical quality assurance setup (if one exists)? Who is responsible, and how many?*

**R. H.:** Traditionally retailers and brands typically have a quality Vice President or Director and one or more quality managers. This team sets standards, reviews testing and inspection reports to make decisions on whether or not to accept goods. Many times they audit product on the store floor to make sure quality standards are upheld. In most cases the Quality organization reports up through Sourcing.

We are starting to see a number of retailers and brands bring Product Development and Technical Design into the quality organization. This new position is Vice President of Product Development & Quality and Compliance. This reports up through Product Development/Design. In almost every case, the compliance component reports directly (or dotted line) through legal/risk management. Social Compliance (CSR) usually reports through legal/risk management.

Leading manufacturers usually have a large quality organization. The quality director or manager (who reports directly to the highest levels of the company) is responsible for the management systems and practices to meet or exceed customer expectations. There are typically one or more quality engineers that develop manufacturing process control plans and work to improve processes based on data provided from the tests and measurements specified in the control plan, as well as feedback from customers. Several auditors or inspectors monitor all steps of the manufacturing process, from material receipt through to packing. They perform checks on random samples as outlined in the control plan. It is important to note that individuals performing so-called "100 percent inspections" at the end of the production line are part of the manufacturing process itself and not quality assurance.

**Interviewer:** *Concluding thoughts: tell me where you see quality assurance heading as it relates to the fashion industry supply chain.*

**R. H.:** While every company (retailer or brand) claims that Quality is a strategic, foundational, imperative—"we strive to provide our customers with the highest quality products and experience possible"—the reality is most view the quality functions mentioned above as tactical/transactional and low value add. For many "Quality" is assumed. Retailers and brands claim that "our teams design, develop, and source the highest quality products possible." Every factory owner claims to make "high-quality" products. I'm sure all believe this to be true and have good intentions.

The reality is, Quality cannot, and should not, be assumed. Customer expectations are higher today than ever before. Customer feedback on products (through social media and online reviews) is instantaneous. The "race to the bottom" (squeezing the last penny out of every garment) is over. Retailers and brands are starting to realize that quality products can be cost-effective and improve sales and brand image.

The future is in two areas: unlocking the value of data and better communication and collaboration (with internal and external stakeholders). The following are two case studies:

- A major US retailer implemented a Technical Collaboration Board to address all quality aspects: Fit, Color, Production, Testing, Inspections, Customer Returns, and Feedback. The board consists of the retailer's top 20 suppliers (brands and private label), internal teams (design, product development, sourcing, and merchants), academics, and third-party test/inspection/audit partners. Historically efforts like this failed because the

"collaboration" went in one direction: the retailer would tell the suppliers they need X and expect the suppliers to comply. This effort has been a true partnership and the results have been outstanding:

- Cycle time (concept to delivery) from "Quality functions" has been reduced by nearly 28 working days.
- Nearly $4 million in cost saving have been realized in 2 years, through process improvements and removal of redundancies.
- Customer feedback (positive) related to product quality has nearly doubled in 2 years (base on online comments and customer return rates).

- A major US retailer (different from the above) set out to "re-invent" its entire quality process. For decades this retailer was considered the "Gold Standard" for quality. Unfortunately, in recent years, primarily due to price pressures, this golden image had become tarnished. A holistic view of the quality process was implemented, linking the results from testing, inspections, and audits. The data collected from these services was analyzed both on a factory level and at a testing and inspection line item level. This intense analysis of data has enabled the retailer to achieve significant improvements in Cost, Time, and Customer Satisfaction.

- Cycle time (concept to delivery) from "Quality functions" has been reduced by nearly 12 working days.
- Over $15 million in cost saving have been realized in 3 years, through process improvements and removal of redundancies.
- Customer feedback (positive) related to product quality has nearly doubled in 3 years (base on online comments and customer return rates). A recent customer

survey comparing national brands (the retailer sells) to their private label brands showed that customers rated the private label 76 percent positive (from a quality perspective) versus national brands at 71 percent positive. This was the first time in the retailer's history that their private label brands outperformed national brands.

The world of retail, brand building, sourcing, customer engagement, and every other facet of business has changed dramatically over the last five years. Every indicator says that this change will not only continue, but accelerate, over the next five years. For all of this change, most retailers and brands still manage and execute their quality functions the same way they did 5/10/15/20/30 years ago. This needs to change, too. The change needs to come from the top. Quality must be viewed (by the CEO) as a strategic imperative and a partner to the business, not viewed as the "police."

## Questions Pertaining to Interview

1. Given the information presented by Mr. Horwitch, have your views on quality and the supply chain been altered? Please describe.
2. Mr. Horwitch discusses quality assurance from the vantage point of the CEOs and states that they see quality as the pillar of their company yet when confronted with the costs associated with maintaining that level of quality, they change their view. As a consumer, does that make you question your trust in certain companies? Is that a cynical view? Explain.
3. Knowing what you now know, how do you think the role of quality should be in the supply chain?

---

## CASE STUDY: Quality Disaster

Quality assurance comes with a price and when done properly has a direct effect on the cost of the finished product. Every time someone touches the product, it costs money: when specifications are drawn up, it costs money; when inspections are performed, it costs money; and so on. The following case shows that proper attention to details goes a long way to satisfying the consumer.

A major brand with manufacturing facilities around the world received a reorder from one of its top-tier customers (a major retailer). The order was in response to a previous shipment that the brand had made and that had sold incredibly well. The brand was eager to please the retail customer and took the order while promising a very tight delivery date in order to capture sales while still in season. The order was for 10,000 knit shirts (100 percent cotton) to be delivered to 200 doors (50 pieces per door). In order to make the delivery date, the brand and the retailer decided to drop-ship the shirts directly to the stores (bypassing the brand and retail warehouse). The brand managed to make the delivery date, but the consumers were not happy with their purchases, and return rates on the drop shipment were running at 80 percent due to poor quality. The consumers claimed that the shirts were shrinking in excess of 20 percent. This was a quality disaster.

### Case Study Questions

1. There could be a wide variety of reasons for this quality disaster. Choose one and describe what went wrong.
2. How could this have been avoided?
3. What steps should both the brand and the retailer have taken to avoid such a problem?
4. Where in the supply chain did the process break down?
5. How could working in a team have prevented such a quality disaster?

# CHAPTER REVIEW QUESTIONS

1. What in your mind makes a quality garment?
2. Does the price of the garment have any bearing on the quality of that garment?
3. If you were setting up a supply chain, what steps would you take to develop your quality assurance protocols?
4. In the chapter several high-profile quality assurance organizations were highlighted. If you had to choose one, which would it be and why?
5. Of the four principles (Six Sigma, lean, quality management systems, ISO 9001) identified in the chapter, is one more important than another? Why?

# CLASS EXERCISES

## Exercise A

1. Break up into teams.
2. Scan the web and identify a fashion company you wish to study.
3. Scan that fashion company's website and develop a visual representation of what the supply chain might look like for one of the products produced by that fashion company.
4. Discuss what processes that company may need to have in place to ensure the consumer a quality product.
5. From the team's perspective, what questions might the fashion company ask to ensure that there is ongoing quality and ongoing improvement?
6. Does this fashion company appear to be a hierarchy, or does there appear to be a partnership with all employees actively engaging in decisions?
7. From the team's perspective, what would a fashion company need to do to assist its employees as they take a more active role in the decisions of the company?

## Exercise B

Create two size specification sheets. Collect two pairs of pants from your closet (preferably the same size). Using an Excel spread sheet or a Word document to develop your own size specification sheets for each pair of pants.

Use the information provided in Table 7.1 as a guide for measuring the actual garment. Compare the two sets of measurements and note the differences (if they exist).

# KEY TERMS

| | | |
|---|---|---|
| quality | Six Sigma | ISO 9001 |
| quality assurance | lean | |
| total quality management | quality management system | |

# REFERENCES

1. American Society for Quality (n.d.), "What Is a Quality Management System (QMS)?—ISO 9001 & Other Quality Management Systems." Available online: http://asq.org/learn-about-quality/iso-9000 /overview/overview.html.
2. Ash, R. W. (1992), "The ABCs of Developing TQM," *Security Management*, 36 (9): 82.
3. Burnes, L. D., K. K. Mullet, and O. N. O. Bryand (2016), *The Business of Fashion: Designing, Manufacturing, and Marketing* (5th ed.), New York: Bloomsbury.
4. Forbes Quotes (2015), *Thoughts on the Business of Life*. Available online: http://www.forbes.com/quotes/473/.
5. Gabor, A. (1990), *The Man Who Discovered Quality*, New York: Times Books.
6. Glorioso, J. E. (1994), "TQM and the Team Solution," *Security Management*, 38 (10): 33.
7. GoLeanSixSigma (2012–2016), *8 Wastes*. Available online: https://goleansixsigma.com/8-wastes/.
8. Hashmi, K. (2000–16), "Introduction and Implementation of Total Quality Management (TQM)," iSix Sigma. Available online: https://www.isixsigma.com /methodology/total-quality-management-tqm /introduction-and-implementation-total-quality -management-tqm/.
9. International Organization for Standardization (2015), *ISO 9000—Quality Management*. Available online: http://www.iso.org/iso/home/standards /management-standards/iso_9000.htm.
10. Lean Enterprise Institute (2000–16), *What Is Lean?* Available online: http://www.lean.org/whatslean/.
11. Mahmood, U., S. S. Zubair, and A. Salam (2015), "Synergic Relationship between Total Quality Management and Marketing Management in Creating Customer's Value," *Journal of Business Strategies*, 9 (2): 99–114.
12. "Principles" (2016), *Business Dictionary*. Available online: http://www.businessdictionary.com/definition /principles.html.
13. "Quality" (2016), *Merriam-Webster Dictionary*. Available online: http://www.merriam-webster.com /dictionary/quality.
14. "Quality Assurance" (2016), *Merriam-Webster Dictionary*. Available online: http://www.merriam-webster .com/dictionary/quality%20assurance.
15. Winn, G. L. (1996), "Walking the TQM Tightrope," *Security Management*, 40 (6).

# Logistics

## LEARNING OBJECTIVES

Upon completion of this chapter you will be able to:

- Examine how logistics impacts the design, sourcing, production, and distribution aspects of the global fashion supply chain.

- Evaluate the role that technology plays in the management of the flow of information throughout the supply chain.

- Assess how collaboration drives efficiencies for internal and external logistic partners.

- Design logistic strategies to mitigate supply chain risks.

- Critique today's role of logistic professionals who focus on data and partner relationships.

# LOGISTICS OVERVIEW

**Logistics management** is the use of technology, data analysis, project planning, and general management skills to enable the efficient movement of inventory and information from the raw material production phase, to the distribution, to the end consumer. Within the warehouse, logistics involves processing orders, maintaining appropriate inventory levels, and transporting goods.[1] Given that the fashion industry, like many other industries, competes on price, service, and accessibility, coupled with the fact that the industry is highly geographically dispersed, logistics is a key factor in ensuring that product is delivered to the distribution channels of brick-and-mortar stores and online venues. Logistics also plays an active role in the transportation of raw materials.

As shown in Figure 8.1, the global logistics sector is comprised of a complex network of freight- and cargo-related entities, such as shipping, warehousing, courier, and road/rail/air freight.[2] The global logistic market's revenue is expected to expand from $8.1 trillion in 2015 to $15.5 trillion by 2023.[3] The global transportation services market is one of the fastest-growing sectors, with more than 7 percent year-on-year growth since 2011.

**Figure 8.1**

**Air, sea, rail, and truck: the multiple means of transportation** Given the geographically dispersed nature of the global fashion supply chain, apparel and footwear products utilize all of these means of transportation.

As worldwide consumption experiences a shift in demand due to a growth in emerging markets and a reprioritization of buying preferences, the global logistics market will see demand move from the traditional Western economies to new areas of opportunity in China, India, other Asian economies, the Middle East, and Latin America. With 42 percent of the global transportation services coming from the United States alone, the United States and Europe are still the dominant global logistics markets.

The road freight segment, which is part of ground transportation, is the largest portion (74 percent) of the global logistics industry. Because of the cost-prohibitive nature of air transportation for many industries, air has been experiencing a decline since 2012. With a projection showing significant growth in cargo capacity by 2017, shipping containers continue to be an important segment of global trade transportation.[4]

## Leading Logistics Companies

As with every industry, there are market leaders in the global logistics sector. United Parcel Services (UPS), founded in 1907 as a messenger service, has evolved to be one of the largest US package delivery companies, with $61 billion in 2016 in revenue.[5] UPS is a leader in the **less-than-truckload (LTL)** delivery service market, which involves small packages that weigh 150 pounds or less. FedEx is an American global carrier service with $50.3 billion in revenue in 2016 based on the company's annual report. FedEx has carved out an area of expertise in international trade services such as customs brokerage and ocean and air freight forwarding services. Deutsche Post DHL is the largest worldwide logistics solutions provider, with 47,000 employees in more than 220 countries in Europe, North and South America, and Asia-Pacific. Exel is a supply chain and logistics company owned by Deutsche Post DHL. With $4.2 billion in revenue, the company has operations in the United States, Canada, Latin America, and South America. For trucking services, J. B. Hunt Transport Services and Schneider National are the leading providers. With revenue of $3 billion, J. B. Hunt employs 16,000 employees and operates over 12,000 trucks throughout the United States, Canada, and Mexico. Schneider National is the largest privately owned trucking company in North America.

# MAJOR LOGISTICS TRENDS

As the sourcing and selling aspects of retail have become more complex, logistics has evolved from low-skill, labor-intensive processes to data-driven, strategic functions that require management skills, real-time information, and collaborative versus transactional vendor relationships. Today's logistics professionals are facing the hurdles of managing a global sourcing business to meet the demands of traditional retailing, fast fashion, and ecommerce business models while also addressing consumers' concerns about socially responsible manufacturing facilities and processes. Additionally, the **B2C**, which includes businesses that sell goods or services directly to the consumer ecommerce market, is causing a tremendous increase in parcel volume because consumers are purchasing with a growing expectation of free shipping. Ecommerce retailing necessitates modifications of warehousing procedures, order fulfillment, and return procedures. Logistics are also being forced to address retailers' movement to use a push versus pull inventory strategy that will enable them to respond to consumer demand.

## Ecommerce

With the growth of ecommerce, regional distribution centers are no longer the central dropoff points for inventory; instead, mini-fulfillment centers are located throughout a retailer's selling footprint. Additionally, the ecommerce market has fueled the rise of time-definite parcel/express delivery service. For these reasons, many retailers have moved to insourcing logistics solutions; an example is Amazon's decision to lease twenty Boeing 767 planes from Air Transport Service Group (ATSG).[6] Amazon has also taken a similar position with its warehousing operation; in 2013 the company opened seven 5,000-square-meter distribution depots to service the UK market. Large retailers are increasingly negotiating with the idea that suppliers hold the inventory and distribute goods directly to retail outlets instead of the retailers assuming the capital costs and overhead associated with the management of large, regional distribution centers. Not only are suppliers assuming the capital and labor costs associated with holding inventory, but they are also incurring additional transportation costs because they are making more frequent deliveries to retailers. This is called **vendor inventory management (VIM)**. However, this additional cost is passed off onto the retailer.

The ecommerce business model has forced warehouses to tackle challenges such as managing leaner inventory levels, fulfilling smaller order sizes, storing larger SKU (stock keeping units) categories, processing quick order turnarounds, and delivering increased customer packaging and value-added services. The concept of warehousing has changed greatly because of increased automation and advanced process management procedures.

Because the delivery requirements for ecommerce orders are centered around individual preferences instead general delivery options such as bulk shipments to one location such as a distribution center, logistics providers are moving away from commoditized service offerings and are increasing their value-added services that primarily support the **individual package market**: deliveries made directly to an individual consumer. This market is continuing to grow in size and frequency of delivery. To pursue a more cost-effective delivery strategy, retailers like Amazon are testing **common locker delivery systems** that require the consumer to pick up items rather than have them delivered to the door. Of course, for a fee, companies will continue to offer same-day delivery to residences.

## Increasing Significance of Distribution Centers

Warehouses are used to store large amounts of inventory for potentially long periods of time. Distribution centers are typically used to hold smaller amounts of inventory to fulfill customer orders and to replenish stores. Because of the order fulfillment process for ecommerce purchases, distribution centers have grown in significance, and retailers have had to relocate their distribution centers close to their customers.

In addition to storing inventory, distribution centers may also provide value-added services such as labeling and customer support for online purchases. Since many ecommerce companies look to enhance the customer experience through their order packaging and delivery services, distribution centers are key in the online customer servicing process.

Because of the need for retailers to keep up with the demands of their consumers for quick delivery turnaround times and for an omnichannel shopping experience, brick-and-mortar retailers have started allocating store space for in-store order pickup and ship-from-store order fulfillment options. These stores have taken on a local distribution center role for these retailers. For example, Gap and the Banana Republic offer the option to shop online and reserve items in the store for pickup. This option is attractive to customers who are looking to receive purchases without the delay and cost involved in shipping items. In 2013, Macy's committed to establishing within 500 of its stores designated space for online order pickup and fulfillment.[7] There is also an opportunity to utilize store personnel to support this aspect of the supply chain. As with every opportunity, there are also areas of concern, such as the impact on the in-store experience, the ability to adequately manage in-store inventory levels, and a retailer's personnel allocation strategy and incentives.

To be able to offer Amazon Prime, a member benefits program for Amazon shoppers, Amazon had to rethink its local distribution network. By paying either an annual or monthly fee, Amazon Prime customers receive member services such access to videos, music, and ebooks. The key feature that significantly impacts the Amazon supply chain network is Amazon Prime's offer of free one- or two-day shipping on most items. According to ChannelAdvisor, an ecommerce solutions and sales data firm, Amazon's distribution network includes 173 supply chain centers around the world. These centers include fulfillment centers (FCs), sortation centers (SCs), redistribution fulfillment centers (RFCs), and "Prime Now" hubs.[8] The "Prime Now" hubs stock Amazon's most requested orders and are located closer to the customer for quick order fulfillment.

## Globalization

While globalization has created an opportunity for retailers to establish a network of sourcing partners around the world, it has also created a networked economy that eliminates the ability to function in isolation. In the past, companies could operate as independent entities that managed direct interfaces to suppliers and customers. Today, companies must collaborate with partners around the world both vertically and horizontally

in their extended supply chain network. Not only is the integration expected on a relationship level, but entities are also being required to integrate their processes and systems. Thus, there are dependencies and additional costs associated with a global supply chain network. As speed continues to be a driving factor for supply chain efficiency, it is the integration throughout the supply chain that will enable companies to achieve this goal. The days of logistics vendors operating in isolation have ended. Logistics companies must collaborate with their carrier partners such as FedEx throughout the global supply chain.

Because of the geographically dispersed nature of the global fashion supply chain, shipping by means of containers is continuing to play a growing role in the movement of goods from production locations to selling markets. Thus, **intermodal goods transport**, the movement of goods without the need to change packaging or documents between modes, is growing for sea to land distribution. For multimodal movement of goods, freight terminals are being established throughout the global supply chain network. In **multimodal transport**, a product will use two or more transport modes, but this is not necessarily a seamless process.

## Continued Pressure of Cost Containment

While the industry is moving more to a collaborative versus a transactional supply chain model, cost pressure is still an important factor in logistics management. Because most ecommerce retailers have essentially moved to a free shipping model and because the movement of raw materials and finished goods is a significant portion of the overall cost of production, there is an ongoing pressure to see how the product can be transported and warehoused with reduced costs. Logistic procedures are constantly being monitored to ensure that resources are being utilized in a manner that drives continuous savings. For example, to contain costs associated with inventory movement and management, shipping companies are turning to **freight pooling**, the distribution of orders to numerous destinations within a geographic area; **zone skipping**, a shipping consolidation method; and **backhauling**, whereby a load of goods is transported on the return trip of a truck or ship.

## Notes from the Field

Logistics is about moving products from point A to point B and very often to several points in between before the product arrives for sale to the consuming public. One of the key elements of logistics is cost. Cost containment can be compromised by other elements of the supply chain, and logistics can mean the difference in a profit or a loss. Our general practice was to ship via sea freight in full containers. One order was running very late, and we did not want to disappoint the customer, who was threatening cancellation, so the decision was made to deliver via air freight. This was not a decision taken lightly, as it increased our freight cost fivefold and ate into our profit considerably, but in the end we preserved the order and our relationship with the customer. Unbeknownst to the customer, it also provided us with leverage to negotiate a better price on our next order with the factory.

As the value-added services of logistics, such as customer service support, specialty packing and delivery services, and return management, increase, and as shipping continues to grow as a cost factor primarily for ecommerce sales, there has been an emphasis on capturing actual per-order distribution costs rather than spreading costs across all orders. To gain a true cost per item, companies are looking to charge inventory storage and handlings costs back to the appropriate cost center. **Activity-based costing**, an accounting practice that increases the visibility of hidden costs on a per-item basis, is being utilized as a management tool to effectively oversee costs associated with internal distribution operations.

## Infrastructure Disruptions

Since **logistics** is essentially the coordination of the movement of inventory and information throughout the supply chain network, there are numerous points of risk and possible disruption that might occur throughout the supply chain. Because of the factors mentioned earlier in the chapter, traditional trade routes are shifting from Europe and the United States and are moving toward the emerging markets of Asia and BRIC (Brazil, Russia, India, and China). Because of this shift in production and selling routes, there is a concern about infrastructure risks due to the quality of service roads, access to logistics service providers, and the increased equipment investment needed to support these new growth markets.

As the land and labor costs along manufacturing coastal areas in heavily manufacturing centers like China increase, there will be a continued movement of production further inland, which will require improvements in road and delivery infrastructure to meet the new demands of inland production facilities.

Natural disasters due to climate change are another factor that is causing concern with regards to supply chain disruption. According to research from BSI Intelligence, a multination service provider, "Approximately 40 percent of all 2014 United States imports originated in countries with a High or Severe risk of natural disaster exposure."[9] The increased frequency of weather-related issues such as floods, hurricanes, and droughts is causing retailers to assess their chain for resiliency and flexibility. BSI also reports that the top five natural disasters, which include tragic incidents such as the Nepal earthquake and Typhoon Komen, which cost many lives in Myanmar, Bangladesh, and India, resulted in a collective loss of about $33 billion of business damages.[10] An additional global threat to the supply chain is the outbreak of diseases such as those caused by Ebola in 2014 and the 2015 rise in the Zika virus, which spread fear for workers' health.

## Political and Economic Volatility

In addition to natural disasters, companies must also look for means to protect their supply chain from threats such as cargo theft, terrorism, labor strikes, political uncertainty, and cybercrime. Each of these factors poses a threat to the resiliency of a company's supply chain. Global cargo theft cost is estimated to grow by $1 billion in 2016, and China, Germany, India, Mexico, South Africa, and the United States will be the areas of most concern.[11]

The 2008 financial crisis in the United States, coupled with the fact that Europe has been in a recession since 2011, has resulted in a significant drop in spending by the world's largest consumers. As a result, retailers have reduced their store base, inventory levels have decreased, and layoffs have occurred for many large retailers. Because of the challenges in the United States and Europe, there has been an adverse impact rippling through the entire global supply chain. As the economy in China continues to show weakness, a potential drop in consumption from this market will also impact the global supply chain.

The industry has also been hampered by labor strikes such as the 2015 West Coast dockworker dispute, which essentially crippled the movement of goods into the West Coast ports. The workers who were on strike represented shipping companies and port terminal operators for twenty-nine ports from San Diego to Seattle. These ports handle about one-quarter of all US international trade, much of it with Asia.[12] There have also been labor disruptions in the foreign labor markets. Labor strikes in China were up by 58 percent in 2015 compared to the previous year. As a result of these strikes, the footwear industry experienced more than an estimated $27 million in losses.[13]

In addition to labor concerns, the industry is also facing ongoing geopolitical issues associated with refugees and the security impact on European supply chains. The influx of immigrants to Southeast Europe from Syria, East Africa, and even Afghanistan is causing European leaders to question the Schengen Agreement, a treaty signed by five of the ten members of the European Economic Community that allowed the free movement of people across mainland European countries. The refugee crisis coupled with terrorist concerns is causing a rethinking of border controls, which would heavily impact the global supply chain because of the delays and additional costs associated with increased monitoring.

## Increasing Regulations
The shipping regulatory environment is experiencing changes that will potentially increase costs and delay the movement of international freight. The International Maritime Organization's SOLAS (Safety of Life at Sea), a treaty that focuses on the safety of merchant ships, requires the verification of gross mass containers before loading. Shippers were concerned that they will not be able to comply with this requirement by the mandated deadline of July 2016. While established to increase safety, minimize environmental risks associated with shipping, and improve maritime security, there is always a cost and time factor involved in the enforcement of these suggested regulations. In addition, the EU's Union Customs Code experienced significant change commencing in 2016 with the goal of replacing and harmonizing existing customs regimes in Europe. These changes will have an impact on shippers, carriers, and freight forwarders. The World Customs Organization, an independent intergovernmental organization, is also providing resources to minimize the adverse impact of this regulation.

# THE ROLE OF TECHNOLOGY IN LOGISTICS MANAGEMENT
To meet the growing demands caused by the request for more time-sensitive deliveries, specialized service offerings, and controlled costs, companies are continuing to turn to technology for automated solutions. Additionally, the need to meet the expectations of an omnichannel retailing experience is causing retailers to seek innovations in the areas of inventory management, order delivery tracking, and customer support. Enterprise-wide systems are needed to provide real-time information for order placements regardless of where a shopper initiates the transaction. Technology is also being deployed to improve data collection, which is becoming increasingly important in the management of complex organizations. As with every industry, big data has become an important factor in providing segmented customer information that supports the ability to source delivery routes and enhance the overall service offerings for a customer.

## Warehouse Management Systems
Warehouse management systems (WMSs) and transportation management systems (TMSs) have been implemented to reduce costs and improve overall servicing levels. Management often turns to WMSs when workload and/or customer specifications exceed the capability of management to evaluate the data in an

efficient manner, or the manual process fails to provide an opportunity to expand capabilities. A typical WMS supports the oversight of daily functions such as planning delivery schedules and allocating resources to move and store inventory within a warehouse. WMSs operate off a database that captures inventory-related information such as **stock keeping units (SKUs)**, an identification code for the size of an item, dimensions, case pack, automatic ID labels, inventory warehouse location, and manufacture date. A key function of warehousing is order picking and packing. If you think about what is required to fulfill an individual online order, you gain an understanding of the warehousing information needed, such as the item warehouse location number, the picking sequence, the type of use (picking, reserve storage, etc.), the type of storage (each, case, pallet), the location size or capacity, and storage/movement restrictions.[14]

In addition to critical details about inventory located in the warehouse, the WMS provides information to support the operations management aspects of moving and storing inventory. To ensure that there are adequate labor and work demands per shift, the warehouse management team must coordinate delivery times with the dock staff workload and organize the sequencing of orders based on the distribution channel, delivery timeline, and delivery. Successful warehouse planning strategies such as cross-docking, postponement, and kitting ensure the optimization of warehouse resources.

The WMS also helps to ensure that the warehouse management team can achieve resource optimization by guaranteeing that processes and procedures are adhered to throughout the warehousing process. In addition to a WMS, management often implements **International Standards Organization (ISO)** 9000, quality management standards that provide process techniques and management tools for organizations that want to deliver a consistent quality that meets a customer's requirements. Communication of information is one of the ultimate purposes of a WMS, and it achieves this goal by using communication technologies like automatic ID technologies that include barcodes, **radio-frequency identification (RFID)** (the use of electromagnetic fields to track items), and mobile computers.

Most WMS packages utilize radio frequency (RF) to support floor and dock operations in the warehouse. RF can be used to facilitate the order-picking process by providing information on an item's location, its size, and its packing requirements, which allow for a variety of picking methods, such as discrete, zone, and batch picking. RF picking supports picking by label and cart, which can be verified by location and SKU barcode scans. The alternative to RF-guided picking is the use of paper lists, which are highly inefficient and reduce overall picking accuracy. An additional benefit of RF picking is that data are created that enable near-real-time inventory and order updates.

While RFID remains slightly cost-prohibitive for small operations and can be somewhat cumbersome to use, especially in piece pick operations, it is still considered important to enhance product authentication, reduce inventory levels, and increase overall cost visibility. There are also voice-directed solutions that support a hands-free picking environment. However, cost is still a deterring factor for voice-directed technologies. As these resources become more commonly used, costs are expected to decrease due to increased volume.

One factor that is slowing the adoption of RFID is the establishment of standards around RFID. Much like barcoding technology, RFID is being hampered by issues of consistency across the supply chain. The **electronic product code (EPC)** is the leading standard for RFID supply chain applications.

Given the complexity of the warehousing process and the dynamic nature of customer expectations, monitoring for consistency and enhanced improvement is vital for success. The final element that a WMS provides is the visibility to monitor and track warehouse performance, which enables management to proactively troubleshoot problems and evaluate performance on an ongoing basis.

## Transportation Management Systems

A **transportation management system (TMS)** is a software that facilitates interactions between an organization's order management system (OMS) and its warehouse management system (WMS) or distribution center (DC).[15] The TMS supports the movement of inbound (procurement) and outbound (shipping) of goods through a series of transportation scenarios that evaluate the most appropriate route, delivery mode, and least cost provider. Additionally, the TMS provides information to support the settlement or payment process using electronic load tendering and track/trace to execute the shipment with the selected carrier.[16] The benefits of a fully deployed TMS are reduced costs due to savings incurred by efficiency in the selected route, load optimization, carrier mix, and mode selection. Because of the increased visibility in the route selection and carrier costs, there are improved savings due to better cost accountability. TMS also provides an opportunity for management to be proactive in troubleshooting issues and implementing last-minute changes to enhance the overall flexibility of the transportation process, which ultimately leads to enhanced service quality and, potentially, greater cost savings.

## Labor Management Systems

Labor management systems (LMSs), which were first introduced in the grocery and food services industries, are used to track and manage the labor aspects of logistics management. LMSs enable companies to break down work tasks, assign employees, and track expected completion time by benchmarking performance from historical task completion data. In addition to being a resource to optimize labor allocation, LMS provides a means for management to implement incentive-based pay. Some of the most challenging forces that drive logistics costs are inconsistency and efficiency within the operations functions. LMS enables workers to do repetitive tasks in a way that ensures consistency and optimal efficiency. For example, with a labor management system a company can define the most efficient route and steps to improve efficiencies within pick-and-pack, the efficiency process of fulfilling customer orders by minimizing the number of steps required.

## GPS and CRM Systems

As with the individual automobile market, global positioning systems (GPSs) provide individuals with location information for directional and tracking purposes; GPSs have enabled companies to manage route selection, monitor delivery times, and lessen the burden of package tracking by allowing consumers to track items themselves. Customer relationship management (CRM) systems enable the tracking of information at the customer level. This information facilitates the tracking of orders and supports customer service inquiries. CRM is also used in combination with supplier relationship management (SRM) systems.

## FUNCTIONS OF INTERNAL LOGISTICS DEPARTMENTS[17]

There are numerous tasks involved in the movement of raw materials and finished goods throughout the entire supply chain process, and there are various internal departments and outsourced relationships that provide these functions for retailers. Procurement and purchasing is the department that is traditionally considered the beginning of the logistics supply chain. It is often an internal department that oversees the procuring of resources such as raw materials, office supplies, goods for store operations, and even travel. This department primarily identifies suppliers, negotiates contracts, establishes payment and delivery, and maintains a vetted supplier list of purchased items, typically by means of purchase orders. Over the years, this department has often aligned with the accounting function with regards to the tracking and management of inventory levels.

## Traffic and Receiving

Inward transport or traffic is the central area of business logistics that manages the movement of goods from suppliers to a company's receiving area, be it a distribution center or a direct-to-consumer location. This area is responsible for identifying the transport supplier, confirming the best route, negotiating the costs and time of delivery, and guaranteeing that all safety and legal requirements are met. The traffic-monitoring function is a key focus because it is traffic that ensures that the right goods get to the right locations at the right time and within the appropriate cost constraints. As supply chains become more customer-centric through ecommerce, the role of traffic has been magnified because retailers are delivering to multiple distribution centers that require an even more precise understanding of customer demand. Traffic also has a significant impact on consumers' ability to obtain products when they want them versus the frustration of products being out of stock. To track the impact of global events on production, companies are creating war rooms for management teams that constantly monitor traffic and production concerns.

The **receiving department** confirms that the items delivered from a purchase order match the quantity, price, and expected delivery date. The receiving department inspects the order for damages and acknowledges receipt of the items.

Once an item is received, inspected, and sorted, the item is then stored in a warehousing facility until it is shipped to a store location or, in the case of ecommerce businesses, directly to a consumer. Same-day delivery and omnichannel selling are causing the traditional warehouse box located in remote areas to be replaced with mini-distribution centers that are located throughout the country. To accommodate online in-store pickup, many retailers like the Gap and Macy's are dedicating selling space for item pickup. Thus, the retail locations are becoming fulfillment/distribution centers.

## Inventory Management and Order Fulfillment

The **stock control department** works with a retailer's planning division to set the policies for inventory. Stock control works to obtain a balance between stock on hand and consumer demand. This function requires data on consumer projections and also an understanding of the costs of holding inventory and the potential impact of missed sales.

Retailers move a large amount of finished goods from warehouses to stores, and even between store locations. The **material handling department** oversees the movement of goods within an organization. The goods are now the ownership of the retailer, and the retailer has the responsibility of transporting the goods from the warehouse to a store location. The material handling department ensures the delivery method to minimize damage or timing delays with the item delivery. Because of the potential for theft, shrinkage is a concern that this department must also address.

With ecommerce retailers, and even catalog companies, the order-picking process is another area of importance within the order fulfillment function. **Order picking** entails the selection of items to be shipped for customer delivery. For an online retailer, order picking incorporates the selection of individually purchased orders versus brick-and-mortar orders that were bulk shipments to store locations. Another area of order fulfillment significance is packaging. Given the costs of manufacturing and transporting goods, retailers place an emphasis on minimizing damaged goods. Proper order packing wraps and packs items to facilitate internal movement and to minimize the labor time spent unwrapping and stocking the selling floor. Once the item is packaged properly, the outward departure area takes goods from the receiving department and distributes them to the consumer.

As with any order, there is a chance that items might be damaged. There is also equipment used in the inward delivery that must be returned to the supplier, such as pallets, delivery cartons, cable reels, and merchandise containers. The **recycling and waste disposal department** is the area that focuses on these concerns. Given the amount of potential waste associated with the packaging of goods, this is an area where retailers can implement socially responsible operating practices.

## LOGISTICS OUTSOURCED RELATIONSHIPS AND SERVICES

To meet the complex needs of a global supply chain, many retailers outsource aspects of their logistics to third-party entities that work with retailers in a variety of contracting relationships. The following is a brief summary of these logistics relationships.

### Contract Relationships

**Contract logistics** or **3PL (third-party logistics)** are generally three- to five-year contract relationships with a logistics provider or third party that handles logistics services such as warehousing, packaging, labeling, transportation, quality controls, and compliance inspections. Since contract logistics offer services for multiple customers, these providers leverage their IT and management talent to offer logistics solutions to a platform of customers. This relationship requires a high level of confidence because the contract logistics partner is assuming responsibility for a major role within a company's supply functions.

As the online market has taken on greater significance, **courier express parcel (CEP)**, the delivery of small parcels, has gained greater importance in the delivery of customer packages. This area is highly time-sensitive and requires an ability for consumers to track parcel delivery.

In the most basic of terms, a **freight forwarder** is a company that arranges for the movement of goods via air or ship. Export freight forwarders are licensed by the International Air Transport Association (IATA) to handle air freight, and by the Federal Maritime Commission to handle ocean freight.[18] While companies are not required to use freight forwarders, a forwarder's knowledge and access to transportation resources can help companies address the compliance and cost concerns associated with the exportation of goods.

Freight forwarders can almost be considered a concierge service for export because they facilitate service options within a network of carriers. Freight forwarding is typically an asset-light business model because freight forwarders buy capacity airlines, trucking companies, and ocean carriers. Freight forwarders maximize capacity by combining deliveries and leveraging management resources across their base of customers.

By working with their customer and the customer's buyer, the freight forwarder ensures that goods are delivered in the specified window of time, at the best cost associated with the means of delivery, and within the stated compliance requirements. Freight forwarders enable retailers to focus on the production of their goods while leaving the details about transporting the goods up to the freight forwarder. The freight forwarder advises on exporting costs such as freight costs, port charges, consular fees, the cost of special documentation, insurance costs, and freight-handling fees.[19] The forwarder also ensures the proper filing of all documentation, such as the **bill of lading**, or B/L. The B/L is a vital document because it establishes the following guarantees:[20]

- Provides evidence of contract of carriage between the "carrier" and the "shipper or cargo owner" to transport the cargo as specified by the sales contract between the buyer and seller.
- Documents that the carrier received the goods from the shipper or its agent in apparent good order and condition.

- Confirms that there is a clean title of goods that enables the goods to be transferred to the holder of the B/L, which then gives the holder of the B/L the right to claim the goods or further transfer the right to another party.
- Ensures compliance with security rules and regulations such as the **Customs Trade Partnership against Terrorism**, a voluntary supply chain security initiative led by US Customs and Border Protection (CBP).

The freight forwarder also advises on the most appropriate mode of cargo and packing logistics based upon the receiver's specifications, point of destination, and category of item being delivered. With access to a network of carriers, the freight forwarder can work relationships to reserve space on vessels, aircrafts, trains, or trucks. The final detail that the forwarder covers is to make arrangement with overseas customs brokers to ensure that the goods and documents comply with customs regulations. Because of fines and possible delivery delays due to customs-related issues, the freight forwarder plays a key role in expediting customs concerns.

# LOGISTIC STRATEGIES TO MITIGATE RISKS

Given the multiple and complex nature of the risks associated with a supply chain network, the following is a summary of strategies that can be used to minimize risks and improve the overall resiliency of the supply chain network.[21]

- Supply chain data management systems should be established to enable quick assessment of internal and external disruptions to a company's supply chain network due to a natural disaster or a significant unforeseen occurrence that impacts the movement and/or production of goods.
- Agility from a process and a corporate management perspective is critical to enable organizations to react to supply chain disruptions within a window of time that minimizes loss. This need for agility further confirms the need for standard operating procedures (SOPs), transparency of key information throughout the supply chain, and

an efficient decision-making process to increase responsiveness.

- Prior to a disaster, it is important for there to be a collaborative working relationship between vendors and the companies placing orders. This includes a shared operating plan to address disasters and a communication guide to support information and decision-making during times of crisis. Companies should have a business continuity management (BCM) plan that will enable operations to continue in the event of a business disruption.
- Supply side risk can include the loss of a supplier, perhaps due to bankruptcy, which calls for changing logistics patterns to work with other suppliers.
- Companies can use **push vs. pull inventory control**. Push uses forecast to predict demand, while pull uses actual order to determine what should be produced. While there are risks associated with both methods, the use of a pulling inventory process is faced with the risk of ensuring the most accurate information within a close to real-time basis. Zara is an example of a retailer that manages the majority of its inventory with a pull method.

## Selection of Ports and Carriers

As with most supply chain management decisions, on-time delivery is the key factor in determining a port or carrier. A **port** is a town or city where vessels can load for purpose of exporting goods and can unload goods for the purpose of importing goods. Since most apparel items are carried by sea, a carrier is often a shipping vessel that contains multiple containers of items. However, the need for on-time delivery also requires that goods may be sent by air. In that circumstance, the carrier is an aircraft.

Retailers tend to use third-party contractors to handle the selection of a port and carrier. Because of the significance of the decision and the need to ensure availability and flexibility in the process, the negotiations to establish the third-party relationship occur very early in the sourcing process.

To ensure on-time delivery and to minimize costs, the port selection decision is often driven by where the manufacturer's factory is located. Given the number of factories that exist in China, six out of the ten largest ports in the world are located in China.[22] These ports

**Figure 8.2**
**The port of Shanghai** This image shows the Huangpu River and the massive city skyline that has developed around this major port.

include Shanghai, Shenzhen, Hong Kong, Ningbo-Zhoushan, Qingdao, Guangzhou, and Guangzhou Harbor.[23] Because of the size of these ports, they are able to accommodate numerous, large vessels and process a heavy volume of shipping containers. As seen in Figure 8.2, ports are often the gateways to vibrant cities that thrive off of the commercial opportunities centered around the business of the port.

In selecting a carrier, one must consider the schedule of the shipping vessel, its capacity, its availability, its minimum item requirements, and of course price. To minimize the risks associated with the selection of a port and carrier, it is necessary to establish certain relationships and determine the volume of items to be delivered. By having a working relationship with a third-party contractor at a port, a retailer is able to navigate some of the issues that might arise due to the geopolitical environment, such as labor strikes, terror threats, and corporate social responsibility standards.

The August 2016 bankruptcy filing of Hanjin Shipping is an example of the risks associated with carrier selection. Prior to its bankruptcy, Hanjin was the seventh largest container shipping company, with a fleet of 98 container vessels in 60 countries and approximately 6,000 employees.[24] With the bankruptcy occurring during the heaviest shipping period of the year, retailers were concerned that their items would fail to arrive in time for the holiday season. To minimize such risks, retailers must continue to focus on relationship building with third-party contractors, vet contractors by assessing their financial capacity and performance history, and maintain an alternative delivery strategy.

# LOGISTICS MANAGEMENT AS A COMPETITIVE ADVANTAGE

*"In this battle for customers, our supply chain and distribution network give us a key advantage."*

MEG WHITMAN, CEO OF HP[25]

Given the competitive and highly fragmented nature of the fashion business, companies continue to seek ways to create a unique advantage. Since consumers are favoring business models that allow for immediacy with regards to product offerings and delivery, an efficient logistics process should enable companies to establish a supply chain network that is agile and responsive to consumer trends. The network should also provide real-time data that enable a company to ensure that tracking and delivery information is current and accurate, manage lean inventory levels because order fulfillment data accurately depict supply and demand, and facilitate omnichannel and mobile shopping habits that encourage consumers to shop anytime and anywhere. The 2014 Supply Chain Benchmark Study by Boston Retail Partners, a retail consulting firm that focuses on IT and strategy integration, reports that 22 percent of North American retailers have merged cross-channel efforts into a single organizational structure instead of separate silos. By focusing on centralized operations with an ability to utilize integrated data, companies are able to offer the product and shopping experience that consumers are expecting in today's retailing environment.

## Significance of Logistics Collaboration

"The essence of supply chain management is the ability to orchestrate collaborative relationships cross-functionally within their enterprises and externally with supply chain partners."[26]

From a logistics standpoint, certain key relationships, as shown in Figure 8.3, must exist to ensure the

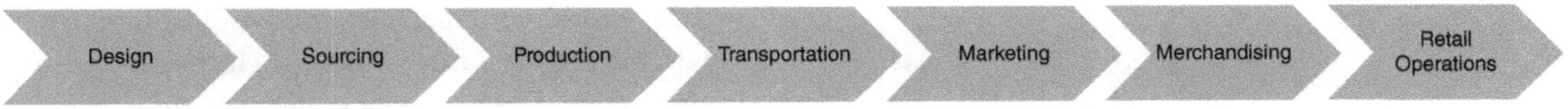

| Design | Sourcing | Production | Transportation | Marketing | Merchandising | Retail Operations |

**Figure 8.3**

**The steps in apparel manufacturing** This diagram shows the multiple steps to bring a design idea from the raw material phase to actual distribution to the customer.

proper movement of ideas, raw materials, finished goods, and consumer information. The design team must gain insight from the merchandising and marketing department with regards to the design calendar and anticipated marketing plans. Once the designer has produced the line patterns, then the sourcing team must confirm fabric availability, review factory capacity, and negotiate delivery times with the factories. The production team will manufacture the goods based on the agreed-upon deadline and item specifications. The production team will also manage the oversight of the compliance process to ensure that the products received meet the government and company compliance requirements. Now that the product is produced, the logistics of the transportation segment of production will require communication with the shipping or air transportation services and customs. To ensure that the products arrive to meet the advertising window and customer expectations, there are communications with the marketing and merchandising departments.

All parties in this process must be working together and have a clear understanding of how their contributions impact the overall production process. In order for effective collaboration to occur, it is key that the supply chain relationships operate on three key elements: trust, information, and leadership.

## Trust

Primarily, there are two types of production relationships that exists for a company: vertically integrated and outsourced. A **vertically integrated** company maintains control of its entire supply chain, meaning the company has in-house design, sourcing, and production teams. Given the resources that are required to support such an infrastructure, vertically integrated companies are usually large manufacturers like PVH, Inditex, and Tommy Hilfiger. A vertically integrated company maintains entire control of the supply chain. Downsides include the fixed costs associated with the infrastructure and human capital

investment, risks related to concentration of production, and possible loss of nimbleness and resiliency. Given the control that exists within this type of relationship structure, the trust factor is driven by an organization's internal culture and the ability to create incentives and goals across departments that allow for harmonious productive engagement throughout the organization. This trust can be further propelled though the transparency of organizational resources, goals, and strategic outlook. If a department performs well, not only does the company succeed, but the individuals of the department benefit, too, and there is a greater probability that the department and organization will reach their long-term goals.

Companies that **outsource** some or all of their production are entities seeking potentially quick turnarounds on garment production, smaller fashion houses, and companies with a business model that places a reliance on lean production. The benefit of outsourcing is the lack of capital investment, but the downside is the lack of production control, which may result in risks and compliance concerns. Depending on the size of the company and/or financial relationship, retailers can establish a collaborative working relationship with sourcing partners, and companies are able to mitigate concerns by implementing proactive monitoring strategies and establishing long-term investment plans such as production commitments across multiple seasons to ensure a dedicated working team for production. A **balanced scorecard** measures performance as part of a process and creates an incentive for vendors to work on a collaborative versus transactional basis. Additionally, if companies instill a production philosophy that they are committed to the value of relationships over price, they will have opportunities to strengthen relationships throughout the supply chain.

## Information

The goal of logistics information is to get the right product to the right consumer at the right time and the right

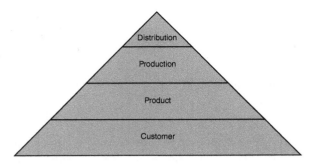

**Figure 8.4**
**Layers of logistics information** Information is the source of insight and the foundation for logistics. The customer, the product, production, and distribution all produce information that is used to support logistics.

price. To accomplish this goal, there are various layers of information, as seen in Figure 8.4, that are relied upon throughout the supply chain systems of customer relationship management (CRM) and supplier relationship management (SRM).

At the customer level, the information shared is about consumer demographics, such as the target customers, their buying preferences, and the ways that these customers engage with the product. This customer information is used to inform the designer and manufacturer about the type of garment to be produced. For example, a luxury designer that is catering toward a consumer that values high-end, specialty items will require the designer to create product offerings that match certain craftsmanship, quality materials, and service expectations. Since fashion is driven primarily by the whimsy of the consumer, customer information informs companies about trends. Fast fashion business models are winning today's consumer because the customer of today is looking for quick turnaround times.

## Leadership

As with any organization, leaders serve as the directional figures that establish the vision, obtain support and resources, and oversee the overall execution of a goal, function, or initiative. This is also the case with supply chain management. An example of where leadership is playing an active role is the movement of companies to focus on socially responsible business practices. Hence, factories are being asked to certify production lines for

socially and environmentally friendly labor practices. While these efforts may cause a slight rise in the cost of production, it is clear that companies are feeling the pressure in the boardroom to meet the demands of today's socially conscious consumer.

Company leadership is also causing supply chain professionals to think about their vendor relationships as collaborative versus transactional. While cost is still the key driver for production, the leaders of retailers are beginning to recognize the benefits of managing their sourcing relationships with a focus on price and longevity. By focusing on a collaborative arrangement, companies are able to work with their vendors to collectively identify and implement opportunities for long-term benefits.

## THE ROLE OF LOGISTICS IN THE PRODUCTION PROCESS

If the supply chain is the lifeline of the fashion industry, then logistics is the blood that flows throughout the system to ensure the delivery of product from concept to consumer. Just as blood provides invaluable nutrients to keep the body moving, logistics provides the data, communication, and transportation for the flow of garments from the raw material phase to the finished product delivered throughout the sales distribution channel. Logistics is all about product availability. Many have described this as "getting the right products to the right place at the right time."[27] Designers can create the most beautiful sketches; however, absent an efficient and accurate production process, the design will never come to life. Just as the designer masters the creative elements of fashion, there is a need to also conquer the logistics of the garment production to actualize the design. While the process may seem quite effortless to the average consumer, the logistics of sourcing includes a complicated, often nonlinear series of actions that require time, an ability to monitor, and most of all, effective communication throughout the supply chain.

A garment moves through several stages before it reaches the consumer. As seen in Table 8.1, the production process for a $9.99 T-shirt is a great example of how a simple item requires multiple vendors, touchpoints, and movements. Because there are several components, vendors, and handoffs that occur throughout the supply

**Table 8.1** Production and Logistics for a Cotton T-shirt

| Production | Logistics |
|---|---|
| 1. The T-shirt starts with the picking of the raw material, cotton. The cotton is most likely harvested in China, India, or the United States. | The cotton must be harvested and delivered to the next step of production. |
| 2. The bolls of cotton are shipped to a gin to be pressed into bales. | Most likely the gin is in the same country where the cotton was harvested, so there is a form of transport by truck or rail. |
| 3. The bales of cotton fiber go to a spinning facility to be spun into yarn. | The move from the gin to the spinner requires a form of transport by truck or rail. |
| 4. The yarn then moves to a mill to be knitted or woven into fabric and wet-processed for its fabric finishing | The move to the mill requires a form of transport by truck or rail. |
| 5. The finished fabric is sent to a garment factory to be cut and sewn. | Depending on the origin of the raw materials and finishing locations, the fabric may require being shipped to Asia or possibly Mexico. Compliance and quality control also occur in this phase of the process. |
| 6. The T-shirt is finally sent to the retailer. | Since most garments are imported, there will be a need for intermodal transportation to reach the retailer. |

This table outlines the steps for the production of a basic cotton T-shirt, from raw material to finished goods.

chain that cause complexity and risks with regards to shipment deliveries, logistics is a vital aspect of the overall production process. A raw material for a garment may be in one county, manufactured in another country, then assembled in another, and ultimately delivered to a consumer in a completely different part of the world. The logistics required form a complex web that requires a continuous source of information as to where the components of the garment exist, if they're available, and when the components will come together to complete manufacturing.

# THE INDUSTRY'S GROWING NEED FOR LOGISTICS TALENT

Supply chain management has been identified by the Department of Labor as one of the fastest-growing areas for career opportunities. For the fashion industry, this growth is being fueled by the rise of ecommerce businesses that are enabling consumers to shop anytime and anywhere with guaranteed delivery times that range from one hour to a standard shipping window. Additionally, many retailers are building sourcing networks around the world to achieve favorable returns and to meet the demands of a global marketplace. The

population around the world is aging, which is causing a global shortage of production workers and management talent. It is not clear how emerging economies that traditionally have not had to transport goods from factories to ports will meet the growing demand for transportation and logistics workers. In the 2014 report by Evotech Capital, it was predicted that there would be 1.1 million job openings between 2013 and 2016 in the US logistics industry. Within this span of time there would only be an estimated 75,000 logistics workers being prepared for the expected 270,000 available jobs.[28] The report also predicted the following annual shortfall of logistics-related talent for the following positions between 2013 and 2016:

- Warehousing and distribution: 125,000 jobs
- Trucking: more than 115,000 jobs
- Industrial engineering: 12,000 openings
- Logistics operations and management positions: 12,660 positions
- Freight rail: 4,530 jobs

Due to the increasingly complex nature of global sourcing, personnel are being asked to perform higher-skilled work that requires an understanding of software, analytics, engineering, and management expertise.

Similar expectations are also being held for hourly workers who input data or are part of the production movement cycle that requires the use of logistics management systems.[29] Because of these factors, there is a need for supply chain professionals who can manage a global vendor base, lead diverse teams, and implement innovative business solutions. At this rate of expected growth, logistics management will be a field of continued opportunities for the foreseeable future. Thus, it is vital that continued certification training and advanced degree programs build learning opportunities that will ensure that these future workers are able to meet the demands of current and future logistics needs.

## CONCLUSION

The logistics function is a complex network of interrelated assets and entities. The coordination of this network supports the successful movement of inventory and information throughout the global fashion supply chain.

Logistics ensures that the right goods get to the right consumer at the right time. As retailers compete in the competitive fashion world, they need to better understand how they can leverage their internal resources and external partners to create a supply network that is efficient, reliable, and able to adapt to the changes of the market. The emphasis on online sales order fulfillment and a seamless omnichannel shopping experience is forcing retailers to increase the agility of their supply chain network while implementing logistics strategies with customer-focused delivery solutions.

Consumer demand is driving the need for logistics to support shorter lead times and more complex delivery options such as same-day delivery. Because of these factors, logistics is continuing to evolve as a key area of significance and employment in the supply chain. In addition, technology is playing a key role in providing supply chain professionals with relevant, real-time data to support management decisions.

## INDUSTRY INTERVIEW: REGINE LAHENS, LOGISTICS DIRECTOR, LOOMSTATE

Regine Lahens is the director of logistics for Loomstate. In this role, Ms. Lahens oversees the entire logistics operations for the company while also leading the customer service department. In addition, Ms. Lahens has established standard operating procedures that support the overall logistics operations for Loomstate. Prior to joining Loomstate, Ms. Lahens was the director of logistics for Eddie Borgo/Outhouse, LLC and Marc Jacobs. Ms. Lahens earned an MBA in supply chain management from Ashford University and a BS from Syracuse University. She teaches in the Global Fashion Supply Chain Management Master of Professional Studies program at LIM College.

**Interviewer:** *What are the big challenges and opportunities that supply chain management faces today?*

**R. L.:** The biggest challenge is the complexity of the expectations from customers as to what a retailer can do from a speed and production capability perspective. The ecommerce platform allows

flexibility that hadn't existed before while at the same time the supply chain has become that much more complex because of reverse logistics and the expectations around speed, speed of production, and delivery to the end user.

In addition to speed, consumers are looking for unique products and service. Each customer is unique and is challenging retailers with their unique request of products, delivery mode, and even consumer engagement. This expectation of customization is putting a strain on the supply chain that doesn't exist with mass market production.

The technological advancements of the supply chain present tremendous opportunities to support improved communication and information throughout the entire supply chain. Technology facilitates the delivery of information that has the potential to be real-time and more accurate than manual tracking of customer and production data. For example, enterprise resource planning (ERP) systems give customers visibility to real-time inventory levels while providing the retailer with current information regarding the needs for inventory replenishment. Real-time data enables retailers to maintain lean inventory levels while having some assurance of their ability to meet consumer demand. For these reasons it is important for retailers and vendors to be able to operate with real-time information.

Technology also supports retailers with the management of multiple stock keeping units (SKUs) to once again project inventory levels and consumer demand. It is important for retailers to understand their sell through, especially when they are managing multiple SKUs. This information enables retailers to avoid the risk of carrying obsolete inventory or even worse, not having enough inventory to meet consumer demand thru inventory replenishment.

The movement to a see-now, buy-now shopping culture is causing retailers to rethink their production lead times, which means these retailers need to consider major modifications to all functions, even the design aspects of the business. The traditional fashion calendar of fall, holiday, spring, and summer is going away to be replaced by season-less buying. Since the majority of manufacturing occurs in Asia, the pressure to reduce lead times is of great concern for retailers. Because Asia shipping of products is four to six weeks, there is a built-in lag between the time orders are placed with the factory

and when the consumer receives the product. A key solution for this will be a further dependence by retailers on third-party logistic companies for trafficking and route planning that minimizes shipping delays.

Logistics are impossible without collaboration. For all of the aforementioned reasons, collaboration is a critical component for success throughout the entire supply chain, from product design to consumer delivery. Because a supply chain comprises many internal partners and external vendors, collaboration is fostered through the development of long-term relationships versus a more short-sided perspective where price is the driving factor.

**Interviewer:** *How is logistics being impacted by fast fashion and ecommerce's push toward same-day delivery?*

**R. L.:** The ability to produce product fast is the name of the game. To meet a fast fashion production schedule, retailers must be able to get access to raw materials in much shorter time. The calendar has to be really tight to shorten lead times. Since so much of the production process is dependent upon multiple variables and vendors, it is key that the production planning is well planned. A delay in any part of the chain will impact the delivery of the finished good. That is why it is important for retailers to have their supply chain strategically located with access to fabric mills, labor, and transportation infrastructure.

Since the majority of retailers are leveraging an online and brick and mortar presence, logistics are needed to support multiple inventory locations and distribution dropoffs. Retailers with multiple stores are increasing their ability to meet consumers' delivery and return expectations by having their retail stores serve also as mini-fulfillment centers.

Carriers like UPS, DHL, and FedEx are enabling retailers to reduce lead times by facilitating nearly next day delivery of samples and finished goods. However, there is a cost for speed that is being pushed into the pricing for consumers to absorb.

**Interviewer:** *Since nearly 90 percent of production occurs outside the United States, what does it mean for companies to maintain a global fashion supply chain?*

**R. L.:** Given the distance and the dependency on various relationships, there is tremendous potential for risk throughout the global fashion supply chain. To mitigate transportation risks, retailers often use multiple carriers. The threat of natural disaster is an area of concern, such as the (2014) Taiwanese disaster and the earthquake in Japan. Both of these disasters destroyed numerous factories. Then, there is also the infrastructure challenges within these countries, such as consistency of energy source, dependable roads, and labor. There are always global risks; some you can and some you cannot plan for, such as visibility to political issues within local areas, language, and cultural differences. While not only being a risk to the business, these issues can significantly impede progress.

Another big issue is the ability to synchronize the production process with its many moving parts. For example, for the production of a handbag the leather may come from Italy, while the bag's hardware (embellishments) might come from China. These pieces must all come together in order to meet the factory production time slot in Japan. In this instance, a delay with any of those pieces might result in a missed production window that ultimately might arise to chargebacks to the factory. However, some factories share responsibility for production delays with the retailer. This is all dependent upon the agreements throughout the supply chain. Not to mention, the potential revenue lost due to the retailer's inability to get the product to the customer on time. Because so much of the supply chain process is segmented but dependent upon one another, synchronization is key.

**Interviewer:** *From your perspective, what is the job outlook for logistics positions?*

**R. L.:** Because the business is changing so quickly, there are new and newly elevated roles that are becoming of significance, such as traffic management. Traffic is basically understanding what demand is like for a product on a location and/or geographic area. With the introduction of omnichannel, consumers have multiple points of purchase, which is causing an advanced level of demand planning and management within the overall traffic function.

Because information is a key driver throughout the supply chain, an understanding of EDI technology is important for many logistics positions. While logistics professionals don't have to know how to program files, it is important to have an understanding of how files/data are laid out, how the information can be manipulated, and how the data can be used to make decisions.

## Questions Pertaining to Interview

1. Beyond speed, what are the other ways that consumer expectations are changing the demands of the global fashion supply chain?
2. What are the operational risks that must be considered with regards to the global nature of the apparel supply chain?
3. Based on the comments from the interview, what are the key experiences and knowledge that individuals should try to obtain to ensure their competitiveness for logistics career opportunities?

### Company Background

Under Armour is the entrepreneurial brainchild of Kevin Plank, a former University of Maryland football star. He started Under Armour out of his quest to improve cotton T-shirts with innovative moisture-wicking performance fibers. Founded in 1996, with its headquarters in Baltimore, Maryland, Under Armour has built brand recognition in the competitive athletic market, which traditionally has been dominated by global brands like Nike, Adidas, and Puma.

In 2015, the company marked its tenth year of being a publicly traded business. The company's 2015 Annual Report commented on the business's robust financial health with the following key financial metrics: 30 percent average top-line growth and twenty-three consecutive quarters of over 20 percent net revenue growth. The company's growth can be attributed to the success of its celebrity endorsements through athletes such as the Golden State Warrior basketball player Stephen Curry, the number one golfer in the world, Jordan Spieth, and the 2015 Super Bowl quarterback, Cam Newton. The company's focus on athletes complements its mission, which is to make athletes better.

Under Armour also gained tremendous lift in the women's apparel sports market when Misty Copeland, shown in Figure 8.5, appeared in an Under Armour YouTube video. Under Armour is known for its savvy use of social media to build brand recognition. The company also does a fair amount of offline promotion through sponsorship of local sporting events.

### Products

While the company started on the basis of a T-shirt, the business has branched into multicategory athletic wear for men, women, and children. The largest product category is apparel. The company has the following gear lines: HEATGEAR, COLDGEAR, and ALLSEASONGEAR. The fitness wear comes in three groupings: compression (tight fit), fitted (athletic fit), and loose (relax fit).[31] With a 57 percent growth in footwear, the company believes that this category

**Figure 8.5**
**Misty Copeland** Here Misty Copeland, the American Ballet Theater's first African American principal dancer, is posing for the cover of the 2014 Under Armour Annual Report.

will evolve into a significant portion of its future business. The Curry Signature basketball line was the lead driver behind the growth. In the company's annual report, Under Armour projects that its footwear offering will become a billion dollar plus business in the near future.

The company's performance focus has made its products a favored brand among professionals and the everyday athlete. A key to the brand's product success has been the numerous patents that the company holds in areas such as accessories, apparel, footwear, innovation, and digital information management. In addition to product innovation, the company has built an internet community of physical fitness enthusiasts who track their meals, workouts, and ongoing fitness quests with the use of the Under Armour Connected Fitness Business. This platform leverages the company's fitness focus through the brand's four mobile application workout sites: UA

Record, MapMyFitness, Endomondo, and MyFitness Pal. The site has 160 million users from around the world, with 1,000 sports fanatics joining each day.

**Selling Channels**
The company has a direct-to-consumer business, which is the major portion of its international growth. As of its 2015 Annual Report date, the company was operating 25 global ecommerce sites with over 200 retail locations around the world, such as the retail locations at the Magnificent Mile in Chicago and the flagship store located in China. Because of the company's focus on its retail store destinations, the Under Armour international business has grown by 69 percent.

In North America, the company owns and operates 140 factory stores located in outlet malls. The business also includes ten regular price retail locations. The company distributes its product through third-party logistics partners located primarily in Canada, New Jersey, and Florida. The company's international stores are run through distribution agreements that provide access to Canada, Europe, the Middle East and Africa (EMEA), Asia-Pacific, and Latin America.[32]

**Supply Chain Network and Sourcing Considerations**
In 2016 the company announced a $5.5 billion redevelopment project to be located in Baltimore, Maryland, the company's headquarters. The founder purchased 100 acres that would be used to house the company's executive functions, operations, design, and manufacturing.[33] This is significant because as of 2013, Under Armour was primarily an outsourced manufacturing operation.

As with most other apparel and footwear brands, the majority of the company's manufacturing is located in Asia (Figure 8.6). The company sources its raw materials from a small textile network of mills located in China, New Mexico, Taiwan, and Vietnam. Similar to the company's manufacturing vendor base, there is significant vendor concentration, with a few factories and mills supporting the business. Under Armour also works with a group of licensees

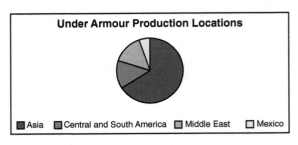

**Figure 8.6**
**Under Armour production locations[34]**

that produce socks, team uniforms, baby and kid's apparel, eyewear, and inflatable footballs and basketballs under the Under Armour brand.

While the company is able to build deep relationships with its sourcing partners by leveraging a consolidated supply chain network, it is also vulnerable to geographic and business risks within the small network of vendors it utilizes. As the company considers the move toward re-shoring several of its sourcing functions, some of these risks will be mitigated. However, the company will now be faced with the challenges of identifying and retaining in-house talent capable of sustaining the product quality and innovative product offerings that the Under Armour customer has valued since the inception of the business.

**Case Study Questions**
1. Given that the Under Armour brand is known for the quality of its product, what logistical concerns might arise with regard to the design, sourcing, production, and distribution aspects of the business?
2. To support the collaboration between Under Armour and its vendor base, what information must be shared throughout the Under Armour supply chain network to ensure that the mills, factories, and transportation resources are able to efficiently and effectively meet the demands of the Under Armour consumer?
3. As Under Armour grows its international presence, what logistical considerations and risks will become increasingly important within the business?

## CHAPTER REVIEW QUESTIONS

1. Draw a flow chart of production for an apparel item. In the chart, detail the role that logistics plays throughout the process. Describe the internal and external departments and companies that carry out these various roles.
2. Figure 8.4 depicts the information of customers, product, production, and distribution. Explain the types of information that each of these areas contributes to the overall flow information for

logistics. Is any of this information redundant? How important is each area of information to other areas?
3. If you were a logistics manager for a small retailer that does production in Asia, what steps would you take to mitigate risks in your supply chain?

## CLASS EXERCISE

Given Under Armour's plan to bring significant portions of its design and manufacturing functions in-house, develop a five-year plan that makes recommendations on how the company should strategically move its manufacturing capabilities in-house. What are the challenges and opportunities? What technical and equipment capabilities are needed to maintain the current level of product satisfaction? What does this mean to the Under Armour workforce? How does this move change the company's logistics strategy?

## KEY TERMS

logistics management
less-than-truckload (LTL)
B2C
vendor inventory management (VIM)
individual package market
common locker delivery systems
intermodal goods transport
multimodal transport
freight pooling
zone skipping
backhauling
activity-based costing
logistics
Schengen Agreement
International Maritime Organization's SOLAS (Safety of Life at Sea)

warehouse management system
stock keeping units (SKUs)
International Standard Organization (ISO)
radio-frequency identification (RFID)
electronic product code (EPC)
transportation management system (TMS)
labor management system (LMS)
pick-and-pack
global positioning system (GPS)
customer relationship management (CRM)
procurement and purchasing
inward transport or traffic
receiving department
stock control department

material handling department
order picking
recycling and waste disposal department
contract logistics or 3PL (third-party logistics)
courier express parcel (CEP)
freight forwarder
bill of lading
Customs Trade Partnership against Terrorism
push vs. pull inventory control
balanced scorecard
ports
vertically integrated
outsource

# REFERENCES

1. Bowersox, D. J., D. J. Closs, and M. B. Cooper (2013), *Supply Chain Logistics Management*, Boston: McGraw-Hill Irwin.
2. Huangon, N. (2014), *Global Logistics Industry Outlook*, January. Available online: https://www.businessvibes.com/blog/report-global-logistics-industry-outlook.
3. Global Logistics Markets to Reach US $15.5 Trillion by 2023, Transparency Market Research, October 2016. Available online:
4. Huangon, *Global Logistics Industry Outlook*.
5. http://www.referenceforbusiness.com/history2/37/United-Parcel-Service-Inc.html.
6. Vanian, J. (2016), "Amazon Steps Up Its Air Delivery Game," *Fortune*, March 16.
7. Ryan, T. (2013), "Macy's, Others Turn Stores into Online Fulfillment Centers," *Retail Wire*, April 3.
8. Berthiaume, D. (2015), "Report: Amazon Fulfillment Center Network Far Ahead of Other Retailers," *Chain Store Age*, October 19.
9. http://bsi-supplychainsolutions.com/en-US/supply-chain-risks/business-continuity/natural-disasters/.
10. Donaldson, T. (2016), "Here Are the Biggest Threats to the Global Supply Chain in 2016," *Sourcing Journal*, March 24. Available online: https://sourcingjournalonline.com/here-are-the-biggest-threats-to-the-global-supply-chain-in-2016-td/.
11. Ibid.
12. Weise, E., and C. Woodyard (2015), "Deal Reached in West Coast Dockworkers Dispute," *USA Today*, February 20. Available online: http://www.usatoday.com/story/news/2015/02/20/west-coast-ports-dispute-union-labor-secretary-tom-perez/23744299/.
13. Ibid.
14. Piasecki, D. (n.d.), "Order Picking: Methods and Equipment for Piece Pick, Case Pick, and Pallet Pick Operations," Inventoryops.com. Available online: http://www.inventoryops.com/order_picking.htm.
15. Curt, B. (2012), "Is a Warehouse Management System Right for Your Multichannel Business?" Multichannel Merchant. Available online: https://www.fcbco.com/hs-fs/hub/163466/file-18223143-pdf/docs/wms_vendor_whitepaper_2012.pdf.
16. Ibid.
17. Evotech Capital (2014), "Overview and Outlook in Logistics Industry," January 1. Available online: http://docplayer.net/35058348-Overview-and-outlook-in-logistics-industry-evotech-capital-1-4-2014.html.
18. https://www.export.gov/article2?id=Freight-Forwarder-What-is-a-FF.
19. http://www.itintl.com/what-is-a-freight-forwarder.html.
20. http://shippingandfreightresource.com/what-is-a-bill-of-lading/.
21. Culp, S. (2013), "Supply Chain Disruption: A Major Threat to Business," *Forbes*, February 15. Available online: http://www.forbes.com/sites/steveculp/2013/02/15/supply-chain-disruption-a-major-threat-to-business/#32f429447757.
22. ITI Manufacturing Staff (2014), "The Five Biggest and Busiest Export Ports in China Manufacturing," *Chinese Manufacturing News*, October 21.
23. http://www.worldshipping.org/about-the-industry/global-trade/top-50-world-container-ports.
24. Journal of Commerce (2017), "Hanjin Shipping." Available online: http://www.joc.com/maritime-news/container-lines/hanjin-shipping.
25. Glatzel, C., and J. Rohren (2014), "Excellence in Supply Chain Management," McKinsey & Company.
26. Bowersox et al., *Supply Chain Logistics Management*.
27. Fernie, J., and L. Sparks (2005), *Logistics and Retail Management: Insights into Current Practice and Trends from Leading Experts*, London: Kogan.
28. Evotech Capital, "Overview and Outlook in Logistics Industry."
29. Singer, T. (2004), "Trends in Warehousing and Distribution," *Deeper Insight ZEBRA Technologies*, November 11. Available online: https://www.impomag.com/article/2004/11/trends-warehousing-and-distribution.
30. Under Armour 2015 Annual Report. Available online: http://investor.underarmour.com/annuals.cfm.
31. Reuters–Under Armour (UA) Company Profile. Available online: http://www.reuters.com/finance/stocks/companyProfile?symbol=UA.
32. Ibid.
33. O'Connell, J. (2016), "When the Titan Wants to Build the Town: Under Armour's Founder Kevin Plank's $5.5 Billion Plan for Baltimore," *The Sun*, July 29.
34. http://marketrealist.com/2014/12/armour-nature-business-product-portfolio/.

# The Flow of Information through the Supply Chain

## LEARNING OBJECTIVES

Upon completion of this chapter you will be able to:

- Identify the various types of information that are needed to meet the production and delivery demands of consumers.

- Develop a perspective on the value of collaborating with internal departments and external vendors to generate accurate, readily available information.

- Evaluate the data management practices that increase the speed and reliability of information throughout the global fashion supply chain.

- Compare information management strategies to reduce supply chain risks.

# SUPPLY CHAIN DATA

Given the competitive nature of the fashion business, coupled with the whimsical nature of the typical consumer, brands are working to create global fashion supply chains that possess speed, agility, and an ability to practice a customer-centric approach when it comes to production and delivery practices. Design teams are able to speed up the design process by making decisions quickly in fabric selection. Speed can also be achieved through efficient manufacturing planning with regards to downtime in factories, production errors, and redundancies with quality control procedures. Because much of what drives fashion—celebrity endorsements, weather patterns, and economic considerations—falls outside of the control of the retailer, brands need flexibility in their supply chain to be able to react to market changes. To achieve agility or slack in the production process, brands look for opportunities to build relationships that enable resources to be optimized while also providing a means to maneuver around unexpected opportunities or market downsides. Today more than ever, the customer is the focal point. We live in a world where individuality is embraced and expressed in our spending habits and apparel selections. Hence brands are looking for opportunities to provide personalized products, services, and experiences that speak to the desire of the individual.

To achieve these goals, brands need to build supply chain networks that enable a flow of information throughout all aspects of the production-to-delivery process, the means to efficiently capture accurate and meaningful data that can be used to support proactive and agile decision-making, and the leadership talent and management expertise to champion the use of information to run their business operations. While it is clear that data are able to solve many of these hurdles, access to data and use of data continue to be a challenge for numerous businesses. A research report by SAP, a German software company that focuses on business operations, provided the following interview responses by supply chain executives on the current and future state of its supply chain and the data that support these operations.[1]

- 74 percent say that insight on what customers desire and would pay for is highly valuable but difficult to access.

- 62 percent say that they have no valuable data from indirect customers, with 34 percent stating that they have no data whatsoever.

- 78 percent say that they have data from direct customers that are less than a week old and valuable; 34 percent say that access to their supply chain data is real-time.

- 70 percent of first movers on the use of customer profitability analysis say they have real-time direct customer data that are highly valuable.

These statistics point out the need for insight into customers to gain an understanding of buying preferences and product substitutions. The study also shows how companies are failing to benefit from real-time information that will further support the agility and efficiency of their supply chain network. However, the companies that are leading the charge in adapting to the demands of a customer-centric market are accessing data on a real-time basis (70 percent of the participants). This is to be expected, because to achieve success with customer segmentation and profitability analysis, companies require data in a timely fashion to allow for analysis and reaction.

During the production, warehousing, and distribution processes, a great deal of data is generated, such as shown in Table 9.1, which includes information such as fabric availability, the number of SKUs, and markdown percentages. Because information is created and used by many different departments and vendor relationships through a brand's supply chain, it can be used for different reasons throughout the supply chain. For example, Table 9.1 shows that finished goods delivery timing is used by both marketing and store operations. Marketing is using the information to plan when the advertising should occur for the product promotions. Store operations uses the information too, but to plan the new inventory delivery dates for the stores. Both departments are using the same data, but for very different reasons.

While there are many uses for supply chain data, the ability to access, and more importantly, utilize supply chain data from a company-wide versus individual department perspective is often hampered for the following reasons: a silo mentality, challenges to collecting the data, and a lack of leadership perspective on the powerful impact of applying supply chain data

| Supply Chain Data | Product Development | Logistics | Marketing | Finance | Merchandising | Store Operations |
|---|---|---|---|---|---|---|
| Raw Material Level | Fabric Availability | Transportation Requirements | Product Insight | Costs | Consumer Preference | Delivery Timing |
| Work in Progress | Production Status | Transportation Requirement | Costs | Delivery Timing | Delivery Timing | |
| Finished Good | Production Status | Transportation Requirement | Delivery Timing | Cash flow | Delivery Timing | Delivery Timing |
| Quality Control Defects | Production Challenges | Potential Delivery Delays | Product Communication & Potential Delivery Delays | Cost | Delivery Timing | Delivery Timing |
| On-time Delivery Rates | Production Challenges | Potential Delivery Delays | Potential Delivery Delays/Tie to Promotion Calendar | Cost | Delivery Timing | Store Layout Planning |
| Number of SKUs | Production Requirements | Transportation Requirements | Marketing Planning | Category Margins | Merchandising Plan | Store Layout Planning |
| Product Sell Through Rate | Product Acceptance | Transportation Requirements | Marketing Planning | Margin Impact | Merchandising Plan | Store Layout Planning |
| Markdown Rates | Product Acceptance | Marketing Planning | Margin Impact | Merchandising Plan | Store Layout Planning | |
| Stockouts | Product Acceptance | Marketing Planning | Margin Impact | Merchandising Plan | Store Layout Planning | |
| Return Rates | Product Acceptance | Marketing Planning | Margin Impact | Merchandising Plan | Store Layout Planning | |

**Table 9.1** Supply Chain Data from Product Development to Store Operations

This table shows the types of data that are collected throughout the supply chain, as well as how the data are used by the different departments of a retail brand.

throughout the entire organization. Chapter 4 gives a clear understanding of the relationships between internal departments and external partners in the supply chain. Because of these relationship dependencies, looking at data throughout the supply chain instead of on a myopic departmental basis is critically important. For example, within retail, one of the most challenging areas of business is the planning of the production calendar. This process requires high-level oversight and information from various departments, such as design, sourcing, marketing, and finance. It would be impossible for a retailer to take a silo approach to plan its production calendar.

**Key performance indicators (KPIs)** are quantitative information that is used to monitor and track progress. For supply chain management, KPIs are metrics that can help management determine important points of information, such as the completion rates for a production line, the defect rate for a product that failed to meet the design specifications, and on-time delivery. KPIs are important because they enable management to focus on the significant factors that drive the business. Figure 9.1 shows how KPIs provide the knowledge to analyze, solve, define, implement, and review organizational outcomes. This ability to zone in on the key drivers is valuable because of the increased need for quicker

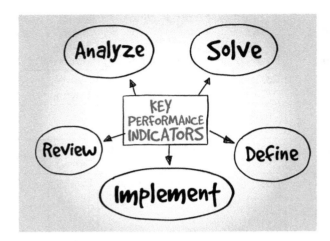

**Figure 9.1**

**Key performance indicators** Key performance indicators provide leaders with insight into the performance of their business. They provide data to analyze, solve, define, implement, and review key organizational decisions.

and more accurate decision-making throughout the supply chain. As repeated throughout this book, speed is a key force in supply chain management. KPIs enable management to make informed decisions more quickly and also enable a company to reduce production time and costs by applying the KPI findings throughout the entire course of the business. Additionally, KPIs provide an opportunity to benchmark performance by working with a set of common metrics over a period of time.

From an apparel manufacturing perspective, KPIs generally fall within the following categories: financial, customer experience, and operating performance.[2] For a retailer, the *financial* KPIs might include the percentages of costs such as production, rework items, and logistics. These financial KPIs tell the story of how production is impacting unit margins and overall company profitability. Given the competitive nature of fashion, KPIs that identify concerns with customer orders, product reception, and returns are also important metrics for management to monitor. As with the financial KPIs, the *customer experience* KPIs are also a means to predict the impact of production on both the unit and company level. Finally, with the exception of luxury items, the typical margins for apparel manufacturing are quite slim. This is why KPIs that focus on *operating performance* are important to enable management to potentially minimize product

defects, ensure better alignment between order production and actual demand, and train workers on real-time data with regards to production concerns. Once again, KPIs are an invaluable way for managers to increase their company intelligence through a consistent monitoring of results.

## Inventory Management Data

Second to labor, inventory is typically the largest cost of a retailer. Therefore, the counting and monitoring of inventory are a key focus of supply chain analytics. Companies rely on inventory management systems to provide visibility to inventory levels, consumer demand, stockouts, shrinkage, customer dissatisfaction, and obsolete items. Because smaller production runs are necessary to accommodate greater sell through for the retailer, while also supporting multiple SKUs to accommodate the consumer's desire for variety, inventory management has grown in its complexity. Additionally, retailers are attempting to use inventory data to learn more about their customers' buying habits, to be able to develop more accurate production forecasts, and where possible, to determine the next big item that their shoppers must have.

## Big Data

The introduction of **big data**, a collection of data from traditional systems such as inventory management and point of sales (POS) systems with digital insight like web purchasing data and online searches, enables retailers to maintain a more complete perspective on their inventory. While inventory management data had traditionally been used to monitor the various stages of inventory such as the raw materials, work-in-progress, and finished goods, the algorithms and integrated systems utilized by big data have enhanced the functionality of this information. As seen in Figure 9.2, instead of being able to only assess information on a one-dimensional basis, businesses can use big data to create customer profiles based on multiple data points such as shopping patterns, style trends, and the correlation of data sets. Big data takes information that was once captured within multiple departments and vendor relationships and enables the information to be looked at in aggregate. It is

**Figure 9.2**

**Big data** This is a graphical depiction of the volume of information that is now available within reach of one's computer screen because of the capabilities of big data to draw upon multiple data sources. Before big data, information was viewed in a silo or would require a laborious process to access and evaluate it simultaneously.

a powerful resource that is dramatically changing how inventory is managed; retailers are utilizing this information to inform their marketing plans, financing considerations, and even store layout: big data can provide insight on what type of store environment works best for a retailer's target customer. Big data can also provide insight on how to think through the life cycle of a consumer to ensure that the retailer is able to best meet customers' needs with the right product, at the right time, at the preferred price.

Among the many challenges that retailers encounter, speed in decision-making is major. The push for reduced lead time coupled with consumers' fashion fatigue—because the social media world is always promoting the next new thing without allowing retailers the time to develop and sell their current inventory—retailers must be able to reduce decision-making time while also increasing their projection accuracy. Big data enables retailers to leverage the customer insight from multiple data sets to drive decision-making that is based on real-time information from multiple data sources. The user-friendly access to multiple data sets is a significant time reducer. In the past, retailers might need to collect data from multiple systems to then come up with data

## Notes from the Field

Data have always been in intrinsic part of the fashion industry. Every Monday morning the retailers would look at their numbers from the prior week. In many instances that was done with pencil and paper, depending on the company's size, and some things never change. Data are still important, but the way we collect data has morphed into what some call "big data" or "data analytics." The numbers are still the key to success, but we have become much more sophisticated in how we collect them. Today's fashion industry is all about "big data"! When I first entered the industry working for JC Penney as a catalog inventory control specialist (CICS), the company was just starting to realize the power of data. One of my responsibilities

was to monitor the sales of catalog items through what was then a new technology. We used a percent done model and could tell in the first few days if the item was a dog (below estimate), on estimate, or a runner (way ahead of sales estimates). One particular item, a quilted flannel men's shirt, started out with a bang, and, based on the data collection and analysis, went from an estimate of 10,000 shirts to 110,000 shirts in the first day! Now the trick was capturing the demand, which we were able to do 98 percent of the time. It was a mad scramble for production and piece goods, but we satisfied 107,800 customers. Data collection and analysis have vastly improved but still have the same goal, satisfying the consumer.

to integrate the information into their decision-making process. Big data simplifies data integration, which significantly reduces the time it takes a manager to produce a report. When there is no process for integrating data, there is a lag in the data collection process. The integrated systems insight of big data supports real-time information access. Today's consumers shop anytime and anywhere, and real-time data is key to servicing their needs.

# Radio-Frequency Identification (RFID)

**Radio-frequency identification (RFID)** has been available and used somewhat in apparel manufacturing since the 1980s. RFID is gaining popularity as an information management tool for retailers who are managing significant volumes of inventory with multiple SKUs and item variations. According to a report by Global Industry Analyst, the RFID market is expected to reach $18.7 billion by 2017, with the current cost of $0.05 per RFID chip expected to see further decrease due to increased market adoption.[3] By using a chip, a retailer is able to track the mill that the material came from, the factory that cut and sewed the item, the cargo vessel that brought the garment to its selling market, the warehouse that stored the item, and the store or ecommerce distribution point that received the item. It is almost like having a GPS for a piece of clothing. Questions that retailers were unable to ask in the past can now be asked because of the information supplied by RFID. For example, if a retailer is continuously experiencing returns with a particular dress because the consumer feels that the material is wearing after one wash, the retailer is able to see whether a particular mill has a pattern of providing defective textiles. RFID also gives retailers insight about the time required to produce particular goods, the cost impact due to delays with various batches, and the geographic location of inventory.

## RFID Omnichannel Solution

To succeed in an omnichannel environment, retailers are turning to RFID for the readily available inventory detail that RFID provides to support the shopper's buying and order fulfillment process. In an omnichannel selling environment, retailers need real-time, accurate information about their stock on hand, the inventory's geographic location, and the inventory that is being produced. Absent this information, they will be unable to create a seamless selling environment with multiple points of customer access.

Before the deployment of RFID and other inventory management systems, retailers would usually inventory their stores twice a year, typically in January after the big holiday selling period and during the summer prior to the holiday push. This was a labor-intensive process in which a sales associate would literally count and tag items by hand. This required the use of additional labor hours because the inventory counting often occurred while the store was closed to avoid any sales disruption. Because the count was being done by hand, there was a great risk that the information would be inaccurate. With the request of a report, RFID is able to provide real-time, accurate inventory detail by category with size, color, and location information. These are the data that a retailer needs to fulfill consumer demand within an omnichannel selling environment. The omnichannel retailer Macy's, which operated 876 stores as of April 2016,[4] needs an automated, simple way to leverage its inventory across its store footprint so that it can sell in-store and online and, if need be, move inventory between locations to balance a store's inventory with its demand.

While RFID is growing in significance in the retail industry, many retailers, because of their size and ability to deploy resources, still manage their inventory by using **universal product code (UPC)**, a unique twelve-digit number assigned to retail merchandise, and a **hangtag system**, the use of item hangtags to maintain an inventory count. While these means fail to meet some of the real-time and speed benefits of RFID, these traditional methods are still a way to give retailers an understanding of their inventory levels.

**Retail shrinkage**, the portion of the inventory that is either lost or stolen during the production or distribution phases, can be a costly drain on a retailer's profit margins and inventory availability planning if a control mechanism is not in place. Annually, retailers lose profits because of employee, vendor, and customer theft. Inventory is also lost because of common error. Shrinkage reduces retailers' margins by 1.45 percent, which is a significant reduction on the already low retail margin that the National Retailer Federation has set: 5.04 percent. Absent shrinkage, the same apparel item could achieve a margin of 6.49 percent, a 28.8 percent higher margin.[5] Given this financial impact, analysis is a high-priority area of focus for manufacturers and in-store operations. Because it makes available inventory location data, RFID is a solution to inventory theft throughout all areas of the supply chain and the in-store environment.

## DATA COLLECTION

We have been discussing the use of data throughout the supply chain. In order to use the data, one must first collect the information. For improved accuracy and timeliness of data collection, the data collection and reporting processes should be standardized. This standardization will enable multiple users to access the information and will also reduce the amount of time needed to collect the data. Dashboards and balanced scorecards (discussed in following text) are examples of data collection methods that support increase information flow throughout the supply chain.

## Dashboards

A **dashboard** is a user-friendly, visual representation of KPIs that informs management at a glance about the performance of a process or function. As demonstrated in Figure 9.3, a dashboard centralizes information into a commonly agreed-upon reporting format that can be shared with multiple individuals on a real-time basis. A continual theme of supply chain management is the need for management to react quickly to customer requests, design defects, production modifications, and

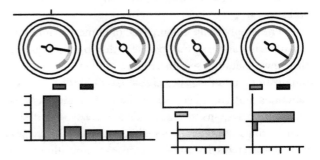

**Figure 9.3**
**A dashboard** This dashboard captures KPIs in a central visual image to quickly give management an overall understanding of the business's performance.

### Notes from the Field

Not only do the retailers use big data to affect decisions, but ancillary groups that operate within the scope of the fashion industry do as well. For these companies and organizations, big data is just as important because information can affect funding, which allows these groups to do the good work that they do. Cotton Incorporated operates as a nonprofit organization and is the marketing arm of the US cotton industry (although it has gone global as well). One stop on my industry tour was with this company. Cotton Incorporated was big on collecting data and analyzing the data to gauge trends in cotton use among consumers. Originally the focus was the United States, but it became a global focus with the globalization of the fashion industry. Cotton teamed up with Tide laundry detergent to study the use of its product on cotton products in Mexico. Collecting data in the early 1990s was an interesting process in Mexico, as much of the data collection relied on door-to-door surveys. The results of the survey were very interesting, as the people surveyed overwhelming said they were using Tide laundry detergent products on cotton apparel. In fact, the results far outstripped the total amount of product that was being exported to Mexico. It appears that when surveyed the respondents did not want to disappoint the people conducting the survey, so they basically told them what they thought they wanted to hear. The point is that data collection has to be analyzed to exclude any potential bias!

projected inventory levels. By pulling this information into a central reporting mechanism, managers can tackle complex decisions because they have access to the KPIs that impact their business. Absent a dashboard or a comparable data collection source, managers would be required to go to multiple systems to collect data and then be forced to evaluate the accuracy and relevance of this information. Dashboards automate this process, significantly reducing the speed and evaluation time needed. With a dashboard, this work has been done in advance, so time can be spent on analyzing data versus collecting it.

The supply chain is composed of numerous internal departments and external partners that often maintain their own operating systems, reports, and means of communication. Dashboards heighten visibility to buried functions and costs because of the limited automation or common systems to support data gathering.[6] A dashboard brings immediate visibility to current inventory levels, projected sales, and per store inventory allocation. This information helps managers to make better and quicker production decisions.

## Balanced Scorecards

A **balanced scorecard** is a strategic performance management tool that creates a way to monitor how an internal department or vendor's performance is operating relative to a retailer's operational and even company-wide goals and objectives. Scorecards utilize visualization to document progress and identify categories of focus. The user-friendly information layout supports ease of use and consistency of information while ensuring access to a broad array of company metrics. Companies often require their vendor partners to use balanced scorecards. Companies tend to use the scorecard to assess compliance in key areas such as sustainable manufacturing processes.

Companies have also used balanced scorecards to maximize profits by looking closely at costs, to optimize resource allocation by evaluating bottlenecks and service gaps caused by improper resource management, and to elevate customer service levels by identifying product defects and unfavorable customer communications.[7] Because the balanced scorecard captures a great amount of information from multiple internal departments and

| Critical Success Factors | Target | Status |
|---|---|---|
| Business Benefit | - Customer car costs reduced by 15% <br> - Market share increase by 5% | ⬤ |
| Financials | - Program budget tracking at or under 100% of planned | ⬤ |
| Schedule | - Milestone 1 = week 3 <br> - Milestone 2 = week 28 <br> - Milestone 3 = week 48 | ⬤ |
| Technology | - Target patents on track <br> - Key technology partners in place | ⬤ |
| Customer | - Product scores 4/5 with target consumer segment <br> - Customer care scored 4/5 with target consumer segement | ⬤ |

**Figure 9.4**

**Balanced scorecard** A balanced scorecard documents critical success factors, operational targets, and status of the business's critical success factors. The scorecard provides management with vendor updates on operating performance.

vendors, companies are able to manage multiple areas of concern and opportunity.

Figure 9.4 is an example of a balanced scorecard that shows the multiple areas of performance about which this company plans to gain greater insight. Performance in each category is measured using a predetermined target, with progress tracked by a red, yellow, and green coloring scheme. At a glance, management teams are able to assess progress, areas of concern, and opportunities for improvement. Since collaboration is a key means of achieving organization goals, the stakeholders of each internal department and vendor must show a common buy-in and understanding of the value and use of the balanced scorecard.[8]

The balanced scorecard aligns the often long-term visionary goals of the organization with the daily process that gets the work done.[9] It provides leaders with the reality of how their company is performing in relation to their vision. Because visions often include an amount of stretch in their projections, the balanced scorecard provides a means to track and monitor progress and even provides insight into how the vision can be modified based on the capabilities of the organization. The balanced scorecard also provides a means to connect internal departments and suppliers that often operate in isolation yet have an interdependent relationship within a company's supply chain network. For example, mills provide the fabric that is used in the production process to create the vision of the designer. While in many instances the mill and the factory are two separate entities, the manufacturing is highly dependent upon the quality of the material, the ability of the mill to deliver the material on time, and the cost of the material. These factors all go into the creation of the scorecard metrics that relate to the operating and production capabilities of the supply chain network.

Multiple factors can potentially impact supply chain internal and external participants, and scorecards are a means to track and monitor the effectiveness of these relationships. A key objective achieved from scorecards is continuous process improvement. By evaluating key categories of operations, manufacturing scorecards provide visibility to sourcing effectiveness and common challenges across a retailer's supplier network. Scorecards are often used when monitoring sustainable business practices.

The following is a list of factors that one should consider when developing a balanced scorecard.[10]

- Identify categories/groupings for the information that you will gather, such as financial metrics, customer impact, operating performance, and management initiatives.
- Minimize the number of metrics to no more than fifteen things to be counted and/or monitored. When developing the scorecard, challenge the company leadership to think broadly about the organization vision and mission and how these goals are played out in the daily work environment.
- Because of the timing of outcomes, the metrics should be an appropriate balance of lead and lag indicators. **Lead indicators** are inputs that typically impact an outcome, such as the number of revised shipping routes to increase on-time shipping deliveries. **Lag indicators** are outcomes of the business, such as the number of items produced, total revenue, and costs.
- To create an effective management tool, the scorecard should focus on company-wide goals

and objectives versus a more siloed approach that monitors individual department performance.

- Scorecards should be reviewed on a frequent basis to ensure that the metrics being captured are still germane to the business and best project the organization's vision.

# PROCESS IMPROVEMENT STRATEGIES

In today's retail environment, there is an ongoing need for process improvements. Additionally, the fickleness of the industry increases the risk of retailers getting stuck with fads that consumers no longer want or being outdone by the market by failing to produce enough items to meet consumer demand.

The Bureau of Labor Statistics reported that there was a drop in labor productivity for apparel and footwear manufacturing between 2014 and 2015. If this trend continues to plague the industry and consumers continue to seek apparel alternatives that require supply chains with increased speed and efficiency, there will be an adverse impact on the industry's ability to meet the demands of the market. To take a proactive stance on reversing this trend, there are a few process improvement initiatives that retailers can embrace, such as lean manufacturing, Six Sigma, and total quality management. In Chapter 7 these same strategies were introduced in the discussion surrounding quality assurance. These strategies serve many different functions in the fashion industry supply chain.

## Lean Manufacturing

Just as with the KPIs and balanced scorecard, it is critical that the retailer have an understanding of the company's mission and vision and how process improvement supports these goals. **Lean manufacturing**, often associated with the automotive industry, is a method of process improvement that focuses on removing waste, also known as **muda**, the Japanese word for wastefulness, out of the production process while elevating job functions to value-added functions and increasing the flow of information throughout the supply chain. **Waste** is any non-value-added activity that a customer doesn't see enough reason to pay for. An area of debate regarding non-value-added activities is compliance testing. Since lean manufacturing focuses on continuous improvement, the manufacturing should proceed without a need for additional testing, which creates costs and increases production lead times. Lean manufacturing is typically suited for repetitive processes like production or assembly lines that allow for opportunities to remove redundant tasks and that drive efficiency with required functions through worker training and workflow redesign.

As discussed in Chapter 7, there are various forms of waste that occur during the manufacturing process. Each area of waste provides an opportunity for management to leverage data collection, training, and collaboration to implement processes and procedures that work to minimize muda.

As shown in Table 9.2, each area of waste has an impact on business operations, affecting costs, customer satisfaction, and operating efficiency. By managing to minimize waste, retailers can meet the demands of consumers in a cost-effective manner. Within each of these categories there are also elements of hidden waste that management might overlook and/or bury into overhead costs, which might falsely impact the profitability of an item and therefore hamper production planning decisions.

Especially for apparel, there are tremendous opportunities for waste throughout the production process, such as water treatment waste for any dying processes used on the material and a wasteful amount of unusable scrap that results from cutting fabric. In additive manufacturing, an interesting area of waste management, there is zero waste because one fits materials to a form instead of starting with a generic piece of material that must be cut into the actual pattern. It also cannot be stated enough how waste not only impacts the operations of the retailer, but also has a potentially detrimental effect on customer relations regarding product availability, cost, and quality.

To ensure the highest standards, lean manufacturing also incorporates the **5Ss: sort, set in order, shine, standardize, and sustain**[12] (from the five Japanese words *seiri, seiton, seiso, seiketsu, and shitsuke*).[13] This process improvement practice focuses on a way to think about discipline in the workplace to instill order in one's physical and mental space and promote a harmonious work environment.

**Kaizen,** a Japanese business philosophy that focuses on process improvement and has the potential to impact an entire organization, is a key component of lean manufacturing. Kaizen provides insights into how to transform a process by guiding management to encourage collaborative decision-making in order to identify innovative solutions that challenge traditional thinking. Kaizen applies the power of thinking out of the box to obtain goals that under ordinary circumstances might seem unobtainable. If, for example, a company wants to produce the same amount of dresses annually while decreasing resources by 50 percent, this can only obtained by approaching the solution with an open mind on how to achieve the goal.

## Six Sigma

Like lean manufacturing, the process improvement concept of Six Sigma was first introduced outside of the apparel industry. It gained popularity at Motorola, the

**Table 9.2** Seven Types of Production Waste[11]

| Area of Waste | Business Impact |
| --- | --- |
| Overproduction | Unnecessary use of raw materials, manufacturing resources, and warehousing facilities |
| Waste of Unnecessary Motion | Depletion of energy resources and potential equipment wear |
| Waste of Inventory | A direct result of overproduction is the production of inventory that fails to fulfill a demand |
| Production of Defects | Waste of materials and labor and possible customer dissatisfaction |
| Waste of Waiting | Idle production time, leading to lost opportunity costs |
| Waste of Transportation | Energy use and extended lead times |
| Waste of Overprocessing | Unnecessary use of resources and potential impact on product quality |

This table outlines how waste occurs throughout the production process.

multinational telecommunications company. The concept of **Six Sigma** originates from a statistical term that validates the thought that "perfection is possible," but with 99.73 percent of the output meeting the range of acceptability.[14] This concept allows for the thinking that operations can reach higher standards and improve performance with results that meet or exceed acceptability.

While Six Sigma can apply to any process, to partake in a Six Sigma effort a retailer would first identify the projects that possess the best returns or are most impactful to the company. Because Six Sigma projects require a commitment of adequate talent management, capital investment, and time, companies should prioritize projects that are aligned with their goals and objectives. Six Sigma projects go through what is called DMAIC: Define, Measure, Analyze, Improve, and Control (Figure 9.5).

As with any strategic initiative, planning is a key to success. Hence, the first Six Sigma phase is "Define": define the project, the project team, and the proposed outcomes. By defining the project, management is able to allocate resources, adjust priorities, and, where appropriate, alter existing operations to create time to focus on the proposed project. Based on the project chosen, the next phase is "Measure." Because of the investment made to execute a Six Sigma project, the measurement aspect is needed to justify continued resources, track outcomes, and, in some cases, make adjustments to ensure that the goals of the project still align with the organization's goals and objectives.

Now that the management team has developed the purpose and scope of the project and adequate thought has been given to the metrics that will be used to track progress, this information will be evaluated in the "Analyze" phase. This is the phase where the project outcomes are tested and assessed for solutions to the problem. The "Improve" phase is where the project solution is tested, either in a pilot or simulated effort. This is the phase during which a company's leadership is able to step back from the data and challenge project participants to think beyond the company's status quo processes and procedures and make recommendations that present an opportunity for innovation to achieve the project's projected goals. This is a key step; companies often fail to change because change requires them to ask the hard questions, challenge the status quo, and, in some cases, suggest talent shifts to achieve the goal. During the piloting period, companies should make sure to provide adequate time and resources to create a test environment that will provide a true indication of how the solution would work in a real-world situation.

If management is satisfied with the results from the "Improve" phase, the next phase is "Control." During the "Control" phase, the project team seeks to identify company participants who will maintain the processes and procedures that were defined and previously tested. This is the phase in which formal standard operating procedures (SOPs) are developed and training occurs. Because of the investment made to get to this phase of the project, it is key that the handoff and/or inclusion of new participants includes a time for buy-in from stakeholders to ensure their willingness to continue to be project champions.

During the final phase of the Six Sigma project (not shown in Figure 9.5), "Synergize," the test environment, project outcomes, and the project's philosophy must be shared throughout the organization. As defined at the beginning of the project, the purpose of Six Sigma is to create game-changing solutions throughout the organization, not just in certain departments. A step in the

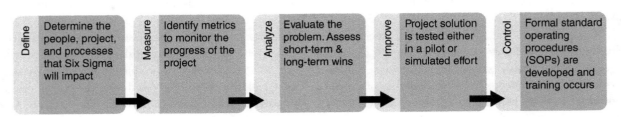

**Figure 9.5**
**DMAIC: Define, Measure, Analyze, Improve, and Control** This figure outlines the five areas of a Six Sigma project and their expected outcomes.

"Synergize" phase might be to identify other company problems that could benefit from the results that the Six Sigma project created. The key to ensuring ongoing process improvement is to create a culture in which the company is constantly looking for areas of growth by applying previous learning.

Professionals are able to obtain industry-recognized belts of accomplishment for the types of projects that they have led and for the amount of knowledge that they know about Six Sigma. There are four levels of belts that an individual can achieve: Master Black, Black, Green, and Yellow. The **Master Black Belt (MBB)** is the most senior person with a recognized area of expertise. This individual has led numerous Black Belt Six Sigma projects, mentored junior candidates on advancing their belt certifications, and served as an advisor to senior leadership teams on the progress and outcome of Six Sigma projects.

A **Black Belt (BB)** is the most senior actively engaged Six Sigma professional. BBs have amassed significance experience in managing Six Sigma projects. They are involved with planning the project scope, identifying resources, and playing an advisory role to more junior belt holders. The BB also oversees a majority of the project reports that are sent to senior management and other project stakeholders. The **Green Belt (GB)** handles somewhat less complex Six Sigma project work that tends to focus less on the statistical analysis aspects of the project. At times, GB functions might overlap with BB functions.

The **Yellow Belt (YB)** is more of a strategic oversight role. These individuals are trained in the Six Sigma functions much like BBs and GBs; however, their role is more of a project champion or stakeholder. These individuals tend to be more important in the later phases of the Six Sigma project, when the focus is on implementation and potential introduction to the rest of the organization.

Data collection and analysis are a key aspect of the Six Sigma process. **Discrete data** are data that can only take certain values. An example of discrete data is information that is counted, such as the number of dresses produced and the percentage of dresses with defects. The item is discrete because it represents one whole unit; you would be unable to say you have only half a dress. Hence, discrete numbers are counted in whole numbers such as zero, one, two, three, and four. In discrete data, there is a finite number of results.

**Qualitative data** is information that can be observed but not measured, such as the color of dresses, the feel of the material, and the appearance of the sample. Qualitative data are represented by numbers and can be reflected in categories of items by a number code. Because consumers often purchase based on the look, feel, and appearance of a garment, qualitative data are often used in combination with discrete data to capture the quality of a garment.

**Attribute data** is information that is presented once a particular condition occurs, for example, the number of dresses that shrink when they are washed. While the number of dresses can be counted, the attribute data is a subset of data on the dress once the condition of washing the item has been met. The key for attribute data is to ensure that outcomes result from comparable environments. If two dresses are washed, one in cold water and one in hot water, the attribute data would not be comparable because of the water variation. Attribute data can also be used to track the impact of marketing campaigns by asking consumers whether they made a purchase because of a coupon they received from the retailer.

Another form of quantitative data is **continuous data**. This information measures the magnitude of something, such as the length of a hemline, the amount of time required to produce a garment, and the amount of give of a piece of fabric. Because consumers often purchase apparel on the basis of an item's quality and consistency, continuous data is an important source of insight in the apparel manufacturing process.

In the world of consumers that shop anywhere and anytime, **location data** are an invaluable source of insight because retailers are able to assess inventory demand and purchasing location. Through online purchases, retailers are even able to determine the device that was used for the purchase. Within the manufacturing environment, location data are able to provide insight about per-factory production, inventory by location, and movement of goods during the transportation phases of production. Companies like Amazon have built their businesses around the insight gained from location data. Location data are also an invaluable customer service tool because retailers are able to use these data to troubleshoot problem deliveries and help sales associates locate inventory.

**Total quality management** (TQM) is a process improvement strategy that works to instill a continuous philosophy of improvement throughout the entire organization. TQM focuses on building customer loyalty through quality service, products, and brand association. Once again, the competitive nature of the fashion industry requires companies to continuously seek opportunities to improve their supply chain efforts. From field notes, they are able to see the numerous errors that can occur during the garment manufacturing process. Since the supply chain is composed of multiple functions, there are also other areas of potential error within the distribution, transportation, and warehousing aspects of production. Through the application of the TQM guides, organizations can think about their operations as a means to retain customers by presenting products that meet expectations for today's consumers.

## ISO 9000

The **International Organization for Standardization (ISO)** is an independent, not-government-affiliated organization with a membership of 163 national standards bodies. The purpose of the organization is on a voluntary basis to promote standards of process innovation through training and leadership guidance. Through the contributions of its membership, ISO has published over 21,000 international standards that impact just about all industries and all areas of operational focus.

ISO 9000 is a set of five guidance standards, of which three standards, ISO 9001, 9002, and 9003, are certifications that organizations seek to pursue. ISO 9000 and 9004 are guidance for the three certifications.

As with the other strategic process improvements mentioned in this chapter, ISO 9000 benefits companies by requiring them to take a reflective, critical look at how they do business and how successful their operations are at achieving improved customer service and providing quality products. Because the ISO certification requires documentation of processes, companies develop extensive standard operating procedures (SOPs). The ISO designation is a company differentiator based on process performance from a global competition perspective.

## CONCLUSION

As today's consumer continues to value fast fashion, unique styles, and custom delivery options, a retailer's supply chain must be able to achieve these goals. Therefore, information is key to identifying fashion trends, sourcing product, and providing the right product at the right time to the right customer. Information is used to support speedier and more accurate decision-making throughout the supply chain. KPIs and inventory management information alert management teams to issues that might impact production and consumer demand. Data collection tools such as dashboards and balanced scorecards further support decision-making by consolidating information from various phases of the production and distribution process—the opposite of a silo approach. Data are able to be analyzed from a company-wide perspective. Since most decisions require input from multiple internal departments and external partners, a company-wide view of data is most beneficial to the decision-making process.

With regards to process improvements, Six Sigma, total quality management (TQM), and ISO 9000 provide management with the tools to continuously monitor and improve production outcomes. For all of these improvement strategies, data are required to evaluate the overall production process.

# INDUSTRY INTERVIEW: MARY A. ALONSO, PRINCIPAL, ALONSO FASHION SOLUTIONS

Mary A. Alonso is the senior product manager for footwear for Fully Beauty Brands, an American plus-size women's and men's apparel and home goods company. Ms. Alonso has P&L (the revenue and cost aspects of the business) responsibility for private label and branded shoe categories. In this role, she plans assortments, merchandises product, and enhances customer experience for both online and catalog orders. Ms. Alonso collaborates with inventory, sourcing, and ecommerce teams to optimize profits. She was the principal for Alonso Fashion Solutions (formerly Strategic Brand Direction). At Alonso Fashion Solutions, Ms. Alonso devised productivity measures to enable ecommerce fashion companies to analyze category sales. She also evaluated market potential and developed target prospects for startup footwear wholesalers.

Ms. Alonso is an adjunct fashion instructor at the Fashion Institute of Technology (FIT) and Berkeley College. She earned her MBA in marketing from Pace University and her BA in psychology from Rutgers University (Douglass College). She also studies shoe production at Tresham School of Footwear.

**Interviewer:** *What role do data play in today's supply chain?*

**M. A.:** Data play a critical role because of the pressure that retailers face to deliver the right product at the right time. In order to achieve this goal, data are essential in planning and forecasting demand and managing how inventory turns impact a company's cashflow. In order to maximize efficiency and increase profit margins, there is a need to be able to integrate all budgeting, order logistics, and sales data. The faster communication of consumer needs allows for a more nimble response to customers. Apart from the availability of data, it is the system advancements that increase the ability to obtain data quickly and accurately.

So far, some of the most impactful types of systems advancements have been around order fulfillment for both online and brick and mortar, merchandising planning software, and logistics platforms. Another technology-based solution is the ability to integrate multiple systems to produce data that is able to inform multiple areas of the business, such as customer services, sales, inventory management, and marketing.

It is not just that there is a wealth of data; it is how usable are these data in impacting a company's people, systems, and culture. For example, data enable a sales associate to know where else an item is located throughout the entire company. Knowing how to use data to get an item to a customer when needed has a positive effect on sales, customer services, and inventory management.

While there are tremendous benefits that come with this access to data, recognition from the senior management team of an organization is key to instilling within the culture of an organization the importance of collecting and maintaining accurate data, meaning that the most basic of functions such as data entry must be accurate. The senior management team can promote the mindset of not seeing data collection as a burden, but as a critical tool to build customer relationships. It is also important to recognize that some of these systems take time for associates to learn and enter data correctly. Absent adequate training, there is a greater chance that the data will be inputted incorrectly.

**Interviewer:** *How has the access to data impacted the way retailers engage with their supply chain vendors?*

**M.A.:** The access to data has had more of an effect on the timeliness of getting products from the warehouse to the retailer. Depending on the level of data that a company shares, data can give the design and merchandising teams at the factory more insight about their customer base. By increasing the access of information throughout the supply chain, customers get new product quicker, retailers have a more efficient means to engage with customers about demand, and there is improvement in order fulfillment, ultimately reducing the potential for missed sales caused by lack of availability. Retailers must keep a focus on inventory replenishment to avoid stockouts.

Data in the product development phase have been quite useful because retailers are able to see how items are performing by collecting reorder data. Sales data are some of the most useful data because you gain insight as to what is working well for consumers. There is planning data, but sales are the actual results of the planning.

Another area of improvement is the transmission of data to and from vendors, such as the automated delivery of product specifications and construction components to factories by means of the web. Remotely, retailers are able to provide guidance on product specifications. While not directly data focused, another area of improvement is computerized pattern grading, which cuts time from manual pattern making. This automation reduces time in the production process by not requiring the product development step of **grading**, the creation of a series of patterns for multiple sizes based off the initial design, for all sizes.

**Interviewer:** *What role has technology played in today's footwear supply chain?*

**M.A.:** The role of technology in the evolution of the footwear supply chain has been pretty much the same as it has been for apparel, with some areas showing significant improvement while others remain pretty much unchanged. However, an area that has seen tremendous advancement has been around 3D printing. Because the proper fit for footwear is multidimensional, it can be hard to fit a shoe. However, 3D printing determines shoe fit against the actual foot.

Other areas where I am seeing technology play a key role is the research and development behind the textiles and other raw materials used to produce shoes. For example, Nike is looking to create a shoe with better breathability but that is still stylish to sit within the athleisure segment. The shoe also features comfort innovations around the use of foam for the insole.

Beyond the production changes, technology is also playing a role in the monitoring of inventory levels. Companies are using RFID for more frequent cycle counts of inventory in production and at stores. RFID is much faster and more accurate than traditional means of inventory management.

**Interviewer:** *Are you seeing the fast fashion craze in the footwear industry?*

**M.A.:** The shoe-selling cycle typically runs around the seasons of fall, winter, resort, spring, and summer. Because of the different components in shoe construction, there are limitations with footwear and fast fashion. The last, the shoe form, is expensive. To recoup the cost of lasts, shoemakers typically design multiple styles off of the same last versus the request of fast fashion which are smaller inventory runs with a greater frequency of new designs. However, larger companies like H&M, which are doing fast fashion footwear like they do their accessories businesses, have limited small runs produced more frequently.

**Interviewer:** *When selecting a factory for shoe production, what do you look for?*

**M. A.:** You want to know what type of product the factory typically produces to determine whether the factory's capability meets the standards of your customers. You must assess whether their strengths align with your business needs. You also want to know whether the factory is able to produce the product within your projected cost constraints.

To manage the risk aspects of production, don't give all of your business to one factory. You almost want to take a portfolio approach to the placement of your production so that you are able to hedge your risk for production delays, errors, and potential conflicts with factory management. You must ask yourself when selecting a factory, who you want to have as your partners.

**Interviewer:** *What job opportunities are being created to support the use of data and technology in the supply chain?*

**M. A.:** Planning roles are increasing in demand. The need is growing for individuals that are able to analyze data quickly and create actionable reporting. As 3D printing continues to proliferate, there will be a growing need for people that can manage 3D production. You will need people with 3D printing skills. That's the demand.

In the US, there is an opportunity for software development to support the production process. If the US wants to bring back jobs, the focus needs to be on the technology skills needed to support a more automated production workforce versus the traditional labor-intensive manufacturing lines. People must be able to use the software that programs the code to be able to run innovative productions like 3D printing.

Another key aspect of today's workforce is that retailers are looking for job seekers to come trained. Gone are the days when companies would pay for training. The current retail environment of low margins and reduced sales is forcing retailers to seek individuals that are able to bring immediate benefits to their business. Therefore, job seekers should be trained on the various software packages that the industry uses, such as merchandise and inventory planning systems.

## Questions Pertaining to Interview

1. In what ways has access to data improved the order fulfillment process? What has this meant for the success of ecommerce businesses?
2. Why has 3D printing seen significant adoption in footwear product development? How will 3D printing impact the apparel supply chain?
3. Is there an opportunity for a fast fashion business model to occur in footwear? If yes, what needs to happen to the supply chain to allow this to occur? If no, why wouldn't the supply chain allow a fast fashion footwear model to happen?

## Company Background

The Rebecca Minkoff brand is an accessible luxury, lifestyle brand for the Millennial shopper, primarily women. The company was founded by its namesake designer, Rebecca Minkoff. Rebecca started the brand by designing fashion-forward handbags. Since its inception, the company has morphed into a full lifestyle brand with offerings that include a ready-to-wear line for women, handbags, footwear, jewelry, accessories, and athleisure. Uri Minkoff, CEO and cofounder, also launched a stylish menswear and accessories brand under the parent company, Rebecca Minkoff.

As an ambitious designer, Rebecca Minkoff started her brand in 2001. After nearly three years of trying to get traction, the company ran out of money. At that time, Rebecca reached out to her brother Uri, a successful businessman, for a loan and some business advice. Not only did Uri invest his savings in the business, but he decided to join the company. This allowed Rebecca to focus on design while Uri could focus on the business operations aspects of the company.

The brand operates three domestic retail stores and two international locations while maintaining a wholesaling presence in over 900 stores worldwide. The brand had gained recognition as being a trailblazer in the industry when it broke the Fashion Week tradition and embraced the "See Now, Buy Now" model that enabled fashion show attendees to purchase the items immediately being shown on the runway rather than wait for the typically three- to six-month production window. The brand is also known for livestreaming its shows. The Rebecca Minkoff brand holds true to its view on creating access to fashion by leveraging technology.

## Wearables

In addition to designing items that speak to an edgy but sophisticated consumer, the brand has gained the eye of major fashion publications and leading retailers because of its success with merging technology and design. **Wearables** are a category

of technology and fashion that are an accessory or apparel item capable of monitoring health and wellness information, offering technology support, and exhibiting smart technology functionality. Because of the brand's focus on Millennials, Rebecca set out to design a fashionable, but functional, wearable creation. In 2015, the brand debuted its first wearable designs, the Notification Bracelet ($120 retail) and the Lighting Cable Bracelet ($58 retail). In addition to being jewelry statement pieces, these accessories were able to serve as a personal assistant, vibrate for incoming calls and text messages, and charge one's phone.

## Connected Store Concept

Given the company's pioneering spirit, it is no surprise that the brand is also taking the lead in creating a smart store that enables retailers to collect purchasing and buying behavior information while the customer is shopping in their brick-and-mortar location. The concept is very similar to the data collected during ecommerce shopping through the use of cookies and other data-gathering technologies.

For the company's New York location, Rebecca Minkoff teamed up with eBay to launch the "connected store" concept. Through a customer tracking system driven off of a customer's phone number, the brand tracks the items selected, engagement within the fitting rooms, purchases, and items left behind. While the shopper is in the fitting room, which includes a magic mirror, the salesperson is able to pair items and make styling recommendations on the basis of previous purchases and the actual store inventory. The magic mirror is a touch screen computer that recreates aspects of the online shopping experience by allowing shoppers to scroll through the store's inventory, look at how outfits are styled, and even place a request to the salesperson to select additional items to be tried in the fitting room.

To track the actual inventory items, all of the clothes and accessories within the store are tagged with an RFID tag. By tagging all items, the store is able to match the customer's selection with its unique identifier, the telephone number, to build a customer profile. RFID also is used to monitor inventory levels and shrinkage. At all times, the retailer has a real-time assessment of its inventory volume.

## Power of Customer Data

The use of customer information enables the salesperson to create a custom experience for the shopper while also continuing to collect the shopper's buying preferences. Because of the information obtained in the fitting room, the retailer is also able to send email messages to customers about items they were unable to purchase because the size or color was not in that location; the retailer can also send messages about new arrivals and style recommendations for future shopping trips.

In addition to providing the retailer with increased information that can be used for future product design and buying preferences, the "connected store" concept enhances the overall in-store shopper experience. As retailers try to compete with access to virtually unlimited product offerings, brick-and-mortar stores are trying to give customers a reason for coming to them by working on the overall customer experience. With the traditional retailing experience, with the exception of high-end, commission-based stores, it was virtually impossible for a salesperson at lower price point stores to create a unique retailing experience. By leveraging the power of the customer data collected in the

"connected store," salespersons are able to tailor the shopping experience by offering curated selections based on customers' previous buying preferences. The Rebecca Minkoff brand has realized an increase of nearly 30 percent of in-store sales due to the advancement in the technology of the "connected store" locations.

The company is working on technology that will ultimately allow customers to check out their items without leaving the fitting room. This solution meets the demands of customers that want increased service with minimal hassle. Time and convenience are key drivers for the Rebecca Minkoff Millennial consumer.

## Case Study Questions

1. How would the planning and production cycle for wearable items be different and similar to that for traditional apparel items? How would these considerations impact a retailer's supply chain network?

2. Given the amount of information that is collected through the "connected store" concept, what are the privacy concerns that might arise? How would a retailer justify its decision to collect this customer information?

3. How might innovations such as artificial intelligence and 3D printing be used in the "connected store" concept?

## CHAPTER REVIEW QUESTIONS

1. How does information support a retailer's ability to offer a seamless selling environment through an omnichannel retailing strategy?

2. Identify six ways that big data and RFID minimize inventory management risks.

3. Describe how each of the process improvement strategies mentioned in the chapter—Six Sigma, total quality management (TQM), and ISO 9000—could be utilized to improve a company's manufacturing capabilities.

4. How can access to timely, accurate information support a retailer's emphasis on minimizing waste?

## CLASS EXERCISE

Debate the pros and the cons of the Rebecca Minkoff "connected store" concept. Address the concerns and opportunities given the following questions. As the company considers rolling out the "connected store" concept throughout its stores, what employee training and customer-related issues do you think the company has to address? Why might employees not be pleased with the "connected store" concept?

## KEY TERMS

key performance indicators (KPIs)
big data
radio-frequency identification (RFID)
universal product code (UPC)
hangtag system
retail shrinkage
dashboard
balanced scorecard
lead and lag indicators

lean manufacturing
muda
waste
5Ss
kaizen
Six Sigma
Master Black Belt (MBB)
Black Belt (BB)
Green Belt (GB)
Yellow Belt (YB)
discrete data

qualitative data
attribute data
continuous data
location data
total quality management (TQM)
International Organization for Standardization (ISO)
grading
wearables

# REFERENCES

1. Davis, M. (2016), "Customer Centric Supply Chain Omnichannel Leaders Plan to Widen the Gap," *SCM World*, April.
2. http://www.strategy2act.com/solutions /manufacturing_excel.htm.
3. Fiorletta, A. (2013), "RFID: The Key to Tracking Inventory for Omnichannel Success," *Retail Touch Points*, September 17.
4. Information provided from Macy's Inc. https://www .macysinc.com/.
5. Lander, S. (n.d.), "Typical Annual Inventory Shrinkage," *Small Business Chronicle*. Available online: http:// smallbusiness.chron.com/typical-annual-inventory -shrinkage-74314.html.
6. SJ Guest Editorial (2015), "Improve Retail Supply Chain Decision Making with Critical Path Management," *Sourcing Journal*, November 18.
7. Murby, L. (2005), "Effective Performance Management Technical Report," INSEAD. Available online: https://www.researchgate.net/file.PostFileLoader .html?id=567b92e96307d9264f8b459d&assetKey=AS %3A310075271385088%401450939113861.
8. Rothberg, A. F. (2012), "Performance Measurement: Understanding Balanced Scorecards," CFO Edge. Available online: http://www.cfoedge.com/resources /articles/cfo-edge-performance-measurement -balanced-scorecard.pdf.
9. Ibid.
10. Ibid.
11. Balakumar, R. S. (n.d.), "Lean Manufacturing in Apparel Industry," Textile Learner. Available online: http://textilelearner.blogspot.com/2015/05/lean -manufacturing-in-apparel-industry.html.
12. Donaldson, T. (2016), "What Exactly Is Lean Manufacturing Anyway?" *Sourcing Journal*, June 20.
13. https://www.cgsinc.com/blog/lean-manufacturing -garment-industry-apparel-business.
14. Atwell, R. (2005), "Six Sigma for the Apparel Industry," August. Available online: https://www.scribd.com /document/277481659/Six-Sigma-for-the-Apparel -Industry.

# Supply Chain Financing

## LEARNING OBJECTIVES

Upon completion of this chapter you will be able to:

- Assess how financing has evolved to meet global and diverse business models within the fashion industry.

- Establish how financial statements function in relation to supply chain financing.

- Evaluate the cashflow implications of supply chain management decision-making and operational outcomes.

# EVOLUTION OF APPAREL PRODUCTION FINANCING

This chapter will compare and contrast the various financing instruments that support the global fashion supply chain. What once started as lending facilities to single, regional garment businesses has progressed to secured and unsecured financing instruments that can accommodate borrowing by multiple vendors in various geographic locations throughout the global fashion supply chain.

In order to provide readers with an understanding of supply chain financing mechanisms, this chapter will provide a basic overview of company financial statements. With an understanding of the various financial statements, the reader of this book will be able to assess the long-term and short-term financial impact of supply chain management decisions. For example, as companies began to move production further from their selling markets, as when the United States shifted production to China, retailers' cash situation was being stretched because the length of time required to receive goods pushed retailers to purchase greater amounts of inventory to avoid **stockouts**, situations in which inventory is unavailable for sale. However, the purchase of additional inventory meant that a greater percentage of cash was being tied up in the cost of inventory for a more extended time. This tightening of cash might mean that a retailer would delay the purchase of equipment or delay other investments that might occur if there were additional cash available. Moreover, the cash invested in inventory was now much more at risk because of the potential for theft, defects, and markdowns, to name a few risk factors associated with a global supply chain. Ultimately, supply chain decisions have a rippling effect throughout the business.

Because an underlying driver of financing is the performance of the borrowing entity, this chapter will also discuss how the performance of a company's supply chain impacts the business's access to capital, borrowing rate, terms of debt repayment, and financing flexibility. The chapter will also discuss financial metrics that track and monitor the efficiency of the supply chain while also evaluating the tactics used by industry to assess the market's acceptance to the goods being produced. Upon completion of this chapter, a student should feel confident discussing the impact of finance on the global fashion supply chain.

As stated in the previous chapters, the apparel supply chain, as shown in Figure 10.1, is a complex network that includes farmers that produce the natural fibers used in apparel production, such as cotton; textile mill owners that convert fibers into bulk fabric; factories that cut and sew the garments into finished goods, conduct quality control on the garments, and pack them; and the

**Figure 10.1**
**Supply chain production cycle** Production moves from fiber, to yarn, to finished goods, to delivery to the retailer.

transportation and logistics companies such as shipping lines, railroads, and truckers that deliver the finished goods to retailers for them to sell the items to consumers. In today's ecommerce world, sometimes the goods go directly to the consumer.

At each step along the way, financing is required to fund the stage of production. Because of the global nature of the apparel supply chain, the types of financing instruments have had to evolve to address international banking practices, multiparty loan holders, and increased risks due to longer production lead times, increased order minimums, and the overall volatility of the retail sector. A survey of international banks by Gartner, a US-based research and advisory firm, found that between 2012 and 2014 the dollar value in supply chain financing transactions had increased from 30 to 40 percent.[1] A significant portion of this increase is due to the fees associated with financing complex, risk-oriented businesses.

The following is a brief overview of financial statements. The **balance sheet** (Table 10.1) is an accounting or a snapshot of a company's assets, liability, and equity for a period of time. The **assets** are the items that a company owns, such as cash, accounts receivable, inventory, equipment, and buildings. Because it is important to understand the liquidity of business, that is, how quickly a company's assets can be converted to cash, assets are broken into long-term and short-term assets. Short-term assets are cash or cash-equivalents or items that can be converted to cash in less than a year, such as inventory and accounts receivable. Long-term assets, or fixed assets, are items that take longer than a year to convert to cash, such as equipment and buildings.

On the other side of the balance sheet are the liabilities. As with assets, **liabilities** are classified into long-term and short-term liabilities on the basis of their time to cash conversion. Short-term liabilities are payables, which often include payments owed to vendors for raw materials and/or labor. Long-term liabilities are items such as mortgages for buildings or long-term leases for production facilities.

The rules of accounting require that a balance sheet must balance. Hence, the difference between a company's assets and liabilities is the company's equity. When a company's assets exceed its liabilities, financing professionals say that there is equity in the business.

From a supply chain perspective, the balance sheet is significant because many of the mechanisms to fund a company's production and any other working capital needs are often financing instruments that either leverage the value of assets or leverage the equity in the business to secure additional funding.

The **income statement** keeps track of a company's revenues and expenses. The revenues are the company's sales, while the expenses are the costs associated with the creation of the sales. While the income statement keeps a record of a company's sales, the cashflow statement captures the movement and/or availability of cash within a company. **Working capital**, which is located on the cashflow statement, is the cash available within a company for daily operating expenses. By evaluating a company's working capital, the cashflow statement enables companies to measure their cash needs and capital constraints.

Much like typical financing for other industries, apparel financing can be broken down into short-term and long-term capital needs (Table 10.2). Short-term capital is essentially working capital, which is the difference between current assets and current liabilities. For an apparel manufacturer, the current assets include balance sheet items such as cash, inventory, and accounts

**Table 10.1** Blueprint of a Financial Statement

Harry's Fashion Business
Balance Sheet
December 31, 2018

| Assets | | Liabilities | |
|---|---|---|---|
| **Short-Term** | | **Short-Term** | |
| Cash | $103,000 | Accounts Payable | $ 7,000 |
| Accounts Receivable | $ 26,000 | | |
| **Long-Term** | | **Long-Term** | |
| Building | $100,000 | Mortgage | $ 10,000 |
| | | **Equity** | |
| | | Owner's Equity | $212,000 |
| **Total Assets** | $229,000 | **Total Liability & Equity** | $229,000 |

**Table 10.2** Short-Term versus Long-Term Financing

|  | Short-Term Financing | Long-Term Financing |
|---|---|---|
| Use | Working capital: wages and inventory | Equipment and real estate |
| Time Period | Less than 12 months | Greater than 12 months |
| Funding Instruments | Line of credit and factoring | Amortized loan |

receivable. These assets are considered current because they were acquired within the last 12-month period. These assets are also the most liquid assets because they can be converted into cash, typically within a 12-month period of time. Current liabilities are also found on the balance sheet. A company's current liabilities include accounts payable, which typically are wages that are due within a 12-month period. An understanding of working capital is important for apparel manufacturing financing because of the types of financial instruments that lenders use to support these asset requirements.

The long-term capital needs for apparel manufacturing are often used to finance capital investments such as equipment and land for factories. The financing for the long-term needs of the business is addressed by long-term loans that are amortized over multiple years. Because of the length of the extended period for a long-term loan, banks reduce their risks by asking the borrower to provide collateral, a secondary means of repayment that a lender can obtain in the event of a default on the loan.

Because the apparel supply chain has grown in complexity due to its movement from regional/local production to global vendor relationships, and because companies outsource versus produce in house, mismanagement of the financing aspects of the business can create a significant working capital challenge for a business. For example, to achieve better bulk production pricing and to ensure that there is an adequate amount of inventory available, companies have moved to holding greater amounts of inventory, which ties up their working capital. If a company's cash is tied up in inventory, this means that there is great potential for obsolescent inventory, which can result in reduced profits due to markdowns. Companies are also trying to manage their cost of financing, which is driven by factors such as their profitability, the quality of their receivables, and access to alternative financing sources. Thus, the management of supply chain financing is a strategic endeavor

that requires a company's management team to think about their supply chain capital needs from a holistic perspective.

Table 10.3 gives the terminology for supply chain financing, which is needed to be able to assess transactions, make decisions about financing considerations, and identify opportunities to improve supply chain performance based on access to financing instruments. For the asset side of the balance sheet, there are the accounts receivable (AR), items that are owed to a business. On the liability side of the balance sheet, there are accounts payable (AP), costs that a business owes. Cost of goods sold (COGS) is the direct costs that are used to make a garment, such as the material and labor costs. Because there is often a lag between when a designer obtains an order and when the designer is paid, there is often a need to seek receivable financing to cover the cost of producing the items for the receivable. While receivable financing is underwritten by the actual receivable, there is still the potential risk that, because of a host of factors, such as cancellations of an order or markdowns, the receivable will not be paid by a buyer. To minimize their risk, lenders seek recourse from the borrower by obtaining a personal guarantee, which makes the loan a recourse financing. For borrowers there is an actual cost of capital, which is important in evaluating the overall profitability of a line based upon the production and financing cost to produce the line. Ultimately, working capital financing is what designers seek to cover the cost of production.

## GARMENT INDUSTRY FINANCING INSTRUMENTS

Typically, the time period from when a designer develops a sketch of a garment to when the garment is available for sale by a retailer is approximately four to six months. Now, with fast fashion and the trend of seasonless selling, the production cycle is getting shorter.

**Table 10.3** Key Supply Chain Financing Terms

| Term | Definition |
| --- | --- |
| Accounts Payable (AP) | Money that a manufacturer owes. A short-term liability that will come due in less than 12 months, such as wages that a factory might owe to its workers. |
| Accounts Receivable (AR) | Money that is owed to a manufacturer for work that it has performed, such as the production of goods for a garment contract. ARs are short-term receivables that come due in less than 12 months. When a designer produces an order, it obtains a receivable from the retailer. |
| Cost of Goods Sold (COGS) | The direct cost attributable to the items sold by the retailer. COGS only reflects the direct cost of production, such as the raw material and manufacturing labor. The labor associated with selling, goods, and administration (SGA) is excluded from COGS. |
| Receivable Financing | When a designer obtains funds in advance by factoring its receivables. The lender extends funds prior to the receivable being paid on the basis of the quality of the receivable. |
| Recourse Financing | Protection for lenders in the event of a default. The lender is able to seek payment from the borrower in the event of a default. |
| Weighted Average Cost of Capital (WACC) | Because there is a cost for the use of capital, WACC measures the use of capital as either a debt or equity instrument. |
| Working Capital | The difference between current assets and current liabilities. Essentially, these are the funds that manufacturers and retailers use to finance the daily operations of the business. |

However, the nature of the business requires significant cash investment up front per season to generate retail sales. Additionally, the global nature of the supply chain means that cash for payment to supply chain vendors will need to pass through many domestic and international borders before a finished good reaches the consumer. Various financial instruments are used to support the short- and long-term capital demands of the business.

## Accounts Receivable and Inventory Financing

Accounts receivable and inventory financing (ARIF) is a form of asset-based lending. For ARIF, borrowers use the value of their receivables or inventory as collateral to finance their working capital needs. This window of time between when a receivable or inventory converts to cash is fairly risky because of the long lead time during the production cycle, the whimsical nature of the retail market, and unforeseen production failures. It is for these reasons that ARIF financing is a fairly costly form of financing. Companies that typically seek ARIF financing lack access

to traditional financing due to their stage of business, sector, and/or even seasonality, all of which impact companies in the fashion and retail sectors. Hence, this is an often-used financing source for these sectors.

The lender collects on the debt through the conversion of the receivable or inventory into cash. Over time, the concept of ARIF financing has evolved to extend beyond the collateralization of accounts receivable and inventory to include other assets such as the machinery related to the production process. As the types of collateral for ARIF have expanded, so too has the use of ARIF. Companies have used ARIF to finance acquisitions, restructure debt, and provide an extending financing facility for distressed company situations.[2] By expanding the types of collateral and use of capital, ARIF has also become capital for long-term financing needs.

## Asset-Based Lending

The spectrum of ARIF varies from collateralized financing to loans without recourse, a loan without collateral. Asset-based lending (ABL) is a formulaic means of financing in which a lender extends credit on the basis of a borrowing formula that is a negotiated discount rate against the actual receivables of the business. The funds that are provided to the borrower from the receivables are called an advance: an advance payment on the receivable. Because these funds are used to run the daily operations of the business, borrowers may contact the lender daily to gain an advance of the funds.

If a fashion designer is awarded a $20,000 order from a publicly traded retailer with a favorable investment grade rating such as Moody's Aaaa (the highest rating this credit-rating firm offers, reflecting minimal credit risk), the lender will extend funds based on the quality of the company that extended the receivable. Because this receivable was written by this Aaaa company, the designer is able to negotiate a favorable discount rate of 25 percent. Because financing is essentially a negotiation, the designer is achieving a more favorable discount rate because of the quality of the receivable.

With ABL, unlike conventional cashflow lending, the borrower is extended funds based on the value of the receivable rather than on the value of the cashflows generated from the lender's business. For highly season-based businesses such as fashion brands, which are also driven by the fickleness of the market, the financing community prefers ABL because the lender's ultimate means of repayment is tied to the quality of the company that extended the receivable; the lender does not have to rely on the importer to convert the receivable into cash. With the aforementioned scenario, the lender will extend credit to the designer net of fees. For the lender, this loan is highly secured based upon the underlying receivable. This is considered a loan with recourse, meaning that the lender would take the collateral in the event of a loan default.

## Factoring

One of the oldest and most common means of ARIF within the apparel industry is factoring of receivables. Factoring is when a company sells its uncollected receivables to a factor, a third-party commercial finance company, in exchange for an upfront payment of cash that is a percentage of the overall receivable. In the previous example of the designer that has a $20,000 receivable from an Aaaa company, the funds would be extended to the designer based on a percentage of what is collected from the Aaaa company for the receivable.

### Notes from the Field

Financing is essential to the success of a fashion business. How you obtain financial backing varies based on how your company is organized and how well it performs. In order to get business, you need to prove that you can produce your orders. For large multinational fashion companies, this is not an issue, but for small startups and midsize companies, it can be a daunting challenge, and you may be living from order to order. Factors were once seen as the lifeblood of the fashion industry, and today they still perform a valuable function, although there are much fewer than in the past. The rate that a factor will charge a customer is dependent on the prevailing interest rates. During the 1980s there was a time when factors were charging 15 to 18 percent interest; this changed the way many small companies did business. I had recently left a large company to work for a small startup, and of course we needed the support of a factor to conduct our business. With the cost of money at those high rates, we were forced to add it to the cost of goods sold. This put us at a distinct disadvantage when negotiating with retailers, as they would ask if we were factored. As a matter of fact, in one particular instance buyers demanded that we reduce our prices. Because buyers don't care about another business's financial issues, they will not assume any additional costs due to interest rates. Luckily, I knew these particular retailers and how they operated, so before they came to the showroom we raised our prices 20 percent, gave them the 20 percent discount, and everyone was happy.

Instead of using a borrowing formula to determine the amount of funds that will be extended, the lender purchases the receivable upfront with no recourse to the borrower. In the event of a default, the lender is unable to go after the borrower's assets to collect on the debt. This means that the lender must conduct its due diligence on the borrower's receivables by assessing the receivable's aging (the number of days that the receivables have been outstanding), evaluating the performance of the designer to fulfill the receivable, and evaluating the underlying economic factors of the industry. Since the lender is relying on the quality of the receivable, the lender must also check to make sure that there isn't significant exposure from the same Aaaa company that extended the receivable. Given that each financing variable implies a certain amount of risk, factoring is considered one of the more costly means of gaining capital.

In a typical factoring arrangement, the client (retailer) makes a sale, delivers the product or service, and generates an invoice. The factor (the funding source) buys the right to collect on that invoice by agreeing to pay you the invoice's face value less a discount, typically 2 to 6 percent. The factor pays 75 percent to 80 percent of the face value immediately and forwards the remainder (less the discount) when your customer pays.

For a percent of the receivable, the factor provides working capital to the designer. Because factoring is essentially purchasing the receivables of the company, the factor may place constraints on the types of receivables that the company is able to extend to orders. Due to the amount of knowledge that is needed to extend factor credit, there typically are companies that specialize in this means of financing. Because the factor has purchased the receivable, the retailer will make payment to the factor on behalf of the designer.

The percentage of the cost that the factor charges is based upon the quality of the receivable. This inverse relationship is captured in Figure 10.2. An established retailer like Nordstrom or Saks Fifth Avenue is considered a quality grade of retailer, whereas a smaller unknown boutique may be considered of less significance. The quality of the retailer is important because this, in addition to the days outstanding, drives the percentage that a factor charges. The greater the value of the retailer, the lower the cost of factoring.

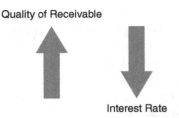

Quality of Receivable

Interest Rate

**Figure 10.2**
**Inverse relationship between quality of receivable and factoring interest rate**

## Pledging Receivables

While not as typical, lenders in the fashion industry also take pledges of receivables from borrowers. Unlike a factored receivable, a pledged receivable remains on the balance sheet of a company, and the loan is not underwritten on the basis of the amount of the receivable. The receivable is placed as a means of collateral in the event that the borrower defaults on the loan.

## Purchase Order Financing

Another means of working capital financing that designers might pursue is **purchase order financing**. Due to the lag that exists between when a retailer takes an order and the purchaser pays for the order, retailers can obtain cash to pay suppliers for the work that is required to fulfill the purchase order. Unlike with factoring, the borrower versus the factor is the entity that the purchase order is paid to upon collection. Purchase order financing gives retailers an ability to meet large orders that might put a capital constraint on the company's cash reserves. A significant benefit of purchase order financing is that it provides the credit-appropriate borrower with flexibility to expand its capacity to accept larger orders without assuming fixed costs prior to growth from increased orders and/or size of order. Because the repayment of the financing is dependent on the borrower's ability to convert the receivable to cash, purchase order financing is typically used by more established companies.

## Supply Chain Financing

As the nature of the supply chain has become more complex, so too have the financing instruments, terms, and sources of finance. In the 1950s, when the raw materials and production occurred on the same shores, financiers were able to exert tighter control by managing financing among common businesses within the fashion industry. However, the movement of production abroad resulted in extended supply chain networks involving business entities that typically had limited previous relationships.

**Supply chain financing (SCF)** was created by the financing community to support the various entities and financing needs throughout the global supply chain network. SCF is defined by the financing community as short-term financing of buyer and seller working capital needs for supply chain management. Because SCF financing is typically extended on the basis of a receivable or invoice that may originate in one country and be reclaimed in another, the use of technology to track and monitor transactions is key. While somewhat new, the practice of SCF is most common in the United States, followed by Europe in the commerce-focused areas of the United Kingdom and Germany. Because of the more traditional financing support offered in cooperative business structures such as the keiretsu, SCF has developed more slowly in Asia than in the United States or Europe; however, China and India are on target to be the fastest areas of SCF expansion in the coming years.[3] The Asian development bank reported that in 2012, the Asian trade financing gap was $425 billion or greater.[4]

SCF includes credit products such as structured warehouse finance, vendor prepay, preshipment finance, postshipment preacceptance, and postshipment postacceptance, including buyer or distribution finance.[5] These financial instruments reflect the length of the borrowing need and the international aspects of the global fashion supply chain.

## Import/Export Financing

In 2013, China produced 43.1 percent of global clothing and 60 percent of the world's shoes.[6] Given the amount of production that comes out of China, the relationship between an importer and exporter must be taken into consideration when one discusses supply chain financing. An exporter is the entity that is sending an intermediate or finished good to another country for sale. An example of an exporter is a factory in China that produces handbags for the US retailer Marc Jacobs. In this case, the factory is exporting the finished goods of a handbag for sale

in the US retail market. The retailer, Marc Jacobs, would be the importer, the entity that is receiving intermediate or finished goods from abroad. The importer is required to pay the cost of the goods, transportation costs, port handling fees, and tariff and import fees. In addition, some countries charge national sales and local taxes and possibly customs fees.[7] That is why when quoting a price for a garment, individuals ask for the **"landed costs"**: all the costs an importer incurs to acquire the good.

**Tariffs**, also known as duty, are the costs that a country charges to import a good. Tariffs are imposed by governments to alter the balance of trade between the tariff-imposing country and the international trading country.[8] Since importing reduces local production, the tariff is a means to recoup the reduction of tax revenue due to the importing of goods. Governments also impose tariffs to protect domestic industries from foreign competition. Countries assess tariffs on the following factors: product value, trade agreements with **export** country, product's country of origin, use of product, and the product's harmonized system code (HS). The HS is a product-naming standard that is produced by the international representative of the customs community, the World Customs Organization (WCO). The HS classifies 98 percent of all goods by the use of a six-digit code.[9]

Each country charges a different tariff for each item category. Because of the variation within the government-imposed costs of duties and taxes, the cost of doing business in a particular city is an important factor when importers look for a country in which to produce goods. Products made in the United States may receive favorable import costs on the basis of the Free Trade Agreement (FTA), a trade agreement that provides incentive for US goods to be exported to one of the twenty FTA countries that fall within the agreement.[10]

## INTERNATIONAL TRADE FINANCING MECHANISMS

While the movement of production throughout the world supports the fashion industry's goal to maximize profit through controlled costs and to pursue new market opportunities closer to sources of production, the global nature of the supply chain creates significant financial challenges regarding the management of cashflow, tax

## Notes from the Field

Tariffs play an important role in world trade. As an importer it is essential that you know and understand the role of tariffs, how to apply them, and where to find the information. The tariff can be a major component of the cost sheet. Tariffs were originally put in place to preserve jobs but are now a major source of revenue for the US treasury and contribute to the revenue of countries around the globe. While exploring new sourcing opportunities, my company through one of our agents discovered a burgeoning manufacturing opportunity on the island of Saipan. Those who know geography and some history will recognize this tiny island located off the coast of Japan, although it is considered part of the United States as a protectorate.

We started to import men's woven sport shirts from factories in Saipan with no tariff because it was considered part of the United States, although there was a rule that we had to leave 51 percent of the value of the garment on the island, which in this case was the labor cost. We managed to bring in over a dozen containers full of shirts before the customs agents here in the United States got curious about how we were importing from halfway around the world with labels that said "Made in the United States." We were abiding by the laws and paying no tariffs, but they were not happy and made us change orders going forward to "Made in the Northern Marianas"!

considerations, and risks. By the sheer fact that globalization means multiple countries with various currencies, there are financial concerns that arise due to currency fluctuations and underlying economic situations in the country of origin. In addition, globalization creates concerns regarding cross-border funding and repatriation of money into the local economy.[11] For these reasons, the financing mechanisms for international trade are constantly evolving to meet the demands of today's global fashion supply chain.

For international trade, there are essentially four financing instruments: cash-in-advance, letter of credit, documentary collection, and open account (see Table 10.4). Each instrument has different payment terms, cost considerations, and levels of financial risk. As with any relationship, there are incentives on both sides with regard to the timing and means of payment. Because the exporter pays the costs upfront to manufacture and distribute the goods, the exporter wishes to receive payment as soon as the goods are produced. However, the importer wishes to make payment on the goods once they arrive from the exporter. The balancing of these two interests is the premise for international trade financing, financial instruments that expedite the payment of goods within a window that maximizes working capital for both the importer and exporter while also managing the risks associated with international trade transactions.

**Table 10.4** International Trade Financing Instruments: Pros and Cons

|  | Pros | Cons |
|---|---|---|
|  | **Exporter (Seller)** | **Importer (Buyer)** |
| **Cash-in-Advance** | Payment received prior to shipment. | Payment made prior to shipment. |
| **Letter of Credit** | No cost to the exporter to obtain the letter of credit. | The importer bears the cost to obtain the letter of credit from the bank. |
|  | **Importer (Buyer)** | **Exporter (Seller)** |
| **Documentary Collection** | Not obligated to pay for goods prior to shipment. | Bank's role is limited and does not guarantee payment. |
| **Open Account** | Pays for goods upon receipt. | Bears the risk of nonpayment. |

## Cash-in-Advance

The most favorable means of payment for an exporter is full or significant cash paid by the importer prior to the transfer of ownership of the goods. Exporters that are offering highly unique and/or favorable order-processing accommodations, such as the acceptance of small minimal order sizes, typically enable an exporter to request **cash-in-advance,** a payment made by the buyer upfront before the goods are received from the seller. Exporters that solely accept orders by means of the internet typically also only accept payment in advance of shipment. Cash-in-advance is paid by means of wire transfer, escrow, and credit card payments. With the exception of the escrow payment, the other means of payment are executed without a third party. In the case of an escrow payment, the importer places the funds with a third-party entity. Once the importer verifies the documents associated with the goods, the importer then gives approval to the third party to release the funds to the exporter.

While cash-in-advance is still used in some instances, most exporters have realized that by requiring cash-in-advance they are limiting their customer base. The cash-in-advance exporters are less competitive because of companies that are unable to meet such a request and because there are financing entities that enable more flexible, credit lending practices to meet the time lag and risk issues associated with international trade.

## Letter of Credit

One of the longest-standing forms of trade financing (since the 1900s) is the **letter of credit (LC),** a trade document between an accepting bank and issuing bank that facilitates the transfer of goods. At the request of the importer, the entity that is buying the goods, the issuing bank agrees to pay the exporter for goods on the basis that they meet the terms and conditions of the purchasing agreement.[12] Typically, the importer extends the LC from its line of credit with the issuing bank. Once a company initiates an LC, the funds for the purchase are frozen. This means that the company is unable to use these funds for any other purchases. The ability to freeze funds is one of the guarantees of the LC.

A letter of credit enables an exporter to rely on the credit and reputation of the issuing bank rather than the importer; this is why letter of credits are used in

international trade transactions, in which there is a limited relationship and market knowledge between an importer and exporter. The accepting bank receives the LC draft on behalf of the exporter, the beneficiary. Because a financing commitment is not extended until the bank receives all of the proper documentation for the goods, including the bill of lading, the buyer's risks are mitigated. It should be noted that the bank accepts the LC on the basis of the documents presented versus the actual goods. For this reason, the importer still must do its due diligence on the exporter to ensure that the exporter doesn't provide inferior goods or items that do not meet the specifications of what was detailed on the LC documentation.

Unlike a letter of credit, a standby letter of credit is not a form of payment. A standby letter of credit is a guarantee of payment to be made. To also ensure payment, an exporter may request that an importer purchase a standby letter of credit. In the event that the importer fails to pay the exporter, the issuing bank of the standby letter of credit will make the payment to the exporter.

There are two types of LCs: revocable and irrevocable. A revocable LC means that the importer has the option of cancelling or changing the LC up until the point of the LC being collected by the importer. An irrevocable LC prohibits the modification of the LC without approval from all parties. Unless stipulated, all LCs are irrevocable.[13] To facilitate the worldwide acceptance of LCs, the International Chamber of Commerce (ICC) publishes internationally agreed-upon standards that govern the issuance of LCs. The LC governing practices are called the Uniform Customs and Practice for Documentary Credits (UCP). It should be noted that the company that initiates the LC has the money frozen to avoid further use of these funds. This mechanism serves as a guarantee for the LC.

## Documentary Collection

While a somewhat cheaper way to facilitate trade financing, **documentary collections** offer importers and exporters a way to receive the documentary information of goods. The bank will extend funds to the exporter from the importer on the basis that the documentation provided will enable the importer to access the goods at the negotiated time and condition. In the event of a default, there is no collateral to offset outstanding payments.

## Open Account

Because the exporter wants to get paid as soon as the goods are finished, and the importer wants to pay once the goods are received, the financing option of an **open account,** when goods are shipped and delivered before the payment is received by the exporter, is least favorable to the exporter. However, the competitive nature of the apparel business forces exporters to consider this means of financing to secure importer business. In addition to assuming the risk of nonpayment from the importer, the exporter has cashflow tied up in the production costs of the garments.

Open accounts are becoming more common as the financial markets tighten and companies lack the ability to pursue other means of financing. Additionally, supply chain management tracking with the use of digital supply chain features is providing a heightened visibility to goods production that enables exporters to feel a sense of comfort when shipping goods without minimum or even partial deposit of goods. Open accounts create a sense of administrative ease that international trade financing lacks an ability to achieve.

# HOW FINANCING IMPACTS THE GLOBAL FASHION SUPPLY CHAIN

Because capital is the key resource that supports the financing of equipment, the purchasing of materials, payments for labor, and the fuel used to transport goods, the supply chain is highly dependent on a company's access to capital and cashflow. Therefore, the way in which a company manages its capital and cashflow has a tremendous impact on the company's ability to meet customer needs to pursue innovation and to leverage its resources to gain a competitive advantage in the industry. While there are tremendous benefits to a global supply chain, there are also significant operating and financial considerations that may have an adverse impact on the business, such as an increase in inventory due to the length of time added to the production cycle for goods shipped abroad, or the drain on cash reserves because an increase in inventory means that the company's cash is being tied up in financing its inventory instead of being converted into working capital. More importantly, there is an increase of overall inventory risk because of the lead time and volume committed to support production abroad. Global production also means that a company is now vulnerable to currency fluctuations, geopolitical considerations, and supply chain disruption due to natural disasters. Thus, it is important to monitor the financial commitment and conversion cycle within a company.

## Cash Conversion Cycle

**Cash Conversion Cycle (C2C) = Inventory Conversion Period + Receivables Collection Period (DSO) – Payables Deferral Period**

The calculation consists of the following steps:

(1) Inventory conversion period = Inventory/Sales per day = # days

(2) Receivables Collection Period (DSO) = Receivables/Sales/365 = # Days

(3) Payables Deferral Period = Payables/Cost of Goods Sold/365 = # Days

**Cash Conversion Calculation = Step 1 + Step 2 – Step 3**

Cash is key to any business; however, the fashion industry places a significant focus on cash because of the industry's volatility, the complexity of the production cycle, and the industry's reactionary nature due to world economics. With that said, supply chain professionals and senior management team members such as the chief financial officer and chief operating officer pay attention to a company's ability or inability to quickly convert its receivables into cash. Once again, the longer that raw materials and finished goods take to be converted into cash, the greater the company's risk of having inventory obsolescence, which could result in markdowns, write-offs, and possible theft. Companies also face a negative financial impact due to a delayed cash conversion cycle because a company's cash is being held from being invested in other projects or general operating activities.

The **cash conversion cycle (C2C)** is a metric that measures a company's efficiency on the basis of how the company manages its working capital, primarily the conversion of inventory and the management of payables and receivables. A company with a lower C2C is more efficient because that company is converting its inventory more quickly.[14] For example, a company such as Zara that turns its inventory quickly is able to utilize its inventory to create cash several times better than the average business in the industry. Not only does a lower C2C mean additional sales, but it also means that the company has greater cash reserves to invest in innovation or is able to utilize its cash reserves to self-fund (instead of borrowing capital), which further improves the company's profitability because it does have to bear the cost of debt service. In addition, the more favorable cash position often results in higher business ratings, which could lead to better vendor terms because the business is considered financially and operationally sound and the company will have access to the capital markets at a cheaper discount rate because of its favorable cash reserves.

The C2C is composed of the following balance sheet items: inventory (asset), accounts receivable (asset), and accounts payable (liability). A high C2C means that there is an ability from the consumer demand side of the business to sell the goods; hence, the slowdown in the inventory turns. An unfavorable C2C may also be caused by a slowing in payments from customers, a driving up of accounts receivable, and/or a reduction in payment terms from a supplier, causing shorter windows to pay receivables. Regardless of the reason for the low (favorable) or high (unfavorable) C2C, it is obvious that a company's C2C is a factor that can be controlled through the tight measurement of inventory levels, the due diligence on customers and effective collection processes to minimize outstanding receivables, and the collaboration mindset with vendors to ensure payable terms that enable companies to optimize their cash position while also making sure that the owner of the payable isn't at risk for extended payable terms.

## Trade Credit

In addition to the cash conversion cycle, retailers also use trade credit to manage the business's cashflow. Trade credit is when a supplier allows a company to purchase supplies with the promise of paying for the supplies at a later date. Trade credit enables businesses to collect the cash from their accounts receivables from their sales before being required to pay for the supplies used to produce these sales. The typical credit terms are net 30 or 60 days. Thus, a business would be required to pay for the supplies within 30 or 60 days to avoid a penalty. The extension of credit is typically granted based on a company's credit rating and reputation in the industry.

Because suppliers are also focused on their cashflow, they also offer discounts for the expedient payment of invoices, such as the payment term of **2/10, N30.** This term means that there will be a 2 percent discount applied to invoices paid within ten days or the invoice total is due within thirty days.

# HOW THE SUPPLY CHAIN'S OPERATING PERFORMANCE IMPACTS FINANCES

Because fashion is primarily driven by the whimsical nature of consumers, who often change their buying habits based on numerous factors such as weather, celebrity appeal, lifestyle changes, and sometimes cost, it is a challenge for retailers to predict in advance what shoppers want. In addition, the internet is creating an expectation that shoppers can shop anytime and anywhere and receive their product whenever they want. It is for these reasons that supply chain performance in the fashion industry has been forced to become quicker with a goal of giving customer-centric satisfaction within a reasonable price parameter. To protect their bottom line, companies are placing greater emphasis on the performance of their supply chain. When all works well in the supply chain, a company is able to achieve a favorable C2C that meets profitable projections and ultimately customer expectations. However, there are a host of financial challenges that arise when a company's supply chain lacks operating efficiency.

Retailers make money by getting the right product to the right consumer at the right time. When this fails to occur, there are markdowns, which reduce the profit margins for an item. These markdowns may occur because a product missed the season, the weather pattern was off, and/or the consumer decided that straight-legged jeans were out and flared jeans were in for the season. For example, the holiday 2015 season was extremely warm during the months of November and December. Because of the weather pattern, retailers were stuck with winter coats and boots that consumers didn't purchase.

When a retailer is faced with inventory that isn't moving, there are additional costs associated with the warehousing of inventory, coupled with the possible costs of disposal. The carrying of additional inventory also impacts a company's balance sheet because cash reserves are tied up, and there is also a potential for inventory write-offs due to obsolescence of the inventory.

The reverse of a markdown is a stockout, when there isn't adequate inventory replenishment. There is demand for the product, but the retailer is out of inventory to meet the demand. Since several retailers' manufacturing is outsourced to Asia, the lead time for garment production often doesn't meet the challenge of an unexpected increase in demand. Hence, there is a missed opportunity cost, coupled with the disappointment from one's customer base, who might decide to shop elsewhere because of the lack of in-season inventory replenishment. Unlike most retailers, Zara reserves a significant portion of its merchandise selection open to be produced in season. Keeping a portion of production open for in-season sales makes Zara flexible to meet the ever-changing trends in fashion.

Another area of production that has the potential to impact a company's financials is quality: quality of the material, fit, and garment construction. Because returns represent a significant cost for retailers, quality management at the production level is imperative. A retailer's quality must also align with the expectations of its target market. According to research from the *Wall Street Journal*, a third of all online purchases are returned.[15] In addition to the potential loss of a sale, there are other costs associated with return items, such as restocking, shipping, and the potential for product obsolescence.

While labor is often the most emphasized production cost, there are several other supply chain costs that a retailer can manage to impact its bottom line. Because textiles represent a significant portion of a good, sourcing for materials is a key factor for a company's profit margin. The sampling and pattern-making processes are key aspects of production that enable the retailer to test a garment for market acceptance and fit. Waste is an area of production costs.[16]

The supply chain is also vulnerable to financial costs associated with theft. Given that supply chains often comprise third-party vendors, international relationships, and often relationships with limited network knowledge, the global fashion supply chain is highly vulnerable to the financial impact of loss from theft or fraud. Additionally, the multiple parts of the supply chain, such as raw materials, production, and distribution, create opportunities for shrinkage to occur throughout the supply chain. For

example, the raw materials of fashion fabrics and trim are easy targets for theft. As one moves further down the supply chain, finished goods while in transit represent items that are also highly vulnerable to theft.

# SUPPLY CHAIN FINANCIAL REGULATORY REQUIREMENTS

With the goal of achieving greater financial accountability and visibility to costs for public companies, the United States enacted Sarbanes-Oxley (SOX) in 2002 after the corporate financial scandals of companies that used off-balance sheet transactions to hide risky transactions that might adversely impact the company's stock price and/or overall financial position. From this regulation came a series of operating requirements that strengthened financial reporting for company transactions. The regulation's requirement to provide oversight of the assessment and management of internal controls is what brought supply chain management under the scrutiny of Sarbanes-Oxley.

Within the regulation, there are two sections of disclosure that impact how CEOs and CFOs report information about supply chain management. Section 401, Disclosure in Periodic Reports, focuses on the reporting of *off-balance sheet transactions*, that is, commitments that are not included on the balance sheet of a company. The concern is over the financial impact that these commitments might have on a company's liability and/or debt outlook. Companies have used off-balance sheet accounting to hide commitments that adversely impact the financial health of the business. For supply chain management, potential off-balance sheet commitments are significant volume purchases for goods, services, or manufacturing capacity. Certain service contracts with ocean carriers fall within the area of disclosure because of the potentially adverse impact that a default on such a contract might have on the business.[17]

Section 404, Management Assessment of Internal Controls, requires that executives confirm their ability and actual success in being able to report internal controls for all aspects of the business. This requirement impacts supply chain professionals because it requires them to document their processes for event identification, risk assessment, and response. Given the multitude of vendor relationships that might exist around the world and the fact that the supply chain has reach throughout an organization, the documentation for supply chain–related internal controls is an extensive area of reporting. The key for reporting SOX issues is visibility to transactions and relationships throughout a company's supply chain. Technology such as enterprise resource planning (ERP) systems and company-wide policies and procedures enable companies to have greater visibility into their supply chain for key risk factors such as supplier concentration, cash constraints, and vendor defects.

Outsourcing is a key solution that many companies use to reduce fixed costs, gain expertise that a company might lack, and/or test new sourcing or manufacturing capabilities. However, outsourcing also creates the potential for contractual relationships and risk situations that fall within the SOX reporting requirements. Supply chain disruptions such as labor strikes and natural disasters are operational challenges that must be monitored, managed, and reported by senior executives for SOX purposes. Given the operationally extensive nature of the SOX mandate, compliance with the regulation helps to strengthen the overall management of the supply chain from a visibility and risk management perspective.

## CONCLUSION

The complex nature of the global fashion supply chain creates a need for funding throughout the various aspects of the supply chain. Because of the lead time for production and the fact that the majority of the production occurs in Asia, there is a need for financing instruments and procedures to facilitate international trade. The other area of financing that retailers must consider is the impact on the overall cashflow of the business. Once again, lead times mean that companies might require payment prior to receipt of sales. That is why early-stage companies often seek financing sources that extend beyond bank financing. The key for financing the supply chain is to ensure that the funding sources are able to support the underlying cost of production.

# INDUSTRY INTERVIEW: CHAD SCHOFIELD, COFOUNDER AND CHIEF DIGITAL OFFICER OF BOXC

Chad Schofield is currently cofounder and chief digital officer of BoxC, a startup that simplifies and shortens the supply chain from manufacturer direct to retailer or consumer anywhere in the world. Previously, Chad was founder and managing director of Three Global, a consultancy that guides and advises companies, trade associations, NGOs, and governments when they are adjusting to the changing realities of international marketing, sourcing, and logistics in the apparel and accessories industry.

As a consultant for USAID/COMPETE Africa, Schofield led strategic planning and global sourcing by developing a branding and awareness campaign, Origin Africa, to promote African apparel exports to the United States and Europe. Additionally, he matched African women co-ops with Western fashion designers and African fashion designers with Western fashion brands for collaborations.

**Interviewer**: *Given the global nature of apparel production, what are the financing instruments that fashion brands use to finance their overseas production? What are the risks associated with these financing instruments?*

**C. S.:** Essentially, the funding instruments for apparel manufacturing fall within four sets of options based upon the size and reputation of the fashion brand: letter of credit, trade credit, factoring, and credit cards. Letter of credit is often used by larger, established fashion brands with orders from blue chip retailers. **Blue chip** companies are entities that have an established reputation; these businesses are known for their market presence and sound financial footing. This is important because the quality of the receivable gains a greater market value based on the retailer's ability to pay the receivable. Receivables from these types of entities are considered solid receivables because of the retailer's ability to pay them. Gap and Walmart are examples of such retailers.

In addition to access to letters of credit, large fashion brands tend also to have relationships with factories where the factory will manufacture their items with 90 days of credit. These factories are extending trade credit to these fashion brands. Therefore, the brand pays the factory after the item has been produced. In some cases, the 90 days may also allow the retailer to collect the funds from the sale of the item before needing to pay the factory. This is one of the additional benefits of being a large fashion brand.

The most common means of financing for fashion brands that produce in China is to use a factor to finance the invoice. Factoring is when a fashion brands sells its invoices to a trade financing company in exchange for access to cash to finance its orders. For example, if we have a fashion brand that has a $10k order from Anthropology, the factor would give the fashion brand 80 percent of the invoice based on the financial strength of the company issuing the invoice.

Once the invoice has been purchased by a factor, then the fashion brand will typically pay 30 percent of the invoice to the factory to start production on the order for Anthropology. The fashion brand will pay the balance of the order once the items have been produced or based on the terms that the fashion brand has negotiated with the factory. Once again, the key to the credit negotiations is the size of the fashion brand and the brand's relationship with the factory. Factories prefer to receive the 30 percent advance payment because factories sometimes find it to be a challenge to collect on letters of credit. This arrangement also works well for the fashion brand because the cost of its production is typically half of the item's retail price. Hence, the fashion brand should have enough cash to produce the order.

Because a factory's decision to extend credit to a fashion brand includes consideration for the size and reputation of the retailer, fashion brands that take orders from small boutiques will typically finance the order by credit card. This enables the factory to receive payment for the item prior to the item being shipped. The biggest risk with this arrangement is potentially the quality of the items being shipped. Since payment is being made in advance of delivery, the fashion brand assumes the risk that the items might be defective and/or not meet the company's compliance standards.

**Interviewer:** *How important is cashflow management with regards to a fashion brand's typical conversion cycle?*

**C. S.:** A fashion brand's management of its cashflow is a delicate balancing act. The first hurdle of a fashion brand's cashflow management is the securing of funds to launch the initial line. For a fashion brand to get started, it first must pay some money to get samples made. Fashion brands that are looking to sell to retailers will typically attend trade shows. At the trade show, the fashion brand will take preorders for the production of its apparel items. By taking preorders, the fashion brand is able to protect its cashflow because it doesn't produce items until it receives an order from a retailer. The preorder amount is the order that gets placed with the factory. If items aren't well received during the trade show, the fashion brand will reduce the assortment to produce only the items that are well received.

Once the fashion brand gets an order from a retailer, the brand can sell the receivable to a factor to get 80 to 90 percent of the receivable in cash. From the money received, the fashion brand can pay the factory and address any other operating expenses

that might arise. Once a fashion brand has covered the expenses of producing samples and attending the trade show to get orders, the brand should be able to cover its cashflow requirements because the brand will be taking preorders that can be sold to a factor to receive operating cash.

An innovation in financing for fashion brands has arisen from the introduction of Kickstarter and Indiegogo campaigns. These online platforms are a means for startup brands to go direct to the consumer to pre-sell items by means of an online financing campaign. The campaign model enables early-stage brands to finance their production by leveraging their social model presence. By taking orders before producing the items, the startup brand is able to manage its cashflow and reduce the risks associated with the buildup of excess inventory. In addition to the reduced inventory risks, this method of financing also avoids costs associated with trade shows and other expenses associated with taking retail orders.

Successful campaigns are typically niche category items such as athleisure apparel. Instead of producing an entire collection, the campaigns that work well are single items that allow the brand to introduce itself to the market. Once the brand has been introduced, then the company can look to expand into additional items. These online, financing campaigns are a means for a new brand to enter the market with minimal risks due to the ability to pre-sell items.

**Interviewer:** *What are the greatest financing hurdles that fashion brands face in today's retailing environment?*

**C. S.:** It is always tough to be a medium- to small-size fashion brand. The hardest part is when a brand is seeing market success, but the brand is not large enough or is not selling to top retailers to get factors to purchase its receivables. This creates a cashflow management challenge with regards to the expansion of the business. It's a size thing. When a brand is big enough, the brand can get a factor to buy a lot of its invoices to enable the business to finance its production. Also, when a brand is big enough, the brand can often dictate the terms of production to a factory. The larger the brand, the less of a challenge with regards to managing and accessing financing.

## Questions Pertaining to Interview

1. What strategies should smaller fashion brands put in place with their factories to ensure that their production is not challenged because of the size of their business?

2. What are the pros and cons of using factors to finance a fashion brand? How can brands protect themselves against risk with factors?

3. Given the importance of social media for financing campaigns like Kickstarter and Indiegogo, at what stage in the startup of a business is it a good time to conduct a financing campaign?

## CASE STUDY: The Zara Gap[18]

### Company Background

The publicly traded Spanish conglomerate Inditex is the parent company of Zara. Amancio Ortega Gaona, one of the richest men in the world, opened the first Zara store in 1975. The company's headquarters are in northwestern Spain in the small town of Artexio. In the middle of this town, surrounded by fishing villages, is a glass building called the Cube. This building houses the management and design teams for Zara.[19] Artexio is also central to the four hundred smaller firms that produce Zara's more basic fashion designs, such as plain T-shirts and undergarments.

Today, Zara has 2,100 stores located in 88 different countries. Through a close communication system that exists between the Zara store base and headquarters production, Zara has created a customer-centric, quick response design process. To execute this style-driven model, Zara employs 200 designers. Additionally, Zara does small production runs to minimize overstock and to create a sense of scarcity for key items. At a scheduled time, store managers place orders for new items, and twice a week new orders arrive at the same time.[20] This order inventory/delivery process is a key communication and supply chain connection that allows Zara to stock the right items for the right customer at the right time.

### Limited Demand Equals Full-Price Sales

This model of limited inventory has fueled a sense of scarce supply that further supports Zara's ability to command full price on 85 percent of its inventory.[21] By locating its stores in trendy cosmopolitan areas and being known for carrying looks right off the runway, Zara doesn't spend money on advertising. The selling model is purely built-up demand and word of mouth. This creates a powerful message to customers that there is always something new to see at Zara and that you shouldn't wait to purchase an item because it may not be there on your next visit. Zara's ability to stay ahead of the average retailer has resulted in Zara being known as the chic fashion destination.

Because of Zara's stellar production and selling performance, the concept of a "Zara Gap" has developed (Figure 10.3). The Zara Gap, as coined by Dr. Hausman from Stanford University, is the arbitrage situation that Zara creates by its deployment of a fast fashion production model that enables it to outperform more traditional retail models. **Arbitrage** is when a company is able to capitalize on a market imbalance and create profitable returns in its favor. For the past ten years, Zara has created an arbitrage situation that has enabled it to outperform other

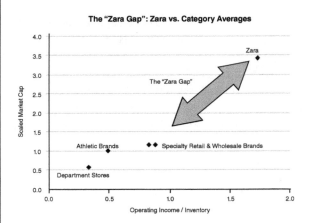

**Figure 10.3**
**The "Zara Gap"**
Source: *Sourcing Journal*, October 28, 2014.

industry players like department stores, athletic brands, and specialty retail and wholesale brands.

A key way to maximize retail profit is to sell more inventory at full price versus having losses due to markdowns. Table 10.5 shows how Zara outperforms its competitors. Because of Zara's ability to run production and selling cycles that maximize the company's in-season selling, Zara is able to achieve a rate of only 15 percent markdowns. Compared to traditional European retailers with over 30 percent markdowns, and traditional US apparel retailers and US department stores with 40 percent markdowns, Zara is clearly outperforming its competitors with regards to the percentage of inventory being marked down.

To ensure that the right product gets to the right store at the right time, Zara ships the majority of its inventory by air. Even with the cost of air freight

compared to shipping, Zara is able to achieve more favorable profit margins because of its savings from fewer markdowns and because it avoids the additional warehousing and transportation associated with excess inventory.

Zara is able to outperform the industry by executing a production strategy that has significantly greater in-season production options versus the typical retailer that has committed the majority of its open-to-buy sometimes six months before items reach the stores. The lack of in-season production capabilities reduces a traditional retailer's ability to maximize its full-price sales. For example, Table 10.5 shows that Zara's production model of sourcing a significant portion of its inventory in season and placing a greater emphasis on store-level demand enables the retailer to have only 15 percent of inventory marked down, which is less than half of the best-performing retail grouping, the European retailers.

**Case Study Questions**
1. What are the critical elements of Zara's supply chain that enable the company to be so responsive to in-season selling?
2. What impact does this business model have on the company's cash conversion cycle? Is the company's current means of cashflow management sustainable?
3. Why do you think other retailers have been unable to create a sourcing strategy similar to Zara's?
4. From a customer's perspective, what are the pros and cons of the Zara sourcing model? How might customer service and brand identify be impacted by Zara's inventory strategy?

| **Table 10.5** Zara versus Traditional Retailers | | | |
|---|---|---|---|
| **Fast Fashion Zara** | **Traditional European Apparel Retailer** | **Traditional US Apparel Retailer** | **US Department Stores** |
| 15% of inventory | 30–40% of inventory | 50–60% of inventory | 60–70% of inventory |
| 15% markdowns | 30% markdown | 40% markdown | 40% markdowns |

Source: *Sourcing Journal*, October 28, 2014.

## CHAPTER REVIEW QUESTIONS

1. Given the lead time for apparel manufacturing, what impact does this lead time have on a brand's working capital?

2. From a supply chain perspective, what can a brand do to improve its cash conversion cycle? How can improving a brand's cash conversion cycle affect the brand's vendors and customers?

3. Why might an early-stage fashion company use factoring over asset-based lending? What are the pros and cons of factoring?

4. What are the financing risks associated with manufacturing goods abroad? What are the various financing instruments used to mitigate these risks?

## CLASS EXERCISE

Based on the information provided in this chapter, what strategies should a fashion brand consider to ensure that the business maintains an adequate cashflow to operate its business? Given the lead time required to produce garments and the fact that the majority of the production occurs abroad, what impact do these factors have on the management of a fashion brand's cashflow position?

## KEY TERMS

stockouts
balance sheet
assets
liabilities
income statement
working capital
collateral
accounts payable(AP)
accounts receivable (AR)
cost of goods sold (COGS)
receivable financing

recourse financing
weighted average cost of capital (WACC)
accounts receivable and inventory financing (ARIF)
asset-based lending (ABL)
factoring
purchase order financing
supply chain financing (SCF)
landed costs
tariff

export
cash-in-advance
letter of credit
documentary collection
open account
cash conversion cycle (C2C)
trade credit
net 30 or 60 days
2/10, N30
blue chip
arbitrage

# REFERENCES

1. Price Waterhouse Coopers (PWC) (2014), "Managing Risk: Supply Chain Finance."
2. Comptroller of the Currency Administrator of National Banks (2014), *Accounts Receivable and Inventory Financing: Comptroller's Handbook*, CreateSpace Independent Publishing Platform.
3. Ibid.
4. Hawser, A., and P. L. Green (2014), "Best Supply Chain Finance Providers 2014," *Global Finance*, July 17.
5. Ibid.
6. "Made in China?" (2015), *The Economist*, March 12. Available online: https://www.economist.com/news/leaders/21646204-asias-dominance-manufacturing-will-endure-will-make-development-harder-others-made.
7. "Tariff and Import Fees" (2016), export.gov. Available online: https://www.export.gov/article?id=Tariff-and-Import-Fees.
8. Investopedia (2015), "What Are Common Reasons for Governments to Implement Tariffs?", April 17. Available online: https://www.investopedia.com/ask/answers/041715/what-are-common-reasons-governments-implement-tariffs.asp.
9. World Customs Organization website. Available online: http://www.wcoomd.org/en/about-us/what-is-the-wco.aspx.
10. Ibid.
11. Hazen, J., C. Conn, and G. Hoffman (2009), "Shift from Letters of Credit to Open Account Using Electronic Supply Chain Management Tools," AFP Annual Conference, October. Available online: https://www.treasurystrategies.com/events/shift-letters-credit-open-account-using-electronic-supply-chain-management-tools/.
12. US Department of Commerce, International Trade Administration (2007), "Trade Finance Guide: A Quick Reference for U.S. Exporters," April. Available online: https://www.trade.gov/media/publications/pdf/trade_finance_guide2007.pdf.
13. "A Guide to Letters of Credit," TD Financial Group.
14. Banomyong, R. (2005), "Measuring the Cash Conversion Cycle in an International Supply Chain," Annual Logistics Research Network (LRN) Conference Proceedings. Available online: http://www.bus.tu.ac.th/usr/ruth/file/C2C%20LRN%202005.pdf.
15. Kim, S. (2013), "Online Retailers Tackle High Rate of Customer Returns," *ABC News*, December. Available online: http://abcnews.go.com/Business/online-shopping-transactions-returned/story?id=21312312.
16. Wisner, P. (2011), "Linking Supply Chain Performance to a Firm's Financial Performance," *Supply Chain Management Review*, May.
17. Craig, T. (2004), "Sarbanes-Oxley Supply Chain Management," *LTD Management*, May.
18. SC Resilience Program Materials. The Canadian Professional Logistics Institute, Supply Chain Resilience Professional, June 4, 2016.
19. Berfield, S., and M. Baigorri (2014), "Zara's Fast Fashion Edge," *Bloomberg*, November 13.
20. Ibid.

# The Retailer

## LEARNING OBJECTIVES

Upon completion of this chapter you will be able to:

- Examine the changing face of retail.

- Describe the various types of retailers.

- Examine how retailers impact the supply chain.

- Consider the reverse supply chain and its environmental effects.

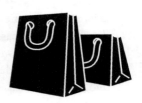

# THE CHANGING FACE OF RETAIL

The global apparel market is valued at over $3 trillion annually, which accounts for 2 percent of the world's gross domestic product (GDP). The labor force required to achieve this level of economic power equates to 57.8 million people worldwide. Of the over $3 trillion in business, a large proportion is exchanged globally through all the various retail channels that exist in today's world (Fashion United 2016: para 1). This chapter discusses the importance of the retailer in the global economy and how retailers affect the fashion industry supply chain. A **retailer** is defined as "a business that sells products and services to consumers for their personal or family use" (Levy & Weitz 2004: 719). It is easy to see that the act of retailing can be traced back thousands of years, with people around the globe using different methods and currency to conduct what is commonly called the retail trade.

In the 1700s, with immigration to the United States increasing, people needed to purchase food, clothing, and other supplies to live in their new home. There were no local stores to go to or malls to visit. Peddlers in horse-drawn wagons were the first retailers to establish themselves in the United States. These retailing pioneers would load up their wagons with goods that they felt were needed by the people along their route and go from home to home selling their wares. In a sense, they were the first trend forecasters, as they would use history and current events to determine what would sell and when. In many respects, they would learn from the people that they would sell to—the consumers—what was needed to survive in the new homes. The country then set up trading posts in what would have been considered high-traffic areas to cater to the multiple families and people passing through a specific route. This was the status quo until the late 1790s, when the local shop began to be developed in cities. The term *clothing store* first appeared in public notices in the Boston area in 1813. Brooks Brothers first opened its doors in 1818 (Figure 11.1).

Once these local stores began to open their doors for business, a new trend began, the department store. A listing of the successive openings of major department stores may be viewed in Table 11.1. Not to be outdone

**Figure 11.1**

**A Brooks Brothers store in a mall setting** This iconic retail store first opened in New York City in 1818 and is still considered a prominent fixture in the retail landscape. Brooks Brothers has been able to change and adapt with its target market while maintaining the rich heritage that is a major part of its retail DNA.

| Table 11.1 Timeline of Department Store Openings | |
|---|---|
| **Year** | **Store Opened** |
| 1826 | Lord & Taylor |
| 1842 | Gimbels |
| 1849 | Famous Barr |
| 1851 | Jordan Marsh |
| 1852 | Marshall Field's |
| 1854 | Carson Pirie Scott & Co |
| 1857 | Macy's |
| 1862 | Stewart's |
| 1867 | Rich's |
| 1869 | John Wanamaker & Co. |

by what we would typically call brick-and-mortar retailers today, Montgomery Ward (see Figure 11.2) opened the first mail-order catalog in 1872, with Sears Roebuck following in 1896. These ventures were made possible by the addition of a formal postal system in the United States that allowed for delivery to individuals. Ward's struggled in the beginning because people were hesitant to trust this mode of retail; then Montgomery Ward himself started to offer a money-back guarantee, and the rest is history.

**Figure 11.2**
**Cover of early Montgomery Ward's mail-order catalog** Yes, you could even buy a house from the catalog! Catalogs revolutionized the way the consumer bought products. Today catalogs are often used as marketing tools to create demand for products, which are then often purchased online and not actually ordered out of the catalog.

Fast-forward to today and the retail landscape has changed dramatically. From small boutiques, individual mom & pops, to the large-format or big box retailers, to the ever-changing mall, retail is changing, not only in the United States but also around the world. An article by IRI Worldwide (2016) noted that "there has been a distinct change in shopper behavior over the past few years with consumers increasingly shifting their purchases to smaller-format and more experience-oriented retail locations while traffic to malls and big box retailers has been declining" (para 1). This change in buyer behavior necessitates a change in retail buying habits because of the need for smaller assortments that are replenished on a quicker turn. These changes have a direct effect on how the fashion supply chain operates. In an earlier article, IRI Worldwide (2015: 2) stated that

> in the late 90's and early 2000's small, local, neighborhood storefronts lived in fear of big box encroachment. The mom & pop shops of the world shut their doors as large format locations drew customers away with low prices, extensive assortments, and the convenience of one-stop shopping. However, following the recent recession, momentum has shifted away from "biggest box" retailing.

Although there is a shift in the retail landscape, the big box stores and the malls are not going away. The real estate is too valuable, so a new breed of retailers is entering this space. Barbara Thau (2016) published an article in *Forbes* titled "The Changing Face of the Mall Dominates Chatter at Retail Real Estate Show." In this article Thau presents research from Dana Telsey of the Telsey Advisory Group and notes Tesley as saying:

> There are more new non-apparel retailers that are beginning to occupy mall space than five years ago, particularly in what is considered prime or "A" mall space such as retailer PIRCH, the upscale, experiential home improvement store, Tesla, the tony car company, as well as etailers that have become retailers, such as Warby Parker, . . . and Bonobos. (para 3)

This phenomenon is not just confined to the United States but can also be seen in the UK with the resurgence of "high street" retailers. A research paper by Deloitte Consulting (2014) suggests that the demand for high street locations is on the increase. The report says that although this is a good sign, it is by no means a declaration of full recovery, as much more needs to occur in order to claim victory. However, the use of technology such as smartphones and mobile devices is contributing to a recovery over and above the competition presented by shopping centers and retail parks.

Many retailers are employing varying strategies to attract and keep consumers. The buzzword in the retail industry in 2016 was **omnichannel**, which describes a multiprong retail strategy in which a retailer uses a variety of channels to create a unique shopping experience for its customers. Omnichannel includes the use of research before a purchase, in addition to providing "channels" such as brick-and-mortar stores, online stores, mobile stores and apps, telephones, catalogs, TV, and any other way the retailer can think of for connecting with the consumer. Today the challenge for every retailer, no matter what size, is how to engage consumers by creating the experience that they now demand.

Technology has played a large part in this shift in consumer buying habits; another contributing factor is retailers' belief that they need to promote their merchandise to attract the customer. The retailer, particularly the department store, has trained the consumer to wait for the product to go on sale. Department stores have adopted the "sale" as a marketing tool to drive traffic into their stores with the hope that the consumer will buy not only what is discounted but also some full-price products. Unfortunately for the consumer, the game is rigged in favor of the retailer, with the overwhelming majority of these "sales" planned into the budget to create the illusion that the consumer is getting a bargain. The retail trade today has entered into a game of psychological warfare to attract and keep its customers. This sale strategy is now fixed in the retail landscape and will prove very difficult to change.

One can look at the changes that Ron Johnson, former CEO of JC Penney (see Figure 11.3), attempted to instill in 2014–2015 to see how sales and coupons have become ingrained in the consumer purchase decision. Johnson's strategy was to eliminate all coupons and drastically reduce the number of sales per year while pricing the products at what he considered a fair price. This did not go over well with the Penney core consumer and was one of the new strategies instituted by Johnson that nearly put the company out of business.

Sudhir Holla (2016), in an article from *Internet Retailer*, created the top ten list of omnichannel trends that are affecting the retail industry:

1. There is greater attention to the supply chain, with greater emphasis on efficiency and reducing operating costs.
2. Physical location matters, but so does the virtual location, especially since consumers are relying on search engines such as Google and Bing.
3. The lines between retailers and brands are becoming blurred. More and more retailers turn to

**Figure 11.3**

**A JC Penney storefront** JC Penney, a long-standing retail fixture in the United States, was teetering on the brink of bankruptcy under the guidance of Ron Johnson. The company has since reversed some of Johnson's mistakes but still has a way to go to gain back the trust of its core customers.

private-label product offerings to reduce costs, while brands invest in a direct-to-consumer model.

4. A trend is described as something moving in a particular direction over a period of time. Mobility has arrived and is no longer considered a trend. Retailers have figured this out and are using the personalization of mobility to enhance targeting efforts.
5. The trend in retail is capitalizing on social media and using it as a marketing tool to enhance sales. This trend rewards the consumer for posting about a product. Engaging the consumer through social media to drive traffic to one's site or retail location actually democratizes marketing and invites the consumer to be a major player.
6. Using technology to personalize offers to the consumer has demonstrated returns on investments. Price is just one element of a personalized pitch to a specific consumer; other incentives are also used.
7. Using technology to track consumer spending is using information to forecast upcoming trends and to actually see firsthand what decisions the consumer is making.
8. Technology can help provide big data, information that industry needs to gain insight about the consumer. The data show what is happening that may not be apparent on a smaller scale. With this information and the greater insight that comes with this

information, decisions may be made that drive the industry in ways never capitalized upon before.

9. Millennials are now the largest consumer group on the planet, surpassing the Baby Boomer generation. All of the trends listed here are and will be directed at the Millennial customer. This is the future of retail; from a numbers point, this is where a large focus will be placed by retailers around the globe. Of course, the next generation's strengths and how they will drive the market in terms of consumerism are yet to be seen.

10. Stores are still evolving. The answer lies with the retailer and its ability to create the experience that attracts customers and keeps them coming back for more. This creativity comes at a cost and must be managed to remain profitable. (adapted from Holla 2016)

All ten of these points are important omnichannel retail trends, but it is no surprise that the number one identified trend focused on the retailer (regardless of the channel) and the supply chain. This is the area where retailers can have a direct impact on the cost of goods sold, particularly as they seek to increase the assortment of private-label program offerings. Private labels are directly controlled by retailers, and therefore retailers also control the supply chain on which private labels are sourced and manufactured. In addition, retailers as buyers can place pressure on the brands and suppliers that they do business with to ensure that their individual supply chains are functioning at peak efficiency so that the retailers can buy the products at the right price. The retail physical location as a destination has not lost its appeal, as consumers still crave the experience of shopping, but it has become for many the last step in the process. Consumers are utilizing search engines to research their intended purchases online, but many still like to touch and feel the product before that final step that is the actual purchase.

In looking at the changing face of retail, Kantar Retail sees the urban landscape as a key to retail success. Smaller-format stores are a trend that will take root in urban areas. Kantar Retail (2016: 8) states that "a number of suppliers and retailers have urban strategies largely aimed at solving the route-to-market complexities of urban selling which is fragmented and complex from

a supply chain standpoint." This newly evolving urban demand chain will become a reality when smart retailers and suppliers use these urban landscapes as testing grounds for new products and new retail store formats. The urban areas will reap the rewards of this trend, and the suppliers and retailers that have planned the supply chains in advance will win the day. Smaller urban formats will require that many big box stores change their supply chain philosophies. These stores commonly buy thousands of pieces of one stock keeping unit (SKU); they will now have to buy tens or hundreds of SKUs.

Like others, Kantar Retail (2016) believes that technology will also continue to change the face of retail and that robotics will have a strong impact, particularly in the area of logistics in the supply chain. By 2025 Kantar believes that robotics will be a major game changer. In addition, Kantar sees two key strategies fueling the retail trade: **demand-chain transparency** and **demand-chain productivity.** According to Kantar (2016), "Walmart won the late 20th century by reimagining supply-chain transparency through sharing accurate, detailed, and real-time data to improve business performance between itself and its trading partners" (9). Kantar looks at demand versus supply and envisions that the retailers that can crack the code for the demand chain will be the winners. With the complexities of digital marketing creating multiple opportunities for the retail community, those that decode the complexities will benefit in the long run. Kantar further discusses a second strategy, demand-chain productivity, and notes that "most major suppliers are focusing on making the dollars they spend creating demand at retail more productive" (Kantar 2016: 9). Retailers around the globe will undertake studies to evaluate how they are spending money to create demand and to bring more focus to the process. Not only are retailers forced to deal with a more complex supply chain, but they are also confronted with further developing their demand chain.

Gone are the days when you could produce a product, put it in the store, and expect the consumer to come in and buy it. All one has to do is look at the many retailers that have gone out of business in your own lifetime and to further research the list of retailers that for one reason or another did not keep up with the trends and stay focused on consumer wants and needs. Table 11.1 listed ten retail stores, and today, in addition to Brooks Brothers, there

Retailers always come and go for a myriad reasons. No doubt we will continue to see considerable change in the field of retailing as the internet continues to gain on traditional retailers. My prediction is that Amazon will soon be the largest retailer. While I was working for a private-label company called Harper Industries, there was an employee who had been with Harper for over thirty-five years, a real industry veteran. One day we were chatting about retailers closing, and he made a bet with me that he could name a retailer that he knew and had done business with that had closed for each letter of the alphabet. After a couple of hours he came back to me and presented me with a handwritten list that included a retailer and sometimes several for each letter. This was in the early 1990s, so some things do not change. Retailers continue to open and close to serve the consumer.

are only two retailers from Table 11.1 that continue to operate, Macy's and Lord & Taylor. During the 1990s Macy's went on an acquisition binge and acquired several of the retailers that appear in Table 11.1, and even Lord & Taylor, which maintains its namesake, was acquired by the Hudson's Bay Company in 2012.

The retail landscape has become very complex, with consumers demanding more transparency, flexibility, value for their dollar, and increased technology. Ecommerce and smaller store formats will continue to expand, creating that special consumer experience; there will also be consolidation of retailers, the use of analytics (big data), and localization. All of these changes are courtesy of the consumer, who has become fully empowered by digital technology. Retail in general is slow to change because change is disruptive and costly. Most retailers are playing catch-up with business models that predate the most recent technology revolution. In this instance the term *retailer* encompasses not only the physical space and the technology being used but also the very people who operate the companies. The winners will be those retailers that anticipate the changes and invest in entrepreneurs who can adjust business strategies to match those of the consumer, and today technology is driving that change.

# RETAILERS' IMPACT ON THE SUPPLY CHAIN

Retailers, regardless of the size and breadth of their products, have a direct and sometimes indirect impact on their fashion supply chains. Retailers are also the link between supply chains and the consumer. It is not possible, within the context of this chapter, to identify every conceivable method by which a consumer can buy a product. The focus, therefore, is on the major sources of retail; we investigate how retailers' buying practices can and do impact supply chains around the globe.

## Who Are the Retailers?

Today there are many retailers in the fashion industry. Table 11.2 lists and describes the different kinds of retailers.

A listing of the various types of retailers and a corresponding general description of these retail establishments has been provided. There is also a more formal classification system known as the **North American Industry Classification System** (NAICS), which classifies every industry and business sector in North America. The system is administered by the US Census Bureau and first started to collect, analyze, and publish statistical information related to the business economy in 1997. The system uses a six-digit code to identify the businesses from which the data are collected.

- The first two digits equal the economic sector.
- The third digit equals the subsector.
- The fourth digit equals the industry group.
- The fifth digit equals the NAICS industry.
- The sixth and final digit equals the national industry.

By way of example, department stores are classified as NAICS Code 452111, and the formal definition that is

**Table 11.2** Kinds of Retailers

| Retailer | Description |
|---|---|
| **Mom & pops** | Small retail format, generally a single owner with a small assortment of product. Generally located in downtown shopping areas. |
| **Boutiques** | Similar to mom & pops; small format, sometimes single ownership, with limited product assortment. Example: women's dresses or men's suits. |
| **Big box retailers** | The term *big box* is derived from the store's physical space: generally more than 50,000 square feet, usually plainly designed, and often looks like a big box. Examples: Best Buy, IKEA; some consider Wal-mart an example of a big box, although in the industry it is considered a discount store. |
| **Department stores** | Large retail establishment with an extensive variety and range of goods, organized into separate departments. All departments are housed under the same roof to facilitate buying, customer service, merchandising, and control. Examples: Macy's, Dillard's, Harrods of London. |
| **Specialty stores** | Retail stores that offer specific and specialized types of items. These stores focus on selling a particular brand or a particular type of product. For example, a store that exclusively sells menswear or a range of apparel for the family would be considered a specialty store. Examples: GAP, J Crew, Ann Taylor. |
| **Chain stores** | Chain stores are retail outlets that share a brand and central management and that usually have stand-ardized business methods and practices covering multiple locations. Examples: JC Penney, Sears, and Montgomery Ward's. Today Ward's is out of business, JC Penney likes to be called a department store, and Sears remains a chain in the eyes of the industry. |
| **Discount stores** | A retail store that sells products at prices lower than those asked by traditional retail outlets. Some discount stores are similar to department stores in that they offer a wide assortment of goods; indeed, some are called discount department stores. Discount stores generally operate on lower profit margins and do not have as many amenities as department or specialty stores. Examples: Walmart, Target, Kohl's, Primark. |
| **Factory outlets** | The original concept was based on the many factories in the United States that produced apparel and/or accessories and that would open a "store" in the factory, generally on pay day, for the employ-ees to buy goods that were left over or damaged. Today the factory outlet is used to sell overruns, excess inventory, and product specifically made to supplement the other products in the store. Exam-ples: Nike factory outlet stores, Coach, Tommy Hilfiger. |
| **Off-price retailers** | The goal of an off-price retailer is to deliver great value on ever-changing selections of brand name and designer fashions at prices generally 20 to 60 percent below department and specialty store regular retail prices on comparable merchandise. Examples: TJX, Ross Stores, Century 21. |
| **Warehouse clubs** | Large-format retailers that carry a wide variety of merchandise, including apparel and accessories. They are no frills and require a yearly fee for entry. Examples: Sam's Club, Costco. |
| **Mail order/ catalog** | These use the mail system to buy and ship products. These products are ordered from the catalog via the internet, phone, or mail and shipped directly to the consumer's home address. Examples: Victoria's Secret, JC Penney, Lands' End. |
| **Television shopping** | Home Shopping and QVC have utilized the TV to engage the consumer 24/7. Consumers view the prod-uct on television and order from their remote, their mobile device, or the phone, and the products are shipped directly to the home. |
| **Ecommerce** | Ecommerce (electronic commerce or EC) is the buying and selling of goods and services over an electronic network, primarily the internet, and includes transactions made via mobile devices and apps. These business transactions are business-to-business, business-to-consumer, consumer-to-consumer, or consumer-to-business. The terms *ecommerce* and *ebusiness* are often used interchangeably. The term *etailing* is also sometimes used in reference to transactional processes for online shopping. Examples: Amazon, Gilt Group. |
| **Kiosks, consignment shops, thrift stores, vending machines** | These are other ways in which the consumer can engage in a retail transaction, and although important in some areas, they do not generally have a great impact on the fashion supply chain. |

Developed by Michael P. Londrigan.

assigned to department stores by the Census Bureau is as follows: "This U.S. industry comprises establishments known as department stores that have separate departments for various merchandise lines, such as apparel, jewelry, home furnishings, and linens, each with separate cash registers and sales associates. Department stores in this industry generally do not have central customer checkout and cash register facilities" (US Census Bureau 2012: para 1).

So, for each of the store groups identified in Table 11.2, there is an NAICS code that provides a formal definition, although for those who work in the fashion industry it is more common to refer to the various retail groupings as discussed in Table 11.2.

## The Impact of Different Retailers

All retailers impact the fashion industry supply chain in some manner. The impact that *boutiques* and *mom & pops* have on the supply chain is more focused on the logistics side, as they would primarily be ordering product from other suppliers such as brands and designers (see Figure 11.4). Typically these types of retailers cannot afford to order large quantities and therefore rely on suppliers that already have stock on hand. One exception could be a design boutique that creates special one-of-a-kind designs. Their impact would be slightly different because they would have to secure fabric and develop patterns, buy findings and trims, and create the end product. In an ideal situation, boutiques and mom & pops would place an order and tell the supplier which shipping method it should use to send the goods on a timely basis. As cost is a consideration in the delivery method, the decision is borne by the retailer. Although logistics may be the primary focus, these retailers can and do impact the supply chain in an indirect way by choosing suppliers that embrace sustainable business practices and that are good corporate citizens. Unfortunately for small-size retailers, this is not always possible, as they are at the mercy of the suppliers that are willing and able to provide product for their stores. With smaller suppliers it is also more difficult to ascertain CSR information, unlike with large, publicly traded companies, which readily provide such information to the general public as well as their trading partners.

Boutiques and mom & pops generally have the responsibility of making sure their suppliers are socially

**Figure 11.4**
**A boutique** These small shops can be found around the globe in residential and business areas and are the backbone of many communities, often providing the consumer with varied choices. They provide a small-store feel with high levels of customer service when done right.

responsible and that the logistical aspect of their business is following reasonable business practices. The lead-up to shipping the order to these customers is where the supply chain would be further impacted, but that is on the manufacturer and is discussed in Chapter 3.

*Big box retailers* play an important role in the retail industry, but because they are more focused on hard goods than on apparel and accessories, we will not discuss their role in the supply chain. Some business professionals see Walmart as a big box retailer, which is not the case; it is considered a discount retail operation and will be discussed along with other discount stores.

*Department stores, specialty stores,* and *chain stores* all have similar impacts on the fashion industry supply chain. These stores buy products to sell in their stores from other parties, whether from wholesalers, brands, or designers. In addition, they create their own products or private labels using a merchandising team or a team product development specialist to source goods for their stores.

If retailers are buying from third parties, the impact on the supply chain is somewhat skewed because those that are providing the products must ensure that all the necessary legal and contractual obligations are fulfilled and must deliver the product in the manner prescribed by the retail purchase order, which is a binding contract. The retailers purchase in good faith from third-party suppliers with the understanding that they are complying with all of the rules and regulations that the retailers have set forth in their vendor compliance manuals. In these manuals the retailers describe how they want to conduct business and advise on any penalties that the third-party suppliers can incur if they do not follow the code of conduct. In these instances the retailers are putting their trust and faith in the third-party suppliers to live up to their end of the agreement. The retailers in turn will ensure that the code is followed by conducting their own inspections or by using third-party agents to inspect facilities and products to ensure adherence to the code.

By purchasing through third-party agreements or "extended value chains," retailers can further impact the supply chain by requesting a change to a style that is already in production, which forces the supplier to stop production, address the change, and potentially push out the delivery date or incur overtime to stay on schedule. These retail groups can place the supply chain at risk by demanding that certain fibers and fabrics be used. Deloitte Consulting (2013) identified several areas of concern for risk management in the supply chain (see Table 11.3). Deloitte Consulting (2013) further states:

> Supply chains are becoming highly sophisticated and vital to the competitiveness of many companies. But their interlinked, global nature also makes them increasingly vulnerable to a range of

| Table 11.3 Risks in the Supply Chain | |
|---|---|
| Macro-environment risks | Potential downturns in the global economy, critical shortages of raw materials (cotton fiber), political instability, newly created regulations, natural disasters |
| Extended value chain risks | Issues with various partners, changes from customers, either financial or product related |
| Internal operation risks | Product development issues, manufacturing, logistics, increased pressure on lead times |
| Functional support risks | Risks in legal, finance, human capital, information technology; shortcomings in these functional areas can lead to issues in compliance or information flow |

Adapted from Deloitte Consulting LLP (2013).

risks. Most executives are concerned about their extended value chain. Executives surveyed are more concerned about risks to their extended value chain—outside suppliers, distributors, and customers—than about risks to company-owned operations and supporting functions. As supply chains have become more interconnected and global, they have also become more vulnerable, with more potential points of failure and less margin of error for absorbing delays and disruptions. Supply chain risk exposure is increasing, and so too is the frequency of problems.

The larger the retailer, the greater the risk, and more attention needs to be paid to the supply chain, putting additional pressure on human capital as well as time and money.

When third-party providers are used for the retailers that fall into the category of department stores, specialty stores, and chain stores, the risk in the supply chain grows in size and scope, and one way to mitigate some of these issues is to create product in house through merchandising, design, and product development teams. The same issues and risks are present with one difference, which is that the retailer has more control over the risks and rewards associated with private-label production. When incorporating private labels into your product mix, you work directly with the supplier (manufacturer) to create the products that you specify. You control the logistics, the finances, the quality, and the selection of materials and trims. The entire sourcing process is controlled in house, and therefore any risks are undertaken by members of your team; conversely, any rewards are celebrated by the same team. The key to private label is buying the right product, at the right time, at the right price, and in the right quantity, which is not an easy feat. The supply chain is complicated and fraught with potential disasters that are too numerous to address in this text. The key takeaway for this group of stores is that there are aspects of the supply chain that you can control, while others are completely out of your control.

Discount stores face the same realities as the store groups already mentioned, with the one major exception, which is the extreme pressure on price. Discount stores buy from third-party suppliers and also create private-label product in house; the difference is that based on their target market and the demographic segment of the population they serve, the price becomes one of the most important aspects of the product offering. As any supply chain industry veteran will tell you, the more price pressure you have, the more opportunity to cut corners and to create potentially dangerous situations.

Factory outlets operate much like department stores and specialty stores, as they assume responsibility for merchandise that does not sell in their full-line stores and supplement the offerings with product specifically made for the outlets, either through private-label offerings or third-party suppliers. The same pressures and issues surrounding the department stores and specialty stores apply to outlet stores. One consideration that does exist is that

## Notes from the Field

As is often said, the best-laid plans often go astray. As just discussed, even with the best-planned supply chain and the most professional people monitoring the chain, things can happen, and you may not always have a good backup plan. Stuff does happen, and it did to me on more than one occasion. While selling a woven shirt program to Eddie Bauer, the supply chain that we had established suffered a significant disruption, one that I would say was totally out of our control. The fabric that was to be used to make the shirts was shipped from the mill via truck (all 20,000 yards) and en route the truck was involved in a crash, resulting in the trailer catching on fire and the total loss of the fabric (luckily the driver escaped serious injury). I had to report to the buyer that we could not honor the delivery because we had to replace the fabric. She was not happy and somewhat dubious as to the cause of the delay until I was able to provide a newspaper report of the accident, which even identified the fabric as belonging to Eddie Bauer. Disruptions in the supply chain are inevitable; it is all about how you and your customer deal with them.

the product that they supplement in the overall assortment may be made from materials different from those in the main stores so that they can achieve a specific price point to attract the outlet consumer. When this occurs, the supply chain must react by finding different materials and possibly suppliers to support these decisions.

*Off-price* retailers are currently a leading force in the retail trade, with continued growth year over year. The majority of the products offered in the off-price arena are bought out of existing inventories from leading brands and designers. In this business model, the supply chain is shortened because the off-price retailer is buying existing product and the supply chain issues that surround sourcing and manufacturing have already been solved by the owners of the merchandise, be it a retailer, etailer, designer, or national brand. In an effort to provide additional goods not readily available, some off-price retailers have resorted to buying assortments from third-party suppliers to supplement merchandise in their stores, and in those instances they face the same supply chain issues as most other retailers.

*Warehouse clubs,* such as Costco and Sam's Club, carry a select assortment of apparel and accessories in their overall assortments, which account for a small percent of their sales, although they do tend to buy in large quantities to support their sales targets while working on reduced margins. Warehouse clubs generally buy from third-party suppliers (national brands, designer labels) and therefore face the same supply chain issues as already discussed. Warehouse clubs have limited associates on the floor and no fixtures and racks to create the same ambiance as a traditional department store, while providing an attractive price point.

*Mail-order catalogs* and *television sales* companies that offer apparel and accessories face the same buying issues as department stores and specialty stores. The major difference is the limited amount of products per page that the catalog house has to merchandise and the limited air time TV companies such as Home Shopping Network (HSN) and Quality Value Convenience (QVC) have to show their products, and therefore the supply chain issues that they encounter are limited in scope. The biggest challenge for a mail-order catalog or TV home shopping channel is making sure it has the product in the right stock keeping unit (SKU) when the customer places the order, so there is constant pressure on the supply chain to be able to fulfill orders the first time and not to run out of stock or create a back order. The issues that surround the supply chains for mail-order and TV shopping channels are similar to those of other modes of retail.

The supply chain issues that face *ecommerce* are no different than those that are discussed on the previous pages. The difference is that with ecommerce sites the size and scope can be vastly different from one website to another. In some instances websites mirror boutiques and mom & pops, while others such as Amazon face supply chain issues that encompass all the possible challenges that a fashion retailer would be confronted with. In fact, it has been predicted that in the not so distant future Amazon will be the single largest retailer of apparel and accessories. Given the differences in size and scope that ecommerce can offer, it is easy to see that the challenges and impacts that these websites can have would be no different than those that all other retailers have, except that they can all be found on the same platform.

*Kiosks, consignment shops, thrift stores,* and *vending machines* were listed in Table 11.2 as examples of additional opportunities for consumers to purchase products. These additional venues do have supply chain implications that are unique to these operations but are not discussed here.

To recap, retailers can impact the supply chain in the following ways:

- Choice of manufacturer through the sourcing process, either through private-label or third-party buying.
- Logistics concerning how goods will be shipped.
- Human capital, which addresses whether or not workers are being fairly paid and treated appropriately and whether or not working conditions are safe. Cost of goods sold, that a fair price is paid to the supplier and a fair price is charged to the consumer.
- Ensuring that all laws and regulations around the globe are adhered to.

## THE REVERSE SUPPLY CHAIN

The forward-looking supply chain creates and brings goods into the retail stores. There is another aspect of the supply chain that needs to be considered: the part of the supply chain known as the **reverse supply chain** (see Figure 11.5). This part of the supply chain siphons off hundreds of millions of dollars in lost margins. The reverse supply chain is made up of all those returns that retailers take in from unsatisfied consumers. The practice has a twofold effect on the retailers' business. First, retailers have to work with an unsatisfied customer, whom they may lose depending on the severity of the issue surrounding the product that is returned. The consumer could be unhappy with the purchase decision and just return the merchandise, in which case there is no harm, as this is a common occurrence. But, if the return results in an unpleasant exchange, the retailer stands the chance of losing that customer forever.

## What Becomes of the Return?

Every year four million pounds of retail returns are shipped off to landfills, according to Environmental Capital Group (see Figure 11.6) (Retail Dive 2016: para 2). Apparel and accessories only make up a portion of the landfill. Other retail products also contribute to this practice. Some say that with the advent of fashion and also the acceptance of throwaway products we are experiencing an increase in the amount of product being "thrown in the heap." This number is expected to continue to grow thanks to the boon in ecommerce, which has apparel return rates that can run up to 40 percent of sales (Dunn 2015).

One reason for the high rate of return is that online retailers make it easy for the consumer to return with policies such as free shipping and free returns. Traditional brick-and-mortar retailers are growing their online

Figure 11.6

**The final resting place of returns** This photo shows a US landfill filled with apparel. Multiply this by the fashion products that are discarded around world, and one can see it is a major source of concern for not only the near term but also for the future of the planet. Increased education on how to properly dispose and/or reuse apparel and accessory products is necessary to help stem this problem.

presence to compete with the likes of Amazon, and the easier they make it for their customers to return goods, the more returns they will have. This text offers much information on sustainability and corporate social responsibility (CSR), and the focus is all on the front end of the supply chain. Retailers are concerned about the supply chain, whose main function is to get products into consumer's hands at the right time, right price, right quality, and right amount. There is, however, limited attention being paid to the back end, or the reverse supply chain. The reverse supply chain also has the ability to put retailers out of business if they do not manage it more efficiently, not to mention the cost to the environment. The place of CSR is clearer today than ever. There needs to be additional attention paid to CSR and the environment.

This problem is not new, but it has received renewed interest as margins continue to shrink at retail and senior executives are looking at every conceivable aspect of the business to boost profits. The issue is not only landfills but also the time, effort, energy, and space it takes to process and hold returns. The challenge for retailers is how to reduce the returns from the start by using sound customer service policies and analyzing the products from a design standpoint to ensure fit and function. Retailers must invest in developing people and systems to handle this approach. This investment will cost money, but reducing the return rate by 1 or 2 percent can pay big dividends in the long term.

Figure 11.5

**Reverse supply chain** This photo represents the thinking that goes into the reverse supply chain. Much thought process and effort are focused on the forward-looking supply chain. In reality the reverse supply chain is just as important.

## Notes from the Field

Innovations in reverse supply chains are happening in more ways than one. Companies are recycling polyester to make new yarn, cotton is being made into insulation, and garments are being repaired more often, but I still remember that while working for JC Penney over thirty years ago they identified apparel returns as a major drain on the cost of goods sold and created a program with their major vendors whereby they would destroy or donate small numbers of returns on soft goods (one piece of this, another of that) at the local store level as opposed to packaging and processing a physical return back to the supplier. Of course, I could not confirm that this practice is still in place today, but it does make sound fiscal sense. The cost associated with returning one or two items was so much greater on both the retailer and supplier side that it made sense to donate or destroy the physical product. How is this for corporate social responsibility!

Retailers that take a serious look at how to improve their reverse supply chains will be in a position to improve their profitability while at the same time improving their stance in the community as it relates to sustainability and corporate social responsibility. For retailers the supply chain has a beginning (sourcing the product), a middle (selling it in their store or online, through TV, catalog, etc.), and an end, which is a satisfied customer or a return. When retailers have too many returns, the bottom line suffers and creates the potential to drive them out of business while filling the landfills of the world.

## CONCLUSION

Retail has an interesting history. The US history of retail is introduced here, along with a discussion of retail in general and the impact of retail on the supply chain locally and on a global scale. Retailers in all forms control the business process. They are the bridge that connects the product to the consumer and that holds the keys in the fashion industry supply chain. Retailers come in many shapes, sizes, and delivery methods, from the small boutique to the superlarge discounter. Although there are many similarities in how various retailers impact the supply chain, each has its own unique set of circumstances. Some retailers choose to be very involved in the decisions up and down the chain, while others leave them up to third parties. The importance of the reverse supply chain is apparent, as it can have a major impact on the profitability of the business and how the consumer views the company. The next time you connect with a retailer to purchase a product or return a product, what questions do you suppose you will consider given the information that you now know?

## INDUSTRY INTERVIEW: MICHAEL GILSON, RETAIL INDUSTRY EXECUTIVE

In this chapter we look at the retail segment and the various types of retailers that make up the fashion industry, as well as how they interact with the fashion industry supply chain. We had the good fortune to speak with Mr. Michael Gilson, formerly of Hudson's Bay Company (HBC), who was directly involved with the supply chain on a day-to-day basis. Hudson's Bay Company is a public company based in Toronto, Canada, with assets that include Saks Fifth Avenue, Lord & Taylor, and Hudson's Bay department stores. As former vice president of Global Sourcing Operations, Supply Chain/Logistics & Wholesale, Michael was responsible for import and wholesale businesses for private and foreign designer brands, in addition to finance, operations, supply chain, logistics, and corporate social responsibility. Michael also serves on the board of directors of Worldwide Responsible Accredited Production (WRAP), an independent, nonprofit team of global social compliance experts dedicated to promoting safe, lawful, humane, and ethical manufacturing worldwide, headquartered in Virginia with offices in Hong Kong and Bangladesh and representatives in India and Southeast Asia. He is also a member of the World Affairs Council, is an authority on customs and importing for the Import/Export Association of Canada, and is on the Advisory Board of LIM College, a business school for the apparel and fashion industry. Michael is a certified public accountant and a champion of Six Sigma methodology and training. He shared his views on several key topics that are relevant to the retail side of the fashion industry supply chain.

**Interviewer:** *There is an old saying in the fashion industry that the "buyer has the pencil," meaning that the buyer can write the orders that control the business. Is this true for the fashion supply chain? Are the retailers in control?*

**M. G.:** Yes, I would say that the retailers are still in control, but I would expand that definition to include retailers and importers. I count HBC, Macy's on the retail side, for example, and importers such as Phillips Van Heusen (PVH) and Vanity Fair Corp. (VF), who would be considered direct manufacturers, to have similar control. But it goes beyond the "buyer" and is really about the brand manager and the entire team that has the control. Of course, the buyer is still a key element in that mix, but more and more companies are adapting the brand management model. From the retail perspective, private label continues to gain importance, with retailers striving for as much as 40 percent of the merchandise mix to be private label. This gives the retailer the opportunity to increase margins.

**Interviewer:** *What impact can the retailer have on the supply chain as it relates to corporate social responsibility? Have you discontinued using suppliers because they did not or could not conform to your policies?*

**M. G.:** Corporate social responsibility (CSR) plays a significant role in the decisions that we here at HBC make on a daily basis. We look at that question from two sides; we have at times eliminated suppliers because they could not conform to our CSR practices, and we have also added suppliers that had strong CSR records in the industry. The decision to drop a supplier is always a difficult one as it could impact (depending on your level of business) the very people that you are trying to help, the workers. So we will give the suppliers several opportunities to improve before making that tough decision. At HBC CSR has legal ramifications and is under the umbrella of global sourcing. The main focus is to not damage the brand in any way, so we have a strong team of auditors both in house and contracted that pay close attention to detail. We view CSR as a partnership with our vendors and we do it because it is good for business and not just for the PR value. We believe that we should always do the right thing regardless if anyone is looking.

**Interviewer:** *Should retailers share more information about their supply chains with the consumer? Does it matter? Do they care?*

**M. G.:** There was a time when we thought this was important and provided a lot of information on our website for the consumer to view. We shared vendor lists, discussed what countries we were in, and the bottom line was that we received very few if any clicks. We believe that it is important to the consumer, but it all depends on who the retailer is. Take a company like Patagonia, who lives and breathes these issues. Their consumers expect this kind of information, not so much from the big department stores who carry hundreds if not thousands of different brands. Let's face it, to provide that information costs money, so we took a step back and decided that it was not an important initiative for us as it did not resonate with our consumers. I go back to the question above; we strive to do the right thing regardless of who is looking.

**Interviewer:** *Trade agreements play a role in the supply chain. How are they affecting your supply chain? What do you see for the future?*

**M. G.:** I would consider this one of the most critical aspects of the fashion industry supply chain facing retailers and importers today. Having your pulse on the various trade agreements and understanding the fine details can provide you with the competitive advantage that everyone is looking for. We have a team of in-house specialists supported by outside trade agreement experts who focus strictly on these issues. With their guidance we can determine what countries we should be in for the short term and also what countries might be viable in the long term. We might take a risk and start developing business in a specific country that has a bill before Congress with the anticipation of a favorable agreement being signed. Free trade agreements (FTAs) as well as other agreements will continue to play a major role in the future of the fashion industry supply chain.

**Interviewer:** *The fashion supply chain has many links. Which do you see as the most important? Why?*

**M. G.:** I would consider the retailer (brick and mortar as well as ecommerce) as the most important link as they are the ones who interact with the consumer and provide the product in their own space. Some might say that it is the manufacturer, but until they can establish a direct link to the consumer the retailer will still be the most important link. Without the retailer providing product to the consumer there would be no need for a supply chain.

**Interviewer:** *Within your organization, which department has the most effect on the supply chain?*

**M. G.:** Within our organization it is the area that is run by the brand management team. The brand managers, in conjunction with buying and sourcing, set the direction for the product that we will carry. The brand managers have to have their pulse on the consumer in order to get it right; then it is up to the rest of the departments to find the best way through the supply chain to provide the consumer with the value that they want.

**Interviewer:** *Does HBC take a holistic view of the supply chain, or is it more compartmentalized?*

**M. G.:** Yes, we do take a holistic view; it is end to end and starts with the brand managers. From there it would go to sourcing to be costed, and if that works, great; if not, we need to look at what we can do to get the cost right. I will say that it is not always possible to achieve the cost needed to properly market the product, and we then make a choice to scrap it or redesign it to fit the price we need to be competitive for the consumer. You have to look at the entire product life cycle to make sure that you are providing value to the consumer.

**Interviewer:** *Crystal ball time. What does the future hold for the retailer as part of the supply chain?*

**M. G.:** Two things stand out in my mind, continued globalization and consolidation. HBC is going global (well, more than United States and Canada), and Macy's is making a foray into China. We will see more and more of the big retailers making these moves. At the same time, we are seeing consolidation on the supply side; there are fewer and fewer large quality producers, and this is forcing us to look at our supply chains in different ways. Both globalization and consolidation will come from mergers and acquisitions, with continued growth in ecommerce. You can look at ecommerce as acquiring another store; it is another way to reach the consumer.

## CASE STUDY: JC Penney

The retail world around the globe continues to change. With an increased emphasis on technology and online sales, retailers are being forced to face new realities. Some retailers are faring better than others when it comes to meeting the new challenges of tomorrow. One challenge that faces all retailers, whether large or small, is how to maintain current customers and grow new ones while remaining profitable. In this chapter we discussed the different types of retailers and how they interact with their various consumers. The focus of this case study is on a US retailer that has strong roots in middle America and has remained fairly consistent with its message and product assortment—that is, until it hired a new president. JC Penney, the retail store that has been known as the department store with a difference, found itself in a serious situation with its retail sales plummeting. This precipitous drop in sales was the result of the vision of one man, Ron Johnson. Mr. Johnson was hired in June 2011 to succeed Myron Ullman as chief executive officer. Ron was fresh off his stint as senior vice president with Apple and previously was vice president of merchandising at Target. Johnson set a casual tone early on, and he was driven to change not only the internal culture at Penney's but the customer culture as well.

Johnson stated that the store needed more designer labels, a strategy he had used successfully at Target. In addition to identifying the need for more designers—something that Penney's has always struggled with—he needed to get the eighteen- to thirty-five-year-old demographic in the stores. To achieve these goals, he needed to address the pricing strategy, the online business, and the home business. One of Johnson's first moves in December 2011 was to buy 16.7 percent of Martha Stewart Living Omnimedia. The companies signed a ten-year contract saying that Penney's could open Martha Stewart shops in its retail space and could sell branded Martha products in the store's home section to give that area a much-needed boost. The second part of this plan hit a snag, as JC Penney found itself in court being sued by Macy's because it too had a licensing agreement with Martha.

February 2012 saw the start of the makeover strategy that Johnson had envisioned, starting with simplified pricing. In 2011, JC Penney ran 590 promotions, which were generally ignored by its customers. The word *sale* was removed from the vocabulary and replaced by "fair and square everyday pricing." Ellen DeGeneres was hired as a Penney spokesperson. The "fair and square" model contained three pricing elements: everyday prices that converted prices to the out-the-door price of at least 40 percent off, monthlong values based on themes such as Back-to-School, and "best prices," which was clearance. Markdowns would be taken on the first and third Fridays of every month. All the merchandise in all the stores was repriced with new price tags ending in "00"; no more would the customer see a "99" cent ending.

Johnson claimed that pricing should be fair and honest—no coupons, no gimmicks, just "fair and square" pricing every day. With the new strategy firmly in place, the first quarter ended in disaster. Comparative store sales declined 18.9 percent, and total store sales decreased 20.1 percent. Ron Johnson stated, "Sales and profitability have been tougher than anticipated during the first thirteen weeks, but the transformation is ahead of schedule . . . While we have work to do to educate the customer on our pricing strategy and to drive more traffic to our stores, we are confident in our vision to become America's favorite store." In mid-May 2012, Michael Kramer, Penney COO, stated, "We did not realize how deep some of the customers were into coupons." Apparently, "coupons were a drug, they really drove traffic." Another realization occurred when Penney's managers stated that their marketing was not working and did not communicate the pricing strategy.

Sales continued to slide, and customers were staying away in droves. The retail department store industry has trained the consumer to shop "on sale," and Penney's was fighting an uphill battle to change the consumer mindset. By the end of May, Johnson had started to see the error of his ways but decided to stay the course with some slight deviations, starting with a revised pricing strategy. Five more Friday sales were planned for the year, including Memorial Day weekend and Black Friday. Additional Friday events would occur during the Back-to-School and Christmas seasons. Even with these additional "sales," the decline continued into the second, third, and fourth quarters.

In the first full year with Johnson at the helm, total store sales declined 24.8 percent, a disaster. With this drop in sales, stores began to close and people were laid off. Throughout the year Johnson had asked the retail and the financial community for time. Johnson stood firmly committed to his vision. Another phase of the plan was to open smaller designer shops and include other notable brands, but everyone was asking the big question: will it be too little too late? This case study poses several questions, and although it has taken place in the past, it can provide a good understanding of retail issues that continue to face the industry.

**Case Study Questions**

1. What are your thoughts about Johnson's initial plan?
2. What were the strengths and weaknesses of the plan?
3. Considering the time when the initial plan was developed (2011), what did Johnson base his decision-making on prior to initiating his plan?
4. Was his plan sound? If not, why not?
5. Where did Johnson go wrong, and what could he have done to change the outcome of his business decisions?

## CHAPTER REVIEW QUESTIONS

1. Which retailers influence the fashion industry supply chain the most? Why and how?
2. How can apparel and accessory retailers reduce their return rates?
3. Which is more important, demand-chain transparency or demand-chain productivity? Why?
4. Which retailers have a strong omnichannel plan in place? What are they doing well? Name three retailers and explain their philosophy for omnichannel.
5. What do you see as the most important change confronting the retail industry today? How will that change impact the future?

## CLASS EXERCISES

1. Identify two major retail organizations and discuss their current reverse supply chain strategies. Compare and contrast these strategies and recommend ways they can improve their current strategies to be more profitable and sustainable.

2. Break up into groups and research various trade agreements. Once the groups have completed their research, come back as a class and discuss findings. What do the trade agreements say? How do these agreements affect the fashion industry and business practices specifically?

## KEY TERMS

retailer
omnichannel
demand-chain transparency
demand-chain productivity
mom & pops
boutiques
big box retailers
department stores

specialty stores
chain stores
discount stores
factory outlets
off-price retailers
warehouse clubs
mail order/catalog
television shopping

ecommerce
kiosks
consignment shops
thrift stores
vending machines
North American Industry
    Classification System
reverse supply chain

## REFERENCES

1. Deloitte Consulting LLP (2013), *The Ripple Effect: How Manufacturing and Retail Executives View the Growing Challenge of Supply Chain Risk*. Available online: https://www2.deloitte.com/content/dam/Deloitte/global/Documents/Process-and-Operations/gx-operations-consulting-the-ripple-effect-041213.pdf.

2. Deloitte Consulting LLP (2014), *The Changing Face of Retail: Where Did All the Shops Go?* Available online: http://www2.deloitte.com/uk/en/pages/consumer-business/articles/where-did-all-the-shops-go.html.

3. Dunn, C. (2015), "Why It's Time for Retailers to Embrace Online Returns," *Entrepreneur*. Available online: https://www.entrepreneur.com/article/246421.

4. Fashion United (2016), "Global Fashion Industry Statistics—International Apparel." Available online: [0]https://fashionunited.com/global-fashion-industry-statistics.

5. Holla, S. (2016), "Top 10 Omnichannel Retail Trends for 2016," *Internet Retailer*. Available online: https://www.internetretailer.com/2016/02/02/top-10-omnichannel-retail-trends-2016.

6. IRI Worldwide (2015), "The Changing Face of Retail: Adapting to Smaller Formats and Embracing E-commerce." Available online: https://www.iriworldwide.com/en-US/insights/Publications/Changing-Face-of-Retail.

7. IRI Worldwide (2016), "Changing Face of Retail." Available online: http://www.iriworldwide.com/en-US/insights/Publications/Changing-face-of-retail.

8. Kantar Retail (2016), *Changing What Matters: Kantar Retail's View of 2016 and Beyond*. Available online: http://www.kantarretail.com/wp-content/uploads/2016/02/Kantar-Retails-View-of-2016-and-Beyond.pdf.

9. Lindsey, K (2016), "Why retail has a growing reverse supply chain problem—and how to fix it." *Retail Dive*. Available online: http://www.retaildive.com/news/why-retail-has-a-growing-reverse-supply-chain-problemand-how-to-fix-it/422136/.

10. Levy, M., and B. A. Weitz (2004), *Retailing Management*, New York: McGraw-Hill.

11. Thau, B. (2016), "The Changing Face of the Mall Dominates Chatter at Retail Real Estate Show," *Forbes*. Available online: http://www.forbes.com/sites/barbarathau/2016/05/31/the-changing-face-of-the-mall-dominates-chatter-at-retail-real-estate-show/#6d0a421124fc.

12. US Census Bureau (2012), "North American Industry Classification System: 2012 NAICS Definition: Sector 44-45 – Retail Trade$^T$ 45211 Department Stores." Available online: https://www.census.gov/cgi-bin/sssd/naics/naicsrch?code=45211&search=2012%20NAICS%20Search.

# The Consumer

## LEARNING OBJECTIVES

Upon completion of this chapter you will be able to:

- Gain an understanding of how today's consumer buying habits and product preferences impact retail strategies.

- Evaluate the role that emerging markets play in the global retail sector.

- Analyze how new and future retailing strategies are influencing the global fashion supply chain.

- Determine what retailers must do with their supply chain and retailing functions to win over today's consumer.

# DOMINANT CONSUMER CHANGES

Throughout the course of this book, there has been a common theme that speed to market at favorable pricing is key to meeting the demands of the fashion industry. In addition, consumers are looking for products that practice socially responsible manufacturing techniques while also achieving a design aesthetic that speaks to the authenticity of the brand. Given these lofty consumer expectations, it is no wonder that the supply chain has grown in its significance as a business differentiator, financial driver, and, most importantly, a means to better meet consumer demand. While there are numerous customer-related factors that are impacting the global fashion supply chain, this chapter focuses on the impact of the Millennial shopper and the evolving demands of emerging markets. These factors suggest that retailers must alter their supply chain to meet the demands of these consumers.

**Figure 12.1**

**A group of Millennials** Because of the number of individuals who fall within this grouping, Millennials have become a key focus for retailers. These consumers are technologically savvy shoppers who are driving key changes in the retailing experience, such as the continuing surge of online shopping and the introduction of new, ecommerce-based business models.

## Millennials

Millennials are a key driving force behind the change in buying habits and consumer expectations. According to a research report by the consulting firm Accenture, the **Millennial generation**, individuals born roughly between 1982 and 2000, is expected to outpace the **Baby Boomer** generation by becoming the largest consumer group. By 2020, Millennials' projected spending will be $1.4 trillion.[1] To put the Millennial projected buying power into perspective, the Baby Boomer generation represents 76 million individuals, whereas Millennials represent 79 million. Figure 12.1 shows an image of Millennials, a diverse group of individuals who are causing retailers to rethink the traditional retailing experience. Because of the sheer number of individuals who fall within the Millennial category, retailers must think of ways to attract and meet the demands of this consumer base. Unlike previous generations, Millennials have distinct buying habits that reflect their adoption of technology, social consciousness, and lifestyle preferences. In 2012, Boston Consulting Group surveyed 4,000 Millennials and 1,000 non-Millennials. The purpose of the study was to identify the distinct buying preferences of the Millennial generation. The following is a summary of the survey findings with regard to Millennial attitudes and behaviors.

The Millennials' comfort with technology, coupled with their openness to online payment systems, has fed the desire for mobile transactions that meet the demands of "I want it fast, and I want it now." The "buy now; wear now" mindset has fueled the design world's move to season-less selling cycles and changed the traditional Fashion Week model to feature items that can be purchased within weeks, compared to the four to six months it took in the former garment production calendar. A report commissioned by the **Council of Fashion Designers of America (CFDA)**, the trade organization that owns the Fashion Calendar, confirmed the consumer's demand for more product with in-season relevancy for the designs that were being presented. Millennials are speeding up fashion's time clock to be more flexible and time-sensitive to their heightened demands.

In 2006, fashion bloggers like Patricia Handschiegel, Susie Lau, and Jennine Jacob began to create their own audience by sharing fashion styles and brand information. The sensation of blogging then moved to the video realm with the introduction of YouTube celebrities who provided curated fashion tips from the perspective of

**Table 12.1** Attitudes and Behavior of the Millennial Consumer[2]

| Attitude and Behavior | Buying Impact |
|---|---|
| "I want it fast, and I want it now." | Immediate gratification and convenience are key. |
| "I trust my friends more than corporate mouthpieces." | Collaboration and self-validation through peers are what drive Millennial sales. The brand's authenticity is important. |
| "I'm a social creator, both online and offline." | Brand affinity can be built around social engagement. |
| "I can make the world a better place." | It's not just about the product; it's also about the cause. |

This table examines how Millennials' behavior impacts their buying preferences.

the everyday individual instead of from the perspective of the *Vogue* and *Mademoiselle* fashion pages. The rise of social media as a means to promote a brand speaks to Millennials' desire to hear from their peers instead of a company spokesperson. Millennials are a bold generation who do not require validation from authority figures—they crave assurance from themselves: hence, the Millennial idea of **"I trust my friends more than corporate mouthpieces."**

Table 12.1 shows how Millennials' behavior is impacting their spending and product engagement. This attitude also speaks to how Millennials shop and use online reviews to support purchasing decisions. Fifty percent of Millennials, compared to 20 percent of non-Millennials, reported using online reviews to influence their buying decisions.[3] Another area of shopping impact is the use of crowdsourcing for products, a means that meets the collaborative nature of Millennials. Websites such as Polyvore, where the Millennial designer Rebecca Minkoff executed a handbag design competition to see what her consumers wanted, have done well in meeting the demands of Millennials.

Not only do brands need to be social online, but they must also engage the consumer through their retailing space to satisfy Millennials' desire to gather together. The popular Millennial athleisure retailer LuLu Lemon offers in-store yoga classes to promote community while leveraging the company's commerce opportunities. Within the online world, community retailing sites and features support the Millennials' desire to be social: hence, brands' use of Facebook pages to garner a favorable nod by means of the "Like" feature.

As Table 12.1 shows, Millennials are known for wanting to improve the world and themselves. They gravitate to causes and seek experiences that fulfill a higher purpose to their being. Because of this need to feel part of something that changes the world, Millennial shoppers are focused on where their clothes are made, the amount of water required to create a pair of jeans, the living wage of apparel workers, and the need for satisfaction in the purchase. Retailers such as Toms, which supports footwear around the world, and Warby Parker, which donates some of its proceeds from glasses sales to aid children around the world, are aligned with the values of the Millennial consumer.

## Emerging Markets

The United States is the largest market for apparel consumption worldwide, and it is also the most saturated and costly market to enter. For these reasons, retailers are looking outside of the United States for future growth opportunities. A report developed by Market Publishers Ltd., a consumer research firm, identifies the top five emerging markets for apparel as Brazil, China, India, South Africa, and Mexico. These markets were projected to achieve an 8.35 CAGR (compound annual growth rate) for 2016.[4] For various socioeconomic reasons that this chapter will explore further, the emerging markets are demonstrating a stronger appetite for apparel consumption. For example, the average urban Chinese household spent 1,902 RMB (or $306) on clothing in 2013, accounting for 10.6 percent of its total annual expenditure, compared to around 3 percent of household annual expenditure in the United States.[5]

Even with an economy that is experiencing significant contraction in leading sectors such as manufacturing and real estate, China is still considered an attractive market for future growth. From a sheer numbers stand-point, China's population of 1.3 billion individuals, or roughly 18 percent of the world's population, makes China a valuable market. With China enjoying the prosperity of over thirty years of 10 percent growth, China's population has benefited from a significant, steady rise in its middle class.[6] As the middle class has grown, so has China's disposable income; in addition, Chinese shoppers are interested in products such as US and European fashions. The result is China's $189.6 billion apparel market.

Chinese consumers are showing an evolution in taste and market sophistication. When the Chinese apparel market first opened to the many brands that gravitated to this emerging market, the Chinese embraced brands with little emphasis on loyalty, individuality, and brand identity. Today's Chinese consumer is not focused on brand logos. Much as in the West, Chinese consumers are looking for products that speak to their market interest. In a 2012 study by McKinsey and Company, 21 percent of the survey respondents that lived in wealthier cities such as Beijing and Shanghai commented that they were interested in brands that demonstrated their unique taste; other cities outside of China expressed a 7 to 10 percent interest in such a buying preference.[7]

Prior to the recent economic slowdowns, the luxury category had done particularly well in China for several of the aforementioned reasons. The Chinese luxury consumer is a worldwide traveler who makes luxury purchases around the world rather than purchasing mainly in China. This is primarily due to the extensive luxury brands that exist extensively outside the Chinese market. In 2012, the Chinese consumer was the largest purchaser of luxury products; however, only 39.28 of those purchases occurred on mainland China.[8] The majority of those purchases occurred in Hong Kong, Macao, and upscale markets outside of China. Much like the middle-class consumer, the Chinese luxury buyer is less interested in branding and more interested in the overall experience and/or the impact of the purchase on the individual, as well as in the value of the investment. The "accessible luxury," a more price-accessible entry-to-luxury market, is another segment of luxury in which US brands such as Michael Kors, Tory Burch, and Coach are seeing outstanding growth.[9] Much like the US market, these brands speak to the aspirations and values of the modern consumer.

Ecommerce is another segment of the China market that has shown tremendous promise. Companies like Alibaba, the online marketplace that in 2014 completed the largest global initial public offering of $21.8 billion, demonstrates the growth potential of ecommerce for the Chinese consumer. Not only has the demographic of the Chinese shopper changed, but the geographic location of the shoppers has also changed. As China's income growth began to spread beyond the major cities to central Chinese locations, the internet began to fill the void of shopping locations throughout those regions. By 2020, China's ecommerce market is projected to exceed that of the United States, the UK, Japan, Germany, and France combined.[10] The features of the internet, such as the product research and reviews, combined with the pricing transparency, are benefits that meet the Chinese consumers' interest in shopping for quality while also pursuing bargain pricing. Another interesting fact, which came out in a research study by KPMG, one of the big four accounting/consulting firms based in the United States, was that as the age of the ecommerce shopper increased, so too did the average value per transaction. This suggests that this market will grow as its shoppers grow in age and discretionary income.

Because of the high volume of luxury transactions in this market, the market can also be flooded with counterfeit products. Popular ecommerce brands have created product authentication mechanisms to address this concern. In addition, the rural and remote nature of the Chinese market raises challenges in logistics. Consumers shop online for convenience, but the logistics of deliveries is a key consideration. Because of the terrain of the Chinese markets that are primarily serviced by third-party logistics carriers, these carriers are challenged to avoid late deliveries, costly transportation, customer servicing concerns, and en route theft. Thus, larger logistic companies such as DHL are making big investments in China to dominate this growing market. In 2016, DHL announced its groundbreaking ecommerce Shenzhen Distribution Center. This facility has the capacity to handle 18 million shipments a year to over 220 countries and territories worldwide. DHL also increased its infrastructure investment in its Shanghai and Hong Kong distribution centers so that it will have the capacity to handle 48 and 71 million shipments, respectively, annually in each of these distribution centers.[11] It is quite apparent that China will continue on its path to becoming a major market for ecommerce transactions.

Following China are Brazil and India, with $36.3 and $15.1 billion revenue in 2014, respectively.[12] While the Brazilian economy is being challenged by its political leadership, an overvalued currency, and health concerns associated with the Zika virus, Brazil is still seen as a favorable apparel market. As in China, Brazilian households are experiencing a rise in disposable income from growth in the country's manufacturing sector. However, the overarching economic concerns within the market are causing retailers to use a cautious investment strategy.

As with many emerging markets, the success of sectors such as manufacturing and, in India's case, services, has created a rise in income to support the growth of a middle-class consumer with a heightened interest in retailing options. Such is the case with present-day India, which is the fifth largest retail market in the world. Of particular interest is the growing market of young consumers between the ages of fifteen and twenty-five. These consumers are focused on trendy styles and on experiencing Western culture. Because of these factors, the apparel manufacturing sector in India is taking advantage of new domestic opportunities, such as the appearance of Indian and foreign brands in many of the country's urban areas. In 2015, New Delhi saw the opening of the US retailer the Gap, the behemoth, fast fashion retailer H&M, and the British fashion brands TOPSHOP and TOPMAN.[13] To support the growth of the Indian market, retail real estate in India is expected to grow significantly; 715 malls were expected to be built by 2017 in II and III tier cities, a classification of city based on market demographics.[14]

Because of the diversity that exists within India—the country is composed of twenty-eight states and seven union territories, all with different styles of dress, purchasing habits, and lifestyle considerations—retail success in India is dependent on the creation of a supply chain network that is able to meet local market demand specifications.[15] In addition to variations in consumer demand, India's supply chain is plagued with low infrastructure investment, minimal technology adoption, and a complex tax structure. India has the second largest road network in the world, with 4.2 million kilometers

## Notes from the Field

Consumers are the lifeblood of the fashion industry, for without them we would not have an industry. In the text we discuss sustainability and CSR, which at times appears counterintuitive to the industry. If we were all sustainable, we would never buy new fashion items, but alas, the consumer is fickle and comes in many different shapes and sizes. My advice to those in sales is to never judge a book by its cover. One holiday season I took a part-time position with Neiman Marcus to make some extra holiday cash. I was assigned to the men's furnishings department. Longtime sales personnel were very territorial and possessive of their clients, and I found this out the hard way by striking up a conversation with a customer only to find out he "belonged" to someone. One busy evening the sportswear department was slammed and my manager asked me to help with the next customer, a woman dressed in ripped jeans and a baggy sweatshirt. The other salespeople in my department were laughing at my prospects of having to leave my post and assist this woman, whom they viewed as a waste of time. I approached her professionally and asked if I could help, and she said she was looking for some sweaters for her husband. I proceeded to tell her about our offerings, and she said she was only interested in cashmere! She bought six sweaters averaging $250.00 per piece, a $1,500.00 order that made my week's commission. When I went back to the department, a few people asked if she bought anything and I told them no, she was just looking. In the retail trade, especially today, you can never tell a person's background, so approach everyone as if he or she could be your best customer.

of roads; however, only 2 percent of these roads are part of the country's highway network. Thus, tremendous investment is required to make the transportation aspects of the market meet the demands of this emerging market.[16]

# HOW CONSUMER PREFERENCES IMPACT SUPPLY CHAIN PLANNING

As seen from our discussion of the Millennial and emerging markets, the two largest segments of apparel growth, these are consumers who want what they want, when they want it, and how and where they want it. This creates a need for supply chains that are **customer-centric**, an approach to business that centers on customer experience and that is built around three key principles: agility, speed, and innovation. To meet these demands, retailers are looking at pull versus push supply chain strategies.

Table 12.2 highlights the differences that exist between a push and a pull strategy. A **push supply chain strategy** uses projected volumes to manufacture goods. Push strategies tend to work best when the retailer has a dominant position in the market and there is minimal variation of goods such as commodity products. Additionally, the push model is consistent with retail's traditional selling cycle that mirrors the four seasons: fall, winter, spring, and summer. By the end of summer, retailers begin to push fall/winter outerwear to the consumer regardless of whether the weather pattern and consumer demand are in sync. The problem with this strategy is that when the fall/winter outerwear is available before there is actual consumer demand, the items sit on the selling floor for an extended period of time, causing the retailer to mark them down. Additionally, once consumers are ready for the fall/winter item, they will have been fatigued from seeing the previous items that were available prior to their period of interest. For the apparel market, the push strategy means longer lead times due to the delay in processing consumer information, which affects production decisions, and minimal opportunity for real-time adjustments because of changes in consumer demand, resulting in increased risks and a greater demand on a retailer's cashflow to support production in advance of actual consumer demand.

For example, winter 2015 sales were tremendously off sales projections compared to the previous year. November 2015 was the warmest month on record, and there was unseasonably warm weather throughout the United States and Europe due to El Niño.[17] As a result, sales of outerwear and boots were down by $421 million from November 1 to December 19, according to a study of 250 retailers conducted by Planalytics, a weather intelligence firm.[18]

Table 12.2 also shows a **pull supply chain strategy**, which is based on actual consumer demand. It is somewhat similar to just-in-time inventory management because the pull strategy plans production based upon actual interests. To achieve the pull strategy, the retailer requires access to consumer information on a close-to, if not real-time, basis, flexibility in production schedules, and access to raw materials to meet a variation in

| **Table 12.2** Push versus Pull Supply Chain Strategy | | |
|---|---|---|
| | **Push** | **Pull** |
| What drives the supply chain process? | **Historical:** Projected customer demand | **Actual:** Customer purchases captured and reported on a close to **real-time** basis |
| How is a company's cash flow impacted? | **Longer Cash Conversion Cycle:** Because cash is tied up longer due to longer lead times | **Shorter Cash Conversion Cycle:** Because product is made closer to the time of sale |
| What types of products work best? | **Commodities** | **Products that require personalization** |
| What is the level of risk? | **Higher:** Inventory subject to obsolescence because of the long lead time | **Lower:** Inventory produced in a shorter lead time and based on actual demand |

This table shows the differences in product planning, cash management, and risk associated with a push versus a pull supply chain strategy.

demand. This pull model enables retailers to be more flexible in their ordering patterns while also creating the opportunity for a fresher-looking inventory and greater potential for full-price sales because the consumer has a shorter buying window. While the rewards of the pull model are great, there is a fair amount of planning required upfront to ensure that the retailer has a means to gain real-time customer information. This customer information is important because a shorter lead time requires that the retailer have a means to still meet the customer's expectation for delivery, and the retailer must ensure that there is production capacity that is capable of being flexible with the timing of finished goods. Because of the challenges of moving a supply chain from a push to a pull strategy, many companies have adopted a hybrid model in which the pull strategy is used for order replenishment. At a minimum, this potentially minimizes markdowns and stores being filled with items that the market isn't pursuing.

## NEW BUSINESS MODELS

In an effort to appease the fashion demands of Millennials, emerging markets, and traditional shoppers, retailers are rethinking the selling channels of brick-and-mortar stores and ecommerce. Because the new models are fundamentally challenging how consumers engage with product, select choices, and even purchase items, these new businesses fall within the category of industry disrupters. Clayton Christensen, a Harvard business professor, defines a disrupter as a business model that displaces existing markets, industry, or technology and replaces them with something that is new and more efficient than was previously possible.[19]

This current era, in which technology meets opportunity, could easily be considered the era of disruption. The hotel industry, which had existed for several years with basic innovations such as room service, electronic check-in, and so forth, was completely turned on its head by the launch of AirBNB, a site that allows individuals to rent their homes like innkeepers. Uber is an online transportation network that enables individuals to become car service drivers on demand. In 2016, *Hamilton*, the play nominated for thirteen Tony Awards, disrupted Broadway by replacing the staid musical format with an upbeat hip-hop storyline that made it one of Broadway's highest-grossing shows.

Just as these mature industries have been forever changed by the introduction of these new business models, so too has the fashion industry been disrupted. Imagine borrowing the latest looks for only a fraction of the cost, and, even better, having the items come right to your door. Rent the Runway, launched in 2009, introduced the concept of sharing versus owning clothes. The high-end segment of the fashion industry has been built around the idea of exclusivity and curated products for a select few. Gilt Groupe and HauteLook, online retailers, made insider fashions available for the average consumer through a site that sold exclusive items through a **flash sale**, a discount or a promotion sale offered for a short window of time by an ecommerce retailer, or a private sale. Shoes of Prey, a global, multichannel brand, invited women to design their own high-heel creations at a reasonable price. Warby Parker made it cool to wear glasses by introducing multiple options on a sleek website. For each of these disruptors, there are tremendous process and technology impacts throughout various aspects of the supply chain, such as product development, selling channels, order fulfillment, and customer service. The remainder of this chapter will explore these new business models and what they mean to current and future supply chain efforts.

## Sharing Economy

By leveraging technology that enables reduced transaction cost and access to consumers through online profiles and marketplaces, the **sharing economy has emerged as a peer-to-peer business model that is worth roughly $26 billion worldwide.**[20] The sharing economy has empowered the average consumer to be either a seller or a receiver of goods by leveraging assets across multiple users. Rent the Runway told consumers that they could have Red Carpet looks without the cost. To achieve this model, the company acquired designer looks, established a company website, and let the world know that for a few bucks, they could rent a gown, evening bag, and jewelry. With a closet full of 50,000 unique fashion items, Rent the Runway has dominated the evening sharing apparel market.[21]

Because of the success of Rent the Runway, this model has been extended into other categories of fashion, such as Gywnnie Bee, a plus-size retailer that provides everyday fashions with the use of a sharing model

and subscription service, and Borrow for Your Bump, an online site that provides stylish looks for pregnant women.

One of the key reasons that these sharing economy businesses are a success is that reverse logistics are employed to ensure that product is received, delivered, and ready for the next shipment within an acceptable window of time. Rent the Runway is able to meet the demands of such a model through its proprietary logistics software, which operates on a just-in-time basis. Rent the Runway credits its ability to meet its ongoing customer demand in a consistent and cost-effective manner to the supply chain processes and procedures highlighted in Table 12.3.

Rent the Runway has established relationships with A-list designers like Bagley Mischka, Nicole Miller, and Marchesa Notte to support the company's inventory needs. By having these relationships and leveraging its buying power, Rent the Runway is able to secure a reliable inventory network to ensure that its consumers have access to the latest evening wear designs. One of the biggest challenges for online sales is clothing fit. Because the Rent the Runway model is built on the exciting premise of receiving the right dress for the right event at the right time, fit is a key element of the business model's success. To address this concern, Rent the Runway uses social media to help its shoppers share their experiences with the sizes of the gowns on real women versus runway models.

As with much of the supply chain process, delivery timing is a key aspect of the process. Order fulfillment enables Rent the Runway to optimize its inventory, ensuring that the evening gown of a customer's choice is available, and in good quality, to be sent to the next

| Table 12.3 Rent the Runway Supply Chain Highlights[22] | |
|---|---|
| **Supply Chain Area** | **Process Description** |
| Collaborative Design Process | In-demand inventory program created through partnership with high-end designers |
| Fit | Through social media shared images provide customers an opportunity to see how designs fit on other women |
| Order Fulfillment | Prioritizes prefulfillment tasks to ensure that inventory is ready and accurately accounted for in the order fulfillment queue |
| Returns | 24-hour return program that includes dry cleaning, repairs, and packaging |
| Data Analysis | Analytics used to assess demand for inventory management and order fulfillment |

customer. This is achieved through Rent the Runway's proprietary order fulfillment technology, which leverages customer analytics to manage inventory and order delivery.

Returns are the heart of the Rent the Runway business model. On the wall of the company's 160,000-square-foot warehouse, which is the nation's largest single dry cleaning facility, the company missions reads, "love. wear. return."[23] The company maximizes its inventory investment by increasing the number of times a Vera Wang gown can be worn. The average Rent the Runway gown is worn thirty times.[24] As proof that the dry cleaning and repair process works, many of these gowns are sold after they have been in use in the company's rental pool. To achieve this high rate of wear, Rent the Runway's dry cleaning technicians and sewing talent specialize in fiber treatments and repair work.

In order to know what is selling best and when those items need to be available, Rent the Runway, like many innovating retail companies, uses big data to solve its inventory management and marketing penetration questions. Through the use of data analytics, the company is able to maintain a constant flow of information between the renter and the company's inventory management, fulfillment, customer service, and even marketing departments. Thus Rent the Runway can monitor its demand in real time versus instead of using projections: a supply chain pull strategy.

## Crowdsourcing Production

In the traditional retailing world, the buyer and merchandiser were the individuals responsible for shopping the international and domestic design markets for the latest trends, executing on an **open-to-buy (OTB) strategy** (a merchandising process that is the budgeted amount of merchandise allocated for a particular store or category of good), and partnering with the visual team to ensure the proper displaying of the merchandise for consumers. The crowdsourcing strategy involves reaching out to one's community of shoppers to test design concepts and/or to request product ideas; it is a winning strategy because it engages the consumer, an attribute in which Millennial shoppers have expressed interest, and can test the potential success of new lines before it makes the costly commitment to fabric, manufacturing,

and marketing. In 2015, American Apparel, the trendy casual brand known for its catchy advertisements and urban locations, reached out to its community to ask designers who focus on American-made products to submit ideas to the company's website. Once submitted, the designs were then reviewed and voted upon by the American Apparel community. Both parties benefited from the additional public relations, and the designers had an opportunity to reach a shopping network that it might have been a challenge to meet.

ModCloth, an online apparel store purchased by Walmart in 2017, has created a feature within its site called Be the Buyer. As virtual buyers for the company, consumers share their likes and dislikes about design options. The benefit to virtual buyers is that if their design is selected, they will be contacted first to buy the item. Because the items are produced in smaller lots, the concept of scarcity creates a built-in market demand. In addition to gaining a sense of what will sell before production begins, the retailer also has a unique opportunity to engage the consumer in a dialogue about the product. In a study by Cotton Inc., a trade association that focuses on the raw material cotton, 68 percent of the shoppers interviewed responded that they typically write product reviews for their purchases. In the same survey, 71 percent of the respondents commented that they use reviews to influence their purchasing decision.[25] Crowdsourcing production ideas give the consumer an input in the production process. 2XU, a high-performance athletic brand, utilizes its crowdsourcing platform to allow its consumer, not a brand manager, to speak to the value of the company's athletic wear.[26] This model appeals to Millennials and other shoppers who seek authenticity in their buying experiences, and it enables brands to leverage the power of consumer selection to market to their customer base for the items being produced.

Crowdsourcing is also impacting the operation side of the business through supply chain innovations with regards to operational performance and risk management. One of the challenging logistical aspects of supply chain management is the ability to optimize one's load. If a trucker has capacity for a full truck worth of deliveries but because of time restraints must make the delivery prior to obtaining a full load of cargo, the cost per delivered item will be higher. Cargomatic, a trucking logistics firm, utilizes technology and its community of truckers to identify excess capacity when scheduling deliveries.[27] The company, headquartered in San Francisco, is considered the Uber of the trucking industry. Companies are also leveraging collective input to identify and mitigate risks throughout the supply chain. By leveraging input from multiple entities, companies are able to develop risk mitigation strategies that provide a greater reach of insight and perspective.

## Subscription Services

A model that had been primarily used in the magazine business has caught the eye of retailers as a means to engage consumers on a monthly basis: **subscription services.** The model plays on consumers' desire to be surprised by monthly deliveries of items selected specifically for them: everyone likes to receive a package in the mail. Many celebrities have entered this market as tastemakers or influencers, such as the actress Kate Hudson and her athleisure brand Fabletics.[28]

Birchbox, the New York retailer that built its business around sending sample beauty products to its subscribers, was an early trailblazer in the modern-day retailing concept of subscription services. From the success of the Birchbox model came etailers such as Stitch Fix, a women's apparel site that offers styling services and monthly product selections, and Trunk Club, the male version of an online styling product company with monthly product deliveries. Subscription services cater to today's shoppers' focus on time and convenience by offering curated product selections without the need to go into a brick-and-mortar store or even to pick out items online. Many sites employ data analytics to assess buying preferences for ongoing product selections. The boxes are also priced at a discount to ensure that if the products were purchased individually, the total selection would cost much more than a subscription box.

Stitch Fix, founded in 2011, is a combination of a styling and subscription service for the busy woman. The company, which has grown primarily by word of mouth and social media, has managed to create a powerful ecommerce brand that has experienced success because of its ability to leverage customer data and supply chain management. On a monthly basis, a Stitch Fix customer receives a box of five items that are selected based on a questionnaire that the customer completes online.

To get the perfect "fix," the questionnaire asks about size, color preferences, lifestyle, and personal interests. Customers only keep the items they like. All other items get returned via the mail. As customers select and return items, Stitch Fix creates a customer profile that enables a personalization of items for future selections. The more you pick and reject, the smarter Stitch Fix becomes at what you like. This is accomplished by the company's technological investments and the leveraging of advanced algorithms.

From a supply chain perspective, Stitch Fix is leveraging customer data to plan its inventory and fulfillment requirements. The company is also leveraging an operating plan that makes possible a simplified but profitable means to build inventory, accept returns, and fulfill orders based on customer insight. Because the company has successfully built an assortment of stylish pieces from over two hundred designers, 70 percent of Stitch Fix shoppers are repeat customers.[29] Since it is expected that a customer will take two out of the five items sent, the return aspect of the Stitch Fix supply chain is another key component in the company's business model.

## Secondhand Sites

The thrift, or consignment, industry, which is a US market of approximately $10 billion in revenue, is driven by a consumer's sensitivity to price and, more recently, the emphasis on sustainability, which promotes the recycling and reselling of finished goods.[30] The market grew tremendously after the 2008 recession, when disposable income tightened, the job market showed extreme uncertainty, and consumer confidence showed minimal tolerance for spending—all characteristics that support the reselling of items to generate cash and the acquisition of goods at an extreme discount.

The auction-based retailer eBay, which launched in 1995, was the original online site that gave sellers a platform to hawk their gently used items to the masses of shoppers hooked on the idea of capturing a bargain or a one-of-a-kind find without leaving the comfort of their home. Since that time, several online sites have entered the market as various iterations of the eBay marketplace, such as The RealReal, a site that combines the thrill of flash sales and the consignment model to obtain top designs such as Jimmy Choo stilettos and an original

Diane Von Furstenberg classic wrap dress. Poshmark leverages the mobile phone to create an easy means to list and buy items without a middleman.

These sites capitalize on excess or unwanted items that serve as inventory for future shoppers. The consignment site ThredUP sends bags to women who wish to eliminate unworn items from their closets. ThredUp will evaluate the item, repair, and clean it, and then place it on the company's website for resale. If an item is unable to be sold because of its condition, ThredUp will either send the item back to the seller or donate the item to charity in the name of the seller. Not only is ThredUp addressing the challenge of accessing affordable clothing, but it is also tackling the often dreaded household chore of cleaning out one's closet.

Because ThredUp relies on its community for inventory and sales, it recognizes the importance of speed in retrieving items for sale and delivering items that have sold. Through data analysis, ThredUp discovered that the more quickly its customers received their package, the higher the purchase price for their next order. To achieve these delivery objectives, ThredUp locates its processing centers close to FedEx hubs. This reduces the time for deliveries while also dramatically reducing transit costs and increasing the customer's overall satisfaction with the ThredUp experience.

## Mcommerce

Ecommerce is the purchasing of items through a company's website on the internet. The next generation of ecommerce is mcommerce, or mobile commerce, the purchasing of items by means of a smartphone or tablet (see Table 12.4). Beyond the age of these concepts, there are several differences that exist between them. Mcommerce supports today's consumer interest in shopping

anytime, anywhere because it doesn't require the use of the internet or a stationary electric source. Mcommerce also provides greater customer engagement because of the technology's ability to engage customers through video sources such as YouTube, Facebook Live, and other forms of social media.

From 2013 to 2014, there was a 58 percent increase in mcommerce transactions, according to a Forrester Research report. In 2014, of a total of $114 billion in mcommerce purchases, $38 billion was made on mobile devices and $76 billion was made on tablets.[32] This jump in mcommerce transactions is driven by consumers' swift adoption of mcommerce for browsing, selecting, and paying for items online. Additionally, retailers have invested significantly to enhance the overall shopping experience from an mcommerce perspective. Retailers are approaching their online presence as a means to excite the customer, harness loyal communities through blogs and customer reviews, and establish an ongoing relationship with consumers that extends beyond the traditional brick-and-mortar experience.

The introduction of ecommerce into retail created an unlimited space to showcase products to individuals around the world. Retailers were no longer confined to their floor space or hours of operation. For example, when the retailer Saks Fifth Avenue decided that it wanted to launch activewear retailing space, it turned to an ecommerce shop. Within the company's website, Saks launched its Activewear Shop, which featured designer sports apparel from T by Alexander Wang, Michi, and Koral Activewear.[33] The Activewear Shop allows Saks to introduce a new product offering without increasing or taking away from its brick-and-mortar floor space while also utilizing social media to promote the retailer's new addition. The internet freed retailers from the constraints of space and time. However, this freedom came

| Table 12.4 Differences between Ecommerce and Mcommerce[31] | |
| --- | --- |
| Ecommerce | Mcommerce |
| Mature concept | Early-stage concept |
| Uses a computer laptop | Uses smartphones, tablets, iPads, and personal digital assistants (PDAs) |
| Requires the use of the internet to conduct transactions | Transactions can occur anywhere there is WiFi access |
| Website serves as the primary means of engagement with a consumer | Able to do videoconferencing to enhance a consumer's experiences |

at the cost of creating a supply chain network that is able to fulfill the inventory and delivery demands of a retailer that has the potential to showcase an unlimited number of product offerings.

In addition, ecommerce also creates a new means to engage consumers and increase full-price purchases. During the fall 2014 New York Fashion Week at the Versace show, attendees were able to watch and purchase at the same time on the brand's microsite #ShowShopParty.[34] In an effort to compete with knock-off brands that copy designs straight from the runway, Versace created a way for consumers to buy what they see during the time of the show. The site was also mobilized so that consumers could truly shop anywhere.

By leveraging the power of social media, Versace drove traffic to the site while encouraging viewers to post on Facebook, Twitter, Pinterest, Google+, and Tumblr. Versace was able to gather real-time customer insight about the line while also creating tremendous buzz. From a supply chain perspective, Versace needed to ensure the availability of the forty items that were being shown so that anxious customers could receive their pieces in the customary quick turnaround time of an ecommerce purchase. By benefiting from mobile commerce, the brand is able to increase full-price sales while creating a meaningful platform to engage customers on the brand's latest collections.

# BUSINESS MODELS OF THE FUTURE

## 3D Printing

**Additive manufacturing** builds product by layering deposited materials (see Table 12.5). It has its origins in the development of rapid prototyping (RP), which

was invented in the late 1980s in the United States. RP utilizes **polymers**, strong, flexible, and durable plastic materials, that are placed in formation through the use of computer-aided design (CAD) data. **3D printing**, which also was created in the 1980s, is the layering of materials to create a design form. As seen in Figure 12.2, 3D printing has evolved to be able to create wearable garments. While it has been around in the fashion industry for some time, the runways are being set a-buzz with it, with 3D fashion showing up on the reality show *Project Runway*, appearing on catwalks with designers like Iris Van Herpen and its 3D-printed collection Voltage, and being sold on retailer websites such as Neiman Marcus.[35] Iris Van Herpen, a Dutch fashion designer, collaborated with Materialise, which held the first 3D fashion week in Malaysia. As the cost and usability of materials such as nylons continue to better meet the demands of fashion, and as more designers embrace the technology, 3D printing will continue to grow in significance in the industry.

Because 3D printing creates its designs through the layering of materials versus the traditional cutting of material, the process is sustainable and green. The fashion industry is traditionally considered to be somewhat harmful to the environment because of the waste in the apparel manufacturing processes, such as dyeing and material waste. Additionally, 3D printing makes small production runs cost-effective, which supports the development of samples, item personalization, and the production for new designers, who often require smaller minimum orders.

Footwear, an area of fashion that often struggles with the challenges of comfort over style, has made tremendous strides with the application of 3D printing for fashion and sports apparel. The win for 3D printing footwear is the ability to cheaply customize the shoe to an individual's foot, a challenge that plagues the industry

**Table 12.5** Traditional Garment Construction versus Additive Manufacturing

| Traditional Garment Construction | Additive Manufacturing: 3D Printing |
|---|---|
| Scraps and waste left at the end of the process | Zero waste |
| Limited construction capabilities | Able to achieve complex garment construction |
| Fit issues still require multiple fittings on multiple body types | Solves fit issues with an ability to fit to form virtually |
| Personalization requires costly, potentially time-consuming tasks | Personalization achieved with the ease of programming |

**Figure 12.2**

**A 3D printed runway garment** 3D printing can produce designs that are fashionable and wearable. 3D printing materials produce unique designs.

because of product defects, returns, and often basic customer discomfort. Current shoes only take into consideration the length, and in some instances, the width of the foot. However, the fit of a shoe is also impacted by an individual's weight, toe placement, and overall bone structure. As Nike so rightfully discovered with the creation of its Vapor Ultimate Cleat American football boot, 3D printing is able to create a high-performance shoe that caters to the needs of the individual athlete.

While the 3D printer brings tremendous upsides to the industry, there are concerns around the possibility of job displacement because the laborious task of garment construction can now be performed by a machine. There are also legal concerns about counterfeiting and copyrighting items, because a significant benefit of 3D

printing is the ability to flawlessly copy items. The effects of 3D printing can substantially be felt throughout the entire supply chain, from the raw materials process to consumer distribution. Additionally, 3D printing takes production control from the retailer and places it with the consumer. This creates a change in the relationship between brand and consumer that will require a different means of engaging and facilitating future transactions. An interesting point to consider is whether there's such a thing as a return in 3D printing, because the printer has the capability to produce to the customer's final specifications. This is why many in the industry consider 3D printing to be the next generation of retail.

## Artificial Intelligence

While it is hard to imagine how the technology that is used to monitor national security, and even cure disease, can be applied to fashion, artificial intelligence is indeed being applied to the workings of the fashion industry. **Artificial intelligence (AI)** is essentially the science of computers that are able to learn. This technology is able to capture customer data to assess buying preferences, behaviors, price sensitivity, and even style preferences to create a profile of a consumer. Because of the scale of research required to make AI fully adaptable in the fashion industry, it will exist more as a platform enhancer than as an individual brand strategy. This is evidenced by the significant investment that companies like Facebook, Google, and Microsoft have made to unlock the capabilities of this advanced technology.[36] AI can become an equalizer like the internet, which enabled all brands to sell online. It can also become a differentiator; only certain brands can fully leverage the technology, such as brands that have been successful in building a brand that is known for enhanced customer experience.

A report by Sonar, the proprietary research arm of J. Walter Thompson, found that consumers are very interested in the use of AI in the retailing experience. Seventy percent of US Millennials and 62 percent of UK Millennials expressed a desire for further AI advancements in product development and consumer engagement.[37] The insight provided from AI, such as predicting a customer's wants, will assist with production planning and inventory management. Amazon, the world's largest retailer, has been hiring talent with an AI background to support the company's apparel and footwear business.

Because of the whimsical nature of fashion, traditional projections only capture a portion of the knowledge needed to make more informed fashion decisions. AI's pattern recognition, combined with the functionality to assess multiple factors simultaneously, makes AI a powerful tool for the fashion business.

After production takes place, AI can also play a key role in helping to determine product distribution. AI provides supply chains with real-time knowledge to potentially support on-demand production. Because fashion is driven by the latest trends, AI's pattern recognition will enable retailers to identify changes in the latest styles and thus proactively manage their outcomes. More importantly, AI assists with providing exceptional customer service because of its ability to plan and learn from previous mistakes concerning an individual consumer's likes and dislikes.

## CONCLUSION

Given the number of potential consumers and the ways in which this market engages with brands, utilizes technology, and values a socially conscious mindset, Millennials are disrupting traditional retailing strategies. The Millennial shopper wants to be engaged in the production and selling cycles through social media while also wanting to reap the benefits of a "buy now; wear now" selling cycle. For these reasons, the Millennial consumer is dramatically impacting retail.

The emerging markets of Brazil, China, India, South Africa, and Mexico are also creating new demands and opportunities for retailers. These consumers no longer purchase for necessity, but purchase for style and social status. Many of these consumers are focused on brands and selling experiences that reflect Western culture. This change in purchasing behavior will impact the type of product offered by retailers. These markets are also very adaptive to the benefits of online retailing.

With a market of shoppers who are becoming increasingly informed through their unlimited access to customer reviews, opportunities to participate in production via crowdsourcing, and even pricing transparency with the assistance of complex search engines, it is becoming key that retailers know their consumers. Through point of sale (POS) transactions, online shopping carts, and frequently visited sites, consumers are beginning to expect that a retailer knows what they want. Additionally, through blogs, Instagram accounts, Facebook, and Pinterest, consumers expect to be engaged by their favorite brands. In order to meet these expectations, retailers must know their consumer. They must understand why consumers purchase from them, what would make consumers purchase more, and what turns a consumer off from a brand.

By having an understanding of their consumers, retailers will be able to leverage new business models, such as sharing and subscription services that meet the product interests of the modern consumer. As we look toward the future of retailing, advanced production and customer insight opportunities such as 3D printing and artificial intelligence will serve as ways to meet the demands of future market interests.

# INDUSTRY INTERVIEW: DAVID MEIR SASSON, COO, DEREK LAM

For this chapter, I had the opportunity to interview David Meir Sasson, the COO of the women's apparel brand Derek Lam. Mr. Sasson also is an Advisory Board member and instructor at LIM College. As the COO for Derek Lam, Mr. Sasson oversees the general operations of the business, which include the supply chain and retail operations. Prior to joining Derek Lam, David was the corporate vice president of financial strategy for Kenneth Cole Productions. In this role, David developed and implemented a restructuring plan for the leather accessories division, rebalancing the operations between Italy and China and achieving $5 million of annual savings. He also designed new development strategies, both in-house and at the factory level, to achieve a better aesthetic coordination among the different divisions of the company. David also held operational roles with the women's apparel retailer Elie Tahari. David earned his MBA from the New York University, Stern School of Business.

**Interviewer:** *How would you describe the Derek Lam customer?*

**D. S.:** Derek Lam offers essentially two brands, Derek Lam and Derek Lam 10 Crosby. The company established these two brands because we wish to serve two different customers. In some categories, we do see some overlap of purchases, but we attempt to merchandise the brands to two separate audiences. Where we see the majority of the overlap is on our ecommerce site.

Derek Lam targets affluent women in the late thirties and forties who shop in upscale metropolitan markets of New York, Chicago, Los Angeles, and Miami. The Derek Lam customer is an educated professional that is seeking insight about her personal style and the fashion world in general.

Derek Lam 10 Crosby is a Derek Lam expansion brand that is targeting the younger market of women between the ages of twenty-five and thirty-five. Crosby tends to be for the Millennial consumer. While somewhat a younger customer, she is a sophisticated, contemporary shopper who is about following fashion trends. She typically buys in specialty stores.

We track the two brands' purchasing behavior from our POS data and customer insight from our ecommerce site.

**Interviewer:** *What are your customers looking for from the Derek Lam brand?*

**D. S.:** From the Derek Lam collection our customers are looking for a design element that is part of the brand. They are looking for strong design and fabric elements. For this customer, the fabric is very important. The Derek Lam shopper is looking for consistency in the brand. Because of the way that we design our product and maintain our retail presence, the Derek Lam consumer knows that the store experience and product will be consistent.

From a supply chain perspective, an emphasis is placed around the selection of fabric. Because the fabric is so key, we tend to design our collections around the fabric. During the design process, we identify the fabric first. If a mill has a long lead time to produce the fabric, we factor this into our design planning. Fabric is key. To ensure consistency with the quality and availability of our fabric we have established strong relationships with our mills. The ability to be able to secure the right fabric within the preferred lead time is more important than the price.

For the 10 Crosby customer, they are looking for what's cool. This customer wants product that reflects the most recent trends. This consumer is less focused on the fabric. They are looking for what's happening now. This customer wants what's in the market now.

From a design perspective, Derek Lam oversees the production of both brands separately.

**Interviewer:** *What are the major customer trends that are impacting your business today?*

**D. S.:** The shift from offline to online is a major focus. We are trying to deal with it from a customer impact perspective. This is a big change. Given how the online market has evolved, we have to be ready for this market. This is also causing us to see a shift from a wholesale to an ecommerce business model. The online customer is not that different from our brick-and-mortar customer. The customer is buying online for convenience.

Because the order fulfillment for online is different, we have made modifications to our operations. Ecommerce is shipped from a separate warehouse because we use a third-party order fulfillment resource. Our third-party partner handles customer service for online and any returns.

Another area of change is in our wholesale business. We see less traffic in the department stores. We are seeing where department stores are carrying inventory in fewer stores. Retailers are tending to focus on their main doors. We expect to see further consolidation in the department store market.

**Interviewer:** *Based on the recent changes with Fashion Week to show in-season designs, what are your thoughts about season-less selling cycles?*

**D. S.:** We are having conversations about this change. There are a lot of discussions about it in the market. While many designers are still doing a spring show in September, they plan to ship still in February. Yes, many retailers are lessening their production time to have product available closer to the time of their show.

At Derek Lam, we are taking more of the European approach. We believe that it really takes time to produce a quality collection because of the fabric lead times and production. Product at the luxury level takes time. The Derek Lam customer believes that high-end fashion takes time and appreciates this. However, for our Crosby consumer, this is a different conversation. For Crosby, we must continue to focus on producing product that meets current trends.

## Questions Pertaining to Interview

1. Because Derek Lam targets two distinct customers, how might this impact the company's sourcing, design, and selling distribution strategies? Are there opportunities for overlap in these markets that might allow for efficiencies in the areas of sourcing, design, and selling distribution?
2. For a luxury brand like Derek Lam, what are the challenges that a growing online market might present? How might the retailer position its brand from an online perspective? Should this positioning be different from its brick-and-mortar presence?
3. In addition to the shift to ecommerce, what other retailing trends are occurring in the women's market that Derek Lam might want to consider? How would these changes impact the company's supply chain?

Trunk Club is an online retailer for premium men's and women's clothing. When the company launched in 2009, it solely targeted the working male professional who lacked the ability or time to coordinate his wardrobe. The company founder, Brian Spaly, also cofounded the successful men's retailer Bonobos. Trunk Club's major selling point is the use of stylists that assist customers with their purchase.

The company is headquartered in Chicago, Illinois. Trunk Club connects customers in person in the following major metropolitan areas: Chicago, Dallas, the District of Columbia, New York, and Los Angeles. The company's physical locations are called clubhouses. Individuals who live outside these cities are able to access a personal stylist by phone or email. In 2014, the company was acquired by Nordstrom Inc. to assist the veteran retailer with a solution for online sales and the growing men's market. Nordstrom was also an investor in the founder's first retail site, Bonobos.

To get started, Trunk Club users would complete an online survey that asks questions about their fashion preferences and lifestyle. Trunk Club offers about one hundred brands that vary by style and price point. Based on the selections provided, a customer's assigned stylist will curate a box of apparel selections to be sent to the customer. Customers are able to try items on in the comfort of their home or at a Trunk Club clubhouse. They keep the items that they like, and they return all selections that fail to meet their approval. The stylist also works with the customer to address questions such as fit, color selections, and garment materials. In addition to offering great customer service, the stylist reduces the company's returns because Trunk Club customers are given insight into items prior to their final selection.

Prior to the acquisition by Nordstrom, Trunk Club maintained a fulfillment center on Goose Island in Chicago, Illinois. In June 2016, the company announced that it would be consolidating its Goose Island fulfillment center into the Nordstrom supply chain facilities located around the country. While the move would result in the elimination of 250 jobs, Trunk Club would have access to an order fulfillment and distribution network that would enhance the company's overall selling strategy. Nordstrom offered to support the transition of the displaced workers. The company's founder commented that the reason for consolidating operations was that the company's spending growth would mean that Trunk Club was quickly outgrowing its current operations. Because Trunk Club already sold some existing Nordstrom brands, the consolidation would further expand Trunk Club's access to the multitude of brands offered by Nordstrom and Nordstrom Rack.

### Case Study Questions

1. Given Trunk Club's business model of having stylists send customers selections and customers having the ability to return items that they don't wish to keep, what does this mean to the company's order fulfillment and reverse logistics processes?
2. So that stylists have a true understanding of the inventory that is available, what real-time information would they need to know about the Trunk Club inventory? What are the risks with such an order fulfillment process? How might these inventory data mitigate such risks?
3. What are the pros and cons of the company's decision to consolidate its fulfillment operations with Nordstrom? How might the Trunk Club customer be impacted?

## CHAPTER REVIEW QUESTIONS

1. What expectations are Millennial and emerging market consumers forcing retailers to address? If you were a retailer, how would you make yourself a preferred retailer for these markets?

2. What are the pros and cons from a supply chain perspective of the new business models identified in this chapter? To capitalize on the pros, what must retailers do, and to mitigate the cons, what must retailers do?

3. What inventory planning risks do you see with each of the identified new business models?

## CLASS EXERCISES

1. Form teams in the class to debate the advantages and the disadvantages of a push versus pull inventory planning strategy. In the discussion, highlight the impact on the consumer.

2. Identify three retailers that could enhance their product offerings by introducing either 3D printing or artificial intelligence into their business model. How would those businesses use these technologies?

## KEY TERMS

Millennial generation
Baby Boomer
Council of Fashion Designers of
    America (CFDA)
accessible luxury
customer-centric
push supply chain strategy

pull supply chain strategy
industry disrupters
flash sale
sharing economy
open-to-buy (OTB) strategy
subscription services
ecommerce

mcommerce
additive manufacturing
polymers
3D printing
artificial intelligence (AI)

## REFERENCES

1. Thau, B. (2015), https://www.vendhq.com/university /retail-trends-and-predictions-2015.
2. Barton, C. (2012), *The Millennial Consumer—Debunking Stereotypes*, Report by Boston Consulting Group. Available online: https://www.bcg.com/documents /file103894.pdf.
3. Ibid.
4. "Top 5 Emerging Apparel Retail Markets Reviewed by MarketLine in Insightful Report Available at MarketPublishers.com" (2013), *Business Wire*, June 11. Available online: http://www.businesswire.com/news /home/20130611006257/en/Top-5-Emerging -Apparel-Retail-Markets-Reviewed.
5. Huang, N. (2015), "China's Apparel Retail Market Sets to Become the World's Biggest," *BusinessVibes*, May 16. Available online: https://www.businessvibes .com/blog/China%E2%80%99s-Apparel-Retail -Market-Sets-Become-World%E2%80%99s-Biggest.
6. S. R. (2015), "Why China's Economy Is Slowing," *The Economist*, March 11. Available online: https://www .economist.com/blogs/economist-explains/2015/03 /economist-explains-8.
7. Wang, H. (2012), "Five New Trends of Chinese Consumers," *Forbes*, December.
8. "China Luxury Apparel and Accessories Market Report, 2012–2015" (2013), November 7. Available online: http://www.prweb.com/releases/2013/11 /prweb11313886.htm.

9. Zakkour, M. (2014), "The China Luxury Downturn Is Real: Global Luxury Brands Must Adjust," *Forbes*.
10. Rauf, H. (2014), "Trends in China's E-commerce Market," *China Briefing*, June.
11. "DHL eCommerce Boosts Its China Footprint with New Investments and Expanded Capabilities" (2016), *PR Newswire*, June.
12. Ibid.
13. ETRetail.com, December 2015. Available online: http://retail.economictimes.indiatimes.com/news /apparel-fashion/apparel/when-global-retailers -knocked-at-indias-fashion-doors-2015-in-retrospect /50378358.
14. Chakrapani, A. (2015), "Consumer Behavior and Preferences of Indian Consumers towards Apparel Purchases in Retail Markets of India," *Innovative Journal of Business Management*, August.
15. "India's Supply Chain Is Improving, But Still Has a Long Way to Go" (2013), *SupplyChainBrain*, February.
16. Ibid.
17. Theilman, S. (2015), "Warm Weather Melting Millions Off Winter Gear Retailers' Bottom Lines," *Retail Industry*, December.
18. Bell, T. (2015), "L.L. Bean and Other Retailers See Sales of Winter Apparel Melt with Warm Weather," *Portland Press Herald*, December.
19. Howard, C. (2013), "Disruptions vs. Innovation: What's the Difference?," *Forbes*.
20. "The Rise of the Sharing Economy" (2013), *The Economist*, March.
21. Galbraith, S. (2013), "The Secret behind Rent the Runway's Success," *Forbes*, December.
22. Ma, Z. (2015), "Rent the Runway: Fashionable Operations," Harvard Business School Open Knowledge, December. Available online: https://rctom.hbs.org /submission/rent-the-runway-fashionable-operations/
23. Greenfield, R. (2014), "Inside Rent the Runway's Dry Cleaning Secret Empire," *Fast Company*, October.
24. Ibid.
25. Salfino, C. (2013), "Apparel Industry Hears Crowd-sourcing's Roar," *Sourcing Journal*, August.
26. Olenski, S. (2016), "3 Global Brands Show How Crowdsourcing Is Done," *Forbes*, March.
27. Watson, K. (2015), "3 Ways Crowdsourcing Is Revolutionizing Supply Chain Management," 21st Century Supply Chain Blog, September.
28. Binkley, C. (2013), "Life & Style—On Style: A Gift to Yourself Every Month—Subscription Services Deliver Boxes of Fashionable, High-End Goodies to Your Doorstep," *The Wall Street Journal Asia*, December 24.
29. Hull, D. (2014), "Q&A: Stitch Fix Founder Katrina Lake, on Melding Fashion and Technology," *The Mercury News*, March 14.
30. "The Thrift Stores in the US: Market Research Report" (2016), IBIS World, February.
31. "Difference between M Commerce and E Commerce," DifferenceBetween.com. Available online: http://www.differencebetween.com/difference -between-m-commerce-and-e-commerce/.
32. Fiergerman, S. (2014), "U.S. Mobile Commerce Hits $114 Billion This Year," *Mashable*, May 12.
33. "Saks Launches Ecommerce Activewear Shop to Round Out Apparel Offerings (2014), *Luxury Daily*, August 12.
34. Jones, S. (2014), "Versace Embeds Instant Ecommerce in Runway Show Livestream," *Luxury Daily*, September 12.
35. Kurutz, S. (2013), "Taking Fashion to a New Dimension," *New York Times*, December 13.
36. Siegel, R. (2016), "Artificial Intelligence and Fashion: A Platform Play," *Loose Threads*, April 10.
37. Arthur, R. (2016), "Future of Retail: Artificial Intelligence and Virtual Reality Have Big Roles to Play," *Forbes*, June 15.

# glossary

**2/10, N30** Term meaning that there will be a 2 percent discount applied to invoices paid within ten days or the invoice total is due within thirty days.

**3D printing** The layering of materials to create a design form.

**5Ss** Five components of lean manufacturing: sort, set in order, shine, standardize, and sustain.

**accessible luxury** Term referring to a more price-accessible entry-to-luxury market.

**accessories** Fashion items such as jewelry and purses that contribute to the overall look of the wearer.

**accounts payable (AP)** Money that a manufacturer owes.

**accounts receivable (AR)** Money that is owed to a manufacturer for work that it has performed.

**accounts receivable and inventory financing (ARIF)** A form of asset-based lending; borrowers use the value of their receivables or inventory as collateral to finance their working capital needs.

**acetate and triacetate fibers** A type of fiber known as a regenerated man-made material. Acetate is developed from cellulose. Commonly seen in linings and even women's lingerie.

**acrylic and modacrylic fibers** Fibers with an uneven surface that are formed by additional polymerization of at least 85 percent by weight of acrylonitrile or vinyl chanide. Used primarily in the manufacturing of sweaters and scarves.

**activity-based costing** An accounting practice that increases the visibility of hidden costs on a per-item basis.

**additive manufacturing** The process of building product by layering deposited materials.

**African Growth and Opportunity Act (AGOA)** A 2000 act aimed at improving the economies of sub-Saharan Africa and improving economic relations between the United States and the region.

**Agreement on Textiles and Clothing (ATC)** A 1995 agreement that mandated a ten-year phaseout of quota protection.

**alpaca** Similar to sheep wool, alpaca fiber is prized for winter wear and has been described as lighter in weight and softer and warmer than sheep's wool.

**American Apparel and Footwear Association (AAFA)** A trade association that focuses on public policy and legislative concerns that relate to the apparel and footwear industry.

**angora** Angora fiber is obtained from the angora rabbit and the angora goat. The hair of the angora rabbit is long and soft. Angora wool is frequently produced from the angora goat, and this wool is often blended with rabbit.

**aramid and polyimide fibers** Fibers that are created via a wet or dry processing technique and spun from the polymer. Protective gear is the end product.

**arbitrage** When a company is able to capitalize on a market imbalance and create profitable returns in its favor.

**artificial intelligence (AI)** The science of computers that are able to learn.

**asset-based lending (ABL)** A formulaic means of financing in which a lender extends credit on the basis of a borrowing formula that is a negotiated discount rate against the actual receivables of the business.

**assets** The items that a company owns, such as cash, accounts receivable, inventory, equipment, and buildings.

**attribute data** Information that is presented once a particular condition occurs, for example, the number of dresses that shrink when they are washed.

**B2C** Includes businesses that sell goods or services directly to the consumer market.

**Baby Boomers** The demographic cohort of individuals with birth years that fall approximately between 1940 and 1964. Noted for the number of individuals that fall within this grouping and their tendencies with regards to buying preferences and behaviors.

**backhauling** When a load of goods is transported on the return trip of a truck or ship.

**balance sheet** An accounting or a snapshot of a company's assets, liability, and equity for a period of time.

**balanced scorecard** A strategic performance management tool that creates a way to monitor how an internal department or vendor's performance is operating relative to a retailer's operational and even company-wide goals and objectives. Scorecards utilize visualization to document progress and identify categories of focus.

**bamboo** Fiber obtained from the bamboo plant; it possesses several qualities such as smoothness and durability. Must undergo a very caustic chemical reaction similar to rayon unless it is retted like flax, which is transformed into a yarn through a mechanical process. Bamboo is largely used in the production of ready-made apparel and home textiles.

**big box retailers** Stores whose physical space is generally more than 50,000 square feet, usually plainly designed; often look like a big box.

**big data** A collection of data from traditional systems such as inventory management and point of sales (POS) systems with digital insight like web purchasing data and online searches; enables retailers to maintain a more complete perspective on their inventory.

**bill of lading** A document issued by a carrier that confirms receipt of cargo for shipment.

**Black Belt (BB)** The most senior, actively engaged, Six Sigma professional.

**blue chip** Refers to companies that have an established reputation.

**board of directors** A body of elected or appointed members who jointly oversee the activities of a company or organization.

**boutiques** Similar to mom & pops; small format stores, sometimes single ownership, with limited product assortment.

**business development department** Department that is charged with developing new business opportunities.

**California Cloth Foundry** A company that has taken a unique approach that borrows from the farm-to-table theme by touting itself as "grown to sewn in the U.S.A.," a completely sustainable American supply chain.

**camel hair** Camel fiber has been traditionally used for the production of winter apparel, most often seen in the development of coats.

**cash conversion cycle (C2C)** A metric that measures a company's efficiency on the basis of how the company manages its working capital, primarily the conversion of inventory and the management of payables and receivables.

**cash-in-advance** Payment made by the buyer upfront before the goods are received from the seller.

**cashmere** Cashmere fiber is obtained from the hair of the cashmere goat, found in Kashmir and Himachal Pradesh in India, Pakistan, Nepal, Iran, Mongolia, and China. At the present time, China is the largest producer of cashmere fiber. It is soft, lightweight, fine, and warm, and the best fibers are harvested from the underbelly of the cashmere goat; considered a luxury fabric.

**Central American Free Trade Agreement (CAFTA)** An expansion of the NAFTA to include five Central American nations (Guatemala, El Salvador, Honduras, Costa Rica, and Nicaragua) and the Dominican Republic; passed by Congress in 2005.

**CEO/president** The person who works with the board of directors to set the goals for the company and, in conjunction with the finance department, creates the budget.

**chain stores** Retail outlets that share a brand and central management and that usually have standardized business methods and practices covering multiple locations.

**China Plus One Strategy** The selection of another area of production in Asia in addition to maintaining production in China.

**click and collect** A purchasing option by which consumers purchase online and retrieve the item from their local store.

**collateral** A secondary means of repayment that a lender can obtain in the event of a default on a loan.

**common locker delivery systems** When consumers pick their ecommerce order from a locker area rather than have them delivered to their door.

**computer-aided design (CAD)** The use of computer systems to aid in the creation and modifications of designs.

**consignment shop** A store that sells secondhand items (typically clothing and accessories) on behalf of the original owner, who receives a percentage of the selling price.

**continuous data** Information that measures the magnitude of something, such as the length of a hemline.

**contract logistics** or **3PL (third-party logistics)** Generally three- to five-year contract relationships with a logistics provider or third party that handles logistics services such as warehousing, packaging, labeling, transportation, quality controls, and compliance inspections.

**corporate social responsibility (CSR)** Refers to companies taking responsibility for their impact on society; specifically, by improving the quality of life for workers and their families in the communities in which they reside as well as society at large.

**cost insurance freight (CIF)** Term used when the seller clears the goods for export and delivers them on board, bearing the cost of freight and insurance to the port of entry named by the buyer.

**cost of goods sold (COGS)** Costs that are used to make a garment, such as the material and labor costs.

**cotton** A fiber that is obtained from the cotton plant. It is the preferred fiber because it is durable. Cotton absorbs moisture, is smooth to the touch, and drapes well.

**Cotton Incorporated** Organization whose mission is to increase the demand for and profitability of cotton through research and promotion while ensuring that cotton remains the first choice among consumers in apparel and home products. The organization is funded by cotton growers in the United States through per-bale assessments on producers and importers levied by the Cotton Board, which reports to the United States Department of Agriculture.

**Council of Fashion Designers of America (CFDA)** The producers of the New York Fashion Week.

**country of origin** The country of manufacture, production, or growth where an article or product comes from.

**courier express parcel (CEP)** The delivery of small parcels.

**customer relationship management (CRM)** Systems that enable the tracking of information at the customer level.

**customer-centric** Refers to an approach to business that centers on customer experience and that is built around agility, speed, and innovation.

**Customs Trade Partnership against Terrorism** A voluntary supply chain security initiative led by US Customs and Border Protection (CBP).

**Cut, Make, and Trim (CMT)** The apparel-manufacturing stage that involves cutting fabric, sewing garments, and putting on finishing touches.

**dashboard** A user-friendly, visual representation of KPIs that informs management at a glance about the performance of a process or function.

**demand-chain productivity** The use of real-time data to ensure a manageable surge in productivity.

**demand-chain transparency** A global system for mediating trust by providing detailed information surrounding the production of apparel and accessory products.

**department stores** Large retail establishments with an extensive variety and range of goods, organized into separate departments.

**design department** The fashion department that applies the art of design and aesthetics or natural beauty to clothing and accessories.

**design process** Conceiving an idea for some artifact or system and/or to expressing the idea in a form.

**digital supply chain** A means to capture sourcing and logistics data remotely while storing this information in a cloud for access by multiple parties.

**discount stores** Retail stores that sell products at prices lower than those asked by traditional retail outlets.

**discrete data** Data that can only take certain values, such as information that is counted in whole numbers.

**documentary collection** A way to facilitate trade financing that offers importers and exporters a way to receive the documentary information of goods. The bank will extend funds to the exporter from the importer on the basis that the documentation provided will enable the importer to access the goods at the negotiated time and condition. In the event of a default, there is no collateral to offset outstanding payments.

**drayage** The costs that one must pay to get the freight out of the port in addition to any other transportation costs to the warehouse or directly to the stores or consumers.

**ecommerce** The buying and selling of goods and services over an electronic network, primarily the internet.

**Educators for Socially Responsible Apparel Practices** A collaborative learning community whose mission is to change curriculum on a global scale to better reflect the current state of Corporate Social Responsibility (CSR) and sustainability in the fashion industry, and to empower students to become change agents.

**elastoester** *See* spandex or elastoester.

**elastomeric fibers** Fibers that are created by cross-linking natural and synthetic rubbers. The resulting fibers are spandex fibers and anidex fibers. These fibers can stretch and recover fully and rapidly.

**electronic data interchange (EDI)** The electronic transfer of information applying a standardized format.

**electronic product code (EPC)** The leading standard for RFID supply chain applications.

**export-processing zones (EPZ)** Designated economic zones that support export production.

**fabric construction** Process that goes from fiber to yarn to fabric. Generally speaking, there are three ways to make a fabric: knit a fabric, weave a fabric, and form a fabric, also called a nonwoven fabric.

**factoring** When a company sells its uncollected receivables to a factor, a third-party commercial finance company, in exchange for an upfront payment of cash that is a percentage of the overall receivable.

**factory outlets** Stores used to sell overruns, excess inventory, and product specifically made to supplement the other products in the store.

**Fair Labor Association** An organization whose main mission is to improve the lives of workers by addressing "abusive labor practices."

**fast fashion** A retailing business model based on the rapid production of trendy designs.

**finance and accounting department** Department that works in conjunction with the CEO/president to develop the top-down budget; it then communicates with each individual department the amount of money it will be allocated to achieve the overall company goals and projections.

**flash sale** A discount or a promotion sale offered for a short window of time by an ecommerce retailer, or a private sale.

**free on board (FOB)** "FOB origin" means that the seller pays for transportation of the goods to the port as well as the loading of the goods. "FOB destination" means that the seller assumes freight costs to the final destination.

**Free Trade Area of the Americas (FTAA)** An agreement that would extend the NAFTA to every country in North America, Central America, South America, and the Caribbean, with the exception of Cuba; is currently being negotiated.

**freight forwarder** A company that arranges for the movement of goods via air or ship.

**freight pooling** The distribution of orders to numerous destinations within a geographic area.

**fulfillment centers** Locations where incoming orders are processed for delivery.

**full packages** Means that the seller (factory) provides all services to bring the product to market, which would include cost of fabric, trims, production, and packaging.

**functional organizational charts** Charts that have at the top the executive, with middle managers below all reporting to the top executive.

**Global Organic Textile Standard (GOTS)** The worldwide leading textile processing standard for organic fibers.

**global positioning system (GPS)** System that provides individuals with location information for directional and tracking purposes.

**grading** The creation of a series of patterns for multiple sizes based on the initial design.

**Green Belt (GB)** Person who handles somewhat less complex Six Sigma work that tends to focus less on the statistical analysis aspects of a project.

**greige goods** Unfinished textiles that are knit or woven in their raw state with no color or finishing added.

**hangtag system** The use of item hangtags to maintain an inventory count.

**Higg Index** A measurement tool developed to measure sustainability performance.

**human resource department (HR)** Department that makes sure that the right people are in the right positions at the right time and for the right cost.

**corporate social responsibility (CSR)** Companies improving the quality of life for those who do not have a voice by improving the lives of workers, their families, and the community in which they reside.

**income statement** Keeps track of a company's revenues and expenses.

**individual package market** When deliveries are made directly to an individual consumer.

**industrial revolution** In America, a period of major industrialization that took place during the late 1700s and early 1800s. This time period saw the mechanization of agriculture and textile manufacturing and a revolution in power, including steamships and railroads, that affected social, cultural, and economic conditions.

**industry disrupter** A business model that displaces existing markets, industry, or technology and replaces them with something that is new and more efficient than was previously possible.

**informal organization** Everyday social interactions among employees that transcend formal jobs and job interrelationships.

**Institute of International Trade** Established in 1935, the professional membership body representing and supporting the interests of everyone involved in importing and exporting and international trade. Offering a unique range of individual and business membership benefits and a world renowned suite of qualifications and training, the Institute is the leading authority in best practice and competence for businesses trading globally.

**intermodal goods transport** The movement of goods without the need to change packaging or documents between modes.

**International Maritime Organization's SOLAS (Safety of Life at Sea)** A treaty that focuses on the safety of merchant ships; requires the verification of gross mass containers before loading.

**International Monetary Fund (IMF)** An international financing organization.

**International Organization for Standardization (ISO)** An independent, not-government-affiliated organization with a membership of 163 national standards bodies. The purpose is to promote standards of process innovation through training and leadership guidance.

**intrapreneuring** "Creating and maintaining the innovation flexibility of a small-business environment within the confines of a large, bureaucratic structure."

**investor relations department** Department that "integrates finance, communication, marketing and securities law compliance to enable the most effective two-way communication between a company, the financial community, and other constituencies"; only pertains to those fashion companies that are publicly traded.

**inward transport or traffic** The central area of business logistics that manages the movement of goods from suppliers to a company's receiving area, whether a distribution center or a direct-to-consumer location.

**ISO 9001** An international standard that documents the requirements for quality management systems. The only standard that certifies quality management systems.

**isolationism** An economic policy that makes a country self-reliant rather than a participant in a global trading market.

**jute** A material that has been used in the textile industry for ages, obtained from the jute plant. Jute has high tensile strength and can be used in packing materials, and in recent years it has become common in home furnishings such as rugs.

**kaizen** A Japanese business philosophy that focuses on process improvement and has the potential to impact an entire organization; a key component of lean manufacturing.

**keiretsu** Large, modern industrial groupings in Japan.

**key performance indicators (KPIs)** Quantitative information that is used to monitor and track progress.

**kiosk** A small structure in a public area used for providing products and services to the consuming public.

**labor management system (LMS)** First introduced in the grocery and food services industries, a system that is used to track and manage the labor aspects of logistics management. LMSs enable companies to break down work tasks, assign employees, and track expected completion time by benchmarking performance from historical task completion data.

**lag indicators** Outcomes of the business, such as the number of items produced, total revenue, and costs.

**land duty paid (LDP)** Term meaning that the seller is assuming the cost of the goods plus freight and the tariff.

**landfills** Disposal locations where waste is buried.

**lead indicators** Inputs that typically impact an outcome, such as the number of revised shipping routes to increase on-time shipping deliveries.

**lean** An approach to the manufacturing process that minimizes waste while endeavoring to create consumer value.

**lean manufacturing** Often associated with the automotive industry, a method of process improvement that focuses on removing waste.

**less-than-truckload (LTL)** A delivery service market that involves small packages that weigh 150 pounds or less.

**letter of credit** A trade document between an accepting bank and issuing bank that facilitates the transfer of goods. At the request of the importer, the issuing bank agrees to pay the exporter for goods on the basis that they meet the terms and conditions of the purchasing agreement.

**liabilities** Items that a company owes money for. Short-term liabilities are payables, which often include payments owed to vendors for raw materials and/or labor. Long-term liabilities are items such as mortgages for buildings or long-term leases for production facilities.

**linen** One of the oldest fabrics known to modern man. The properties of linen are similar to cotton fabric. Linen is a staple in many wardrobes around the globe, especially in arid climates.

**llamas** Llamas produce a soft fiber used in the production of apparel, and courser hairs/fibers are used in the production of rugs and wall hangings.

**location data** Data that provide insight about per-factory production, inventory by location, and movement of goods during the transportation phases of production.

**logistics management** The use of technology, data analysis, project planning, and general management skills to enable the efficient movement of inventory and information from the raw material production phase, to the distribution, to the end consumer.

**logistics** The coordination of the movement of inventory and information throughout the supply chain network.

**lyocell** *See* rayon/lyocell.

**mail order/catalog** Retail formats that use the mail system to buy and ship products.

**margin** A percentage of sales that is derived by subtracting the costs of manufacturing a good from the sales price.

**Master Black Belt (MBB)** The most senior person with a recognized area of expertise.

**material handling department** Department that oversees the movement of goods within an organization.

**mcommerce** Mobile commerce: the purchasing of items by means of a smartphone or tablet.

**Millennial generation** Individuals born roughly between 1982 and 2000.

**modacrylic fiber** *See* acrylic and modacrylic fibers.

**mohair** The hair from the angora goat is called mohair fiber. It is described as possessing warmth and being lightweight, crease resistant, durable, and soft. Because of these qualities it is used in the production of winter apparel, but also in the production of blankets, rugs, and scarves.

**mom & pops** Small retail format stores, generally a single owner with a small assortment of product.

**muda** The Japanese word for wastefulness.

**Multi Fibre Arrangement (MFA)** A 1974 agreement by the United States and EU countries to limit the amount of goods able to be imported from developing countries.

**multichannel retailing** Retailing in which the consumer must opt into a specific channel.

**multimodal transport** When a product uses two or more transport modes.**natural fibers** Hairlike raw materials that are obtained directly from plants, animals, vegetables, and minerals; they are short fibers that are twisted together, with the exception of silk, which is the only natural fiber to come in a filament form. There is a tendency for natural fibers to break during production.

**near-shoring** The movement of production closer to the consumer; allows for sourcing to take place closer to the point of manufacture, which enables a company to cut its lead times.

**net 30 or 60 days** The typical terms for trade credit.

**Nike** A publicly traded sports apparel and equipment company.

**North American Free Trade Agreement (NAFTA)** Agreement made in 1992 to eliminate barriers to trade and to support the cross-border movement of goods among the United States, Canada, and Mexico.

**North American Industry Classification System** A system that classifies every industry and business sector in North America according to a six-digit code.

**nylon** A material that is made of polyamide. It is resistant to wrinkling, does not absorb water, and dries quickly. Nylon has many uses in the fashion industry in both apparel and accessories, not to mention home furnishings.

**OEKO-TEX® Standard 100** A standard that tests for controlled substances and chemicals known to be harmful in textiles, raw materials, and end products.

**off-price retailers** Stores that deliver great value on ever-changing selections of brand name and designer fashions at prices generally 20 to 60 percent below department and specialty store regular retail prices on comparable merchandise.

**offshore manufacturers** Factories that exist in countries or locations outside the company's home country.

**OIA Sustainability Working Group** An organization that assists companies in achieving environmental and socially best practices.

**omnichannel retailing** The integration of multiple selling platforms to enable consumers to engage wherever they choose.

**open account** When goods are shipped and delivered before the payment is received by the exporter.

**open-to-buy (OTB) strategy** A merchandising process that is the budgeted amount of merchandise allocated for a particular store or category of good.

**order picking** The selection of items to be shipped for customer delivery.

**organizational chart** A formal chart that illustrates the key players in an organization.

**Original Brand Manufacturing (OBM)** Factories that produce and sell their own lines of garments.

**Original Design Manufacturing (ODM)** Apparel-manufacturing stage that encompasses the CMT and OEM stages of garment manufacturing while also assuming the responsibilities of garment design.

**Original Equipment Manufacturing (OEM)** Stage of the apparel-manufacturing value chain that typically focuses production activities on creating a finished good.

**outsourcing** The use of a vendor to fulfill an aspect or all of a company's production process or service offering.

**Partner Africa** A leading nonprofit social enterprise driven by a mission to improve the livelihoods of workers and producers and to enhance access to global markets.

**PDAs** Devices that combine the functionality of a computer, a telephone, the internet, and networking.

**pick-and-pack** A fulfillment process in which the individual components of an order are gathered to complete the order.

**polyester** An important synthetic fiber. The manufacturing process uses melt-spinning so the size and shape can be adjusted for specific applications. Polyester has multiple uses in the fashion industry, from dresses to shirts and blouses. Its application, however, extends far beyond the fashion industry, and it has many industrial uses.

**polyimide fiber** *See* aramid and polyimide fibers.

**polymers** Strong, flexible, and durable plastic materials that are used in additive manufacturing.

**polypropylene** This is a vinyl polymer, similar to polyethylene. The structure has a methyl group attached to every other carbon in the backbone chain. It is excellent for base layers while hiking and camping in cold weather.

**polyvinyl chloride (PVC)** This leather look-alike is used to simulate leather products in the fashion industry.

**port** A town or city where vessels can load for the purpose of exporting goods and can unload goods for the purpose of importing goods.

**procurement and purchasing** The department that is traditionally considered the beginning of the logistics supply chain. It is often an internal department that oversees the procuring of resources such as raw materials, office supplies, goods for store operations, and even travel. This department primarily identifies suppliers, negotiates contracts, establishes payment and delivery, and maintains a vetted supplier list of purchased items, typically by means of purchase orders.

**product developers** Individuals who oversee the decisions for the day-to-day operations while interacting with the design team to ensure that the integrity of the design vision is maintained.

**product organizational chart** Chart that represents a structure in which there may be a number of top executives, each responsible for his or her own product.

**production** The process by which concepts are made into salable physical products.

**public relations (PR) department** Department that helps shape public opinion of a company by providing positive news stories on the company's CSR practices as well as general news that consumers are interested in. If and when there is a negative story surrounding the company, the PR department will respond to the situation to maintain the company's profile.

**pull supply chain strategy** A strategy that is based on actual consumer demand.

**purchase order financing** When the borrower rather than the factor is the entity that the purchase order is paid to upon collection.

**push supply chain strategy** A strategy that uses projected volumes to manufacture goods.

**push vs. pull inventory control** Push uses forecast to predict demand, while pull uses actual order to determine what should be produced

**PVH Corp** A global apparel company that is well known in the industry for its social and environmental emphasis as well as its philanthropic efforts.

**qualitative data** Information that can be observed but not measured, such as the color of dresses, the feel of the material, and the appearance of the sample.

**quality** A set of product features that are used to create expectations for a specific product and are measured against a set of predetermined standards.

**quality assurance** The various activities that are undertaken by a company to ensure that the overall quality of the finished product meets established criteria.

**quality management system (QMS)** A collection of business processes focused on consistently meeting customer requirements and enhancing their satisfaction.

**quotas** Restrictions on the quantity of textiles and apparel being imported into the country for certain categories, such as men, women, and children.

**radio-frequency identification (RFID)** The use of electromagnetic fields to track items.

**ramie** Ramie fiber is obtained from the ramie plant. It is costly to produce but is useful in the production of sewing thread, filter clothes, fishing nets, and packaging material.

**raw materials** In apparel manufacturing, the materials from which cloth is made.

**rayon/lyocell** This includes textile fibers and filaments composed of regenerated cellulose, excluding acetate. It is produced from naturally occurring polymers. The fiber is sold as artificial silk, and it has a serrated round shape with a smooth surface. It is a hybrid because it starts out as a natural product but then undergoes a harsh chemical process to create a usable yarn.

**ready-to-wear** Factory-made versus custom-made clothing.

**receivable financing** When a designer obtains funds in advance by factoring its receivables.

**receiving department** The department that confirms that the items delivered from a purchase order match the quantity, price, and expected delivery date; inspects the order for damages and acknowledges receipt of the items.

**recourse financing** Protection for lenders in the event of a default.

**recycling and waste disposal department** Department that deals with items that might be damaged and the equipment used in the inward delivery that must be returned to the supplier, such as pallets, delivery cartons, cable reels, and merchandise containers.

**regional organizational chart** Chart that depicts a larger national or global organization that is represented by regional executives.

**re-shoring** Bringing production back from a foreign country to the home country.

**retail shrinkage** The portion of the inventory that is either lost or stolen during the production or distribution phases.

**retailer** A business that sells goods to the public in relatively small quantities for use or consumption rather than for resale.

**reverse supply chain** All the returns that retailers take in from unsatisfied consumers.

**sales and marketing department** The department that promotes and establishes a business in its market based on products and services the business is offering.

**sales channel** A means to reach consumers.

**Schengen Agreement** A treaty signed by five of the ten members of the European Economic Community that allowed the free movement of people across mainland European countries.

**shareholders** Those individuals and corporate investors who have taken a stock position in a company; they own stock that has been purchased through a brokerage house.

**sharing economy** Collaborative consumption that is typically facilitated by online social platforms that enable a lower per use cost than individual consumption.

**silk** The only natural fiber that comes in a filament form. The discovery of silk in China dates back centuries. Silk is produced by caterpillars often called silk worms. Silk fiber has a unique sheen. It is very smooth to the touch while exhibiting strong tensile strength.

**Six Sigma** A disciplined, data-driven approach and methodology for eliminating defects (driving toward six standard deviations between the mean and the nearest specification limit) in any process, from manufacturing to transactional and from product to service.

**Social Accountability International** An organization whose main mission is to ensure human rights in the work environment. To accomplish this mission, it develops structures and processes in the work environment to protect workers.

**sourcing and production department** Department that is composed of logistics, quality assurance, CSR/sustainability, and legal/security; responsible for developing and executing a plan to procure product.

**sourcing** The act of finding and developing a supplier base that has the capacity to provide the goods and services required to serve the intended target market.

**soybean** Fiber from soybean is lustrous and strong and dyes easily. Moreover, it is soft to the touch and lightweight. It is ideal for use in summer wear, underwear, sleepwear, sportswear, children's wear, and home textiles. As with any new fiber, the cost of production is high because the demand is low.

**spandex or elastoester** A manufactured material that is both lightweight and can be stretched over 500 percent without breaking.

**specialty stores** Retail stores that offer specific and specialized types of items.

**spider silk** Silk produced from spiders. Since this is relatively new, the production costs are quite high, so there is limited production and use in the fashion industry.

**staging goods** Separating production of a garment into various stages of production.

**standard shipping containers** Steel shipping containers with standardized dimensions.

**Stella McCartney** An English fashion designer who values CSR and sustainability. Born September 13, 1971, she is the daughter of former Beatles member Paul McCartney and American musician, photographer, and animal rights activist Linda McCartney.

**stock control department** Department that works with a retailer's planning division to set the policies for inventory; works to obtain a balance between stock on hand and consumer demand.

**stock keeping unit (SKU)** An identification code for the size of an item, dimensions, case pack, automatic ID labels, inventory warehouse location, and manufacture date.

**stockouts** Situations in which inventory is unavailable for sale.

**strategic line planning** A systematic approach involving all aspects of a fashion company to develop a line of apparel or accessories for an intended target market.

The approach is based on research of past, current, and future trends.

**subscription services** When customers receive a monthly delivery of items selected by the retailer and are charged based on the service offered; example is magazine business.

**supplier base** Those key companies (factories, mills, trim suppliers) that would be considered integral parts of the overall supply chain and that play a key role in the organization's ability to deliver the goods when the buyer needs them.

**supply chain financing (SCF)** Short-term financing of buyer and seller working capital needs for supply chain management.

**sustainability** Meeting the needs of the present without compromising the future.

**Sustainable Apparel Coalition** A coalition that focuses specifically on footwear and textiles and works to prevent environmental harm and to create positive outcomes for people and their communities.

**sustainable development** *See* sustainability.

***Sustainable Fashion*** A groundbreaking book by Janet Hethorn and Connie Ulasewicz that sets out to help the reader understand what is currently going on in the fashion industry as it relates to sustainability.

**synthetic fibers** Chemically produced fibers that are made by joining monomers into polymers through a process called polymerization. They are made in a filament form—a long continuous strand—so that they run better on the equipment.

**tariffs** Also known as duty, the costs that a country charges to import a good.

**television shopping** A retail format in which consumers view the product on television and order from their remote, their mobile device, or the phone, and the products are shipped directly to the home.

**thrift store** A store selling secondhand clothes and other household goods, typically to raise funds for a charitable institution.

**TOMS** A shoe company that focuses on both the environment and corporate philanthropy.

**total quality management (TQM)** A process improvement strategy that works to instill a continuous philosophy of improvement throughout the entire organization.

**Trade and Investment Framework Agreement (TIFA)** Agreement established in 2012 by the United States and South Africa to analyze the future outlook on trade and investment.

**trade credit** When a supplier allows a company to purchase supplies with the promise of paying for the supplies at a later date.

**Trans-Pacific Partnership (TPP)** A trade agreement initially between Pacific Rim countries and the United States, Canada, Mexico, Chile, and Peru to strengthen trade among these countries by eliminating tariffs on textiles and garments; goal is to increase trade; in 2017 the United States exited the TPP.

**transportation management system (TMS)** Software that facilitates interactions between an organization's order management system and its warehouse management system or distribution center.

**trend** A general direction in which something is developing or changing.

**trend forecasting** The ability to predict trends using data that relate to colors, fabrics, textures, materials, prints, graphics, beauty/grooming, accessories, footwear, street style, and other styles that will be presented on the runways and in the stores for future seasons.

**triacetate fiber** *See* acetate and triacetate fibers.

**uniform product code (UPC)** A standard means to recognize the product manufacturer, product category, and selling country.

**United States Agency for International Development (USAID)** A US government agency responsible for delivering humanitarian aid.

**universal product code (UPC)** *See* uniform product code.

**vending machine** A machine that dispenses small articles such as candy bars and drinks when a coin, bill, or token is inserted. Vending machines have seen growth in recent years to include apparel, accessories, flowers, and even frozen yogurt and French fries.

**vendor compliance** Describes documents that spell out a company's requirements, expectations, and penalties.

**vendor inventory management (VIM)** When suppliers hold the inventory and distribute goods directly to retail outlets instead of the retailers assuming the capital costs and overhead associated with the management of large, regional distribution centers.

**vertically integrated** A business model in which the supply chain of a company is composed of its internal production departments instead of external vendors.

**Warby Parker** A company whose goal is to offer designer eyewear at an affordable price.

**warehouse clubs** Large-format retailers that carry a wide variety of merchandise, including apparel and accessories. They are no frills and require a yearly fee for entry.

**warehouse management system** A software application that supports the daily operations of a warehouse.

**warehouse management system** A system that supports the oversight of daily functions such as planning delivery schedules and allocating resources to move and store inventory within a warehouse.

**waste** Any non-value-added activity that a customer doesn't see enough reason to pay for.

**wearable** An accessory or apparel item capable of monitoring health and wellness information, offering technology support, and exhibiting smart technology functionality.

**weighted average cost of capital (WACC)** Measures the use of capital as either a debt or equity instrument.

**wholesale department** Department in a fashion company that would have a responsibility to sell its product to various outlets.

**wool** A fiber that has traditionally been used in the textile industry, obtained primarily from sheep. Wool fabric is soft, provides warmth, and is easily dyed, making it a consumer choice for winter apparel.

**working capital** Located on the cashflow statement, the cash available within a company for daily operating expenses.

**World Trade Organization (WTO)** An intergovernmental organization that regulates international trade.

**World Wide Web (WWW)** An information space where documents can be accessed by the internet.

**Worldwide Responsible Accredited Production** An organization whose mission is to ensure that workers are safe and treated in an ethical way.

**yak** The yak, found in the Himalayas in India and Tibet, supplies hair that offers warmth for colder weather.

**Yellow Belt (YB)** A strategic oversight role. These individuals are trained in the Six Sigma functions much like BBs and GBs; however, their role is more of a project champion or stakeholder.

**zone skipping** A shipping consolidation method in which packages are held and aggregated until the quantity reaches a full truckload.

# credits

Chapter opening icons by Yelena Safronova/Fairchild Books

## Chapter 1
1.1  Keith Bell/Shutterstock.com
1.2  Keystone-France/Gamma-Keystone via Getty Images
1.3  Istock.com/Sami Sert
1.4  iStock.com/jamesjames2541
1.5  Rex Rystedt/The LIFE Images Collection/Getty Images
1.6  Anton Marrast/Shutterstock.com
1.7  DOCTOR BLACK/Shutterstock.com

## Chapter 2
2.1  Lipnitzki/Roger Viollet/Getty Images
2.2–2.6  Fairchild Books

## Chapter 3
3.1  ROBERT MILLER/AFP/Getty Images
3.2  Rachel Murray/Getty Images for Amazon
3.3  360b/Shutterstock.com
3.4  Ken Wolter/Shutterstock.com
3.5  Featureflash Photo Agency/Shutterstock.com
3.6  California Cloth Foundry
3.7  iStock.com/KreangchaiRungfamai
3.8  Monkey Business Images/Shutterstock.com

## Chapter 4
4.1  Jan Hyrman/Shutterstock.com
4.2  Fairchild Books
4.3A  Yelena Safronova/Fairchild Books
4.3B  Yelena Safronova/Fairchild Books
4.4  Yelena Safronova/Fairchild Books
4.5  iStock.com/PeopleImages
4.6  iStock.com/diego_cervo
4.7  VasutinSergey/Shutterstock.com
4.8  iStock.com/ipopba

## Chapter 5
5.1  Everett Historical/Shuttestock.com
5.2  iStock.com/Willrow_Hood
5.3  iStock.com/FatCamera
5.4  iStock.com/andrearenata
5.5  Matusciac Alexandru/Shutterstock.com
5.6  iStock.com/visoook
5.7  Developed by Michael P. Londrigan/Fairchild Books
5.8  iStock.com/enviromantic
5.9  Developed by Michael P. Londrigan/Fairchild Books
5.10  iStock.com/trinetuzun
5.11  iStock.com/Rostislav_Sedlacek

## Chapter 6
6.1  iStock.com/pandemin
6.2  iStock.com/LewisTsePuiLung
6.3  iStock.com/Farid_Ahmed
6.4  iStock.com/3dmentat
6.5  iStock.com/tupungato
6.6  iStock.com/Oktay Ortakcioglu
6.7A  mimagephotography/Shutterstock.com
6.7B  Iakov Filimonov/Shutterstock.com
6.8  iStock.com/fototrav
6.9  egd/Shutterstock.com

## Chapter 7
7.1  iStock.com/matremors
7.2  iStock.com/pixdeluxe
7.3  Abd. Halim Hadi/Shutterstock.com
7.4  iStock.com/gerenme

## Chapter 8
8.1  iStock.com/adventtr
8.2  iStock.com/urf
8.3  Fairchild Books
8.4  Fairchild Books
8.5  lev radin/Shutterstock.com
8.6  Fairchild Books

## Chapter 9
9.1  dizain/Shutterstock.com
9.2  Alvaro Cabrera Jimenez/Shutterstock.com
9.3  Yelena Safronova/Fairchild Books
9.4  Fairchild Books
9.5  Fairchild Books

## Chapter 10
10.1a  iStock.com/BCFC
10.1b  iStock.com/TJArmer
10.1c  iStock.com/sbayram
10.1d  iStock.com/goodgraphic
10.1e  iStock.com/bizoo_n
10.1f  iStock.com/JaysonPhotography
10.2–4  Fairchild Books

## Chapter 11
11.1  iStock.com/Wolterk
11.2  Chicago History Museum/Getty Images
11.3  iStock.com/ljhimages
11.4  iStock.com/melaniekjones
11.5  iStock.com/rs-photo
11.6  Gigira/Shutterstock.com

## Chapter 12
12.1  iStock.com/Rawpixel
12.2  Cem Ozdel/Anadolu Agency/Getty Images

# index

transportation management systems, 143–44
warehouse management systems, 142–43
Loomstate, interview of Regine Lahens, 152–54
luxury, 220
lyocell, 82

## M

McLean, Malcolm, 4
mail order/catalog, 205, 209
make detail sheet, 125, 126
margins, 20
Master Black Belt (MBB), 170
material handling department, 145
material resource planning (MRP), 5–6
Mathews, Brett, 54
mcommerce
    ecommerce vs., 227
    mobile commerce, 227–28
measurement, 127
measuring garments, 127
Messura, Mark, 93–95
microfiber, 81
Millennial generation, 218
Millennials, 53, 203, 218–19, 230
mobile shopping cart, 9
modacrylic, 82
ModCloth, 225
Modi, Narendra, 25
mohair, 84
mom & pops, 205, 206
Montgomery Ward, 3, 201
mood board, 88
Morgan, James, 103
MPJL, 76–77
muda, 167
Mulroney, Brian, 29
multichannel retailing, 10
Multi Fibre Arrangement (MFA), 21, 27
multimodal transport, 140

## N

natural disasters, 111, 141
natural fibers, 82–84

natural resources, apparel manufacturing, 28
near-shoring, 11, 109
net 30 or 60 days, 190
NFI Global, 103–4
Nike, 25, 46, 47, 57, 116, 155, 229
North American Free Trade Agreement (NAFTA), 29–30
North American Industry Classification System (NAICS), 204, 206
nylon, 82

## O

OEKO-TEX® Standard 100, 91
off-balance sheet transactions, 191
off-price retailers, 205, 209
offshore manufacturers, 22
OIA Sustainability Working Group, 48–49
Oliver, Keith, 3
omnichannel, 201
    model, 106
    retailing, 10
    RFID, 164–65
    trends of, 202–3
online sales, 10
open account, 187, 189
open-to-buy (OTB) strategy, 225
order fulfillment, 145
order picking, 145
organizational charts
    of fashion company, 62–63
    key players in, 64–65
    of publicly traded company, 64
    of small fashion company, 64
    types of, 63–64
Original Brand Manufacturing (OBM), 29
Original Design Manufacturing (ODM), 29
Original Equipment Manufacturing (OEM), 29
Orlicky, Josef, 5
outsource, 149
outsourcing, 192

## P

Partner Africa, 26

PDAs (personal digital assistants), 9
pick-and-pack, 144
Plank, Kevin, 155
political climate, 110
political volatility, logistics, 141–42
polyester, 82, 89
polyimide, 82
polymers, 228
polypropylene, 82
polyvinyl chloride (PVC), 80, 82
ports, 147
Premiere Vision, 87
price, 111
Pritzker, Penny, 92
process improvement strategies, 167–71
    ISO 9000, 171
    lean manufacturing, 167–68
    Six Sigma, 168–71
proclivity to natural disasters, 111
procurement and purchasing, 144
product
    shipping choices, 112–13
    strategic line planning, 109, 110–12
product developers, 67
production, 100, 101
production process, logistics in, 150–51
production waste, 168
product lifecycle management (PLM), 124, 127, 129
product organizational chart, 63
Project JUST, 107–8
public relations (PR) department, 72
pull supply chain strategy, 222–23
purchase order financing, 185
push supply chain strategy, 222–23
push vs. pull inventory control, 147
PVH Corp (formerly Phillips-Van Heusen Corporation), 44

## Q

Qmilch, 84
qualitative data, 170
quality, 120–22
    approaches, 122–23
    case study of disaster, 134
    definition, 121